Money Doctors

Can economics help make the world a safer financial place? Are there any trends in the way that crisis advice has been dispensed over time? What can we learn from case studies? How is consensus about policies that reduce financial vulnerability built? These are the main questions that this book seeks to answer.

Money Doctors brings together internationally respected specialists from economics, history and political science such as Harold James, Louis Pauly, Stephen Schuker, Charles Wyplosz, Eric Helleiner and Kenneth Mouré. First providing a short history of money doctors, the book then goes on to cover such themes as:

- financial crisis management
- the IMF and policy advice
- the Russian experience
- contemporary money doctors

The book shows that there is still a long way to go before international financial advice develops into something that is truly helpful in the long term. This book is the first to use a broad historical coverage and Marc Flandreau has pulled together a stimulating, comprehensive and authoritative volume that will be of great interest to students and academics involved in international finance and banking. Perhaps more importantly, the lessons learned from the book will go on to help future money doctors and the recipients of their advice.

Marc Flandreau is Professor of Economics, Institut d'Etudes Politiques de Paris, France. He is also co-editor of *Gold Standard in Theory and History*, also published by Routledge.

Routledge International Studies in Money and Banking

Money Doctors

The experience of international
financial advising 1850–2000

Edited by Marc Flandreau

LONDON AND NEW YORK

First published 2003
by Routledge
11 New Fetter Lane, London EC4P 4EE

Simultaneously published in the USA and Canada
by Routledge
29 West 35th Street, New York, NY 10001

Routledge is an imprint of the Taylor & Francis Group

Typeset in Baskerville by Taylor & Francis Books Ltd
Printed and bound in Great Britain by TJ International,
Padstow, Cornwall

British Library Cataloguing in Publication Data
A catalogue record for this book is available from the British Library

Library of Congress Cataloging in Publication Data
Money doctors : the experience of international financial advising
1850–2000/[edited by] Marc Flandreau.
(Routledge international studies in money and banking; 26)
Includes bibliographical references and index.
1. International finance–History. 2. Monetary policy–History.
3. Financial planners–History. I. Flandreau, Marc. II. Series.

HG3881.M5873 2003
332'042–dc21   2003046520

ISBN 0–415–32154–9

Pour Antoine, Servane et Julien

It's a mutual, joint-stock world, in all meridians.
We cannibals must help out those Christians.
(Herman Melville, *Moby Dick*)

Contents

Illustrations

Tables

Figures

Contributors

Roumen Avramov is programming director for economic research at the Centre for Liberal Strategies, Sofia, was a member of the Board of Governors of the Bulgarian National Bank, 1997–2002, and was previously with the government's Economic Coordination Agency and the Bulgarian Academy of Sciences. He is author of *The 20th Century Bulgarian Economy* (Sofia: Centre for Liberal Strategies, 2001); *120 Years of the Bulgarian National Bank, an Annotated Chronology* (Sofia: Bulgarian National Bank, 1999); *Economic Transition in Bulgaria* (Sofia: Agency for Economic Coordination and Development, 1994); editor of the five-volumes series *Bulgarian National Bank – Archival Documents, 1879–1989* (Sofia: National Archives of Bulgaria and Bulgarian National Bank, 1998).

Patricia Clavin is reader in Modern History at Keele University, England. Her most recent book is *The Great Depression in Europe* (London: Palgrave, 2000) and she is currently working on a major study of the history of the Economic and Financial Organization of the League of Nations funded by the Arts and Humanities Research Board (AHRB).

Marc Flandreau is Professor of Economics at the Institut d'Etudes Politiques de Paris and an expert in international macroeconomics and economic history. He has published extensively in the *Journal of Economic History*, *Explorations in Economic History*, the *Journal of International Economics*, and the *Journal of Money Credit and Banking*. He is co-editor (with Barry Eichengreen) of *The Gold Standard in Theory and History* (Routledge, 1997) and the author of *The Glitter of Gold: France, Bimetallism and the Emergence of the International Gold Standard 1848–1873* (Oxford University Press, 2003).

Elisabeth Glaser is a historian of international relations, has taught at the University of Cologne and at Georgetown University, and works part time as a psychotherapist. Among her most recent publications are "The Making of the Economic Peace," in M. Boemeke, G. Feldman and E. Glaser (eds.), *The Treaty of Versailles: A Reassessment after 75 Years* (New York, 1998); and "The Role of the Banker in Transatlantic History: J.P. Morgan & Co. and Aid for the Allies, 1914–1916," in E. Glaser and H. Wellenreuther (eds.), *Bridging the Atlantic: The Question of American Exceptionalism in Perspective* (New York, 2002).

Eric Helleiner is Canada Research Chair in International Political Economy at Trent University, Peterborough, Canada. He is author of *States and the Reemergence of Global Finance* (Cornell, 1994) and *The Making of National Money: Territorial Currencies in Historical Perspective* (Cornell, 2003), and co-editor of *Nation-States and Money* (Routledge, 1999).

Nadezhda Ivanova holds a masters from the New Economic School, Moscow, and from the Center for Economic Research, Tilburg University. She has worked at the Russian–European Center for Economic Policy, a TACIS Program undertaking in Moscow, contributing to macroeconomic analyses and policy design, and writing for *Russian Economic Trends*. She is currently completing a Ph.D. thesis at the Graduate Institute of International Studies in Geneva.

Harold James is Professor of History at Princeton University, was educated at Cambridge University, and was a fellow of Peterhouse, 1978–86. He has visiting professorships at Geneva, Munich, and St. Gallen. He is the chair of the editorial board of *World Politics* and author of *The German Slump: Politics and Economics 1924–1936* (Oxford, 1986), *International Monetary Cooperation since Bretton Woods* (New York, 1996), and *The End of Globalization* (Cambridge, MA, 2002).

Kenneth Mouré is Professor of History at the University of California in Santa Barbara. He is the author of *Managing the Franc Poincaré: Economic Understanding and Political Constraint in French Monetary Policy, 1928–1936* (Cambridge University Press, 1991) and, most recently, *The Gold Standard Illusion: France, the Bank of France, and the International Gold Standard, 1914–1939* (Oxford University Press, 2002).

Louis W. Pauly is Professor of Political Science and Director of the Centre for International Studies at the University of Toronto. In 2002 he was awarded a Canada Research Chair. A graduate of Cornell University, the London School of Economics, New York University, and Fordham University, he has held management positions in the Royal Bank of Canada and served on the staff of the International Monetary Fund. His publications include various books and co-edited volumes, including *Governing the World's Money* (Cornell, 2002); *Democracy Beyond the State? The European Dilemma and the Emerging Global Order* (Rowman & Littlefield and University of Toronto, 2000), *The Myth of the Global Corporation* (Princeton, 1998), and *Who Elected the Bankers? Surveillance and Control in the World Economy* (Cornell, 1997).

Stephen A. Schuker is William W. Corcoran Professor of History at the University of Virginia. He is the author of *The End of French Predominance in Europe* (Chapel Hill: University of North Carolina Press, 1976) and *American "Reparations" to Germany, 1919–33: Implications for the Third-World Debt Crisis* (Princeton: Princeton Studies in International Finance, 1988). Most recently, he has edited *Deutschland und Frankreich vom Konflikt zur Aussöhnung. Die Gestaltung der europäischen Sicherheit, 1914–1963* (Munich: Oldenbourg Verlag, 2000).

Charles Wyplosz is Professor of International Economics at the Graduate Institute of International Studies in Geneva, where he is Director of the International Center for Money and Banking Studies. He is also Director of the International Macroeconomics Program of the Centre for Economic Policy Research (CEPR). Previously, he taught and served as Associate Dean for Research and Development at INSEAD, and directed the Ph.D. program in Economics at the Ecole des Hautes Etudes en Science Sociales in Paris. He is currently a member of the "Conseil d'Analyse Economique" of the Prime Minister of France, of the French Finance Minister's "Commission des Comptes de la Nation," of the Group of Independent Economic Advisors to the President of the European Commission, of the Panel of Experts of the European Parliament's Economic and Monetary Affairs Commission, and of the "Bellagio Group." A frequent consultant to international organizations, he advised the government of the Russian Federation during the period 1993–7.

Acknowledgments

It is a pleasure to acknowledge the financial support of our sponsors, and mainly that of the grant "Action Concertée Incitative" on "Money Doctors: The History, Theory and Policy of International Financial Advice" which Mathilde Maurel and I obtained from the French Ministère de la Recherche in 2000. This grant was supplemented by research monies from the CERI (Centre d'Etudes des Relations Internationales), support for which Nicolas Jabko, a research fellow at CERI, deserves all credit. Nicolas also helped in improving the quality of the volume by writing detailed comments on several papers. It is a great pleasure for me to thank Nicolas and Mathilde for their dedicated work and their decisive contribution to the success of the project. Several institutions also supported the project formally or informally. It is a great pleasure to thank the Ecole Normale Supérieure in Paris, and especially its former director Monique Trédé, the Institut d'Etudes Politiques de Paris, and the Service d'Etudes de l'Activité Economique. The smooth organization of the meetings owes a lot to the remarkable efficiency of Ignacio Briones, a Ph.D. student at the Institut d'Etudes Politiques de Paris. Christiane Lacoste and Marie-Annick Payen must be praised for logistical efficiency and their warm welcome "chez Charles Rist." Nicolas Couderc, a Ph.D. student at the University of Panthéon-Sorbonne, provided sterling help with the manuscript. I am thankful to Rodrigo Abd from *La Nacion* for the cover picture.

Finally, I want to thank all the colleagues who took part in the collaborative effort, either as authors, discussants, or just sitting there, for all of them made a contribution, and all of them must be credited for the success of what turned out to be a very exciting intellectual experiment. These were: Roumen Avramov, Mike Bordo, Albert Broder, Patricia Clavin, Luca Einaudi, Jan Fidrmuc, Giorgio Fodor, James Foreman-Peck, Curzio Giannini, Elisabeth Glaser, Eric Helleiner, Nadezhda Ivanova, Nicolas Jabko, Pierre Jacquet, Harold James, Lars Jonung, Jean-Pierre Landau, Mathilde Maurel, Ken Mouré, Louis Pauly, Stephen Schuker, Jérôme Sgard, Pierre Sicsic, and Charles Wyplosz. To all of them, many thanks!

Introduction

Money and doctors

Marc Flandreau

On December 29, 1926, in Saint Louis, Missouri, where the annual meetings of the American Economic Association were taking place that year, the association's president, Edwin W. Kemmerer, a renowned international financial expert, delivered an address which he emphasized was not "epoch making." But his talk on "economic advisory work for foreign governments" takes on, with hindsight, a considerable significance. Kemmerer – the "money doctor" *par excellence* – was giving a casual discussion of his practice, reviewing

> the field of work usually covered, the method of work which has been found to give the best results; the attitude of the governments and the public toward foreign advisers; the extent to which the advice given is followed; and the type of economic fallacies which most obstruct the work of foreign advisers.
>
> (Kemmerer 1927: 1)

In so doing, he dealt in effect with a number of topics that have now come to the fore in the international policy debate. Essential in the modern controversies on the international financial system is the extent to which well-meant and well-given advice can improve the stability of global capitalism – and thus the relevance of "money doctors."

When Kemmerer gave his talk, international financial advice was by no means a new thing. After a period of infancy during which experience had been accumulated, international economic advice was in the mid-1920s a fully recognized professional activity. The pioneer money doctor was, arguably, Jean-Gustave Courcelle-Seneuil, a French economist who looked for better places after Napoléon III's coup. Courcelle-Seneuil landed in Chile in the 1850s, where he became a lecturer in political economy (European professors were, back in those years, much in demand) and contributed to the drafting of the free banking law in this country: like many other economists, he opposed government intervention and argued that free banking was preferable to a monopoly over notes issues. While Courcelle-Seneuil had been driven out of his country by political turmoil and gave advice in a fairly tranquil country, later money doctors reversed the trend. They generally came from stable countries and traveled to crisis-laden nations.

In effect, the crises of the second half of the 19th century contributed a lot to the progresses of money doctoring – the policy-oriented and emergencies-focused version of what we would call today international monetary economics, and the topic of this book. On the one hand, these crises provided life-size "experiments" which were intensely discussed in countries that happened to concentrate both economic expertise and capital – these were typically Western European nations as well as the United States in the later period. On the other hand, the crises created a demand for cleaning up the mess which financial and exchange rate crises left behind in ailing countries – these tended to be the weaker nations of Latin America, as well as those of Eastern and Southern Europe. Thus the experience of financial crises gave, at the same time, knowledge of how problems arise and insights on how they can be resolved.

From a metaphorical point of view, expert advice to foreign governments as a branch of applied economics has to do with the medical practice. Money doctors inherited an old tradition in economics, dating back to François Quesnay and the physiocrats in the 18th century, and which in the 19th century was illustrated by Clément Juglar, among others. This tradition resisted the gradual rise of an economic science taking physics as its role model, emphasizing concepts of equilibrium and progressing through deduction. Quesnay, Juglar (who were both physicians) and followers preferred to look at the economic organization of a given country as a consistent whole, just as the human organism, and favored inference. For their late-19th-century counterparts, economic problems such as exchange crises were the *symptoms* of deeper flaws which economists *as doctors* had to address. This is how the international macroeconomist, when operating in emergencies, became a "money doctor."

But merely emphasizing the physician nature of the money doctor would not do justice to a multifaceted role. That the countries where the expertise and the money were located were not the same as the ones where problems were experienced was a key shaping factor of international financial advice, and is still a characteristic feature of the practice today: the uneven distribution, throughout the world, of money, ideas, and problems produced a division of tasks – money and ideas on one side, problems and needs for reform on the other side. This imbalance is, from a functional point of view, what gave rise to the advising relation. In fact the international dimension of economic advice is a distinctive trait and may serve to delineate its contours. Economics, as a social science, has always involved advice and recommendations. In their works, Petty and Child, just like Smith, Malthus, Ricardo, Marx, or Keynes, all sought to give advice on what ought to be done. Social sciences, of which economics is one branch, rests on the application of rational discourse to the analysis and solution of society's problems, and relies on logic and empirical evidence. But almost always, the target audience of the works of the "standard" economists was the home government whose policies they criticized in the name of the universal good. Their ideas, when they conquered foreign publics, did so through the teachings of local writers who had read the foreign ones: the views of Adam Smith and Richard Cobden, for instance, were acclimatized in France through the works of Jean-Baptiste Say and Michel Chevalier.

Money doctors, by contrast, traveled abroad. To understand why money doctors must be frequent flyers, it is important to realize that the international flows of expertise they provide are complements to international flows of money (international capital flows), which are desperately needed when crisis hits: consider what happens in a country whose currency is subjected to a run. The money supply shrinks while velocity increases, deposits go abroad, prices rise, interest rates – both real and nominal – increase, as agents require a risk premium for holding currency. The result has always been popular pressure for easing the monetary policy. The problem, however, is that if authorities lower the base rate the flight may accelerate. Hyperinflation is just one block away. Economic experts may have a lot to say at that stage. They may explain that, despite political pressure, it is an increase in base rates which is needed, also pointing out that the money problem is, after all, just one symptom of deeper difficulties. Beyond the control of money supply, fiscal consolidation is needed, and beyond the tightening of money supply, "structural reforms" should follow. But this is probably as far as expert advice can go. And to a large extent, many ailing countries do realize by themselves that this is what needs to be done. Their motive for resistance (and thus the cause of macroeconomic problems in the first place) is that reforms, budgetary austerity, and monetary diet are always costly, at least over the short run. But politicians typically care about the short run and their reelection. This is how expert advice becomes entangled with international lending and how the economist becomes a money doctor. One potential sweetener for the bitter medicine could be money which the crisis-hit country would receive: an inflow of capital, by providing means to check an ongoing crisis, relieves some of the short-term pressure and makes the patient more willing to undergo the painful treatment.

But why should foreign money travel towards a crisis-hit country while domestic capital is fleeing? The very heart of the crisis is an *outflow* of capital. The key notion here is that crisis lending may be profitable, either by mitigating the costs of an uncoordinated run, or in a more direct straightforward way: in global finance, a country is an asset whose price can be talked down or up depending on the perception of policy actions undertaken by the government as well as on the actual effects of these policies. Talking up a depreciated nation could become a profitable business, provided that one makes sure that "appropriate" (whatever is meant by that) policies will be undertaken. And thus the money doctors are brokers between local authorities and foreign investors: the money doctor speaks the price language of the investor and is thus best placed to convey to the borrowing governments what are the appropriate workouts. On the other hand, from his knowledge of the precise economic situation of the lender he is probably in a very good position to customize those very workouts.

We thus reach the possibly controversial conclusion, well echoed in the following collection, that a defining feature of money doctoring is its tight association with crisis lending. *The money doctor is truly part of the process of brokering money against reforms.* What may be changing over time and space is the capacity in which money doctors take part in the trade: but their participation at the joint between capital and reforms is what defines their role. This implies that the narrow interpretation of international advice to foreign governments as a branch of economic science is naïve at best. Any attempt to portray money doctoring as some technical, independent activity misses the point. Because the money doctors provide guidance and support to policies which in turn influence market appreciation of countries' creditworthiness, their recommendations are bound to attract the attention of material interests. Even if these interests are not directly involved, they shall involve themselves.

In fact, who has the money and who gives the advice are such tightly related activities that it would be almost possible to tell the story of money doctoring by following the ebbs and flows of global finance. The emergence of American money doctors after 1900 and their swift success in driving out European ones in several parts of the world cannot be unrelated to the rise of U.S. financial institutions as global players. This view is obviously in sharp contrast to Kemmerer's suggestion that the American success owed a lot to the honest, disinterested U.S. approach mirrored in

> the well founded belief, in many countries, that the United States is not looking for political aggrandizement and is less likely than most great powers to exploit the services of her nationals, who advise other governments, as a means of extending her political power.
>
> (Kemmerer 1927: 2)[1]

Yet the chronological coincidence between the ascent of U.S. money doctors and the rise of the U.S. as an international creditor rivaling then surpassing England and other European markets at the turn of the century suggests that when countries called the money doctor they sought perhaps something other than disinterested advice. In fact the main advantage of international advice is that, in one way or another, it is fundamentally *interested*. Kemmerer himself, for all his intellectual curiosity and genuine desire to help out countries, was nonetheless on the payroll of the New York firm Dillon, Read and Co.

That funds and advice are complements inevitably brings politics into the picture. We said that international support is secured in exchange for "proper" actions. It is possible to describe the exchange of money for reforms, of which the money doctor is the broker, as an "implicit contract" meant to provide borrowers with appropriate "incentives." But the point is that, by definition, there is no reason why the scope of such contracts should be limited to actions belonging to a narrow economic realm. Theoretical economists and economic ideologists alike may describe modern "conditionality" (as these contracts are now known) as meant to maximize some well-defined economic welfare. Conditionality would then foster "good investment" (Tirole 2002) by the borrowing nation. Yet the welfare function of the creditor has not the same arguments as that of the debtor. Of course, one cannot stay rich when one's debtor gets poor. But the link between both parts is loose and long, and the temptation to use international advice as a way to achieve political ends, to "look for political aggrandizement," has proven hard to resist – and for good reasons. Even today, after a long process of bureaucratization and depersonalization of international financial advice, the influence of leading financial and political powers is still strongly felt. While in principle the same therapies would be expected to be applied across the board, politics shapes specific remedies depending on the strategic importance of ailing nations. Some countries are more equal than others, and money doctors who are sent to attend one of the "privileged" nations are invited to dispense their advice with an appropriate measure of restraint: the recent study by Barro and Lee (2002), which shows that who is chosen in International Monetary Fund (IMF) programs is significantly affected by geopolitics, is an illustration of this point.

We thus reach a conclusion which might appear obvious to some: namely that at the very heart of money doctoring is an inseparable combination of economics and politics. The economic dimension defines the structural constraints faced by the various players involved in financial turmoil (range of opportunities, set of eligible policies). The political dimension, on the other hand, shapes the incentives of ailing countries, markets, and international lenders. Moreover, the dovetailing influences of economics and politics in the way international financial advice is dispensed do vary over the long run. It would thus seem that a historical approach to money doctoring is the most appropriate way to explore this relation. It enables us to observe time-varying, or instead time-invariant, features of money doctoring. And this is not because of the traditional polite claim that the three disciplines display certain cognitive biases. Rather, the point is that history, economics, and political science all provide key insights into the various facets of money doctoring – to repeat, a political activity that involves economic analysis and has a long-term record.

This observation was the starting point of the research project of which this book is a milestone. Our working hypothesis was that, at a time when the role of money doctors, and especially those working with international financial institutions, are the subject of a heated international debate (Stiglitz 2001), the time was ripe for encouraging a more systematic assessment of their role. This project began with an attempt to understand better the trends and cycles in international financial advising. We wanted to be able to gauge its potential, its flaws, and possible reforms. There is an embarrassing dearth of information on this crucial topic, despite some recent and path-breaking contributions (Drake 1994; Rosenberg and Rosenberg 1999; Pauly 1996). As remarked by Emily and Norman Rosenberg, "even basic information on pre-World War II financial advising has never been compiled, assessed or interpreted" (1987: 59). In order to attract attention to the topic and encourage future research, we thus decided to bring together scholars from economics, political science, and history in a kind of field study whose topic was the money doctors.

One initial question we had in mind was to be able to determine whether the efficiency of the cures applied by money doctors had improved over time: have money doctors become significantly more efficient in restoring the health of the "patients" that they are called to attend? A better science should in principle mean better treatments and a longer life without disease, and one would want to believe that economics, as a science, has improved over time. But *prima facie* evidence (see Bordo *et al.* 2001) suggests that the frequency of financial crises has not decreased. This could be because the size of the challenges, such as the degree of global capital mobility, has increased: as cars get faster, more accidents occur. But we know from work following the pioneering paper of Bayoumi (1990) that international capital mobility is barely as high today as it was a century ago.[2] This suggests that it is the design of cures – i.e. the way international financial advice is dispensed in relation to funds – rather than their content – the intrinsic "quality" of policy advice – which is the most important facet of money doctoring. As a result, this book has become an exploration of the institutional mechanism through which international expert advice is being produced, dispensed, and absorbed.

To deal with those questions, a workshop met from December 14 to 16, 2000, in Paris. The meetings began in the Service d'Etude de l'Activité Economique, a Paris research center created by Charles Rist, the famous interwar money doctor whose old chair quietly participated in the discussion. The moot point of the views on money doctoring, as it emerged from the discussion of preliminary drafts, was a realization of the defining interaction, described earlier, between economics and politics. The diversity of experiences taken under consideration also outlined how the practice of money doctoring has evolved historically. It appeared that the organization of the world's economic and political order played a decisive role. While on the surface the history of money doctoring is that of an increasing "bureaucratization" of expert advice, with individual bankers and advisers giving way to multilateral agencies, deeper currents can soon be identified, which tell a less linear and in effect more circular story. Until 1900, money doctors had not specialized. Their role was largely embedded within the operations of (European) financiers – especially leading investment banks – who fulfilled a number of proto-IMF functions. These financiers had definite views on what ought to be done to achieve economic development and were concerned about supporting the "good policies." Their experience contributed to developing a body of expertise which was taken up by the American doctors after 1900 and burgeoned after World War I.[3] The failure of the League of Nations to reform crisis lending and international advice by putting them under the common multilateral structure outlined the need for international cooperation and played a decisive role in shaping the IMF. The postwar context of the Cold War and de-colonization led money doctors to relax the stringency of their medications in favor of more context-sensitive, accommodating kinds of financial reform package. This, however, occurred in a setting where capital controls were pervasive, thus allowing for more varied experiences. The end of the Cold War, and the financial liberalization that preceded it, facilitated the emergence of a regime which by many aspects brings memories of pre-1914 operations. The rebirth of the phoenix of international finance outlined the need for a sweeping consensus on the reforms required to achieve financial stability on a country-by-country basis – a consensus known as the "Washington consensus." At the same time, the recent evolution of the policy debate on the importance of relying on market solutions to deal with crises (as opposed to, say, transforming the IMF into some kind of lender of last resort) implies that a large part of the expertise with crisis lending is likely to be recaptured by international investment banks. And this movement is mirrored by a number of proposals which put international financial markets in a position which is not so dissimilar to the one they occupied a century ago.

The rest of this volume is organized as follows. Part I ("The long run: the institutionalization of a practice") provides a broad historical triptych that highlights secular trends in money doctoring. Flandreau's chapter (Chapter 1) traces the origins of latter-day conditionality, before World War I, in the relation between borrowing governments and European financiers. The chapter argues that crises, in an era that was chiefly concerned with containing moral hazard, retained an essential pedagogical role. It also emphasizes the rationale for a widespread tendency towards "relationship banking" as an attempt to improve the quality of creditors' monitoring of borrowers. Schuker's chapter (Chapter 2) deals with the interwar period, which saw the first attempt at organizing money doctoring within an international agency, the League of Nations, at a time when "traditional" advisers were still in operation. The paper underlines the rampant problems of cooperation and coordination both among the various groups of advisers and within those groups. These contributed to the eventual failure of international advice. James's chapter (Chapter 3) traces the evolution of money doctoring during the post-World War II era, when international crisis lending became organized under the auspices of the IMF. James argues that the IMF quickly realized the importance of cooperation of local authorities and began to promote the concept of "ownership" in countries that asked for IMF stabilization assistance. Contrary to the conventional wisdom that ownership is a very recent development, the idea that structural reforms will work best if countries own up to stabilization measures has accompanied all IMF lending since 1945 and has been a distinct feature of its most successful programs.

Part II ("Case studies: physicians and politicians") moves into specific experiences and provides careful discussions of the interplay of politics and economics. In Chapter 4, Wyplosz and Ivanova deal with the Russian default of 1998. They show how politics counteracted economic logic. While the hyperinflation problem of the early 1990s was successfully tackled, deeper political reforms were postponed. For the IMF, Russia was too big – or too dangerous – to fail, and local politicians were unable to address the flaws in the fiscal system. Speculators willing for a time to buy high-yield Russian government bonds only delayed an inescapable collapse. In Chapter 5, Mouré discusses money doctoring in the context of aid to Romania in the 1920s. He shows that behind a veil of "technical" expertise one can easily identify the quest for political power. French money doctors acting on behalf of the Bank of France truly sought to make the best of a political context (especially rivalry between British and French central banks) which in the end turned out to be a major constraint. In Chapter 6, Glaser looks at money doctoring in Chile – a money doctors' favorite. She shows that money doctors were called in as part of a domestic political game, with stabilization plans being used as a weapon in Chilean domestic political debates. While doctors in Chile often complained that politics ruined their work, it appears that local politics had been the main reason for the phone call in the first place. Finally, in Chapter 7, relying on French and Bulgarian archives, Avramov surveys the long-run experience of Bulgaria with conditionality, between 1900 and 2000. He outlines its gradual depersonalization, as Bulgaria moved away from French creditors' direct control towards monitoring by the League of Nations. At the same time, the persistence of domestic problems and an enduring approach to policy-making that favored state intervention produced strikingly stable patterns.

The last part of the volume (Part III, "Experts agree") takes a look at the "multilaterals." It studies how consensus is built within multilateral agencies and how this influences the way "appropriate policies" are identified and implemented. In Chapter 8, Clavin investigates the less than successful contribution of the League of Nations to reflationary policies after 1929. The paper shows how a lack of legitimacy led experts to try to reach out to the broader international public. It also underlines the difficulty of producing analytical work in a highly politicized context: it is basically impossible for international financial institutions to develop their own research and policy agenda. In Chapter 9, Helleiner investigates how U.S. money doctors implemented Keynesian expansionary doctoring in Latin America in contrast to the orthodox recommendations of the French and British experts in their respective "spheres of influence." Finally, Pauly (Chapter 10), while focusing on the comparatively recent IMF experience, provides, in what may be read as a conclusion to the entire volume, a perspective on money doctoring which corresponds to the majority view as it emerged from the workshop. He shows that the political context of "funding" countries – especially the U.S. – has proven a more significant factor in the development of conditionality than the nature of problems in recipient countries. In the end, as this "Introduction" has suggested, the experience of money doctors is determined by push factors.

Notes

1   The somewhat naïve vision that a distinctive trait of European capital export in the 19th century was its highly politicized nature is also at the heart of another contemporary's book, namely Feis (1937). On this matter see Rosenberg and Rosenberg (1999).
2   See Flandreau and Rivière (1999) for a survey.
3   A look through the bibliography of some classic textbooks, such as Conant's (1915), underlines the considerable contribution of European experience to American advice.

References

Barro, R. and J.-W. Lee (2002) "IMF Programs: Who Is Chosen and What Are the Effects?," *NBER Working Paper No. 9851*, May: 47.

Bayoumi, T. (1990) "Saving–Investment correlations, Immobile Capital, Government Policy, or Endogenous Behavior," *IMF Staff Papers* 37(2): 360–87.

Bordo M., B. Eichengreen, D. Klingebiel and M.S. Martinez-Peria (2001) "Is the Crisis Problem Growing More Severe?," *Economic Policy* 16(32): 51–82.

Conant, C. (1915) *A History of Modern Banks of Issue, with New Chapters on the Federal Reserve and the Banks in the European War*, 5th edn., revised and enlarged, New York and London: Putnam.

Drake, P.W. (1994) *Money Doctors, Foreign Debts, and Economic Reforms in Latin America from the 1890s to the Present*, Wilmington, DE: SR Books.

Feis, H. (1937) *Europe, the World Banker. An Account of European Foreign Investment and the Connection of World Finance with Diplomacy before the War*, New Haven, CT: Yale University Press.

Flandreau, M. and C. Rivière (1999) "La Grande Retransformation: Contrôles de capitaux et intégration financière internationale, 1880–1996," *Economie Internationale* 78(2): 11–58.

Jenks, L.H. (1927) *The Migration of British Capital to 1875*, New York: Knopf.

Kemmerer, E. (1916) *Modern Currency Reforms: A History and Discussion of Recent Currency Reforms in India, Porto Rico, Philippine Islands, Straits Settlements and Mexico*, New York: Macmillan.

Kemmerer, E. (1927) "Economic Advisory Work for Governments," *American Economic Review*, March, XVII(1): 1–12.

Pauly, L. (1996) *The League of Nations and the Foreshadowing of the International Monetary Fund*, Essays in International Finance No. 201, Princeton, NJ: Princeton University.

Rosenberg, E. and N. Rosenberg (1987) "From Colonialism to Professionalism: The Public–Private Dynamic in United States Foreign Financial Advising, 1898–1929," *Journal of American History* 74(1): 59–82.

Rosenberg, E. and N. Rosenberg (1999) *Financial Missionaries to the World. The politics and Culture of Dollar Diplomacy 1900–1930*, Cambridge, MA: Harvard University Press.

Stiglitz, J. (2001) *Globalization and its Discontents*, New York: W.W. Norton.

Tirole, J. (2002) *Financial Crises, Liquidity, and the International Monetary System*, Princeton, NJ: Princeton University Press.

Part I

The long run

The institutionalization of a practice

1 Crises and punishment

Moral hazard and the pre-1914 international financial architecture

Marc Flandreau

C'est avec ces femmes qu'Oreste
Dépense l'argent de Papa.
Papa s'en fiche bien – au reste,
Car c'est la Grèce qui paiera!

(These are the women Orest
Spends Daddy's money with
Daddy doesn't care anyway
For he knows that Greece will pay!)
(Libretto from *La Belle Hélène*, a French
musical by Jacques Offenbach, 1864)

This chapter's basic premise is that the 19th-century international financial order rested on two principles. The first was the notion that moral hazard was a formidable evil. That concern was a consequence of the Western principle of laissez-faire, which flourished and expanded during that century. The permissive and inefficient Leviathan had been replaced by an open society which was based on individual responsibility. In its positive form, the fear of moral hazard was rooted in the Darwinian belief that only the fittest could survive, that the weakest did not deserve support, and that appropriate reforms and policies, not a helping hand, were what was needed. In its religious version, it came along with the notion that sinners had to suffer to earn their redemption.

The second building block provided intellectual foundations. It was the belief in universalism and causality, inherited from 18th-century European Enlightenment. Universalism implied that there were economic laws that were valid everywhere, so that no country – contrary to what Russian nationalists were already saying – could claim to be an exception. These laws, once identified, could provide guidelines for the establishment of a "sound" currency. Causality implied that crises had their roots in the functioning of the economy, so that they could be explained by reference to the events that had surrounded them: crises were the consequences of decisions taken in normal times. In short, international macroeconomics was a *science*: the actual French name was "*science des finances.*"

The political and intellectual principles went hand in hand. Science and morality were reinforcing each other. This point of view was widespread, and largely shared by people with influence. It was at the center of a consensus between those actors involved in the macroeconomy from an international point of view. These consisted of two main groups. On the one hand were international financiers, ranging from stock exchange people to the leading investment bankers, who underwrote new government bond issues and had an important advising role in the process. On the other hand were the government officials in charge of running their country's institutions in the ministries of finance and proto-central banks. The exchanges between the two communities were numerous and important, facilitating the flow of information and fostering a common understanding.

Academia also participated in the debate, although its role was not prominent, especially in Europe. It is not that the questions that were being discussed had little relevance for the subject of Political Economy – much to the contrary. However, there was a gap between the academic state of the art, which recognized a number of simple principles such as the quantity theory, and the practical requirements of actual international financial problems. These problems were the subject matter of a discipline that had been mostly developed by practitioners with strong links with either governments or financial institutions: often, these experts made their way into the academic world by writing books or becoming lecturers, rather than the other way round. Prominent authors (some of whom are often remembered as "economists") included, from West to East, Charles A. Conant, a former U.S. Treasury representative in London in the period of the dollar stabilization of the 1870s; Léon Say, the French Minister of Finance, architect of the 1871–2 successful payment of the war indemnity to Germany and Rothschild *protégé*; Paul Leroy-Beaulieu, the editor of *L'Economiste français*; Ludwig von Mises, the Austrian ultra-orthodox Finance Minister of the early 20th century; and Arthur Raffalovich, the Paris-based financial chronicler, occasional lecturer, but, most prominently, the Czar's Paris agent for financial matters.

These contemporaries had to come to grips with the real-life problems of the pre-1914 era, not with the subsequent myth which emerged in the interwar period of an absolutely tranquil period. The decade of the 1890s deserves special attention, from that point of view, for its was paved with international and national crises. While other turbulent periods had been experienced, the 1890s were to be remembered as a difficult time for the international financial system, and left deep impressions in the architecture of global capitalism. The decade opened with the Argentinean default, followed by other suspensions of interest payments in Greece, Portugal, and Brazil. Banking crises occurred, both in "sound" countries such as Britain, the U.S., Australia, and in "problem" nations such as Portugal and Argentina, or Italy. Exchange rate turmoil followed, with massive devaluations in Greece, Portugal, Argentina, and Brazil. "Twin" or "triplet" crises, as they are now known, were becoming a fact of life.

Thus the popular textbook vision that the pre-1914 era was a wonderful place where crises just never happened because countries believed in the merits of rules and carefully adhered to gold is a plain lie. Behind the facade of the gold standard, the men of the previous century had to construct mechanisms that would serve to limit the occurrence of crises and help to deal with them once trouble was in. This chapter addresses this issue in the following way: the first section reviews the "origin" of crises from the vantage point of contemporary analyses, emphasizing the contribution of earlier experiments in shaping a monetarist approach in which the quantity theory and later the tax-based theory of money played a central role. The second section reviews the remedies applied, showing from a discussion of the stabilization plans of the period that they involved a mix of macroeconomic workouts and institutional reform. Finally, the third section shows how the monitoring of macroeconomic policies operated: we find that it rested upon a bilateral relation between bankers and customer states, with routine support being transformed into extensive help in problem periods, but with reasonable conditions that reflected the information which bankers had on their client's outlook. The conclusion makes a number of points on the importance of these findings for the analysis of the role of money doctors.

Diseases: the origin of crises

Fiscal misconduct, the quantity theory, and exchange depreciation

Just like the modern "early-warning indicators" literature, the macroeconomic wisdom of 19th-century experts was based on history. A number of "episodes" became the source of case studies, which in turned served as models to interpret later crises. These models carried lessons, which in turn served to shape policy recommendations. This way of looking at evidence was the natural approach of the time: leading underwriting banks worked that way (Flandreau 1998, 2003b), officials thought that way, and economists wrote that way. Defining experiences included the French *assignats* hyperinflation during the Revolution and the British floating of the pound during the French wars.

To contemporaries, a common feature of these episodes was the presence of a fiscal channel which had fed back on monetary policies. In all cases, it was the predation of monetary policies by governments which had caused an exchange rate depreciation that had in turn magnified other difficulties. These problems were naturally seen as being at the root of the difficulties experienced by countries with floating currencies such as Russia, Austria-Hungary, and the nations of Southern Europe and Latin America. For instance, observers noted that in Russia the National Bank had been set up in 1860 as a state institution with an initially quite restrictive cover system. This rule had been quickly emptied of its significance when the Treasury started to circulate its own notes along with those of the bank. Moreover, short-term advances to the Russian state were unlimited, because the state controlled the discount rate and thus could force the bank to take as many Treasury bills as it wanted. As Conant put it: "The Bank of Russia has been so entirely a mere organ of the State from its foundation to the present time that its history is closely bound up with that of the paper issues of the government."[1] The Austro-Hungarian case revealed similarities. Until the late 1870s, the central bank of the dual monarchy was the private Bank of Austria. The strict rules on specie backing were annihilated by the Treasury, which could short-circuit the bank and issue its own notes: in 1877 the outstanding government issues totaled 350 millions of florins, whereas the mean circulation of the bank was 286 millions in 1875 and 316 millions in 1880. According to one observer: "As long as the State got involved in the business of issuing paper, disorder predominated. The coexistence of two circulations, emanating one from public treasuries and the other one from a private institution, has been a source of difficulties."[2]

While large Central and Eastern European empires, or federal governments such as the U.S., took the direct and brutal route of issues of fiscal notes, the treasuries in Southern European countries preferred the more gradual routes of central banks' advances. This was the case in Italy in the war of 1866. Again, in the late 1880s, fiscal problems developed in a number of heavily indebted states because gold deflation increased the real burden of interest service (Flandreau *et al.* 1998); the response was to increase facilities granted by central banks. For instance, in 1887 both Portugal and Greece loosened the constraints on short-term advances. The process accelerated after 1890; on that date, the Spanish government decided that the bills issued to finance the Treasury's overseas expenses would be discounted by the Bank of Spain, which was further forced in 1891 to grant a 150 million peseta credit to the state. In Portugal, Greece and Italy, short-term advances were granted to the Treasury in exchange for deposit of government bonds. The results were the suspension of convertibility and exchange rate depreciation. These experiences, and the way they were told, shaped an analysis of exchange crises which relied on the role of debt monetization and the quantity theory.

While modern economists keep discussing the validity of the price-specie flow mechanism to characterize the operation of the 19th-century monetary system, the consensus view among pre-1914 writers was that it was of little interest.[3] For practitioners, it was obvious that the Hume–Ricardo self-equilibration mechanism, while dubious for convertible currencies, was of no use at all for inconvertible ones since these were left out of the analysis. Instead, the consensus view was reflected in works such as Leroy-Beaulieu's *Traité de la Science des Finances* (1879). The book contained a classic treatment of the role of government policies in influencing the money supply and had a considerable impact on subsequent writers – chiefly Conant and Lévy. The backbone of the analysis was the quantity theory. The quantity theory, initially developed to explain the behavior of prices in a pure commodity money system, was adapted to inconvertible regimes, this time to explain the determination of the exchange rate: the domestic supply of banknotes determined the value of the currency, measured by its price on the foreign exchange market.

According to Leroy-Beaulieu, emergencies or, more generally, fiscal problems created a need for considerable, immediate and cheap resources, which in some cases neither taxes (because they are too slow to collect) nor bond issues (because in extreme circumstances they are only granted a very high interest rate, if at all) could bring.[4] The only way to get those resources was seigniorage: "when opportunity knocked," states thought of central banks "as institutions meant to lend to the Treasury, especially since, almost everywhere, these institutions have been granted special privileges."[5] The creation of paper money out of proportion to the bank reserves implied exchange rate depreciation. Contemporaries conceded that over the short run these new issues would bring "a veil of prosperity, a fake and short lived expansion," so that they might be met with political support.[6] Yet new issues were often called in to continue the boom and this amplified exchange rate depreciation. Such was the ruthless "Law of the acceleration of paper issues and depreciation."[7] Soon enough, new issues could not keep up with exchange depreciation as the *assignat* hyperinflation had demonstrated. Only if the public understood that the fiscal machine rather than the printing press would be the instrument of choice to finance public expenditure would they give some trust to the currency; contemporaries obviously adhered to what modern scholars call the "tax-based theory of money."

The "reverberation" of financial crises

The belief that economic laws were mostly driven by "fundamentals" went along with a general distrust that there was such a thing as "pure" contagion in the modern sense – that is, that otherwise sound and solid countries might collapse as a pure result of external events. The early 1890s suggested that there was indeed some form of association between crises: the Argentinean default, after triggering problems in London, was followed by difficulties in a number of other countries. Recently, economists have debated the point of deciding whether there was "contagion" (see Mauro *et al.* 2002 and Trinner 2000 for opposite views). In the late 19th century, the word "contagion" did not exist as such and contemporaries preferred the word "reverberation." Crises initiated in some part of the world could lead investors to take a closer look at their portfolio or abruptly change their mind regarding the international investment: Lombard Street could become a carrier.[8] Other channels of transmission included the dynamics of emigrant remittances. Fenoaltea (1988) shows the close link between Italy's financial stability and emigrant remittances. Similarly, the numbers reported by Lains (1999) show the declining sterling value of remittances from Portuguese emigrants to Brazil to their home country, caused by the depreciation of the Brazilian currency.[9]

But the point is that, according to contemporaries, the "reverberation of the Baring crash over Europe, America and Australia" merely amplified existing troubles, but did not cause them. According to Conant, "circumstances which might have impaired American and Australian credit *under any conditions* were *emphasised* by the general distrust aroused by the Baring failure."[10] Thus the Italian problems of the early 1890s had their true origins in cronyism or, to use the words of the time, "evils generated by corruption among her bankers and public men." But these deeper flaws were merely revealed and magnified by "the prevailing distrust" that followed the Baring collapse and "intensified by the return of Italian securities and the steady outflow of gold [under the pressure of a depreciated currency]."[11]

Sound countries, by contrast, were to survive. For instance, the financial market analysts at Crédit Lyonnais (a leading underwriter in the Paris market) noted that Austria and Hungary had suffered from German sales of their securities which resulted from the heavy involvement of German banks in Latin America. Since the securities of the Latin American republics depreciated heavily after 1890, cash-strapped German banks were reported to be selling the firmer bonds of the Habsburg monarchy, thus causing instability in their price as well as in the florin exchange rate.[12] But the Habsburg monarchy, in contrast to what had happened in Italy, Portugal or Greece, had been able to weather the crisis because it did not have fundamental problems. In the end, the general feeling was that well-behaved countries would never be seriously threatened by such movements, since, in the end, a creditable nation would always find someone prepared to hold its bonds. Only misbehaving countries would experience trouble.

Raffalovich's reading of the aftermath of the Baring crisis is illuminating in this respect:

> There was a repercussion effect that affected a number of highly indebted States living on expedients, spending for military and infrastructures more than they could afford to, financing their deficits through official or secret loans, paying coupons with the help of bankers, through advances that were later consolidated in new loans. When bankers decided that they would stop lending, one saw, without an expensive war, in the middle of the peace, the credit of several states collapsing under the weight of their own errors.[13]

The point here is that, while crises were "brutal facts," they had their virtue as well: it was to remind governments "in a straightforward and striking way of the existence of economic laws which one does not violate without the risk of being punished."[14] The implicit philosophy was the same as the old wisdom of political economists such as John Stuart Mill, according to whom "[p]anics do not destroy capital" but "merely reveal the extent to which it has been previously destroyed by its betrayal into hopelessly unproductive works."[15] To be immune from disease one had to be sober in the first place.

Advantages and pitfalls of exchange rate flexibility

Contrary to the modern prejudice according to which floating was just not an option before 1914, there was a good deal of discussion regarding the most desirable exchange rate policy. By the late 1890s, contemporaries had understood that gold convertibility was no protection against fiscal or monetary misbehavior. They knew that the link between the gold standard and international financial stability was weak: throughout the entire century, so many countries had adopted a gold standard only to leave it soon after in a debauch of paper printing. Nor was it a necessary condition either: countries such as Austria-Hungary had been able to operate a fluctuating exchange rate system without damaging their credibility (Flandreau and Komlos 2001; Jobst 2001). Finally, the intrinsic virtues of the gold standard were far from obvious: contemporaries realized that the deflation of 1873–95 could in part be traced to insufficient gold output, and this led to calls for an adoption of bimetallism. It is only when gold became an inflationary standard that its appeal became widespread – obviously not for matters of orthodoxy (Flandreau *et al.* 1998).

The controversy over exchange rate regimes was initiated by Austrian, Russian, and German writers. It coagulated in the early 1890s, when two commissions of experts were gathered in Vienna and Budapest to discuss the stabilization of the florin.[16] The notion that the quantity theory ruled exchange rate determination meant that there was a mechanism to price the currency even when convertibility did not prevail. Moreover, inconvertibility, because it disconnected the currency from foreign monetary shocks, enabled one to conduct monetary policy without the constraints imposed by a fixed exchange rate regime. According to Walther Lotz, the flexibility of the exchange rate was a kind of "Chinese Wall" erected around domestic monetary policy (1889: 1,288): the value of the currency would in the end reflect the underlying monetary policy, itself geared towards domestic imperatives rather than foreign forces. As a matter of fact, more recent research has shown that inconvertible currencies were able to insulate themselves from the international cycle which participation to the gold standard induced (Flandreau and Maurel 2001).

At the same time, a number of authors emphasized that the policy of inconvertibility could entail some difficulties. While convertibility entirely stabilized the exchange rate and connected the value of the currency to that of convertible ones – and thus to their problems too – floating could create mirror-image troubles since it exposed the currency to all kinds of idiosyncratic vicissitudes. The quantity theory determined the value of the exchange rate over the "medium run": over the very short run, however, the trade balance, the payments of dividends to foreign creditors, and the income from foreign holdings or emigrant remittances, the invisible balance, etc. were perceived as causing the exchange rate to move in a somewhat erratic fashion.

These erratic moves could be magnified by speculation. The focus on the fiscal origins of exchange depreciation led contemporaries to consider the role of expectations in determining exchange rate dynamics. Not only current money issues but also future ones mattered. This introduced a relation between anticipated deficits and current depreciation. Expectations translated into exchange rate depreciation, since in the end these would have to be financed by printing money. This mechanism – which from an analytical point of view was seen as a refinement of analysis rather than an alternative view – was especially emphasized by financial economists and practical men who dealt with actual exchange rate movements rather than general theory. Evidence of an understanding of this link may, for instance, be found in bank archives. For instance, commenting on the behavior of the Spanish peseta during the 1898 war against the U.S., Crédit Lyonnais' economists wrote:

> In 1898, the gold agio [i.e. the exchange rate of the peseta in terms of gold]
> was not determined by the current circulation but by the circulation people
> expected to take place as a result of the war. Since the State was to ask from
> the Bank the means that it needed, all the events relating to war were inter-
> preted by the public as if new issues had already taken place, while all those
> pertaining to the peace as if new issues were becoming implausible.[17]

Similarly Raffalovich emphasized that

> the course of exchange also reflects the opinion one has on State solvency,
> on the budgetary situation, on the general economic condition, and on
> foreign policy. This is the "sentimental" or "moral" aspect of exchange rate
> dynamics, while the other factors are more "physical."[18]

In some cases, in order to deal with exchange rate volatility, forward markets developed to manage the resulting uncertainty. However, the first forward markets typically had short horizons, so that it was quite difficult to get cover over the longer run. And we find no evidence of a supply of swaps for bond-holders. This could become a serious problem for domestic agents with large foreign obligations. Indeed, international debts were typically denominated in a limited number of currencies because of the liquidity services that these curren-cies provided (Flandreau and Sussman 2002). A downward movement of the exchange rate meant a higher bill when coupons had to be paid. As described by Leroy-Beaulieu, a "floating currency could become a problem when a large portion of the foreign debt is being held abroad."[19] Governments worried about short-term "speculations," and there were accusations that agents were taking adverse bets on the currency, thus putting the country's finances at risk. One famous instance was the conflict that developed between the Russian govern-ment and Berlin bankers, who were bearish on the ruble and were selling it short before foreign payments were done, in anticipation of the exchange depreciation that the purchase of foreign exchange by the government would cause. In 1894, using a number of foreign agents, the Russian Finance Minister Witte began buying secretly in Berlin the ruble notes that were used for forward speculation. When Berlin bears realized that there was a tension on the spot rate and that they might get squeezed, it was already too late. On the day of reckoning, they had to go to St. Petersburg to negotiate a settlement with the Russian authorities.[20]

The Russian experiment may be thought of as a lesson on how a government can defeat adverse speculation. It is also a reminder that governments tend to be very concerned about speculation when they rely heavily on foreign capital. It is probably no coincidence hat the Russian squeeze occurred in 1894: it closely followed the less happy experience of Southern European countries in the early 1890s. The sovereign defaults of Greece and Portugal of 1893 and 1892, respec-tively, could be traced to the exchange crises that had followed the Baring collapse. The deteriorating borrowing prospects had led these countries to resort to seigniorage, but since most of the Greek and Portuguese debts were denominated in gold, exchange depreciation pushed up the debt service (see Figures 1.1 and 1.2). Since inflation did not follow immediately, the ratio of interest service to tax revenues increased. Additional credits were initially used to continue servicing the debts. But as adjustment required rising taxes, while at the same time the gold value of the new taxes declined, it was not long before default occurred. As a result, a certain fear of floating developed, especially in developing countries. As Leroy-Beaulieu had concluded more than ten years before the Portuguese and Greek defaults, the mixture of exchange rate volatility and a large public debt issued abroad could be deadly, so that in the end one had to choose between only two courses of action – either put checks on external borrowing, or make sure that the convertibility of the currency would never be seriously questioned.[21] And thus the overall suggestion, in a world where international borrowing was perceived as an essential ingredient of development, was that a fixed exchange rate was perhaps to be recommended.

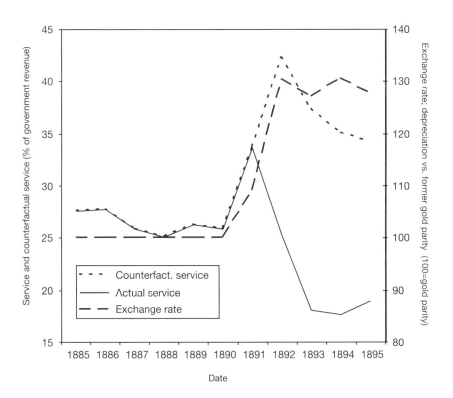

Figure 1.1 Exchange depreciation and sovereign default: Portugal

Note: Counterfactual service is debt service (as % of government revenue) that ought to have been paid, given the current exchange rate, had not default taken place. Actual service is service that was actually paid (as a result of default).

Figure 1.2 Exchange depreciation and sovereign default: Greece

Note: Counterfactual and actual service: see Figure 1.1

Cures: stabilization workouts, institutional fixes, and emergency finance

In this section, we turn to a discussion of the remedies that were implemented to stabilize ailing economies. They inform us, perhaps even more than a discussion of the existing views regarding the sources of instability, of the beliefs of the time, since the therapies employed rested on an analysis of problems: the role of inappropriate macroeconomic policies was seen as the heart of difficulties and thus inspired prescriptions.

Turning back the clock: stabilization as repentance

Here again, views were heavily influenced by the early experiences of large powers such as Britain, France, or the United States. These countries' past financial troubles had emerged from military conflicts which had put a strain on public finances. Stabilization had meant a return to "normality," which implied, inasmuch as the exchange rate was concerned, a return to the old parity. If the goal was to bring the exchange rate back to its pre-crisis level, then macroeconomic policy had itself to turn back the clock of history by restoring the initial conditions. In other words, the state was responsible for mopping up the paper issues – preferably by running surpluses that could be used to repurchase the outstanding excess money supply. Raffalovich's discussion of the ways to "go back to the good currency," for instance, emphasized that, "from a fiscal point of view, one had to restore the balance through fiscal surpluses, since the State needs were what brought in the crisis and disease" in the first place.[22] Alternatively, a stabilization loan – or, to use the language of the time, "consolidation loan" – could be issued. Consolidation loans were used to lengthen the maturity of government liabilities: the short-term debt the government had accumulated by circulating paper certificates or possibly interest-bearing Treasury bills was transformed into a long-term "funded" debt. The rationale for this clearly emphasized the liability aspect of money: the state had obtained from the circulation a short-term "credit" which needed to be paid back once the emergency was over. The result was a contraction of the supply of notes. It induced what in English was eloquently called a process of "starving" (Conant 1915). Starving the demand for money led domestic agents to find other ways to accumulate balances, for example by selling international securities in order to accumulate gold.[23] This propped up the value of the currency on exchange markets at the same time as gold flowed in. Once the situation was brought under control, the currency could finally be pegged, either by reintroducing straight convertibility, or by using foreign exchange interventions to defend the parity[24] – from which we may conclude that contemporaries were routine users of the monetary approach to the balance of payments.

"Starving" had been a key ingredient of virtually all adjustment programs implemented during the 19th century. The British stabilization of 1821, the American experience after 1873, the Italian experience of 1884, etc. had all rested on this principle. It was used again for the exchange rate stabilization programs of Austria-Hungary and Russia of the 1890s (respectively in 1896 and 1897). These programs were intensely discussed and became a testing ground for existing theories. They involved a mix of fiscal effort and monetary restraint.[25] Figures 1.3 and 1.4 illustrate these experiences by documenting the evolution of the cover ratio and the fiscal performance of these two countries, along with those of Italy, which followed suit in 1902 and adopted very much the same strategy. The benchmark year is the date when stabilization was implemented (i.e. successful pegging of the currency), and the performance is examined before and after the stabilization took place. The cover ratio in a given year is represented as a fraction of the cover ratio in the year the currency was stabilized. As can be seen, writers at the turn of the century were basically summarizing the historical evidence. Successful stabilization programs had all gone along with a fiscal effort and a drastic decline in the supply of high-powered money in relation to the reserve. While it appears that the fiscal pressure was released after the stabilization, the monetary effort was maintained.

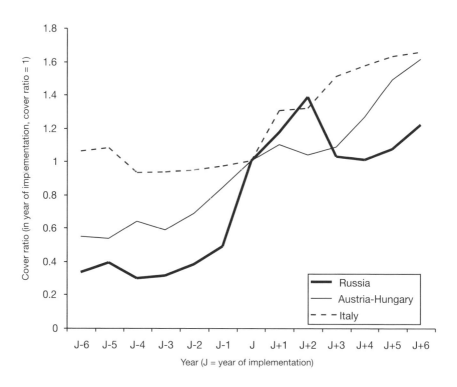

Figure 1.3 Cover ratios and stabilization programs

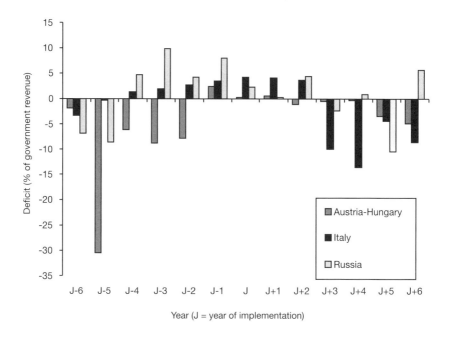

Figure 1.4 Fiscal performance and stabilization programs

Within this general consensus view on how stabilization should be achieved, there was nonetheless a measure of debate regarding both the sequencing and precise policies that needed to be applied. Various authors attached various weights to the different parameters of the stabilization equation, and thus could differ in their recommendations. In some cases violent controversies developed. One debate was on the degree of short-term fiscal effort needed. In practice, there was no reason why there should have been any preliminary accumulation of surpluses. As long as the fiscal situation was brought under control, and provided that existing indebtedness permitted it, there was no reason why one should not be allowed to borrow the funds necessary to implement the stabilization rather than to save them: as a matter of fact, we saw that the fiscal effort was typically released just after the stabilization had been achieved. This means that in order to secure the funds to stabilize the currency a government could issue additional securities and use them to consolidate the note issues it had forced into circulation. This spread the resulting fiscal effort out over an extended time period. On the other hand, a number of writers emphasized that fiscal effort was required by the "moral" aspect of exchange rate determination: "the good opinion one has of public credit shall facilitate the operation."[26] One possible interpretation is that investors had to make sure that a given government was able to demonstrate a capacity for tightening its belt. If foreign resources were merely used to stabilize the currency while adding to outstanding public obligations, there was a risk that monetization would resume in the very near future. In such a case the stabilization funds would truly mean a net deterioration – not an amelioration – of the borrower's prospects: the modern word is "credibility."

Similarly, the degree of monetary effort was under debate. First, depending on the parity chosen as an anchor for the stabilization program, a greater or lesser amount of price deflation was needed. Returning to the old parity was costly as it meant forcing a downward movement of prices. Contemporary sources show that it was widely understood that starving policies slowed domestic activity down and increased unemployment. This explained why a number of countries such as Austria-Hungary and Russia eventually decided to stabilize their currency on a new, devalued exchange rate. At the same time, achieving a stabilization program without inducing an increase in reserves by reducing the supply of money put the country at risk of a quick reversal of money inflows. This was a direct threat to exchange rate stability. The issue was brought up in the debates that surrounded the Japanese stabilization of 1898, where it was recognized that no change in the level of prices would be induced by the chosen exchange rate. When subsequent current account deficits put pressure on the reserve and called for the negotiation of foreign loans, observers remarked that the foundations on which Japan had laid its gold standard were perhaps not deep enough.[27] Again, a bit of recession appeared inescapable.

The question was thus of determining the optimal mix of international reserves borrowing versus starving. For instance, while discussing the official report of December 1904 on the stabilization of the Mexican currency on a gold basis, the *Economist* contrasted the starving policy to the reliance on an international loan on the basis of their different short-term and long-term costs. The starving policy had been the report's recommended action. The *Economist* did not dispute that such a policy was feasible:

> it is permissible to trust that when [silver] coinage shall have been suspended, the necessity of an increase in the circulating medium will begin to be felt, and that of itself will cause gold to flow into the Republic, for only in exchange for gold will silver dollars be coined and the currency augmented.

But the British journal emphasized that

> this method of starving the circulation in order to impart a scarcity value to the silver dollar cannot fail in practice to cause disturbance and dislocation of trade, with results probably much more costly to the country than would be the raising of a loan for the creation of a gold fund.[28]

Thus, an exceedingly strict monetary policy would induce a recession. And in practice, many countries followed Russia and Austria's lead in stabilizing their currency on a lower, devalued parity. In practice, the measure of devaluation depended on a mix of political factors that reflected the relative power of the various interest groups involved, as currency depreciation was always met with the fierce opposition of rentiers.[29] In any case, the conclusion is that discussion of the costs of stabilization was not an invention of the interwar period: some element of "proto-Keynesianism" stood in the way of simple macroeconomic orthodoxy. Moreover, that such views were developed in journals such as the *Economist* shows that these concerns were fully internalized by conservative investors.

Institutional fixes: from central bank independence to the privatization of public finances

The previous discussion of the degree of monetary or fiscal effort needed to signal a change in macroeconomic policy provides a natural transition to an analysis of the debates surrounding the accompanying institutional reforms. These reforms, we saw, proceeded from the notion that problems developed in the fiscal process before infecting the money supply and eventually the exchange rate. To curb such difficulties, remedies needed to be applied upstream, by making sure that the central bank would be made independent, or, in a more extreme form, by using an international agency to control the fiscal process.

No view could be more distant from the actual concerns of the 1890s and 1900s than the modern prejudice according to which central bank independence was the normal state of affairs before World War I and the "cause" of the period's stability. In the years immediately preceding the world war, the protection of central banks against political pressures was seen as the result of a patient construction which had only recently met with success. The doctrine of central bank independence developed in advanced countries during the first half of the 19th century. It was a product of the liberal notion that there needed to be checks and balances on government power. While parliaments controlled the door of deficit, it was important that banks of issue would not let the window open. As a result, the charters of the first banks of issue – such as the Bank of England, the Bank of France, or later the Bank of Belgium – made sure that the amounts the state could borrow from them would be statutorily limited. Independence was fostered by incorporating the bank of issue as a private company, or by assigning it the constitutional goal of preserving the value of the currency.

The experience of France's payment of the war indemnity to Germany in 1871–3 was a turning point. The large payments which the state had to make, and which were achieved through bond issues, nonetheless implied substantial short-term liquidity problems which a number of politicians thought would be fixed by putting the Bank of France under government control. France's premier Adolphe Thiers, however, resisted these calls, and preferred to go through a contractual route, with the period of reimbursement of bank loans being specified at the same time they were granted. The French government made sure that it would pay back the loans on the due dates, and even in advance, in order to impress the public. At the end of the process, a triumphant Thiers could claim that "the Bank saved the State, because it was not a State Bank," clear evidence that the costs of time inconsistency were perfectly understood.[30]

From that point on, the doctrine was gradually illustrated through new case studies but not fundamentally changed. It acquired the status of a dogma. In 1889, Octave Noël's (1888) monograph on banks of issue discussed it in detail. The doctrine was also at the heart of Conant's *History of Modern Banks of Issue* (1896), which emphasized that "the currency of a commercial country should be regulated by commercial conditions and not by the whims of politicians."[31] In 1897 the parliamentary commission in charge of discussing the renewal of the privilege of the Bank of France provided evidence that there was a correlation between exchange rate instability and close relations with the state, and used this to argue that the Bank of France should remain a private concern.[32] Finally, in 1911 Raphaël-Georges Lévy, a leading monetary expert, systematized the "theory that calls for the separation of the central bank from the State" (Lévy 1911: 157). According to Lévy, central bank independence was an absolute prerequisite for exchange rate stability: in his opinion, banks of issue could render services to public treasuries inasmuch as their "existence [is] more independent, and their administration more separated, from that of the State. The less public authority gets involved in the management of the banking system, the better national credit and wealth are protected."[33] The natural extension of this view was the creation of a super-central bank, located in a neutral country, in which one may see the blueprint for the Bank of International Settlements.

As a result, it is not surprising to find that the reform of the statutes of the central bank was traditionally an important step in any stabilization program. Restricting our focus to the 1890s only, we find that this kind of institutional reform was present in all the experiences under study. In Austria-Hungary, full independence was a central aspect of the 1892 reform package aimed at stabilizing the florin. It was decided that the outstanding government paper money would have to be repurchased gradually, and that the Treasury would no longer be allowed to issue notes. Statutory advances were kept to a minimum and government bonds were not part of the reserve. The bank could still invest in public securities, but strictly for reasons of profit, and it could not be forced to do so. Despite some resistance from the treasuries of Hungary and Austria, the bank was able to make sure that the reforms would indeed be implemented. Italy followed after the crisis of 1893. The crisis had emerged from a combination of capital flight caused by the Baring problems and the discovery of a network of connected lending which had involved the former banks of issue, the state and local politicians. The Bank of Italy was transformed into a monopoly of issue to handle the mess and make sure that such a situation would not be able to occur again. It was decided to impose tight limits on central bank credit to the government, for both the short and long term. A strict cover ratio was introduced, and defined in a way that explicitly excluded government bonds. The stabilization of the ruble in 1897 included similar features. While the bank remained under state control, the government could no longer exploit the bank at will. The reserve was protected by one of the highest cover ratios on the continent, and parallel issues on the government account were ruled out.[34] Finally, Greece followed suit in 1898. As part of the stabilization implemented under the auspices of international powers, automatic advances from the bank to the state were ruled out in 1899 and investment in public securities was kept at its 1885 statutory maximum of one-third of the outstanding note issues.

Even in those countries that did not peg to gold, such as Spain, but that nonetheless sought to stabilize their currency, a similar institutional trend took place. The debate on stabilization began under the Villaverde ministry at the turn of the century. It was decided in 1902 that the short-term advances which had been granted to the Treasury should be gradually reimbursed. A formal contract between the bank and the treasury (the so-called *convenio*) provided for this. While investment in public securities was still unlimited, the Treasury made a substantial effort to consolidate its balance sheet and repurchase the former advances. As a result, the government share in central bank credit declined and the proportion of specie in the reserve increased: specie (gold and silver) represented 80 per cent of the note issue in 1909. Portugal, finally, was the only country where no serious effort was made to separate the central bank from the state. Until the eve of World War I, the Portuguese Treasury continued to draw on the Bank of Portugal.[35] This easy door to debt monetization was never shut down, and the political turmoil of the last years before the war led to a return to automatic central bank credit, and a resulting depreciation of the Portuguese exchange rate. On the eve of World War I, Lévy emphasized that Portugal was one of the countries with the least independent central bank.

International control should be seen as a limiting case of the same basic principles. Such schemes implied a loss of sovereignty, which states were always reluctant to accept, and which, for that reason, creditor countries could be reluctant to impose. Withdrawal of fiscal authority from the hands of an inept agent and its transfer to an external authority were generally perceived as the necessary responses to extreme difficulties. In Egypt, the Ottoman Empire, and Greece, international control arose as a combination of two factors: on the one hand, domestic problems led to bankruptcy; on the other hand, the international political situation created an opportunity for multilateral creditor action. The various schemes rested on the notion that in some extreme circumstances it was better to "privatize" not only the central bank, but the administration of finances as well. If the ability of the country's leaders to manage their accounts was so poor that they could not be trusted to do so, it was better to appoint some independent agent to make sure that the funds were used "appropriately."

In practice, these schemes all involved restrictions on the country's sovereignty. In Egypt, the government entirely surrendered its sovereignty regarding the management of its assets and the allocation of its expenses. In the Ottoman Empire, the administration of taxes was placed under the control of an independent council and out of the reach of the Ottoman government by the decree of September 1881 (Herbault 1901: 26). The council was controlled by the representatives of the holders of Turkish bonds. The Ottoman government could not change the tax system without the consent of the council, since a number of taxes were earmarked for the service of foreign obligations.

The Greek experience is particularly significant because it involved a greater domestic ingredient. For years, Streit, the Governor of the National Bank of Greece, had fought an uphill battle against domestic politicians who sought to control the money supply. Greece's defeat against Turkey and subsequent indemnity, occurring at a time when Greek's unilateral default had shut down its access to Western financial markets, put the Greek government in a dead-end. The evacuation of Turkish troops implied a measure of cooperation with creditors. The domestic balance of power was entirely reshaped, and Streit was appointed to chair the International Financial Commission for Greece.[36] The commission opted for the privatization of tax collection. This gave birth to the famous Société de Régie des Monopoles de la Grèce, which was itself placed under the direct surveillance of the International Control Commission. The income of this Société was earmarked for service and amortization of the debt, with government revenue acquiring junior status.

The extreme forms of institutional reform implied by international control admittedly corresponded to very specific situations. Reviewing the three experiences discussed above, Herbault emphasized that control had been motivated by Turkey's "political weakness," Greece's "unfortunate war" and Egypt's predicament, which made it prey to Franco-British appetites and rivalry (1901: 50–1). In general, however, sending gunboats was not easy (not as easy as is now supposed). Herbault thus favored what would today be called "market" solutions. Bondholders, he argued, had a weapon in their ability, through various associations (the Council of Foreign Bondholders in London, the Association

Nationale de Porteurs de Valeurs Etrangères in Paris), to shut down financial markets to defaulting borrowers. In addition, their "relations" and their lobbying of European foreign offices put them in such a position that they could force borrowers to accept clauses that would ensure the transfer to creditors of the management of some public monopolies in case of trouble. Herbault predicted that such solutions would give "excellent results," especially because they did not have the "humiliating character of formal control by a foreign power" (Herbault 1901: 51). Similar creditors' solutions were set to work in the Balkans, with the Serbian monopolies on the one hand and the monitoring of Bulgarian macroeconomic policies by French bondholders on the other (see Chapter 7).

Bridging trouble: funding loans, exchange stabilization funds, and financial innovation

While bondholders played an important role once there was trouble, private banks, and especially investment banks, appear to have been associated with crisis prevention. Adverse shocks could jeopardize fiscal balance: a decline in the price of primary commodities, a fall in foreign remittances, the adoption of protectionist policies in export markets, or an outright confidence crisis following a war or a revolution sent government bonds south. If one was unable to meet one's obligations there was a risk of retaliation by investors (including legal action by the bondholders), which could only worsen the situation. When such "funding crises" were in sight, the price of public securities fell dramatically in anticipation of the incoming mess, meaning that it was becoming more difficult to get money from the stock exchange. States could then resort to overdrafts granted by investment banks, and that served to maintain a record of interest payments. The advances were to be repaid or consolidated through new bond issues once stabilization was achieved.[37] Investigating the balance sheet of the Banque de Paris et des Pays-Bas for the period 1885–1913, Flandreau and Gallice (2003) found extensive foreign overdrafts that were granted to foreign "official" borrowers. In particular, the governments of the so-called "peripheries" of Southern Europe and Latin America relied extensively on the short-term funds of top European institutions; this is especially perceptible in the 1890s, which were years of financial turmoil. Alternatively, funding loans could be arranged. These were securities backed by some collateral such as gold deposits and arranged with bankers, who took a large share of the issue. Unlike the overdrafts, the funding loans often remained on the market for a long time after the crisis had receded. In this way Greece arranged a funding loan with Hambro in spring 1893 that was secured through gold transfers to London. Brazil did something similar in 1898 with the Rothschilds, again with gold being secured in London.[38] In a different vein, access to the market could be reestablished by the use of foreign power guarantees. The Greek loan of 1898, issued under the auspices of the International Control Commission, was guaranteed by England, France, Germany, Russia and the Habsburg monarchy.

Unsurprisingly, its yield rivaled and even surpassed those of the best signatures in Europe.

As mentioned above, the source of the disturbance was often the foreign exchange market, with its destabilizing oscillations. In such cases, temporary fixes could be desirable, as they provided ways of keeping the situation under control. There is ample historical evidence of support from private banks to monetary institutions in order to deal with exchange crises. For instance, in 1855–7 the Bank of France relied on a pool of private banks with international connections to purchase gold reserves abroad (Flandreau 2003a). Gille describes the support provided by the French Rothschilds to the Bank of Italy in 1864–5.[39] Reis (1999) shows that throughout the 1870s and 1880s the Bank of Portugal stabilized its gold reserve through overdrafts granted by foreign banks (Baring was one). Conant recounts that a run on the Imperial Ottoman Bank (Turkey's currency board) in 1895 was checked by a gold loan from the Bank of France.[40] And the accounts of Banque de Paris et des Pays-Bas display extensive overdrafts to such institutions as the Bank of Spain.[41]

There is also evidence of formal crisis support through the creation of exchange stabilization funds. One example was the famous Syndicat des Francs. The syndicate was a peseta stabilization scheme created in 1903 and aimed at preventing the payment of gold coupons by Spanish debtors to foreign (mostly French) investors from destabilizing Spain's precarious exchange rate balance. It thus sought to coordinate, under the auspices of the Bank of Spain, the foreign exchange purchases of the private concerns (railways and mining companies) and the government (state bonds) in an orderly fashion.[42] Technically, operations were conducted through the creation of a lending facility that was negotiated with two French banks.[43] The central bank had to provide the various concerns with the sums which they had stated in advance, drawing on the credit line rather than from the market.[44]

Finally, financial innovation could in some cases be used to deal with financial problems. For instance, the experience of the "twin" crises of the 1890s had shown how exchange depreciation, by raising the burden of external liabilities, had triggered a debt crisis. But, as contemporaries realized, the same mechanism that had made the exchange rate the lever of capital flight and sovereign default could be worked backward provided that the link between the external value of the currency and the burden of external obligations was appropriately designed. In this instance, this took the shape of the 1898 stabilization program of the drachma, implemented under international supervision. The program – designed jointly by foreign financiers and the governor of the Bank of Greece – involved a drastic debt reduction and conversion in paper drachma; however, a provision was introduced that coupon payments would be improved in proportion to the recovery of the exchange rate. In other words, the interest service, while essentially made in drachma, would be increased as the exchange rate recovered. Figure 1.5 shows the effects of this arrangement: as the exchange rate improved, so did the coupon and of course of the price of the Greek bonds. Capital flowed in, and Greece's external equilibrium was restored. Brady-type solutions were born.

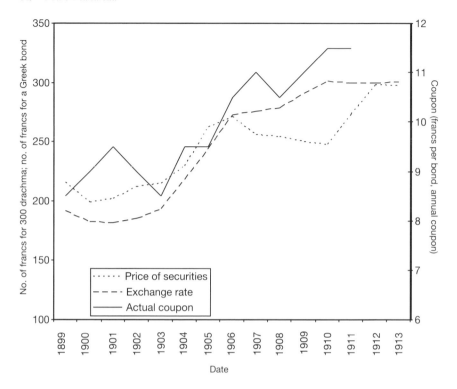

Figure 1.5 Stabilization in Greece

Source: *Le Rentier*, various issues; Archives, Crédit Lyonnias

Monitoring: private banks' supervision between cooperation and competition

The previous discussion of various forms of international support brings up the issue of monitoring, since it is clear that no financier in his right mind would agree to provide funding without a measure of control on how the monies are used. Otherwise, funding loans would have turned out to be just another form of Ponzi finance. In this section we discuss the precise channels through which the perceptions of desirable policies were communicated to policy-makers.

Bankers as confessors: relationship banking before 1914

At a very broad level, the marketplace where the bonds of sovereigns and quasi-sovereigns were being traded provided information on what investors thought of the appropriateness of domestic policies. Investors devoted increasingly larger amounts of resources to get timely and accurate information. Information was processed with avidity. This motivated a number of innovations. In 1871 the Crédit Lyonnais set up its large research department (Flandreau 1998). Similarly, bondholders' lobbies provided for the circulation of facts and figures about borrowers.[45] Envoys could be sent to examine the macroeconomic outlook of heavily indebted countries.[46] The effects of market perceptions on the price of public securities can be felt; when one examines the factors that determined the risk premiums charged in those years on borrowing governments, one finds that "fundamental" measures of debt sustainability loomed very large (Flandreau *et al.* 1998). As James de Rothschild explained in a letter to the Austrian Finance Minister Beust, "the price of government bonds is the exact measure of the credit which a state deserves."[47] This ensured that, in a broad sense, there was consistency between the perception of policies which states pursued and the borrowing conditions they faced.

This discipline of the secondary markets was complemented by the direct "primary" relationship between borrowers and bankers. This is a key dimension of the pre-1914 international financial architecture, and, surprisingly, it is one which is little discussed. The study of the relations between bankers and borrowing governments is often left to biographical research or authors of bank histories, despite its relevance for an understanding of the way the system operated. In other words, the economics of pre-1914 sovereign lending remains to be understood. However, from the historical evidence it is possible to outline a number of features whose attempted interpretation may in turn shed some light on the issue.

Throughout the 19th century, leading investment banks – the prototype was the Rothschild Bank – and a few deposit houses with an investment arm played a prominent role in introducing foreign securities to the London and Paris markets. Because of their standing and position these bankers could offer a wide array of services to both investors and borrowers. They underwrote new loans, gave macroeconomic advice to borrowers, counseled them on debt management; they informed governments of the "requirements" of the market. They also acted as bankers for the government, paying coupons on their behalf, providing short-term advances until the debt was actually issued, or, increasingly after the turn of the century, taking the proceeds of the loans with them and running the borrowing governments' current accounts. On the other hand, as investment banks, they provided information to their clientele of investors, helped their customers to assess the risks, gave indications of how to manage their portfolio, and so on.

Their outstanding position at the crossroads between demand and supply naturally provided bankers with a way of inducing borrowers to adopt certain policies, since the continued supply of services in the end rested on the adoption of appropriate policies. From that point of view, their position was quite different from that of bondholders' syndicates, which behaved mostly like lobbies and used retaliatory devices such as legal actions, political pressure, or attempts to exclude defaulting states from stock market listing. While the bondholders' associations were able to inflict penalties on bad governments and might thus have reduced the incentive to default in the first place, investment banks provided support on a regular basis and were thus able to manage a kind of conditionality lending which rested on positive incentives. Unlike the bondholders, who used a stick, the investment banks had carrots.

One striking feature of the relation between banking firms and borrowing governments is the link that seems to have often existed between given banks and given states over extensive periods of time. Gille's (1967) study of the French Rothschild show that this one bank provided money and advice to its almost exclusive sovereign customers Piedmont and Sardinia (later Italy), the Habsburg monarchy, and, albeit only at an early stage, Spain. In a similar fashion, there was a privileged relationship between the London Rothschilds and Brazil: the bankers underwrote virtually all the loans floated by this country between 1880 and the 1900s. Similar links also existed between banking houses Gibbs and Huths and Chile, between Shröder and the state of Sao Paolo, between Crédit Lyonnais and Russia, and, possibly most infamously, between the Barings and Argentina. At the turn of the century, the author of a noted critical pamphlet declared:

> Each bank has its clientele of foreign states, it has its influence zones. This is known as the "game preserves". These preserves are jealously defended, its rights do not suffer any reduction, and trespassers are asked to walk away. One cannot do business with a foreign government without the authoriza-tion of the landlord.[48]

The observation of special relations between a limited number of bankers and given states discussed in the previous paragraph raises an intriguing ques-tion, which may be formulated as follows: everybody knows that the collapse of Baring resulted from its overexposure to Argentinean securities. But, as far as we know, nobody has ever wondered why it was *only* Baring which took a deadly beating in the Argentinean default: basic prudence should have implied that the bank would not take a long position in one state whose frailty it knew only too well, precisely from its close relation with it. One simple answer would be that some gigantic mistake was made. At a deeper level, however, the exposure of Baring to Argentina had been a fact of life in the preceding decade, just like the exposure of other investment banks to their main client. That must have reflected deeper motives.

To understand the emergence of the pattern described above (and which the literature on the economics of banking calls "relationship banking") it is useful to review several features of the business of sovereign lending. One was the problem of information, already referred to. Borrowers have a natural inclina-tion to use the disclosure of information in a strategic way. They are little inclined to have fully transparent accounts. As a result, public returns typically concealed evidence from market participants, so that the "market" as such could only rely on second-hand information. This created an incentive for banks to acquire information beyond what was publicly available, but this came at a cost, since banks had to organize themselves to achieve this end (Flandreau 1998). In the first half of the 19th century this was done by developing close contacts with local officials. The links could in some cases be extremely tight: one of the first post-unity Italian finance ministers had been the Rothschild house correspondent. In the second part of the 19th century these efforts were extended through data gathering; some bankers sought to assess the accuracy of public returns, fostering systematic comparisons. But the point is that there was a cost that had to be incurred to beat the market.

The second key aspect of this information-gathering process was that each new loan created by itself an externality: it improved the information of the banker who had concluded the deal. Each contract gave an experience of the negotiating counterparts, consolidated the personal network, and gave a number of useful tips that would give an informational edge in the future. One Portuguese official reportedly explained to Crédit Lyonnais in 1898 how the Portuguese accounts were fudged (Flandreau 1998). Finally, this private information, which enabled its recipient to better interpret and better analyze future situations, was bound to remain private: there was no reason why this expertise should be disseminated, as it represented a strategic asset for the lucky banker.

The combination of these three features (costly information, information increasing with the number of interactions, and the confidential nature of information) is known to form the basis of relationship banking (Berger 1999; Boot 2000). The relationship emerges out of the scale economies resulting from the repeated interaction. Rather than having all bankers competing on all issuers, and thus tending to under-invest in information gathering, relationship banking provides extra incentives for each banker to take a close look at his client.

Under such a regime, the quality of the information gathered by the banker improves through a number of channels. One direct effect of close relations is the better quality of information flows. This is magnified by the fact that, since the balances of the borrower are kept in the books of the lender, the latter always knows the exact cash situation of the former. An indirect channel is that this situation induces the borrower to disclose more information than he would otherwise. Governments could, by talking directly to their banker, conceal their short-term problems from the marketplace and thus prevent adverse moves in bond prices, while at the same time working on solutions to sort out pending problems. The privileged banker, on the other hand, had time to assess the situation – for example to decide whether the problem was one of illiquidity or insolvency – and arrange for some form of finance. It is no surprise, from this point of view, that the funding loans of Greece and Brazil were provided by their respective privileged bank. In return for confessing their sins, the governments received very precise and detailed instructions on how to earn their redemption.[49] The banker was a confessor.

Of course, all schemes aimed at solving informational or monitoring problems are only "second-best" solutions, and as such they display unavoidable flaws. Relationship banking suffers from two potential and opposite problems. One, known in the theoretical literature as the "soft budget constraint problem," is the risk of inadequate monitoring by the lender, who under-invests in information gathering and fails to provide the borrower with adequate incentives. The other, known as the "hold-up problem," arises when the information monopoly of the bank is such that a considerable rent can be extracted from the borrower.

The soft budget constraint problem implied that the community of investment banks needed to make sure that each member would do its job properly, and thus behave in the interest of investors. The ability to induce the "monitors" to behave well was closely related to the degree of competitive pressure on the lender side (see Boot and Thakor 2000 for a theoretical discussion in the context of corporate lending). Relationship banking is subject to a pervasive free-rider problem: once a bank has done its homework and has issued the bonds of a given sovereign, there is a temptation for other banks to join in and take their share of the gains without investing in information. Weak states, taken in the midst of fiscal trouble, were typically calling all bankers at once, trying to live on short-term credit until default inevitably occurred. In the archives of Crédit Lyonnais we find evidence of Portugal in 1876, albeit a customer of Baring, turning to the French bank and waving the bait of a change in privileged relations. Similarly, in the years preceding its collapse in 1890, the Argentinean government turned alternately to French and German sources of finance, thus increasing the competitive pressure on its main banker Baring.

While the extent to which the fall of Baring had to do with competition among lenders remains to be determined, there are strong grounds to believe that reduced competition is key to preventing the appearance of the soft budget constraint problem. In a regime of limited competition, the relationship bank takes a disproportionate share of the underwriting. It will thus make both greater profits if the job is performed properly and greater losses in the opposite case. If support is granted while the situation is beyond repair, the privileged banker will take the beating. This may account for the emergence of the "game preserves" described by Lysis (1908). On economic grounds, it makes perfect sense that bankers as a group would want to make sure that there were no trespassers on each bank's preserve. The extent to which they were successful in so doing must have remained imperfect. In fact the improvement in the macroeconomic position of the vast majority of states after the turn of the century (Flandreau *et al.* 1998) meant that in general the bargaining terms were moving in favor of governments. The monitoring role was somewhat eroded, something which traditional investment bankers such as Nathaniel Rothschild interpreted, in their own words, as a decline in moral standards.[50]

Reputation could be another mechanism mitigating the emergence of a soft budget constraint problem. The reputation of investment banks with a long record of sound banking was at stake if it turned out that they had in effect cheated the market. This certainly played a role in inducing the older, more conservative houses to be, on average, somewhat more careful than the younger ones, and in principle it would suggest that highly reputable banks were, other things being equal, able to secure better conditions for their customers – a factor which again worked against competition and free riding. Obviously, no mechanism could entirely prevent accidents from happening, as the Baring episode reminds us. But in a sense these were the inevitable casualties, given that full insurance against misbehavior and information manipulation could not be provided – but only incentives reducing their likelihood.

At the other end of the spectrum, the "hold-up" problem, was probably less serious from the point of view of international financial stability. Borrowing governments could quickly demonstrate their relative creditworthiness by displaying a record of timely coupon payments and financial stability. As soon as this was done, bankers rushed to get the opportunity to lend. An example of this was the way the French government, after exclusively relying on the Rothschilds in order to issue the first part of the 1871 indemnity loan, switched to a broader syndicate for the second part, with a resulting drastic reduction in fees. Another example is the way the Austrian state, after having exclusively worked with the Rothschild European network, gradually repatriated the floatation of their loans after the 1890s. It came to rely increasingly on domestic saving institutions, against which its bargaining position must have been much stronger. One could not be held captive by a bank for long.

In the end, however, the important conclusion is that pre-1914 international support and conditionality were shaped by the policies and organization of "investment" bankers, who, because they provided finance to governments in normal times, were in a position to acquire information that helped them, in turn, to form their own operational distinction between illiquidity (problems that could be solved provided help was given) and insolvency (problems that could not). From a functionalist point of view, international banks had a very important role that was quite distinct from the global financial markets, which priced sovereign risks, or from bondholders' associations, which came after the fall. Investment bankers, by contrast, were those who got the emergency call.

Diminishing expectations: competitive conditionality

The previous discussion of the role of competition in shaping monitoring suggests that recommendations were also influenced by competitive pressure. To illustrate this point, we focus on a debate that was initiated by Crédit Lyonnais' chairman Henri Germain. In March 1902 Germain circulated a study entitled "How to Stabilize the Peseta without a Stabilization Loan"; the paper was issued at a time when the Spanish authorities were trying to restore their currency after the crises of the late 1890s.[51] The pamphlet gave rise to a debate in which the economic establishment of continental Europe participated. In particular, it triggered a series of replies published in the business newspaper *Il Sole* by the former Italian Premier and Finance Minister Luzzatti.

Germain's report relied on empirical work done by Lyonnais' research unit. In line with what we described earlier, it emphasized the role of excessive money supply in causing the depreciation of the peseta. The case had been documented by showing a tight association between the money supply and exchange rate changes. The relationship was very stable and could be used as the basis of a macroeconomic adjustment program. The "innovation" in the Lyonnais proposal, however, was its claim that stabilization could be implemented without relying either on a loan or on the traditional "starving" policies. The trick rested on a reallocation of the money supply, which reduced the number of large banknotes and increased the supply of small ones. Since the smaller notes competed with silver coins in daily payments, they were bound to drive specie out, bringing about a contraction of the money supply without any need for fiscal surplus or external borrowing.[52] Quite importantly, the advice was given on "pure academic" grounds: Germain signed "Membre de l'Institut" – that is, he signed as an expert, not as a financier.[53] The paper stirred opposition. Theoreticians complained that the insights which Germain was putting to work were "not new."[54] Others suggested that the contraction of the money supply would cause just as much domestic disruption as if it had been achieved through a more classic tightening of monetary policy.[55] Luzzatti was much more critical, considering that the measures recommended were too soft. According to him, there was an "intimate" relationship between the budget, the reserve, and a sound currency: for a given money supply, a country with stronger finances was bound to have a higher exchange rate than one with weaker finances, because the resulting discredit in foreign markets would send the foreign price of government securities below their domestic level, thus causing arbitrage operations: foreign purchases by domestic residents would lead to sales of the currency and cause a depreciation of the exchange rate.[56] With its excess of paper money, Spain had deteriorated its credit. Could it restore it without some effort? Or, to put it in another way, without repentance could there be absolution?

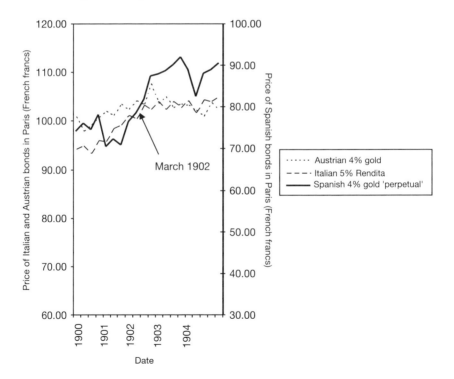

Figure 1.6 Spanish bonds and Germain's comments

Source: Le Rentier, various issues.

The "experts" Luzzatti and Germain continued to debate about theory, emphasizing the need to "diagnose" the "disease" in an appropriate fashion in order to design the appropriate "therapy," and calling themselves "true fellows of science." But nobody was fooled by the academic ring which Germain had sought to give to his proposal. Similarly, it was only too obvious that Luzzatti had other things in mind than a pure theoretical case. Italy was stabilizing its currency that very year, and for this it used, as we have seen, the traditional package of fiscal consolidation and monetary austerity. Thus, as economics were being discussed, the public reached for its wallet. It was generally perceived that Germain's move was very meaningful because it signaled an overall good opinion of the Lyonnais on Spain's outlook, or at least a preparedness to endorse and support its policies.[57] As one observer noted, "This proposal is modestly signed: Henri Germain, *membre de l'Institut*.... But Mr Germain cannot prevent the public, when he signs *membre de l'Institut*, reading nothing other than Chairman of the Executive Office of Crédit Lyonnais."[58] This opinion was also shared by the Spanish side, which welcomed such an interest as good news for the country. As the Spanish counterpart of the *Economist* wrote: "In addition, it is very important to note that M. Germain, with his advice and counseling in financial matters, has favored and helped various countries, among which is Russia, in their monetary and financial difficulties."[59] In the end, as one journalist ironically noted, with so many "doctors" with an interest in Spain's "recovery," it was pretty clear that its exchange rate problems would soon be over: "Do not worry: by one medicine or another, the exchange rate disease cannot wait longer to start healing, if for no other reason than the fact that there are so many rich doctors who find their interest in the patient's recovery."[60] Holders of Spanish bonds could "rejoice, for having found such a protector, they could look to the future with relief."[61] The price of Spanish securities soared (see Figure 1.6).

Self-insurance: the Witte doctrine

In the previous section, we reviewed the borrowing countries' practice of having their privileged bankers take care of their account as part of the bankers' monitoring role. It might be useful, before we bring this chapter to a close, to take a debtor's view for a while and discuss the implications of the specific monitoring regime that existed before World War I for the behavior of resource-scarce governments. The fact is that some debtors found the friendliness and help of foreign bankers less than satisfactory, and as a response began accumulating very large balances abroad, above and beyond their strict needs.

The champion of this policy was Russia, which, under Count Sergei Witte, the iron Finance Minister, had begun accumulating balances in the 1890s and early 1900s. Since this policy was initially met with domestic criticism, Witte had to explain its rationale on several occasions.[62] According to him, the policy had grown out of a critique of the "flawed" theory according to which a state would go beyond its prerogatives in "accumulating pecuniary reserves." The traditional view was that budgets should be balanced. Surplus had to be spent, or used to pay back the public debt. Holding a balance, even one that would earn an interest, entailed a cost for taxpayers since the price at which loans were contracted typically exceeded the price at which the deposits were made. Figure 1.7 illustrates this by constructing a measure of the opportunity cost of Russia's balance between 1900 and 1914.[63] As shown, the average cost of holding a reserve was somewhere around 200 base points a (2 per cent interest rate on the overall foreign balance).

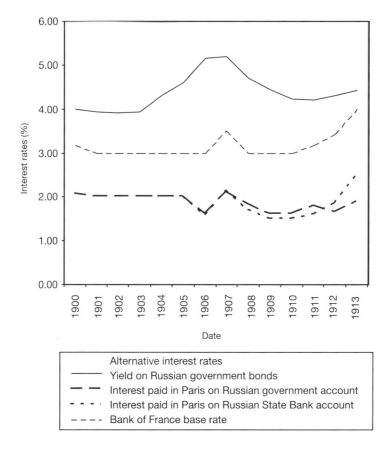

Figure 1.7 The cost of self-insurance

Source: Crédit Lyonnais archives

Witte argued that this expense was necessary. While conceding that states with "small debts" or those whose debts were "primarily held at home" could safely avoid accumulating foreign holdings, he emphasized that this course of action "would be imprudent in Russia, since our country has so large a debt of which so much is held abroad." One reason was the need for strategic money holdings. The market, especially the foreign market, was only generous with those who did not need money; thus funds were always more cheaply acquired when they were not needed than when the state had a pressing need for them.[64] Another reason was the need for precautionary money holdings. A bad harvest had to be met with grain imports, which the state had to finance. But this could destabilize the external balance if international means of payments were not readily available.[65] Finally, foreign balances ruled out credit rationing as they were a collateral on which states could always draw. Witte explained this in reference to Russia's political influence and sovereignty. International conflicts created a sudden need for resources which might not be found in an emergency.[66] Therefore, the holding of balances was an "insurance premium" against various risks. This insurance "purchase[d] for the country a protection against enormous tax increases that would result from financial disasters, and provide[d] the State with the means to buffer without delay regional calamities."

The interpretation of the origins of self-insurance provided here suggests several lessons. One is that the constraints and limitations of the pre-1914 monitoring regime were understood and priced by governments, who reacted by seeking ways to avoid being put under the control of creditors. In a sense, this was fully consistent with the ideas with which this chapter opened: namely that Moral Hazard had to be eliminated, which in turned meant that foreign help could not in general be free. Another lesson is obviously the role of politics. The Witte doctrine was a tight combination of political and economic considerations. It seems obvious that Russia's determination to limit external interference had to do with both its political ambitions and domestic problems. The sharp contrast between the record of Argentina and that of Russia suggests that within a common economic framework political positions could lead to quite contrasting behavior and results.

Finally, one may speculate on the implications of self-insurance for the operation of the pre-1914 international monetary system. Obviously, the demand for insurance should increase when people get richer. It might thus be fairly understandable that the growth of international balances in Russia, Japan, and other countries occurred precisely when the financial situation of borrowing governments experienced the cyclical improvement outlined by Flandreau *et al.* (1998), and which coincided with the post-1896 gold inflation. Thus, one effect of the private monitoring regime of the pre-1914 period would have been to induce a pro-cyclical tendency for states to purchase more insurance when their situation improved and less when their prospects deteriorated. If sustained, this conclusion would go a long way to explaining the highly cyclical stability of the gold standard.

Conclusion

This chapter has surveyed the theories and policies of financial crises before 1914. From a theoretical point of view, the discussion highlights the persistence of problems which have, across time and space, shaped the international advising relationship. In effect, the chapter has shown (somewhat discouragingly) how little has been learned over a century of crises. The basic interpretation of financial crises in the late 19th century is not strikingly different from the one that still prevails today. The debate over the appropriate mix of fiscal and monetary adjustments is still on the agenda. There would certainly be people who would be prepared to agree that International Monetary Fund (IMF) adjustment programs may be called "starving" policies. Moreover, it seems that contemporaries already knew about some dangers which we seem to have only recently relearned. One is the risk of floating with a large debt denominated in a foreign currency: this has caused several crises both recently and in the more distant past.

From a historical point of view, just in the same way as we saw people reacting to the crises that they experienced in the 19th century, and then, more specifically, in the 1890s, there was a keen continuity between the pre-1914 experience and the design of subsequent policies, most notably by the League of Nations. Everything happens as if the responses of every period were shaped by the most recent crises. In particular, the League would undoubtedly share the late-19th-century writers' wisdom that the source of the evil was the budget, and that no stabilization could take place unless the central bank was made independent of the government – thus its famous and often criticized insistence on central bank privatization.

It is probably from a political point of view that the differences between the pre-1914 set-up and the modern one are the most striking. The bilateral confidential relationship that united bankers and governments has been replaced to some extent by a more multilateral system, with the IMF as a centerpiece. This has occurred gradually, with the League of Nations undoubtedly emerging as an attempt to overcome some of the flaws of the pre-1914 monitoring regime discussed here. While the creation of multilateral agencies has made headway in helping to fix coordination problems, they have also created their own difficulties. Back in the pre-1914 years, the "normal"-times banker was also the one in charge of dealing with crises. This probably meant higher rewards for disclosing information. Separating the crisis management role from other attributions has probably created other difficulties, which our own time is currently dealing with.

The shortcomings of the current set-up have increased the pressure on multilateral agencies. Many voices now support a broader use of "market" solutions. This chapter has shown that many of these "new" suggestions to "bail in" lenders, to develop bankruptcy procedures with bondholders, or to encourage "self-insurance" emerged "naturally" in the pre-World War I order.[67] But the historical experience is that such recipes were not enough to guarantee global financial stability, and they led to an attempt to improve the system by increasing the role of multilateral agencies. There is a real danger, in reacting to recent history, that the lessons of the more remote past will be forgotten.

Notes

1 Conant (1896: 235) described it in the first edition of his book.
2 Lévy (1911: 142).
3 This was obvious, for instance, in Nogaro's (1905) undergraduate lectures, where he emphasized that the connection between exchange rate, relative price movements, the trade balance, and bullion flows was not as simple as was posited in Ricardo's inter-

pretation of Hume's "thought experiment," which was concerned with tracing the effects of a sudden and massive increase in one country's money supply. Hume suggested that offsetting flows of bullion (working, for example, through the trade balance) would eventually restore the balance. Ricardo derived from it a theory of the "normal" operation of a specie system, with relative prices triggering bullion flows. It is obvious from the case of Nogaro, however, that academic writers did not have a fully fledged alternative.

4 Raffalovich suggests as a possible list: "war, revolution, waste of resources, insufficiency of tax receipts" (Raffalovich 1901a: 3).

5 See Raffalovich (1901b: 2).

6 Raffalovich (1901b: 3). This interesting quote suggests that it is not that 19th-century international macroeconomists did not know about one key prediction of the Mundell–Fleming model (that monetary expansion brings domestic prosperity by boosting demand), but, rather, that they did not believe in it.

7 Raffalovich (1901b: 3).

8 A recent paper which puts the operation of leading financial centers at the heart of the transmission of problems from country to country is Calvo (1999).

9 There is evidence that contemporaries understood the importance of this channel. Raffalovich explicitly writes about the aggravating role for Portugal of the "repercussion of the Brazilian crisis."

10 Conant (1915: 668–9).

11 Conant (1915: 669).

12 Archives du Crédit Lyonnais (hereafter Arch. CL). Similarly, Conant argued that "[t]he shock drove Austrian securities homeward from Germany as a result of the scramble for ready cash in the Berlin market" (1915: 669).

13 Raffalovich (1901a: 16–7). The French word for repercussion was "*contrecoup*."

14

> The fall of powerful banking houses, stock market crashes, are brutal facts that remind us in a concrete and striking way that there exist economic laws that one does not violate with impunity. Studying crises is interesting. It provides some dramatic episodes and brings practical lessons. It is not that we may praise ourselves for being able to prevent or avoid those crises, but that they bring a number of rules which individuals and governments may profitably use.
>
> (Raffalovich 1901a: 1)

15 As quoted in Powell (1916: 325, fn. 1).

16 See Conant (1896).

17 Arch. CL, 73248.

18 Raffalovich (1901b: 3, fn. 2). It is interesting to remark that "fundamentals" are identified with physical phenomena (and thus physical laws), while expectations are interpreted as a more social phenomena. The fact is that experts reckoned that, while agents were forward looking, they could also be wrong.

19 Leroy-Beaulieu (1879, vol. 2: 579–80). Leroy-Beaulieu in fact had in mind precisely the experience of Russia.

20 On this, see Raffalovich's (1920) detailed account.

21

> This burden is very heavy, because it is an almost entirely external debt. Its weight thus depends on the exchange rate. It rises in terms of crises. The existence of an inconvertible paper regime renders this burden untimely and painful. Assume that as a result of political anxiety or risks, or again because of some economic crisis, the paper ruble, which is the currency in Russia, depreciates by 20 per cent. This is equivalent to an increase of 20 per cent of the service. States should thus be very careful when they borrow abroad.
>
> (Leroy-Beaulieu 1879, vol. 2: 580)

22 Raffalovich (1901b: 4). This view was pervasive. In the Lyonnais discussions of what needed to be done to stabilize the Spanish exchange rate after 1898 we read: "In order to bring back the peseta to its parity, one only needs to restore the situation that prevailed between 1874 and 1891. During those years, the exchange rate stood at par, while the Law prescribed that the cover ratio should be at least 1/4 and that total note circulation should not be in excess of 700 millions." "In restoring the legislation of 1874...one will restore the situation of 1874" (Arch. CL, 73248).

23 The emphasis on starving implies that contemporaries understood that the change in relative prices worked through relative money demands, not through the balance of trade. In other words, the monetary approach to the balance of payments, not the price-specie flow mechanism, was what was relied upon. See Conant (1896) as well as the articles by Willis in *Sound Currency* (1899a, 1899b).

24 This clearly shows that 19th-century applied economists believed in the monetary approach to the balance of payments rather than in Ricardian relative prices–trade balance effects. (See Nogaro 1905.)

25 Raffalovich (1901b).

26 Raffalovich (1901b: 4).

27 Bourguin (1897), Conant (1915: 562–3).

28 *Economist*, December 17, 1904: 2,049. The *Economist* reacted to the plan that had been circulated by the Mexican minister Limantour. The issue raised by the *Economist* had been at the center of a fierce controversy that pitted together the various members of the Commission on International Exchange, in which early money doctors Conant and Jenks participated. The report of the commission was published as *Report on the Introduction of the Gold Exchange Standard into China and Other Silver Using Countries* (2 vols., Washington: Commission on International Exchange, 1903–4). On this controversy, see Conant (1915).

29 Raffalovich argued that the longer the period of float the more difficult it was to stabilize – probably, one would say, because market participants had already adjusted to it: "those who want to withdraw paper money from circulation meet the opposition of those who want more credit and higher prices, especially if convertibility had been introduced long ago" (1902b: 3). The political economy of the new parity typically involved conflict between holders of government bonds (who favored revaluation) and industrial interests.

30 Quoted in Lévy (1911: 24).

31 Conant (1896: vii).

32 *Journal officiel de la République française*, 1897: "Discussion générale": 1,268–77; "Discussion des articles": 1,277–80, 1,285–94.

33 Lévy (1911: 625).

34 It is interesting to compare Conant's 1896 description of the Bank of Russia as an abject agent of the Russian state to the one included in the 1915 edition of his book: "The history of the Bank of Russia is of interest," he wrote, " because it is the most successful instance on a large scale of a bank of issue owned by the State, and because it carried through in the closing decade of the nineteenth century the most serious operations ever undertaken in Europe for the restoration of stability of exchange upon a gold basis" (Conant 1915: 251).

35 Technically, the Treasury could undertake buybacks at a depreciated price, deposit the bonds at the bank and then draw short-term advances against the bonds, using them as a collateral at face value.

36 Conant (1896).

37 Of course the outcome depended on the actual efforts made by the country under review: while Greece defaulted soon after the funding loan was arranged, Brazil "courageously adhered" to the set of stabilization measures that were defined under pressure from Rothschild (Conant 1915: 504).

38 See *Economiste Européen*, March 11, 1898, XIII. Both funding loans were made at a nominal interest rate of 5 per cent. Burdett's *Stock Exchange Official Intelligence* does not provide information on the actual yield. Since the yield on outstanding Greek bonds was above 20 per cent in the first half of 1893, and that of Brazil in 1898 went above 15 per cent, it would be interesting to know whether the guarantees did improve borrowing terms as they should have.

39 Gille (1967: 422).

40 *Bankers Magazine*, December 1895: 726.

41 Flandreau and Gallice (2003). Note that the central bank cooperation that allegedly prevailed before 1914 should be understood within the broader framework of these private schemes. The fact is that all these schemes were typically profitable for the lender. (See Flandreau 2003a.)

42 Arch. CL, 73244/2, "Le Syndicat des Francs." According to Conant, the goal was thus to create a cartel between these interests so that institutions in need of foreign exchange would "not bid against one another for bills at a higher price" (Conant 1915: 317).

43 The goals of the Syndicate were initially leaked by a Catalonian business newspaper, the *Diario de Barcelona*.

44 While it was reported that the scheme had indeed permitted temporary mitigation of exchange rate fluctuations, the 50 million francs of the lending facility were quickly run down and in the end proved unable to contain exchange rate depreciation once the facility was exhausted. The episode suggested to observers that intervention schemes that were not backed by substantial reform were essentially useless in the absence of genuine stabilization efforts. (On this see Mitjavile 1904; Fochier 1905; and *Economiste Européen*, January 24, 1904, XXV: 156).

45 The British Corporation of Foreign Bondholders had a large reference library which investors could get access to.

46 Such was the case, for instance, of Major Law, who was sent to Greece by the British Foreign Office under pressure from the bondholders.

47 Quoted by Gille (1967: 486).

48 Lysis (1908: 105).

49 Gille (1967) describes the insistence that James de Rothschild displayed towards the policy adjustments he expected from the Italian government. Similarly, Ferguson describes how Brazil's stabilization plan was notified to the country in 1898 (Ferguson 1999: 871).

50 As Ferguson describes, after 1900 the Rothschild position "came under attack in both Chile (from the Speyers and Deutsche Bank) and Brazil (from Shröders)" (1999: 871).

51 *Le Change espagnol au pair, sans emprunt*, Arch. CL.

52 Conant (1896, 1915) traces the origins of this idea back to a paper by Max Wirth.

53 The "Institut" was the Institut des Sciences Morales et Politiques, a kind of social sciences Académie Française created in the first half of the 19th century.

54 Leroy-Beaulieu, *Journal des Débats*, April 23, 1902.

55 Siegfried, *Le Matin*, April 27, 1902.

56 Luzzatti obviously had in mind the Italian experience and the violent arbitrage operations which had accompanied it.

57 As a matter of fact, Germain's proposal did not conceal its positive assessment of Spain, a country "which had made genuine sacrifices" and "balanced its books."

58 *Le Mouvement financier*, April 16, 1902.

59 *El Economista*, April 12, 1902.

60 *Le Mouvement financier*, April 16, 1902.

61 *Le mouvement financier*, April 9, 1902

62 See, for example, Witte, "Report on the Empire's Budget": "De la nécessité pour la Russie d'avoir une encaisse importante. Avantages que comporte une encaisse importante au moment de réaliser un emprunt. A quel moment la Russie doit-elle

emprunter?" (annotated translation, Arch. CL, 73216). ["On the need for Russia to hold a large reserve. Advantages of a large reserve when one needs to borrow. When should Russia borrow?"]

63 The opportunity cost of holding the reserve is measured by the cost of the loans that would not have had to be made had the reserve not been accumulated. The revenue from Russian deposits is measured using the figures from Crédit Lyonnais' accounts. Contemporaries indicated that the typical rate at which deposits were taken was 100 base points below the Bank of France base rate.

64 "There is a great difference between the situation of a state which, having holdings, can wait for better conditions and one which, without those holdings, has to accept the lender's terms."

65 "Where shall the State find the means that are necessary to help [the] population if the administration merely balances its books and does not save anything for the rainy days?"

66

> The political destinies of a first class power such as Russia tightly link its life to those of other nations. Wherever important political events take place, and whatever the countries whose interests they involve, these events have almost always an effect on Russia. They are sometimes directly determined by the course of action we take. In other cases they lead us to take steps that protect our country's position in the world. The first result of this impact of political events is, obviously, the need to collect the means necessary to deal with the situation.... Generally, needs resulting from political events are unpredictable and, when they occur, absolutely urgent. From [which] we see that, if we did not have reserves, we would see ourselves, in such a circumstance, [having] either to sacrifice political interests, or to borrow at any price. But then, experience shows that states, like individuals, are often offered loans at attractive prices when they have no use for them, while by contrast, regardless of their solvency, they sometimes just can't find resources at an affordable price, when they need [them] urgently. In such situations, the lack of a pecuniary reserve might cause to the State a political prejudice.

67 Such proposals include Mussa (2000) and Feldstein (1999).

References

Berger, A. (1999) "The Big Picture of Relationship Finance," in J.L. Blanton, A. Williams and S.L. Rhine (eds.) *Business Access to Capital and Credit: A Federal Reserve Research Conference*, proceedings of a conference held in Arlington, Virginia.

Boot, A. (2000) "Relationship Banking: What Do We Know?" *Journal of Financial Intermediation* 9: 7–25.

Boot, A. and A. Thakor (2000) "Can Relationship Banking Survive Competition?" *Journal of Finance* 55(2), April: 679–713.

Bourguin, M. (1897) "L'Etalon d'or au Japon," *Revue d'économie politique* XI: 703–25 (part I); 816–48 (part II); 899–916 (part III).

Calvo, G. (1999) "Contagion in Emerging Markets: When Wall Street is the Carrier," draft.

Conant C. (1896) *A History of Modern Banks of Issue, with an Account of the Economic Crises of the Present Century*, 1st edn., New York and London: Putnam.

Conant, C. (1915) *A History of Modern Banks of Issue, with New Chapters on the Federal Reserve and the Banks in the European War*, 5th edn., revised and enlarged, New York and London: Putnam.

Feldstein, M. (1999) "A Self-Help Guide for Emerging Markets," *Foreign Affairs* 78(2), March–April: 93–109.

Fenoaltea, S. (1988) "International Resource Flows and Construction Movements in the Atlantic Economy: The Kuznets Cycle in Italy, 1861–1913," *Journal of Economic History* 48(3), September: 605–37.

Ferguson, N. (1999) *The World's Banker, a History of the House of Rothschild*, London: Weidenfeld & Nicolson.

Flandreau, M. (1997) "Central Bank Cooperation in Historical Perspective: A Sceptical View," *Economic History Review* L: 735–63.

Flandreau, M. (1998) "Caveat Emptor: Coping with Sovereign Risk without the Multilaterals 1871–1913," *CEPR Discussion Paper*, no. 2004; forthcoming in M. Flandreau, C.-L. Holtfrerich and H. James, *International Financial History in the Twentieth Century: System and Anarchy*, Cambridge: Cambridge University Press, 2003.

Flandreau, M. (2003a) *The Glitter of Gold. France, Bimetallism, and the Emergence of the International Gold Standard*, Oxford: Oxford University Press.

Flandreau, M. (2003b) "Le service des Études financières sous Henri Germain: une macro-économie d'acteurs," in B. Desjardins, M. Lescure, R. Nougaret, A. Plessis and A. Strauss (eds.) *Le Crédit lyonnais 1863–1986*, Geneva: Droz.

Flandreau, M. and F. Gallice (2003) "Paris, London, and the international money market 1885–1913: the case of Paribas," unpublished manuscript.

Flandreau, M. and J. Komlos (2001) "How to Run a Target Zone? Age Old Lessons from an Austro-Hungarian Experiment," *CESifo Working Paper*, no. 556, September.

Flandreau, M., J. le Cacheux and F. Zumer (1998) "Stability without a Pact? Lessons from the European Gold Standard," *Economic Policy* 26: 117–62

Flandreau, M. and M. Maurel (2001) "Trade Integration, Financial Integration, and the Correlation of International Business Cycles in the 19th Century: Just Do It," *CEPR Discussion Paper*, no. 3087.

Flandreau, M. and N. Sussman (2002) "Old Sins: Exchange Rate Clauses and International Borrowing in History," paper presented at the IADB–Harvard Conference "Currency and Maturity Matchmaking: Redeeming Debt from Original Sin," Washington, November.

Fochier, E. (1905) "La Circulation fiduciaire et les crises du change en Italie et en Espagne," in L. Polier, P. Alglave, P. Cahen, P. Cauwes, M. Bourguin, L. Brocard, E. Dolleans and R. Lafarge (eds.) *Questions monétaires contemporaines*, Paris: Larose & Tenin.

Gille, B. (1967) *Histoire de la Maison Rothschild*, vol. II, Geneva: Droz.

Herbault, N. (1901) "Le Contrôle international en Egypte en Turquie et Grèce," *Congrès International des Valeurs Mobilières*, Législation, no. 166: 51.

Jobst, C. (2001) *How to Join the Gold Club. The Credibility of Austria-Hungary's Commitment to the Gold Standard, 1892–1913*," unpublished Diplomarbeit, Universität Wien.

Lains, P. (1999) *L'Economie portugaise au XIXème siècle. Croissance économique et Commerce extérieur, 1851–1913*, Paris: L'Harmattan.

Leroy-Beaulieu, P. (1879) *Traité de la Science des Finances*, 2 vols., Paris: Guillaumin.

Lévy, R.-G. (1911) *Banques d'Emission et Trésors Publics*, Paris: Hachette.

Lotz, W. (1889) "Die Währungsfrage in Österreich-Ungarn und ihre wirtschaftliche und politische Bedeutung," *Jahrbuch für Gesetzgebung, Verwaltung und Wolkswirtschaft im Deutschen Reich* 13(4): 1,265–303.

Lysis (pseudonym) (1908) *Contre l'Oligarchie financière en France*, Paris: Bureaux de la Revue.

Mauro P., N. Sussman, and Y. Yafeh (2002) "Emerging Market Spreads: Then versus Now," *Quarterly Journal of Economics* 117(2), May: 695–733.

Mitjavile, H. (1904) *La Crise du change en Espagne*, Bordeaux: G. Gounouilhou.

Mussa, M. (2000) "The IMF Approach to Economic Stabilization," *NBER Macroeconomics Annual 1999*: 79–122.

Noël, O. (1888) *Les Banques d'émission en Europe*, Paris: Berger-Levrault.

Nogaro, B. (1905) *Le Rôle de la monnaie dans le commerce international et la théorie quantitative*, Paris: V. Giard & E. Brière.

Pareto, V. (1893) "L'intervention de l'Etat dans les banques d'émission en Italie," *Journal des Economistes* 14(1), April: 3–28.

Powell, E. (1916) *The Evolution of the Money Market, 1385–1915*, London: Financial News.

Raffalovich, A. (1901a) "Les Crises commerciales et financières depuis 1889," *Economie politique, no. 22*, Paris: Congrès International des Valeurs Mobilières.

Raffalovich, A. (1901b) "Les Méthodes employées par les Etats au XIXème siècle pour revenir à la bonne monnaie," *Economie politique, no. 58*, Paris: Congrès International des Valeurs Mobilières.

Raffalovich, A. (1920) *Le Marché financier, les dettes publiques et l'inflation pendant la guerre*, Paris: Guillaumin.

Reis, J. (1999) "An Art, Not a Science? Central Bank Management in Portugal under the Gold Standard, 1854–1891," mimeo, Instituto de Cienciais Sociais, Lisbon.

Trinner, G. (2000) "Capital Flight, Contagion or Isolation? International Capital and the Brazilian Encilhamento, 1889–1894," mimeo, Rutgers University.

Willis, H.P. (1899a) "The Austrian Monetary Reform," *Sound Currency* 6: 114–28.

Willis, H.P. (1899b) "Monetary Reform in Russia," *Sound Currency* 6: 82–110.

2 Money doctors between the wars

The competition between central banks, private financial advisers, and multilateral agencies, 1919–39

Stephen A. Schuker

World War I produced a caesura in the history of international finance. The previous half-century had witnessed rapid industrialization in the world's leading nations, the rise of managerial capitalism, and the development of financial intermediaries capable of coordinating domestic economies and lending abroad on a large scale.[1] Contemporaries, especially those who had not examined adjustment mechanisms closely, attributed the smooth working of international exchanges to spreading acceptance of the classical gold standard (see, for example, Kemmerer 1944).

The war undermined both the political institutions and the conceptual framework that had sustained the credibility of the system (Eichengreen 1992). Liberal governments of the early 20th century still had underdeveloped tax bureaucracies, and the belligerent countries resorted to deficit finance to meet unprecedented expenses. The resulting inflation distorted relative prices. It also disrupted existing patterns of commerce and investment. State controls replaced free trade. Outside the United States, the gold standard, as it had traditionally operated, broke down. Britain, France, and America maintained firewalls by pegging their exchanges while hostilities lasted. Once those temporary arrangements ended, all European currencies depreciated against the dollar to a greater or lesser degree. The disordered exchanges served as one barometer of the shifts in financial power, changes in industrial competitiveness, and structural adjustments in trade patterns that had taken place during the war.[2]

The postwar years provided increased scope for "money doctors" of several sorts to help recast the international financial system. Throughout the prewar era, the London "City," as the undisputed leader among financial centers, had channeled long-term capital flows, accommodated trade, and provided shipping and insurance services worldwide. Joint-stock and merchant bankers in the City developed considerable expertise in defusing financial crises and in acting as lenders of last resort.[3] London bankers continued to boast unrivaled expertise in trade finance after 1918; Wall Street never developed a comparable acceptance market in the interwar years. Nevertheless, the deterioration in the balance of payments obliged the Bank of England to restrict long-term loans to non-

Commonwealth countries, at first through capital controls and later through moral suasion, irregularly for most of the 1920s (Moggridge 1972: 199–227). By 1930 Great Britain had already concentrated 58.7 per cent of its portfolio investment within the Empire.[4] Accordingly, even after the immediate postwar emergency had passed, public borrowers in Europe and Latin America had to seek reconstruction loans through international cooperative arrangements or directly on the American market.

During the 1920s, League of Nations agencies, central banks, investment banks in the money centers, and academic economists played complementary, if occasionally competitive, roles as "money doctors" to deficit countries. Some theorists contend that the international economy remains stable and most efficient when a single hegemon provides the coordinating function.[5] Charles Kindleberger has famously argued that no country undertook the responsibilities of the hegemonic stabilizer in the 1920s. Britain no longer possessed the clout to act as the lender of last resort, the buyer of distress goods, and the discounter in a crisis. The United States lacked the political institutions, educated public sentiment, and proportional involvement in world trade that would oblige it to take Britain's place (Kindleberger 1980). All the same, in the 1920s, private and central bankers, international civil servants, and consulting economists alike made efforts to fashion an informal cooperative system. Until the Depression struck, those informal networks registered modest success in overcoming political stalemates, relieving liquidity crises, and recycling capital to where borrowers might employ it efficiently – or, at worst, where it might promote systemic stability.

How did the "money doctors" change their postulates and practices from the prewar to the postwar period? Marc Flandreau demonstrates that late-19th-century economic theorists and the investment bankers who applied their ideas possessed a surprisingly modern grasp of the causes of, and remedies for, structural disequilibrium. They understood that fiscal profligacy, whether deriving from fiat money creation or compulsory advances by central banks, led over time to inflation and an imbalance in relative prices. They acknowledged that capital flows responded to maladjustment much more quickly than trade flows. They realized that, as forward-exchange markets developed, expectations played an increasingly significant role in such movements. Finally, they imposed a form of "conditionality" on official clients in less-developed countries by regulating their access to capital markets.

Whether under fixed or flexible exchange rates, money-center bankers managed the flow of financial information. They examined the fiscal performance of adjusting countries, assessed their "credibility," and distinguished between illiquidity and insolvency. Almost always, they proposed a reform package that included fiscal stabilization and limits on high-powered money. Though aiming to make a profit in the long run, they assumed risk by damping down the contagion of financial crises. Thus they provided a public service. In short, without extensive oversight from their home governments, they performed a function much like that of interwar money doctors or their post-1945 successors at the International Monetary Fund (IMF) (see Chapter 1).

Globalization reached a peak in the generation before 1914. By most measures, it would not approach those levels of integration again until the 1990s (O'Rourke and Williamson 1999). The interdependence of economies increased. That enhanced the ability of money-center bankers or consortiums to impose Western notions of private property, the rule of law, and the obligations of contract. This implied the transmission of cultural values as well as the institutional rules that emanated from them. In their own interest, the bankers encouraged the responsibilities of rulers to subjects in polities overseas or on the European periphery that had heretofore operated along strictly Hobbesian lines. Political scientists describe this development, perhaps too clinically, as the "convergence of expectations" in the international regime (Lipson 1985: 3–33).

The convergence, naturally, remained imperfect. Governments in lending countries rarely deployed military force to reinforce market discipline on misbehaving states. Countries that flouted financial conventions in one decade regained access to capital markets in the next.[6] Still, money doctors had an incomparably easier time performing their duties in the generation before World War I than after it. First of all, financial relations among the major countries remained relatively stable. As will be discussed below, that stability derived more from common discipline and active management of the system than from the intrinsic merits of gold convertibility itself. But stability at the center allowed money doctors to focus their ministrations on the periphery. With occasional exceptions, they could work to restore the finances of Portugal, Spain, and Greece, the Ottoman Empire and Latin America, even Austria and Russia, without endangering their own economies. Moreover, as Flandreau and associates have shown, new gold supplies after 1896 set off a gentle inflation that moderated real debt burdens everywhere. Even absent effective taxation, debtor governments did not need to rely so heavily on seigniorage. They perceived increased advantage in accepting the market discipline involved in adhering to the gold zone (Flandreau *et al.* 1998).

If the assumptions and techniques of money doctors did not change radically as a result of the war, the political context in which they operated was transformed. Not only had the gold standard discipline and the web of understandings that sustained it fallen into disuse, but globalization went into reverse. Wartime barriers to the free flow of capital, goods, and labor persisted stubbornly during the 1920s and mounted further in the adverse economic climate of the Depression decade (James 2001). What's more, the financial center failed to hold. Every country except the United States (and arguably the United Kingdom) had emerged as a deficit land in 1919, in need of external help to restore its fiscal equilibrium. Traditional remedies proved inadequate and sometimes counterproductive. For example, the sheer magnitude of social disruption and decline of wealth in most combatant nations ruled out the venerable deflationary nostrum of compressing the money supply back to previous levels as a corrective for fiscal profligacy. When France adopted such a "starving" scheme through the 1920 François–Marsal Convention, the Banque de France yielded to temptation and eventually cooked the books.[7]

Finally, notions of moral standards and social justice underwent a transformation, in the West and among the rest. Revolutionary regimes in Russia, Mexico, and the Ottoman Empire thumbed their noses at traditional property rules and got away with it. Their success emboldened other countries that encountered payments difficulties to do likewise (Lipson 1985: 84–5). Lenin may never have said in so many words, "The capitalists will sell us the rope with which we shall hang them." Yet, almost everywhere, exporter lobbies prevailed over bondholder interests. The ability of money doctors to take the concerns of existing investors into account while shaping stabilization plans in defaulting countries declined accordingly.

Within Western societies themselves, the notion of financial "credibility" underwent a transformation. When the Pujo Committee of the U.S. House of Representatives investigated the so-called money trust in 1912, J.P. Morgan, Sr. explicated the traditional concept to the committee counsel. "Is not commercial credit based primarily upon money or property?" asked the muckraking Samuel Untermyer. "No sir," Morgan shot back; "the first thing is character."[8] The Morgan partners and like-minded confrères in other banking centers marshaled similar rhetoric in the 1920s. "England will go back to the gold standard because that is the honest thing to do," observed Russell Leffingwell of Morgan's in 1923. "All Keynes and that ilk can say about social justice is beside the mark."[9]

Socialist and Labour parties, which commanded the increasing adherence of the urban proletariat, industrial unions, intellectuals, and the progressive middle class, disagreed. It is difficult to chart the precise trajectory of social change. Yet over the course of the interwar decades, public opinion in every industrial country came to rank full employment, maximum output, and provision of government services ahead of faithfulness to financial obligations, at home or abroad. This marked a reordering not merely of political, but also moral, preferences, and money doctors had to take account of it.

Prosopography

Interwar money doctors hung their respective hats in many agencies, public and private. They formed, however, a remarkably cohesive social group. A large number became acquainted while assigned to the interallied agencies set up to coordinate allocations of food, shipping, and vital resources during the war. Others got to know each other while raising American loans or handling procurement for the Allies. Still others met initially as expert advisers at the Paris Peace Conference. The personal links forged in wartime comradeship endured and frequently facilitated a common approach to problems. To give just a few examples, Arthur Salter, Jean Monnet, and Dwight Morrow worked together in 1917–18 on the Allied Maritime Transport Council. Salter then served as head of the League of Nations Economic Section; Monnet became deputy secretary-general of the League and subsequently a banker for Blair & Co., handling stabilization loans; and Morrow returned to his Morgan partnership, though paradoxically he emerged as the main antagonist to bankers' views of debt refunding when appointed ambassador to Mexico.

At the 1919 Peace Conference the leading Morgan partner, Thomas W. Lamont, advised the American delegation in Paris on reparations, while Assistant Secretary Russell Leffingwell performed economic analysis for the Treasury Department. Five years later, both men had switched to analogous duties in the private sector. Lamont represented the bankers at the 1924 London Conference to reschedule Germany's reparation debt; Leffingwell elaborated the economic projections at home, this time as a partner at Morgan Corner. Leffingwell's wartime assistant, S. Parker Gilbert, effectively ran the U.S. Treasury as Mellon's undersecretary in the early 1920s, and then was tapped by Leffingwell to become Agent-General for German Reparations before elevation to a Morgan partnership himself. Another Lamont protégé, Jeremiah Smith, turned up as commissioner-general for the League reconstruction of Hungary.

Governor Benjamin Strong of the New York Federal Reserve Bank (FRBNY) developed a personal friendship as well as a strategic alliance with Montagu Norman, governor of the Bank of England. Earlier, Strong had learned his trade at Bankers Trust, a frequent participant in Morgan syndications; and Henry P. Davison, the anchor partner at Morgan's in the older generation, had become the joint patron of Strong, Lamont, and Morrow when all four adorned the same social circle in the New Jersey suburb of Englewood. Norman, meanwhile, enjoyed the closest of personal relations with J.P. Morgan, Jr. and his New York partners, as well as with Edward Grenfell, the leading light at Morgan, Grenfell. A Threadneedle Street regular, the latter served thirty-five years as a director of the Bank of England, including two terms on its inner Committee of Treasury. Lamont collaborated with one key partner of Lazard's London branch, Robert Brand, in abortive negotiations for post-Versailles reconstruction loans, and he worked with the latter's compeer Robert Kindersley on German currency reform five years later. Still another Lazard partner, Frank Altschul of the New York branch, conceived the anti-speculative action that Morgan's executed in 1924 to save the franc, notwithstanding the tendency of old-school bankers to consider such operations *ultra vires*. Owen D. Young, the conceptual point man for the Americans on the Dawes and Young committees of 1924 and 1929, wore another hat as director of the FRBNY. Charles G. Dawes, the first American delegate to the 1924 Committee of Experts, not only remained personally close to Sir Josiah Stamp, his British counterpart; their respective children united in matrimony.[10]

One could extend this prosopographical analysis indefinitely. Even some Germans gained limited entrée to the dense web of interconnections as wartime animosities subsided. Carl Melchior, financial counselor to the German delegation at Versailles, struck up an intimate relationship with John Maynard Keynes and drew the latter into monetary advising in Berlin. Max Warburg, Melchior's partner, became a logical interlocutor on New York markets because his brother Paul, a co-founder of the Federal Reserve, maintained close links with Kuhn, Loeb & Co. Academics, of course, moved in less exalted social circles, but even there personal connections reinforced a commonality of outlook. W.W. Cumberland and Arthur N Young, successively foreign trade advisers at the U.S.

State Department, had done graduate work with Edwin W. Kemmerer at Princeton. The two brought Kemmerer into the Washington axis as a consultant on Latin American monetary problems and later as staff adviser to the Dawes Committee. Cumberland and Young, like their predecessor Arthur Millspaugh, eventually left the department themselves for lucrative careers as financial advisers to foreign governments.

The rise of New York as a financial center inevitably meant that lawyers would advance from technical advisers in the preparation of flotations to principals in the dispensation of financial advice. In no other nation, as Alexis de Tocqueville classically observed, has the legalistic cast of mind penetrated so deeply into institutions and culture alike. The career of John Foster Dulles, a senior partner of Sullivan & Cromwell in the interwar years, illustrates that conflation of law and finance emblematically. As a legal adviser to the American delegation at the Paris Peace Conference, Dulles essentially drafted the reparation terms of the Versailles Treaty. In the 1920s he crafted many of the agreements through which Americans bankrolled state and municipal borrowers in Central Europe, Latin America, and Asia; on the side, he counseled Washington regarding the vexed question of priority between private and reparation debt. Through his intimate friendship with Jean Monnet, among other connections, Dulles became deeply involved in debt workout negotiations throughout the following decade.[11]

Only when the Depression overwhelmed traditional banking structures did a true outsider penetrate the closed circle of the financial cognoscenti, and then with unfortunate results. In the early 1930s Ivar Kreuger, the Swedish match king, mobilized credits for Germany and a dozen other countries in return for the concession of match and telephone monopolies. The normally sober *Economist* waxed lyric about a potential complement to the League of Nations Finance Committee: "Technically this conception of wedding the acquisition of markets to the provision of capital for borrowing governments was an inspired notion, which seemed to hold all the 'inevitable simplicity' of great ideas." The innovation seemed less genial after the match conglomerate went bankrupt; Kreuger committed suicide when accounting fraud came to light. In retrospect, Keynes had over-dramatized by claiming that Kreuger lay crushed "between the icebergs of a frozen world which no individual man can thaw and restore to the warmth of normal life." Still, the Kreuger collapse served as one more indicant of a gradual shift in the tectonic plates of international finance. Increasingly, as the Depression decade proceeded, it became clear that the greatest of merchant houses and private banks lacked the scale and scope to succor defaulting debtors. Solutions could emerge, if at all, only at the level of governments.[12]

The prerequisites for monetary reconstruction

It is hardly surprising that continuity in personnel resulted in substantial consensus on the prerequisites for monetary reconstruction after 1918. The Cunliffe Committee on Currency and Foreign Exchanges after the War, chaired by the governor of the Bank of England, embraced the basic assumption that the British government should balance the budget, reinvigorate capital markets, and restore sterling to convertibility at the prewar par as soon as that became feasible. Only the timing of the requisite policy measures remained open for serious debate.[13] Ralph Hawtrey, the civil servant who drafted the bulk of the Cunliffe Report, may already have doubted whether precious-metal reserves would prove adequate to reinstitute the gold bullion standard; significantly, Hawtrey shortly emerged as one of the earliest advocates of the gold-exchange variant (Kindleberger 1984: 332–3). Officially, however, the Cunliffe Report embraced David Hume's price-specie-flow model, under which gold movements and internal price changes would automatically balance external accounts.

Economic historians have long acknowledged that the late-19th-century gold bullion standard involved substantial hands-on management. It did not function so differently from postwar gold-exchange arrangements as textbook models would incline us to suppose. Paper currency and bank deposits accounted for 90 per cent of world monetary circulation by 1913, gold for merely 10 per cent. Monetary authorities in nations on the periphery already held sterling and dollars as de facto substitutes for gold reserves, albeit not to the extent practiced later. Moreover, countries in deficit infrequently forced wages and prices down through higher discount rates in order to adjust the trade account. Nor did they ship gold to creditors, except as a last resort. Instead, capital movements accommodated deficits or surpluses for long periods without requiring rectifications on current account. The regime worked satisfactorily most of the time because bankers in the financial centers adhered to a common doctrinal ethos and shared a commitment to sound money. The London City buttressed mutual agreement on the rules of the game by training elites from abroad as well as by extending counter-cyclical credits and facilitating trade.[14]

Critics of the gold standard point out that regime credibility required political as well as economic harmony. The much-touted advance of democracy meant that labor unions and trade associations could make it hard for postwar governments to sacrifice domestic interests for abstract balance-of-payments goals (Eichengreen 1992: 4–12). And yet postwar experience drove home the parallel lesson that fiduciary inflation and external adjustment through currency depreciation set in motion a cumulative, often irreversible, downward spiral. The margins for government policy choices had narrowed in both directions.

Even the strongest proponents of the gold standard did not claim that it would bring about automatic price stability. Precious metals varied in price like all other commodities. Kemmerer reminded the Dawes Committee that the purchasing power of gold in terms of a basket of commodities had risen by 50 per cent from 1873 to 1896 and then fallen back to the original level by 1913. The purchasing power of gold had tumbled another 60 per cent from 1913 to 1920; the trend reversed owing to postwar deflation, and the value of gold rose by 66 per cent from 1920 to 1924.[15]

Nevertheless, conventional thinking held that the restoration of confidence through a common monetary standard would itself facilitate trade revival despite a residual maladjustment of prices. Russell Leffingwell of Morgan's roundly criticized the maverick economist J.M. Keynes for considering price changes a disease instead of a symptom. Urging a prompt British return to gold in 1923, Leffingwell likened postwar disturbances to a simple bank run:

> When a bank's doors open again after a period of trouble, there are always heavy withdrawals at the outset by people who have been prevented from making withdrawals by the suspension. The trick is to pay everybody very promptly, and…to assure the world that the bank is open to stay.[16]

In short, while statesmen, bankers, and economists might differ about the quantity theory of money or the methods of accommodating political constraints, most conceded that the world needed some agreed blueprint for stabilization (Silverman 1982: 40–61).

At the Paris Peace Conference of 1919, American experts acknowledged that the war-ravaged European Allies required credits to purchase commodities, restore transport facilities, and overcome production bottlenecks. They perceived that Germany and the Habsburg successor states also needed working capital and help in mastering hyperinflation. However, President Wilson had stood firm against French schemes for pooling raw materials during the war. And afterward his economic team rejected the disguised contrivance of Louis-Lucien Klotz, the French finance minister, for pooling war costs through a "financial League of Nations." The American authorities likewise dismissed the British Treasury plan, authored by J.M. Keynes, for recycling American resources to Europe by means of a guarantee of German reparation payments to the Allies. As Assistant Secretary Leffingwell encapsulated domestic sentiment, Americans believed that they had "performed heroic deeds and borne great sacrifices" to save Europe from "annihilation by the Hun." They did not propose to maintain taxation at wartime levels in order to cancel war debts or to pay German reparations through the back door. The Treasury had secured permission to assist Europe during the post-Armistice transition only through intensive lobbying. The Republican-led Congress would never write a blank check along the lines of the Klotz plan or the Keynes plan to recycle American surpluses (Schuker 1976: 176–7).

The practical question, as Leffingwell expressed it, was whether Europeans possessed "adaptability enough and vigor enough to work out some business transactions and [to] interest American businessmen in their financial and economic restoration." In May and June 1919, Lamont explored those possibilities with Robert Brand, Jean Monnet, and other European colleagues. If the Europeans would block out national requirements and arrange guarantees, the Morgan team at home would found a giant trading corporation grouping the main export industries to extend credit and meet vital needs on a generous scale. The New York bankers had in mind an administrative structure in Paris roughly along the lines given substance a generation later by the Marshall Plan. Such arrangements would enable the better-situated European nations to address monetary stabilization themselves. Lamont intimated, however, that the offer came with political strings attached. The Americans insisted not only on Open Door principles in third countries, but also that American credits be employed for the purchase of American goods. If the British needed liquidity beyond that, they should draw down their overseas holdings. In effect, Wall Street demanded a financial condominium that would encroach on British preserves in Latin America and the Far East. As Lamont expressed the idea in his inimitable silky manner, "America has ample credit resources, Great Britain has wonderful credit machinery all over the world. Why not make a combination of the two?"[17]

Both Whitehall and the City bankers poured cold water on the idea of an export syndicate given the terms on offer. The U.S. Congress subsequently provided a modest consolation. It eased the requirements for foreign-trade financing in a limited way by statute. The 1919 Edge Act permitted Federal Reserve member banks to set up foreign-trade investment corporations exempt from antitrust constraints, and Paul Warburg achieved a modicum of success in shipping raw materials to Germany through his International Acceptance Bank. American producers of wheat, cotton, copper, oil, and fertilizers met Europe's commodity needs through a variety of singular expedients (including speculation in depreciated currencies) during 1919–21. Yet although the cumulative trade surplus approached $9 billion in those years – and helped mitigate a fall in domestic demand – Washington steered clear of formal institutional efforts to stabilize currencies overseas.[18]

In any event, the window for ambitious ventures quickly closed. The British wager that they could hold their own against the inroads of U.S. finance overseas proved correct, at least in the short run. In Latin America, for example, British institutions successfully resisted a competitive thrust from the burgeoning branch system of the National City Bank (Parrini 1969: 101–37). A number of British, Dutch, and German bankers organized the Amsterdam Memorial in 1920 in order to foster a public consensus for war-debt forgiveness; Paul Warburg and like-minded bankers proclaimed it "a mortification and a crime" that the United States would not put its shoulder to the wheel.[19]

Such rhetoric played poorly on Main Street, however, as business failures multiplied during the U.S. business depression of 1920. It took no special insight to realize that the Amsterdam Memorial spokesmen had an agenda of their own. German-Americans sought to undermine the reparations settlement, and neutrals who stigmatized "political debts" as counterproductive hoped to recoup their commercial loans and revivify trade with the Reich. Soon enough, the American election season produced a recrudescence of popular isolationism. Attempts at monetary reconstruction overseas would have to proceed piecemeal, or not at all. The delay, in any case, yielded compensating advantages. With the benefit of hindsight, most analysts consider the postponement of stabilization desirable as well as inevitable. Richard Meyer points out that formal devaluation before European nations had repaired wartime damages might have led to a choice of exchange rates inappropriate for normal conditions. On the other hand, forced deflation to restore the prewar par would have produced intolerable shortages of domestic goods (Meyer 1970: 7, 157).

The limitations of multilateralism

In the absence of a trans-Atlantic deus ex machina, the League of Nations arranged a conference of thirty-nine nations at Brussels in September 1920 to articulate the principles that should govern monetary reconstruction. One should not exaggerate the political importance of that confabulation. The largest creditor and the greatest defaulter, namely the United States and Russia, would for different reasons have no truck with emanations of the League. The Germans were still officially excluded. And the French resented the overbearing role of the British Treasury in shaping the agenda. Robert Boyce has likened the proceedings to "sermons against sin."[20] All the same, the League bureaucracy regarded the resolutions that the Brussels Conference unanimously adopted as "the Law and the Prophets" for money doctors everywhere.

Although the term "conditionality" had not yet come into vogue, the Brussels precepts encapsulated the common wisdom of the day (League of Nations 1945: 9–13). Nations seeking to stabilize must balance their ordinary budgets through taxation and meet extraordinary expenses through loans raised out of savings. Central banks of issue should be insulated from Treasury influence, with international supervision if external financing was required. The Dutch banker C.E. ter Meulen elaborated an international credit scheme providing that deficit governments earmark the customs or other hard-currency revenues to meet the service costs on foreign stabilization loans (Silverman 1982: 283–8). The League of Nations Financial Committee opened an office in London to solicit ter Meulen credits on a wholesale basis. Yet, unsurprisingly, no potential lenders showed up. After eighteen months, the League terminated the effort in embarrassment.

The League Financial Committee then shifted to targeted attempts at helping deficit countries one by one in those geographical areas where its writ would run, namely Central and Eastern Europe. The Financial Committee eventually played a constructive role sponsoring rehabilitation of Austria and Hungary, particularly after the Bank of England found it expedient to operate under League cover. Working through Sir Otto Niemeyer in London and Arthur Salter in Geneva, the British pulled the leading strings at the Financial Committee. Austria's initial attempts to obtain a loan on ter Meulen principles by pledging the Gobelin tapestries carried the overtones of comic opera; the House of Morgan regretted that the deal might create a "pawnbroking impression."[21] Nonetheless, in the final analysis, Whitehall perceived a political interest in ending financial chaos in Vienna and keeping French influence out. Once League officials produced a scheme for budgetary reform, and when Austria pledged customs revenues and accepted foreign control of its central bank, Montagu Norman threw himself into the effort. The Bank of England discounted Austrian Treasury bills in March 1923. Some months later, it floated a long-term loan for Austria in tandem with the House of Morgan.[22]

The next year, after Salter masterminded an accommodation between Hungary and its Little Entente creditors, the Bank of England again took the lead in floating a loan for Hungary. The Austrian stipulations served as a model: Hungary undertook financial reform, raised matching funds internally, accepted an American commissioner-general, and created an autonomous central bank with Norman's close associate, H.A. Siepmann, riding herd as adviser (Sayers 1976: 171–3). Subsequently, the League provided its imprimatur for small-scale syndicated loans to resettle Greek and Bulgarian refugees and to complete currency reform in Estonia and Danzig.

Despite the presence of a League administrative apparatus, in several cases for a decade or more, League reconstruction generally failed. Attempts to prevent renewed capital flight proved unavailing. Hungary, Greece, and Bulgaria defaulted outright in the early 1930s; Austria avoided technical default only because the creditors granted fresh advances under duress. Royall Tyler, who represented the Financial Committee in Budapest over fourteen years, waxed philosophical about the outcome. "In particular," he observed,

> the words *pledge, security, mortgage*, and *guarantee* may create the wrong impression…in the mind of the holder. A moment's reflection makes it clear that the implementation of such pledges cannot be achieved in the same conditions…as in a domestic loan, unless the pledged assets or revenues are situated outside the national territory of the borrower.

The specific terms of the loan contract made little difference: "As long as both sides have a will to collaborate, no one looks at a contract, and as soon as either side starts claiming rights under a contract, collaboration is at an end."[23] In modern parlance, the Geneva authorities failed to sustain domestic coalitions that asserted "ownership" of their structural adjustment programs.[24] Given the closely imbricated agricultural, banking, and social crises that convulsed Eastern Europe, however, a more felicitous outcome scarcely seems imaginable.

The Young Committee on German Reparations set forth another cooperative model in 1929 by proposing a Bank for International Settlements (BIS). The BIS would act in the first instance as a trustee for German outpayments and provide a forum where central bankers could exchange views. Montagu Norman hoped that the BIS might develop additional functions, and Emile Francqui of Belgium and Hjalmar Schacht of Germany each roughed out analogous ideas. W. Randolph Burgess, on loan from the New York Fed to the Young Committee, then adumbrated an ingenious plan to create special-drawing rights deriving from reparation payments at the BIS. That facility could be used to increase global liquidity when gold production lagged behind the needs of trade.

The League Gold Delegation had just begun to study the possibility that the world stood at the brink of crippling deflation. Experts disagreed whether an inadequate supply of new gold or falling industrial production costs had the greatest effect on prices, and the three successive reports of the Gold Delegation failed to clarify the matter. The Burgess plan suggested how a combination of creative thinking and enlightened cooperation might produce solutions for otherwise intractable monetary problems. There seemed no obvious reason why the "gold fetters" of which Keynes later spoke so disdainfully need lead ineluctably to deflation.[25] Burgess's seniors on the Young Committee waxed enthusiastic. Still, nothing practical came of the plan. President Hoover, furious that the Young Committee had accepted a link between debts and reparations contrary to his instructions, blocked Federal Reserve participation in the BIS. In the end, the BIS served as a useful club for central bankers, but it accumulated neither the financial resources nor the authority to address massive defaults in the 1930s.[26]

Central bank cooperation and conflict

While the Geneva and Basle institutions registered scant success as money doctors, the central banks compiled a stronger record, at least before the winds of Depression blew their achievements away. Indeed, the period 1924–31 figures as the great age of central bank cooperation.[27] Benjamin Strong, governor of the New York Fed, began to cultivate his opposite numbers in London and Paris as early as 1916. In the 1920s, he devoted much of his energy to collaborating with Montagu Norman of the Bank of England in herding the key countries toward a stable-currency regime. A generation later, Allan Sproul, also a president of the FRBNY, would complain that "the United States has a funny central banking system, with most of the power in Washington, and most of the knowledge in New York."[28] Strong likewise labored chronically under the captious criticism of small-town bankers who dominated the Federal Reserve Board in his day. Herbert Hoover, as secretary of commerce, derided Strong as a "mental annex to Europe" who had initiated easy-money policies in 1924 and 1927 primarily to assist his European "allies."[29] In fact, Strong insisted, domestic and foreign imperatives worked together in both episodes: lower discount rates stimulated business and relieved hard-pressed Western farmers at the same that they opened U.S. markets to foreign borrowing and laid the foundation for monetary rehabilitation abroad. Strong readily conceded that a central bank must privilege domestic monetary management in the event of conflict.[30] In that spirit, the New York Fed advocated restrictive measures in 1928–9 to curb stock-market speculation, even though higher rates would place additional pressure on sterling.[31]

The biographers of Lord Norman, governor of the Bank of England, have fulsomely documented his tactical alliance with Strong, yet they understate his gnawing jealousy of U.S. financial preeminence.[32] From the beginning of his tenure, Norman burned with nationalist fervor to restore the place of sterling in international transactions. Norman framed the central bank resolutions for the 1922 Genoa Conference with a political purpose in mind. Under his proposed "gold-exchange standard," only the lead countries in the monetary system would maintain reserves entirely in gold. The others would hold part of their reserves as foreign-exchange claims on gold centers and stabilize domestic prices through cooperative credit policies.[33] Strong felt mounting qualms about the suggested scheme. It might facilitate a pyramiding of credit on limited gold holdings. Even more alarming, if major countries undertook to manage the system by preventing fluctuations in the price of gold, that might amount to "handing a blank check to some of the impoverished nations of the world…whose government finances are in complete disorder."[34]

Strong evaded a central bank conference to institutionalize such a system and argued instead for tackling stabilization country by country sequentially – what John H. Williams (1947) would later denominate the "key currency" approach. Bank of England records suggest that Norman really aimed to link as many nations as possible to sterling, even before the pound had returned to gold. When the Dawes Committee drew up a Reichsmark stabilization plan in 1924, Norman fought a rearguard battle to avoid basing the new currency on the dollar. "I am aware…that sterling is depreciated in terms of gold," he lectured the head of the Netherlands Bank,

> but it remains the main basis on which European exchanges are operated, and I am most strongly of the opinion that, as Europe obtains no financial assistance or cooperation from America, Europe should no further attach herself to the basis which for the present America controls.[35]

Nonetheless, Norman saw the return of sterling to the prewar par in 1925 as his finest accomplishment. He labored indefatigably to arrange a Federal Reserve Bank credit and a Morgan loan to ensure a smooth return. The London authorities had multiple reasons for hurrying stabilization before relative prices became fully aligned, but international considerations placed high on the list.[36] Not merely Germany, but also South Africa, Australia, the Netherlands, and Switzerland planned an imminent return to gold. As Winston Churchill explicated the policy considerations underlying the Treasury view in May 1925:

> If the English pound is not to be the standard which everyone knows and can trust,…the business not only of the British Empire, but of Europe as well, might have to be conducted in dollars…. That would be a great misfortune.[37]

Following sterling's return to gold, Strong and Norman continued their collaboration to stabilize the continental countries between 1925 and 1928. At the same time, Norman endeavored to foster central banks in the British Dominions.[38] Although France stabilized de facto in 1926 without obtaining either outside Treasury or central bank loans, Strong provided moral support and quietly detailed Robert Warren to render technical assistance. (For reasons of *amour propre*, the French hesitated to acknowledge publicly just how much help they needed.)[39] The cooperative ventures to stabilize Belgium, Italy, Poland, and Rumania, by contrast with the French operation, have come in for trenchant criticism.

The negative evaluations focus less on the monetary aspects of stabilization than on the political conditions in which they took place. Most of those operations, after all, followed some variant of the financial model adumbrated in 1920 at Brussels. They involved balancing the budget, consolidating the floating debt, shoring up the prerogatives of the target country's central bank, and selecting a realistic exchange rate. In return the foreign central banks provided their imprimatur by subscribing to a credit and by tapping the capital markets for a follow-on long-term loan. Richard Meyer contends that, although visible official intervention may prove indispensable from time to time, neither Belgium, Italy, Poland, nor Rumania absolutely needed the credits and loans accorded to them except for development purposes. In practice, the target countries played the participating banks off against each other to obtain the least onerous conditions and the minimum of control (Meyer 1970: 16–160). In other words, the money doctors proved too eager to register political success. Hence bargaining terms moved in favor of individual client nations at the expense of the global financial architecture.

Belgium, for one, took advantage of its diminutive size to stabilize below purchasing-power parity; when France followed suit, that aggravated the putative misalignment of sterling.[40] By contrast, Italy was allowed, for reasons of prestige, to stabilize at a high rate that proved unsustainable at full employment. In addition, Montagu Norman, carried away perhaps by the Morgan interests' admiration of Fascist efficiency, dropped his insistence on central bank independence in Rome.[41] The Polish and Rumanian stabilizations, even worse, exposed the political fissures among the central banks. Allowing political sympathies to warp his judgment, Norman collaborated with the Reichsbank's Hjalmar Schacht in an effort to impose the odium of League control on Poland. The Poles, professing to find the Americans "disinterested," warded off that threat, first by inviting Professor Edwin Kemmerer to investigate, and then by placing themselves under the protection of the FRBNY and a second-tier American bank syndicate. The Poles obtained the funds they desired without accepting fiscal discipline and with a mere simulacrum of control. Not surprisingly, after providing a transitory stimulus, the spigot of new loans turned off (Pease 1986: 40–129).

A controversy over Rumanian stabilization completed the alienation between the London and Paris central banks. Norman, invoking precedent, sought to force Rumania to accept League dictation. Governor Moreau complained to Premier Raymond Poincaré that Threadneedle Street practiced financial "imperialism" all over Europe and employed the Financial Committee at Geneva as the instrument of that "domination."[42] The franc had meanwhile regained de facto stability, and the British grew increasingly dependent on the Banque de France not to draw down sterling balances in London. The French bargaining position had therefore improved. Moreau seethed with outrage when Norman, pretending that nothing had changed, still sought to block France from combining political influence with economic leadership in the Little Entente.

Benjamin Strong deemed the whole matter a tempest in a teapot. The sums at issue were small. Nevertheless, the New York Fed thought it best in principle to encourage France as a capital lender. In the end, the Rumanians got their money without serious reform, and relations between Paris and London continued to worsen. The Bank of England would never again rely on French bona fides, even when a crisis of momentous proportions arose in 1931. The breakdown of cooperation between two key money centers had large implications. By 1927 it had dawned on insiders – even those who had not studied prewar experience closely – that the gold-exchange standard did not adjust to shocks automatically. Rhetoric aside, the central bankers presided in effect over a managed-currency standard.[43] No doubt France's policy of gold accumulation constituted the gravest perceived threat to sterling's stability and thereby to systemic equilibrium. Yet the Rumanian contretemps exposed the manifest political limits to central banks acting as money doctors more generally.[44]

Wall Street to the rescue?

While central banks set the tone, the leading investment banks of the 1920s provided the bulk of the capital for foreign loans. The most important ones, like J.P. Morgan & Co. and Lazard's, maintained representation in all three major money centers and offered one-stop shopping for countries in need of financial assistance. Morgan's still figured incomparably as the dominant banking house of the era. Specializing in "relationship banking," it had strengthened its position by representing the British and French governments during the war and by overseeing purchasing as well as the first mass marketing of foreign loans.[45] Although the Wilson administration began with a deep populist suspicion of Morgan influence, it came increasingly to rely on the talents and contacts of the firm. Thomas W. Lamont assumed a commanding position in the economic group that assisted President Wilson at the Paris Peace Conference (Glaser 1998: 371–400).

Nevertheless, the partners at 23 Wall Street became somewhat troubled during the 1920s by the quasi-public duties that the institutional structure of capitalism had thrust upon them as private citizens. "The Morgan firm is an anachronism," Dwight Morrow once admitted; "it is accountable to nobody but its own sense of responsibility." Partly as rationalization, J.P. Morgan preferred to think of himself as a type of high-level bond salesman, "simply an expert…upon the marketability of securities."[46] Even in private correspondence, the partners preferred to speak of the investment markets' requirements, and of themselves as their mere interpreters.

At the same time, American finance underwent massive structural change in the postwar decade. The transmogrification of Wall Street ultimately circumscribed Morgan leadership. Having witnessed the government's success in mass marketing Liberty Bonds in 1917–18, bankers no longer placed their flotations among a small coterie of the wealthy. Instead, they tapped the burgeoning savings of the middle class. Upcoming firms hungry for business, chief among them Dillon, Read & Co., Harris, Forbes & Co., and Halsey, Stuart & Co., repeatedly undercut Morgan's position by offering easier conditions on foreign loans packaged for retail distribution. The security affiliates of national banks, with deeper pockets than private bankers, took a growing share of the debenture business as well as leading in stock placement. Although Morgan's and its East Coast "establishment" allies continued to set the terms for high-visibility loans to West European governments, their ability to impose conditionality on smaller flotations elsewhere declined (Carosso 1970: 240–99). Challengers stood ready to meet the public appetite for securities without finely calibrating risk against return. As one of the new breed unashamedly told a Congressional committee, "The banker is like the grocer. He supplies what the customer wants."[47]

In 1921 the Harding administration sought to impose public oversight on foreign loans. Commerce Secretary Hoover repeatedly pressed to enlarge that scrutiny. But State and Treasury Department officials feared that, if they passed judgment on any loans as a business proposition, they would incur a potential legal liability for those flotations to which they posed no objection. They accordingly restricted themselves to passing on the political appropriateness of loans (for example to nations that had failed to fund their war debts). When the speculative boom of the middle 1920s threatened to get out of hand, bureaucrats became uneasy about the volume of German and Latin American flotations for unproductive purposes. Still, aside from cautioning the borrowers indirectly, they dared not interfere.[48]

When Congressional committees called them to account in the 1930s, the Morgan partners justly boasted that only two of their own issues had ever gone into default. The exceptions were the Dawes and Young loans, which they had floated at the behest of the U.S. government. Certainly the House of Morgan concentrated on relationship banking and gave a wide berth to risky syndications for most developing countries. At State Department behest, Lamont traveled to the Far East in 1920 to secure Japanese adherence to the International China Consortium, yet the firm confined its own Asian lending in the following years to Japan.[49] Maintaining a prewar ethos that bid fair to disappear among the newer Wall Street conglomerates, J.P. Morgan prided himself on applying strict moral as well as financial criteria to the activities of the firm. Ten years after the war, he resisted pressures to consider a lucrative contract advising the Deutsche Reichsbahn. "From what I see of the Germans," he counseled his partners in the home office, "they are second-rate people, and I would rather have their business done for them by somebody else."[50] All the same, on occasion Morgan's fared no better than less prudent lenders when it encountered the problem of political risk. Marc Flandreau suggests that, even in the 19th century, relationship banking did not foster a very effective form of conditionality.[51] The weaknesses of such arrangements became spectacularly more open in the world after the war, as the Mexican example demonstrates.

In 1921 Lamont had the misfortune to become chairman of the International Committee of Bankers on Mexico. Over the next two decades he spent more time defending the interests of external creditors dispossessed in the Mexican Revolution than on any other matter. He visited Mexico City in October 1921 with the hope of making President Alvaro Obregón a refunding offer he could not refuse, but departed with empty hands. Having observed the success of the Bolsheviks in repudiating foreign obligations, the Mexican negotiators perceived no need to pretend they might make macroeconomic adjustments. "I did not think any government of modern times would so frankly proclaim its complete dishonesty or its abandonment of all decent finance or morals," fumed Jack Morgan from his suite at the Paris Ritz. He congratulated Lamont disconsolately on at least "getting out before they stole your pocketbook or watch."[52] Ever the preternatural optimist, Lamont resumed talks with the Mexican finance minister in 1922 and reached an apparent understanding on annuities secured by oil export taxes and railway revenues. The Obregón regime sought U.S. recognition and hoped to restore its credit rating in order to qualify for a new loan – all without yielding the essence of its revolutionary claim to subsoil rights.

To no one's great surprise, the 1922 agreement did not stick. When the *Yanquis* failed to cough up new money, Finance Minister Alberto Pani withheld Mexican remittances on the grounds (still unusual in the postwar decade, but increasingly common from the Great Depression onward) that "human rights" trumped "legal" considerations. One partial default followed another. In 1930 Ambassador Morrow, placing national-security concerns above bondholder interests, fought to scuttle a revised agreement worked out by his former partners on the ground that it provided no comprehensive settlement of Mexican obligations, both foreign and domestic. The 1930, 1931, 1938, and 1942 refundings proved no more durable than their predecessors, particularly after Washington began to advertise its "Good Neighbor Policy" for Latin America. Neither portfolio investors nor the oilmen recovered more than a miniscule fraction of their original investments or accrued interest. Twenty years along in the process, Lamont reminded a new Mexican finance minister of his boyhood experience seeing a woman skinning eels alive. When he remonstrated, the woman replied: "Oh, they get used to it." As money doctors found so often in the interwar era, political risk loomed larger than financial risk.[53]

Academics and freelancers

Consulting economists constituted the fourth category of "money doctors" between the wars. The Progressive era in America popularized the idea of disinterested public service. Reformers held that the rigorous application of scientific principles could produce advances in public administration as striking as those in the hard sciences. The same generation saw the rise of economics as a credentialed, professional discipline at U.S. universities. Economists made equal theoretical advances elsewhere, of course. And the British were the first to institutionalize independent economic advice to government with the formation of the Economic Advisory Council in 1925 (Howson and Winch 1977). But the unique status of the "expert" became a particular ingredient in American popular culture, where economists, like other social scientists, obtained recognition in the media and special admiration as authorities in their field.[54]

Europe boasted some well-known independent economists too, but it was not always transparent who employed or what motivated them. Charles Rist carried out a number of missions to Eastern Europe – to Rumania in 1927–8 and to Austria in 1931 – nominally wearing his expert hat, but in practice representing the French government, which sought to extend its influence in the region on the cheap.[55] Russell Leffingwell of Morgan's derided "publicist-economists" like Keynes, Gustav Cassel, and Verrijn-Stuart, who made their living mostly through journalism or speculation and who thought, "in their wisdom," that they could control the price level better than the Bank of England or the Federal Reserve. Those iconoclasts' advocacy of a managed currency made them *persona non grata* in orthodox banking circles during the 1920s. From the Peace Conference onward, moreover, the French perceived Keynes as a highly adroit polemicist who placed his unusual talents and knowledge in the service of German diplomacy.[56]

Keynes nurtured a close relationship with the Hamburg financier Carl Melchior throughout the post-Versailles lustrum, and like-minded German industrialists subsidized the influential *Manchester Guardian Commercial* supplements in which the Cambridge economist purported to present a neutral analysis of European stabilization issues. Keynes found himself drawn into the vortex of *haute politique* when Melchior's shipping friend Wilhelm Cuno of Hapag became chancellor of the Reich. In November 1922 the Reich government cast about for a mechanism to head off a declaration of default by the Reparation Commission. It decided to invite seven "independent financial experts," including Keynes and Cassel, to make recommendations for stabilizing the Mark. Arriving in the German capital early, Keynes advanced his own ideas in finished form while his fellow experts were still engaged in "preliminary nail-biting." He persuaded the majority to support a two-year reparation moratorium as a precondition to thorough-going monetary reform, just as the host government desired.[57]

In June 1923 Keynes again rode to the rescue. This time he visited Berlin surreptitiously and worked with Cuno, Melchior, and Foreign Ministry officials preparing a crucial German reparations note. Then he scurried back to London to praise his own handiwork in *The Nation and Athenaeum*. The alternative to the Cuno offer, he warned, would be a reign of tribute and rapine extracted by France, "as the Goths did in the fifth century."[58] It is hard to imagine that Keynes failed to catch on to indications that the Reich government had sustained the hyperinflation as a matter of national policy. After all, Cuno did not mince his words about stabilization in private conversation with his Hamburg friends. Shortly afterward he confessed: "If the reproach is made that we didn't get our tax system in order, well naturally our wish had been to solve the reparation problem first and the tax problem only afterward."[59] What satisfaction did Keynes derive from his German ventures? He kept his pulse on exchange rates and used that knowledge to advise a British textile firm as well as to speculate for King's College and on his own account, but those were secondary gains. Mostly, one can speculate, he acted for the narcissistic gratification of pulling the strings behind the scenes and advancing a political cause in which he believed.

Rather more prosaically, a number of academic economists in the United States turned their expertise to the modernization and reform of monetary conditions abroad. Professor Edwin W. Kemmerer of Princeton figured as the most prominent of his cohort. Other foreign advisers, including W.W. Cumberland, John Parke Young, Arthur N. Young, Arthur Millspaugh, and Frank Fetter, were either Ph.D. students or close colleagues of Kemmerer (Curti and Birr 1954). Kemmerer obtained his first experience as a money doctor in the Philippines, where he served as currency adviser to the U.S. mission in 1903, shortly after receiving his Ph.D. (Glaser-Schmidt 1988: 359–75). Between 1917 and 1934 Kemmerer led financial missions to seven Andean countries as well as to South Africa, Poland, China, and Turkey – in short, to an assortment of nations that lay in the U.S. sphere of influence or disdained potentially humiliating advice from the League. Although Kemmerer, along with Joseph Davis of Harvard, won public plaudits advising the Dawes Committee on German currency reform, he specialized in the transfer of American expertise to developing countries. Indeed, Emily and Norman Rosenberg portray the Kemmerer missions as velvet-glove colonialism, suitably repackaged for liberal sensibilities (Rosenberg 1999: 59–83). While not wholly wide of the mark, that interpretation does less than justice to third-world business notables who embraced modernization as a way to leverage economic growth on their own initiative.[60] In any event, Kemmerer preached the same type of orthodox reform program adumbrated by the Brussels Conference and applied by the League Financial Committee. He cast that program, however, as part and parcel of a more ambitious modernization project. He advocated balanced budgets, scientific collection of taxes, the elimination of corruption and subsidies, the equilibration of exports and imports, and, most important of all, the creation of an independent central bank as a stepping-stone to adoption of a currency linked to gold.[61]

Kemmerer habitually arrived on site with a team including accountants, customs specialists, and men skilled in public administration and finance. He marketed a style of modernization that appealed to local elites who favored an open, export-oriented economy, and in that way pioneered the "ownership" adjustment programs that would become best practice at the IMF half a century later. At the same time, Kemmerer missions provided a stamp of approval to reassure potential U.S. investors. Although the relationship remained secret, Kemmerer accepted an annual retainer from Dillon, Read & Co. from 1924 onward (conflict-of-interest standards were less rigorous then than they have since become).[62] Notwithstanding the efforts of the Kemmerer teams to maintain academic integrity, State Department officials feared by the later 1920s that the publicity attending his missions often facilitated irresponsible borrowing for unproductive purposes (Rosenberg 1999: 155–65). As it turned out, without deep structural and social change in borrowing countries, the Kemmerer reforms tended not to stick. Like IMF programs in a later era, they signaled the creditworthiness of borrowers, but they provided no guarantee of sustainability if commodity prices turned down or political preferences changed (Drake 1994: 128).

Conclusion: disintegration of the reconstructed order

The Great Depression swept away the financial edifice laboriously reconstructed in the 1920s. The gold-exchange standard collapsed; increasingly economists began to question the expediency of restoring it. In the United States, France, and even in England, the respective Treasuries acquired increased leverage at the expense of central banks. In the United States, the Glass–Steagall Act of 1933 worked in tandem with the implosion of capital markets to undermine the functions and prerogatives of private investment banks. There was "no business doing" either in New York or London, lamented J.P. Morgan disconsolately as late as 1938.[63] The Latin American nations that Kemmerer had advised used the excuse of falling commodity prices to suspend his reforms, even though some of those same nations experienced an unprecedented industrial boom (Díaz Alejandro 1983: 5–40). Certain independent financial advisers, for example Arthur Young in China, continued to find employment, but New Deal silver policy undercut whatever wisdom Young could dispense on the spot (Young 1963). In short, the Depression decade offered little scope for the ministrations of money doctors, even in the major countries.

Britain proved a notable exception to the rule. The British Treasury rejected the novel reflationary ideas of Keynes, yet it relied heavily on other economic expertise in crafting its recovery strategy of balanced budgets and easy money. The Bank of England extended its purview not only to advise Commonwealth central banks but also to foster financial rehabilitation at firm level through its Securities Management Trust.[64] Elsewhere, populist governments of every stripe exuded suspicion of the ideology and cultural assumptions embraced by money doctors even when they had to call upon their carefully circumscribed expertise. Franklin D. Roosevelt crafted his bombshell message denouncing the "old fetishes of so-called international bankers" and torpedoing stabilization at the 1933 World Economic Conference without advice from anyone except his Dutchess County neighbor, the gentleman apple grower Henry Morgenthau. Declaring that the bankers had "fooled" him over abandoning gold, he turned the next fall to a heretical agricultural economist, George Warren, for counsel on devaluation. The country was in "agricultural revolution," he maintained; it could stand losing its bonds, but not its homes and farms. When Undersecretary of the Treasury Acheson sniffed that "no reputable economist agreed with the milk farmer who was proposing this," Roosevelt delightedly appropriated the slogan: "the program of a milk farmer."[65]

Economic policymaking in Germany and France also reached phantasmagoric levels at times. Reichsbank President Hjalmar Schacht insisted that Hitler had one idea about finance and a very good one indeed. "It was, leave it to Schacht."[66] In fact, although Hitler lacked the time to read Keynes and Cassel, he repudiated liberal economics and talked of overcoming "a monetary system already attacked by Moses and Christ." He aimed somewhat vaguely at a full-employment socialist economy deriving its innermost essence from a new "moral understanding" and "ethical conviction," in the management of money and credit as in other spheres. He would employ Schacht so long as he proved useful to maintain the credibility of the Deutsche Mark abroad; after that "the Moor would have done his duty."[67] The French Popular Front also created a mental universe far removed from Brussels Conference ground rules. The voluble meridional orator Vincent Auriol, finance minister in 1936, envisaged a simple solution to an imbalance in French external accounts: "*Les banques, je les ferme; les banquiers, je les enferme.*"[68] For good measure, Auriol ordered a telephone tap to monitor conversations at the Banque de France.[69] The civil servant at the Finance Ministry who executed Auriol's orders conceded privately that "the financial aspects of the government's plan are completely subordinated to their social ideas."[70] The measures taken did not increase government credibility, and three devaluations followed within the next two years, leading to rumors of foreign machinations among those already conspiracy-minded. The precepts of the 1920 Brussels Conference had little appeal in a world suffering from mass unemployment, the atrophy of world trade, capital controls, competitive currency devaluation, and premonitions of a new war to come.

Significantly, the default experience of the major creditors in the 1930s, as contemporary analysts recognized, depended mostly on the geographical distribution of their assets. Systemic default in Central and Eastern Europe, China, and Latin America took place in part for political reasons. Countries in the British Commonwealth suffered from the same economic ills as comparably situated nations elsewhere. All the same, they avoided default. In 1935 London Stock Exchange loans issued seven years earlier for Empire governments stood on average at 119 per cent of par, loans for corporations at 116 per cent of par, and even loans for commodity producers at 84 per cent of initial value.[71] Obviously the Dominions that generated an export surplus with Great Britain helped preserve export markets by maintaining a reputation as good borrowers. But it is too simple to say that those borrowers crudely weighed the pecuniary advantages against the costs of delinquency. The imperial visionaries who crafted the Ottawa Agreements of 1932 saw preferential tariff arrangements as a first step toward the larger coordination of trade, migration, and capital movements. The bankers and industrialists who managed the system mutually shared schooling, training, and moral assumptions (Drummond 1972: 17–120). The multiple linkages of interest and sentiment that bound the Commonwealth together evidently militated against interruptions of debt service on grounds of political expediency. Common values proved a more durable tie than the technical stipulations of the money doctors.

In summary, few interwar money doctors, individual or institutional, registered a lasting success. But it does not follow that their failures derived from unsophisticated theory or inadequate technique. Money doctoring always figures as a complex enterprise. It requires political as well as economic judgment. IMF money doctors of the current day have access to better statistics and more elaborate econometric models than did their interwar predecessors. Yet they too must wend their way among conflicting political pressures. Money doctoring, like skillful landscape architecture, requires vision and planning, but also ongoing attention to detail and a modicum of luck. A perfect storm can devastate the most artfully designed construction. To put this another way, the outcome of any macroeconomic stabilization program depends on the specific structure of the economy and the prospects for political accommodation within the target society.

It has become fashionable nowadays for economists to blame the breakdown of the world economy in 1929–33 on the purported rigidities of the gold-exchange standard.[72] The perspective of contemporaries rested on closer acquaintance with the political contingencies that underlay the monetary regime. "The gold standard is sound policy," Leffingwell advised his contacts on the Court of the Bank of England in 1929, "but it is not an insurance policy against all the ills the body political is heir to."[73] The Great Depression brought about a change in political sensibilities that 21st-century economists take virtually for granted. The old model, Eichengreen and Jeanne remind us, hypothesized that "excessively expansionary monetary and fiscal policies were widespread problems." Inflation created chronically overvalued currencies and, with incomplete liberalization of capital markets, limited the ability of central banks and governments to borrow.[74] Enter the money doctors.

In the second-generation model to which current practitioners adhere, central banks and governments are assumed to "maximize a welfare function" in which "domestic variables like output, employment, and the stability of the banking system" outweigh the commitment to any exchange-rate peg. As Eichengreen and Jeanne explain the situation in the value-neutral diction characteristic of the profession today, "the government may be prepared to pay the cost of opting out of its exchange-rate commitment when a high level of joblessness increases the urgency it attaches to the pursuit of reflationary measures." What's more, heightened devaluation expectations under those circumstances can add a devaluation premium to interest rates. An external shock has feedback effects on both unemployment and currency stability. The quantitative data indicate that this is precisely what happened in England in 1931.[75] The premises of bankers from the 1920s about "honest money" have only limited applicability in such a brave new world. That is why the progenitors of the IMF began talking from the outset about allocating the burdens of structural adjustment fairly between debtor and creditor nations (James 1996: esp. 27–84, 309–466). Who adjusts, how, and how much becomes a function of political bargaining.

Notes

1 Feis (1965); Milward and Saul (1977); A. Chandler (1990).
2 Brown (1940, vol. 1: 7–164); Hardach (1977).
3 Kindleberger (1978); Cassis (1992, 1994); Kynaston (1994–99, vols. 2 and 3).
4 Royal Institute of International Affairs [RIIA] (1937: 142–326).
5 Keohane (1980, 1984).
6 Lipson (1985: 37–64); Platt (1968).
7 Lachapelle (1932); Netter (1994). Arthur Raffalovich, who played a central role in the turn-of-the-century "starving" debate, also helped shape public opinion toward the François–Marsal scheme. Compare the discussion in Guyot and Raffalovitch (1921) with Flandreau's treatment in Chapter 1 of this volume. (Raffalovich is published as Raffalovitch in France.)
8 Strouse (1999: 13).
9 Leffingwell to J.P. Morgan, 10 Sept. 1923; analogous comments concerning France in Leffingwell to N. Dean Jay, 16 Oct. 1925, both in J.P. Morgan-Partners file, J.P. Morgan Papers, Pierpont Morgan Library, New York.

10 See Monnet (1978); Salter (1967); Duchêne (1994); Roussel (1996); Nicolson (1935); Schuker (1976); Boyle (1967); Case and Case (1982); L. Chandler (1958); Jones (1964); Lamont (1994); Chernow (1990, 1993); Burk (1989); Ferrari Bravo (1990); Schuker (1980: 124–6). The author thanks J.P. Hannon for providing evidence from the Frank Altschul Papers, Sterling Library, Yale University, showing Altschul's paternity of the 1924 plan to support the franc.
11 Tocqueville (1969: 264–70); Glendon (1994: 257–94); Pruessen (1982).
12 Shaplen (1960); Gäfvert (1979); quotations from "The Kreuger Tragedy," *Economist*, 19 March 1932.
13 Moggridge (1972: 17–28); Kindleberger (1984).
14 Bloomfield (1959); Triffin (1964); Lindert (1969); Bordo and Eichengreen (1998).
15 Quoted in Dawes (1939: 89–90).
16 Russell C. Leffingwell to J.P. Morgan, 10 Sept. 1923, Morgan-Partners file, J.P. Morgan Papers.
17 Schuker (1993: esp. 385–9); Hogan (1977: 20–37).
18 Warburg (n.d.: 33–65); Holtfrerich (1986: 1–32); League of Nations (1943).
19 Warburg to Brand, 22 Mar. 1920, Box 22, Robert Brand Papers, Bodleian Library, Oxford.
20 Boyce (1987: 39).
21 Chernow (1990: 247).
22 Sayers (1976: 163–71); März (1984).
23 League of Nations (1945: 31, 33).
24 For the post-1945 doctrine of local "ownership" of structural adjustment programs, see Chapter 3.
25 J.M. Keynes, *Essays in Persuasion* (1932: 288); cited in Eichengreen (1992: 21).
26 Sayers (1976: 346–59); Case and Case (1982: 434–54); Schuker (1983: 122–30); Link (1970: 438–85); Johnson (1997); Crocker (n.d.).
27 L. Chandler (1958); Clarke (1967).
28 *New York Times*, 6 Feb. 1966, Sec. 3, F3.
29 L. Chandler (1958: 254–5).
30 Strong to Norman, 22 Feb. 1923, FRBNY; Clarke (1967: 31).
31 L. Chandler (1958: 427–70); Clarke (1967: 144–68); and, especially, on Norman's trip to New York, Charles Hamlin Diary, 4–6 Feb. 1929, Box 16, Hamlin Papers, Library of Congress.
32 Clay (1957); Boyle (1967).
33 Clarke (1967: 35–44; 1973: 4–18); Sayers (1976: 156–63).
34 Strong to Norman, 14 July 1922, Benjamin Strong Papers, FRBNY.
35 Norman to Vissering, 14 Jan. 1924, G3/180; elaboration of this standpoint in OV 34/117, Bank of England.
36 Moggridge (1972: 37–112); Clarke (1967: 77–107).
37 Quoted in Kindleberger (1984: 341).
38 Sayers (1976: 201–10); Plumptre (1940).
39 L. Chandler (1958: 360–80); Moreau (1954); Mouré (1991).
40 Van der Wee and Tavernier (1975); L. Chandler (1958: 332–59).
41 L. Chandler (1958: 381–90); Sayers (1976: 193–5); Lamont (1994). For documentation and analysis from the Italian side, see De Cecco and Francesco Asso (1993).
42 Moreau (1954: 488–9).
43 For an explicit acknowledgement of that fact, see Strong to Norman, 19 Oct. 1927, Benjamin Strong Papers, FRBNY.
44 Meyer (1970: 100–37); L. Chandler (1958: 403–22); Mouré (1991: 46–79); Kunz (1987).
45 Burk (1988: 199–211; 1989); Forbes (1974, 1981).
46 Schuker (1976: 141, 277).
47 Garrett (1932: 13).

48 Feis (1950); Hogan (1977: 78–104); Schuker (1988: 35–40).
49 Cohen (1978); Lamont (1994: 153–70, 236–7, 414–7).
50 J.P. Morgan to J.P. Morgan & Co., 30 August 1929, file 36, J.P. Morgan Papers. Although Morgan's expression grates on modern ears, bankers felt no obligation in the interwar era to address questions of borrower credibility in politically correct terms. No doubt Morgan saw himself as appraising a political culture rather than voicing a prejudice. On the context, see Mierzejewski (1999, vol. 1: 297–326).
51 See Chapter 1; also Flandreau (1998).
52 J.P. Morgan (Morgan Harjes tel. 81.447) to Lamont, 24 Oct. 1921, file 36, J.P. Morgan Papers.
53 Lamont (1994: 175–86, 197–200, 280–7, 385–90, 487–9); Smith (1972); Hall (1995).
54 Ross (1991); Haskell (1977, 1984); Larson (1977); Furner and Supple (1990); Rosenberg (1999: 187–218).
55 See Chapter 5; also Soutou (1976: 219–39).
56 Leffingwell to Morgan, 29 Oct. 1923, Morgan-Partners file, Leffingwell to E.C. Grenfell, 15 Aug. 1929, file 176, J.P. Morgan Papers. The classic biographies by Skidelsky (1992) and Moggridge (1992) project their hero's later veneration backward. For the French contemporary view, see Crouzet (1972: 6–26). On Cassel, note Predöhl (1972).
57 Kocherthaler Notizen für das Tagebuch, 2–9 Nov. 1922, Band 196a, Nachlass Max Warburg, Brinckmann-Wirtz & Co., Hamburg; Robert Brand correspondence with Keynes and Karl Ritter of the Auswärtige Amt, Boxes 25 and 49, Brand Papers.
58 Melchior–Keynes–Cuno correspondence, May/June 1923, in FI/2, Keynes Papers, Kings College, Cambridge; Melchior Notiz für das Tagebuch, 24 May and 4 June 1923, Band 147b, Nachlass Warburg; *The Nation and Athenaeum*, 16 June 1923.
59 Notiz Max Warburg, 1 Aug. 1923, Band 157a, Nachlass Warburg.
60 For examples of such modernizing elites, both before and after World War I, see Beatty (2001) and Chapter 6 in this volume.
61 Drake (1989; 1994: 59–132); Rosenberg (1999).
62 Rosenberg and Rosenberg (1994: 59–83, esp. 74).
63 J.P. Morgan to Russell C. Leffingwell, 18 July 1938, Morgan-Partners file, J.P. Morgan Papers.
64 Peden (2000: 247–302); Middleton (1985).
65 Freidel (1973: 470–89); George F. Warren Diary, 20 Oct.–2 Nov. 1933, Box 5, George F. Warren Papers, Cornell University. Roosevelt could have made better use of James Harvey Rogers, a more sophisticated economist on his own ideological wavelength. Unaccountably, he and Henry Morgenthau chose to sideline Rogers.
66 Sir Walter Layton Diary, 31 Mar.–3 Apr. 1933; cited in Schuker (1988: 71).
67 Turner (1985: 260–3).
68 "I close the banks, I jail the bankers" (Lefranc 1965: 366n.).
69 H.A. Siepmann, memorandum of conversation with Cariguel, 7 July 1936, OV45/86, Bank of England. Popular Front partisans insisted in defense that central bank independence required central bank neutrality. The Bank of France had undermined its claim to independence by subsidizing a political campaign against devaluation (see Mouré 1995: 341–62).
70 Rowe-Dutton memorandum of conversation with Wilfrid Baumgartner, 17 July 1936, OV45/86, Bank of England.
71 RIIA (1937: 322, 356–63); Schuker (1988: 125–30).
72 For an elegant exposition of the party line, see Temin (1989).
73 Leffingwell, 29/2420 for E.C. Grenfell, 15 Aug. 1929, file 176, J.P. Morgan papers.
74 Eichengreen and Jeanne (1998: esp. 1–4, 31–2).
75 *Ibid.*

References

Bank of England (1924) OV34/117, German Gold Discount Bank.

Bank of England (1924) G3/180, Governor's Letters.

Bank of England (1936–7) OV45/86, Banque de France.

Beatty E. (2001) *Institutions and Investment: The Political Basis of Industrialization in Mexico before 1911*, Stanford, CA: Stanford University Press.

Bloomfield, A. (1959) *Monetary Policy under the International Gold Standard, 1880–1914*, New York: Federal Reserve Bank of New York.

Bordo, M. and B. Eichengreen (1998) *The Rise and Fall of a Barbarous Relic: The Role of Gold in the International Monetary System*, National Bureau of Economic Research Working Papers Series, no. 6436, Cambridge, MA.

Boyce, R. (1987) *British Capitalism at the Crossroads, 1919–1932*, Cambridge: Cambridge University Press.

Boyle, A. (1967) *Montagu Norman: A Biography*, London: Cassell.

Brand, R. (n.d.) *Papers*, Oxford: Bodleian Library, Oxford University.

Brown Jr., W. (1940) *The International Gold Standard Reinterpreted, 1914–1934*, 2 vols., New York: National Bureau of Economic Research.

Burk, K. (1988) "Finance, Foreign Policy and the Anglo-American Bank: The House of Morgan, 1900–1931," *Bulletin of the Institute of Historical Research* 61(145): 199–211.

Burk, K. (1989) *Morgan Grenfell, 1838–1988: The Biography of a Merchant Bank*, New York: Oxford University Press.

Carosso, V. (1970) *Investment Banking in America: A History*, Cambridge, MA: Harvard University Press.

Case, J. and E. Case (1982) *Owen D. Young and American Enterprise: A Biography*, Boston, MA: D.R. Godine.

Cassis, Y. (ed.) (1992) *Finance and Financiers in European History, 1880–1960*, New York and Paris: Cambridge University Press.

Cassis, Y. (1994) *City Bankers, 1890–1914*, Cambridge and New York: Cambridge University Press.

Chandler, A. (1990) *Scale and Scope: The Dynamics of Industrial Capitalism*, Cambridge, MA: Belknap Press.

Chandler, L. (1958) *Benjamin Strong, Central Banker*, Washington, DC: Brookings Institution.

Chernow, R. (1990) *The House of Morgan: An American Banking Dynasty and the Rise of Modern Finance*, New York: Simon & Schuster.

Chernow, R. (1993) *The Warburgs: The Twentieth-Century Odyssey of a Remarkable Jewish Family*, New York: Random House.

Clarke, S. (1967) *Central Bank Cooperation, 1924–1931*, New York: Federal Reserve Bank of New York.

Clarke, S. (1973) *The Reconstruction of the International Monetary System: The Attempts of 1922 and 1933*, Princeton, NJ: Princeton University, International Finance Section.

Clay, H. (1957) *Lord Norman*, New York: St. Martin's Press.

Cohen, W. (1978) *The Chinese Connection: Roger S. Greene, Thomas W. Lamont, George E. Sokolsky and American–East Asian Relations*, New York: Columbia University Press.

Crocker, S. (n.d.) *Papers. "Young Plan Days"*, Washington, DC: Library of Congress.

Crouzet, F. (1972) "Réactions françaises devant les conséquences économiques de la paix de Keynes," *Revue d'histoire moderne et contemporaine* 19: 6–26.

Curti, M. and K. Birr (1954) *Prelude to Point Four: America's Technical Missions Overseas, 1838–1938*, Madison, WI: University of Wisconsin Press.

Dawes, C. (1939) *A Journal of Reparations*, London: Macmillan.

De Cecco, M. and P. Francesco Asso (eds.) (1993) *L'Italia e il sistema finanziario internazionale, 1919–1936*, Rome: Laterza.

Díaz Alejandro, C. (1983) "Stories of the 1930s for the 1980s," in P. Aspe Armella, R. Dornbusch, and M. Obstfeld (eds.) *Financial Policies and the World Capital Market: The Problem of Latin American Countries*, Chicago: University of Chicago Press.

Drake, P. (1989) *The Money Doctor in the Andes: The Kemmerer Missions, 1923–1933*, Durham, NC: Duke University Press.

Drake, P. (ed.) (1994) *Money Doctors, Foreign Debts, and Economic Reforms in Latin America from the 1890s to the Present*, Wilmington, DE: Scholarly Resources.

Drummond, I. (1972) *British Economic Policy and the Empire, 1919–1939*, London: Allen & Unwin.

Duchêne, F. (1994) *Jean Monnet: The First Statesman of Interdependence*, New York and London: Norton.

Eichengreen, B. (1992) *Golden Fetters: The Gold Standard and the Great Depression, 1919–1939*, New York: Oxford University Press.

Eichengreen, B. and O. Jeanne (1998) *Currency Crisis and Unemployment: Sterling in 1931*, National Bureau of Economic Research Working Paper Series, no. 6563, Cambridge, MA.

Federal Reserve Bank of New York (FRBNY) (n.d.) Benjamin Strong Papers.

Feis, H. (1950) *The Diplomacy of the Dollar, First Era: 1919–1932*, Baltimore, MD: Johns Hopkins Press.

Feis, H. (1965) *Europe, the World's Banker, 1870–1914: An Account of European Foreign Investment and the Connection of World Finance with Diplomacy before World War I*, New York: Norton.

Ferrari Bravo, G. (1990) *Keynes: Uno studio di diplomazia economica*, Padova: CEDAM.

Flandreau, M. (1998) *Caveat Emptor: Coping with Sovereign Risk without the Multilaterals*, London: CEPR DP 2004.

Flandreau, M., J. Le Cacheux and F. Zumer (1998) "Stability without a Pact? Lessons from the European Gold Standard, 1880–1914," *Economic Policy* 26, April: 115–49.

Forbes, J. (1974) *Stettinius, Sr.: Portrait of a Morgan Partner*, Charlottesville, VA: University Press of Virginia.

Forbes, J. (1981) *J. P. Morgan, Jr., 1867–1943*, Charlottesville, VA: University Press of Virginia.

Freidel, F. (1973) *Franklin D. Roosevelt: Launching the New Deal*, Boston, MA: Little, Brown.

Furner, M. and B. Supple (eds.) (1990) *The State and Economic Knowledge: The American and British Experiences*, Cambridge: Cambridge University Press.

Gäfvert, B. (1979) *Kreuger, riksbank och regeringen*, Stockholm: LiberFörlag.

Garrett, G. (1932) *A Bubble That Broke the World*, Boston, MA: Little, Brown.

Glaser, E. (1998) "The Making of the Economic Peace," in M. Boemeke, G. Feldman and E. Glaser (eds.) *The Treaty of Versailles: A Reassessment after 75 Years*, New York: Cambridge University Press.

Glaser-Schmidt, E. (1988) "Amerikanische Währungsreform in Ostasien und im karibischen Raum, 1900–1918," *Amerikastudien* 33: 359–75.

Glendon, M.-A. (1994) *A Nation under Lawyers*, New York: Farrar, Straus & Giroux.

Guyot, Y. and A. Raffalovitch (1921) *Inflation et Déflation*, Paris: Librairie F. Alcan.

Hall, L. (1995) *Oil, Banks, and Politics: The United States and Postrevolutionary Mexico, 1917–1924*, Austin, TX: University of Texas Press.

Hardach, G. (1977) *The First World War, 1914–1918*, Berkeley, CA: University of California Press.

Haskell, T. (1977) *The Emergence of Professional Social Science*, Urbana, IL: University of Illinois Press.

Haskell, T. (ed.) (1984) *The Authority of Experts: Studies in History and Theory*, Bloomington, IN: Indiana University Press.

Hogan, M. (1977) *Informal Entente: The Private Structure of Cooperation in Anglo-American Economic Diplomacy, 1918–1928*, Columbia, MO: University of Missouri Press.

Holtfrerich, C.-L. (1986) "U.S. Capital Exports to Germany, 1919–1923 Compared to 1924–1929," *Explorations in Economic History* 23: 1–32.

Howson, S. and D. Winch (1977) *The Economic Advisory Council, 1930–1939: A Study of Economic Advice During Depression and Recovery*, Cambridge: Cambridge University Press.

James, H. (1996) *International Monetary Cooperation since Bretton Woods*, New York: Oxford University Press.

James, H. (2001) *The End of Globalization: Lessons from the Great Depression*, Cambridge, MA: Harvard University Press.

Johnson, H. (1997) *Gold, France, and the Great Depression, 1919–1932*, New Haven, CT: Yale University Press.

Jones, J. (1964) *Josiah Stamp, Public Servant: The Life of the First Baron Stamp of Shortlands*, London: I. Pitman.

Kemmerer, E. (1944) *Gold and the Gold Standard: The Story of Gold Money, Past, Present and Future*, New York: McGraw-Hill.

Keohane, R. (1980) "The Theory of Hegemonic Stability and Changes in International Economic Regimes," in O.R. Holsti, R.M. Siverson and A.L. George (eds.) *Change in the International System*, Boulder, CO: Westview Press.

Keohane, R. (1984) *After Hegemony: Cooperation and Discord in the World Political Economy*, Princeton, NJ: Princeton University Press.

Keynes, J. (n.d.) *Papers*, Cambridge: King's College, Cambridge University.

Kindleberger, C. (1978) *Manias, Panics and Crashes: A History of Financial Crises*, New York: Basic Books.

Kindleberger, C. (1980) *The World in Depression, 1929–1939*, Berkeley, CA: University of California Press.

Kindleberger, C. (1984) *A Financial History of Western Europe*, Boston: Allen & Unwin.

Kunz, D. (1987) *The Battle for Britain's Gold Standard in 1931*, London and New York: Croom Helm.

Kynaston, D. (1994–9) *The City of London*, 3 vols., London: Chatto & Windus.

Lachapelle, G. (1932) *Le Crédit public*, Paris: Berger-Levrault.

Lamont, E. (1994) *The Ambassador from Wall Street: The Story of Thomas W. Lamont, J. P. Morgan's Chief Executive. A Biography*, Lanham, MD: Madison Books.

Larson, M. (1977) *The Rise of Professionalism*, Berkeley, CA: University of California Press.

League of Nations (1943) *Europe's Overseas Needs 1919–1920 and How They Were Met*, Geneva: League of Nations.

League of Nations (1945) *Reconstruction Schemes in the Inter-War Period*, Geneva: League of Nations.

Lefranc, G. (1965) *Histoire du Front Populaire*, Paris: Payot.

Lindert, P. (1969) *Key Currencies and Gold, 1900–1913*, Princeton, NJ: Princeton University, International Finance Section.

Link, W. (1970) *Die amerikanische Stabilisierungspolitik in Deutschland 1921–32*, Düsseldorf: Droste Verlag.

Lipson, C. (1985) *Standing Guard: Protecting Foreign Capital in the Nineteenth and Twentieth Centuries*, Berkeley, CA: University of California Press.

März, E. (1984) *Austrian Banking and Financial Policy: Creditanstalt at a Turning Point, 1913–1923*, New York: St. Martin Press.

Meyer, R. (1970) *Bankers' Diplomacy: Monetary Stabilization in the Twenties*, New York: Columbia University Press.

Middleton, R. (1985) *Towards the Managed Economy: Keynes, the Treasury, and the Fiscal Policy Debate of the 1930s*, London: Methuen.

Mierzejewski, A. (1999–2000) *The Most Valuable Asset of the Reich: A History of the German National Railway*, 2 vols., Chapel Hill, NC: University of North Carolina Press; vol. 1, 1999; vol. 2, 2000.

Milward, A. and S. Saul (1977) *The Development of the Economies of Continental Europe, 1850–1914*, London: Allen & Unwin.

Moggridge, D. (1972) *British Monetary Policy, 1924–1931: The Norman Conquest of $4.86*, Cambridge: Cambridge University Press.

Moggridge, D. (1992) *Maynard Keynes*, London: Routledge.

Monnet, J. (1978) *Memoirs*, London: Collins.

Moreau, E. (1954) *Souvenirs d'un gouverneur de la Banque de France: l'Histoire de la stabilisation du franc, 1926–1928*, Paris: M.-T. Génin.

Morgan Jr., J. (n.d.) *Papers*, New York: Pierpont Morgan Library.

Mouré, K. (1991) *Managing the Franc Poincaré: Political Constraint in French Monetary Policy, 1928–1936*, New York and Cambridge: Cambridge University Press.

Mouré, K. (1995) "Le Chef d'orchestre invisible et le son de la cloche officiel: The Bank of France and the Campaign against Devaluation, 1935–1936," *French History* 9/3: 341–62.

Netter, M. (1994) *Histoire de la Banque de France entre les deux guerres, 1918–1939*, Pomponne: M. de Tayrac.

Nicolson, H. (1935) *Dwight Morrow*, New York: Harcourt, Brace.

O'Rourke, K. and J. Williamson (1999) *Globalization and History: The Evolution of a Nineteenth-Century Atlantic Economy*, Cambridge, MA: MIT Press.

Parrini, C. (1969) *Heir to Empire: United States Economic Diplomacy, 1916–1923*, Pittsburgh, PA: University of Pittsburgh Press.

Pease, N. (1986) *Poland, the United States, and the Stabilization of Europe, 1919–1933*, New York and Oxford: Oxford University Press.

Peden, G. (2000) *The Treasury and British Public Policy, 1906–1959*, Oxford: Oxford University Press.

Platt, D. (1968) *Finance, Trade, and Politics in British Foreign Policy, 1815–1914*, Oxford: Clarendon Press.

Plumptre, A. (1940) *Central Banking in the British Dominions*, Toronto: University of Toronto Press.

Predöhl, A. (1972) *Gustav Cassel, Joseph Schumpeter, Bernhard Harms: Drei richtungsweisende Wirtschaftswissenschaftler*, Göttingen: Vandenhoeck & Ruprecht.

Pruessen, R. (1982) *John Foster Dulles: The Road to Power*, New York: Free Press.

Rosenberg, E. (1999) *Financial Missionaries to the World: The Politics and Culture of Dollar Diplomacy, 1900–1930*, Cambridge, MA: Harvard University Press.

Rosenberg, E. and N. Rosenberg (1994) "From Colonialism to Professionalism: The Public–Private Dynamic in United States Foreign Financial Advising, 1898–1929," in P. Drake (ed.) *Money Doctors*, Wilmington, DE: Scholarly Resources.

Ross, D. (1991) *The Origins of American Social Science*, Cambridge: Cambridge University Press.

Roussel, E. (1996) *Jean Monnet, 1888–1979*, Paris: Fayard.

Royal Institute of International Affairs [RIIA] (1937) *The Problem of International Investment*, New York: Oxford University Press.

Salter, A. [Baron] (1967) *Slave of the Lamp: A Public Servant's Notebook*, London: Weidenfeld & Nicolson.

Sayers, R. (1976) *The Bank of England, 1891–1944*, Cambridge: Cambridge University Press.

Schuker, S. (1976) *The End of French Predominance in Europe: The Financial Crisis of 1924 and the Adoption of the Dawes Plan*, Chapel Hill, NC: University of North Carolina Press.

Schuker, S. (1980) "The Collected Writings of John Maynard Keynes," *Journal of Economic Literature* 18 (March): 124–6.

Schuker, S. (1983) "American Foreign Policy and the Young Plan," in G. Schmidt (ed.) *Konstellationen internationaler Politik 1924–1932*, Bochum: N. Brockmeyer.

Schuker, S. (1988) *American "Reparations" to Germany, 1919–1933: Implications for the Third-World Debt Crisis*, Princeton, NJ: International Finance Section, Department of Economics, Princeton University.

Schuker, S. (1993) "Origins of the American Stabilization Policy in Europe: The Financial Dimension," in H.-J. Schroeder (ed.) *Confrontation and Cooperation: Germany and the United States in the Era of World War I, 1900–1924*, Providence, RI: Berg Publishers.

Shaplen, R. (1960) *Kreuger: Genius and Swindler*, New York: Knopf.

Silverman, D. (1982) *Reconstructing Europe after the Great War*, Cambridge, MA: Harvard University Press.

Skidelsky, R. (1992) *John Maynard Keynes*, vol. 2, *The Economist as Saviour*, London: Macmillan.

Smith, R. (1972) *The United States and Revolutionary Nationalism in Mexico, 1916–1932*, Chicago: University of Chicago Press.

Soutou, G. (1976) "L'impérialisme du pauvre: la Politique économique du gouvernement français en Europe Centrale et Orientale de 1918 à 1929," *Relations Internationales* 7: 219–39.

Strouse, J. (1999) *Morgan: American Financier*, New York: Random House.

Temin, P. (1989) *Lessons from the Great Depression*, Cambridge, MA: MIT Press.

Tocqueville, A.de. (1969) *Democracy in America* (ed. J.P. Mayer), New York: Doubleday.

Triffin, R. (1964) *The Evolution of the International Monetary System: Historical Reappraisal and Future Perspectives*, Princeton, NJ: International Finance Section, Department of Economics, Princeton University.

Turner Jr., H. (1985) *Hitler: Memoirs of a Confidant*, New Haven, CT: Yale University Press.

Van der Wee, H. and K. Tavernier (1975) *La Banque Nationale de Belgique et l'histoire monétaire entre les deux guerres mondiales*, Brussels: Banque Internationale de Belgique.

Warburg, J. (n.d.) "History of the Warburg Family," unpublished mss., *Paul Warburg Papers*, New Haven, CT: Sterling Library, Yale University.

Warburg, M. (n.d) *Papers*, Hamburg. Brinckmann-Wintz & Co.

Warren, G. (n.d.) *Papers*, Ithaca, NY: Cornell University.

Williams, J. (1947) *Postwar Monetary Plans and Other Essays*, New York: AA Knopf.

Young, A. (1963) *China and the Helping Hand, 1937–1945*, Cambridge, MA: Harvard University Press.

3   Who owns "ownership"?

The IMF and policy advice

Harold James

The International Monetary Fund (IMF) has frequently given policy advice in situations characterized by political instability. Indeed policy failures and political problems are often associated with each other, and tackling the concrete problems of appropriate policy-setting also involves a much broader task of establishing legitimacy. There are two possible – but alas contradictory – ways in which policy advice from the outside and the establishment of political stability may be related. First, a government in an unstable and uncertain position may use an external agent as a scapegoat and try to shift the burden of responsibility for unpopular stabilization measures outside the political system. The IMF becomes in this scenario a very plausible external whipping boy. It can also be used in struggles within the government, as hardliners on stabilization try to use the external advice to capture government policy. The second alternative sees the formation of responsible policy as essential to political and economic stabilization, and advice from the outside as merely a help in reaching a new consensus on appropriate policy. This is the vision that dominates in the official description of recent IMF programs, which emphasize the need to create "ownership" of a program.

Both these positions have their problems. In the first case, when the external agent is used as a whipping boy, there is likely to be no sustained effort at policy reform, and a constant danger of backsliding. In addition, this mechanism works as a deterrent for other countries. There was a neat example from an institution which behaved – as Louis Pauly (1996) has very plausibly argued – in some ways similarly to the later IMF, the League of Nations. In the early 1920s, the League had conducted two programs with countries newly created after the First World War which were very vulnerable politically and had experienced hyperinflations (Austria and Hungary). The League's stabilizations involved drastic budget cuts, which threatened political stability by laying off tens of thousands of civil servants. The experience was so unsatisfactory that subsequently other candidates for stabilization (such as Poland) turned to the capital markets instead.

The problem with the second approach is that it may frequently lead to no reform, or bad results, and the civic or political unity that produced the consensual "owned" solution is then likely to collapse in mutual recrimination.

A modern self-image of the IMF is that "in the bad old days" the institution was prepared to be used as a whipping boy, but that today it emphasizes "ownership." It is worth looking at the history of the institution in order to ascertain how the discussion of fund advice, national policy autonomy, and the appropriate role of international institutions has developed. In fact, the historical trajectory is quite complicated and does not really correspond to the modern myth.

The most successful early stabilizations, in industrial countries in the 1950s, emphasized the "ownership" dynamic. It was in the 1960s and 1970s that Fund-imposed conditionality became a substitute for political reform, and that the IMF consequently became a very contested institution. Some of these developments are associated with broader changes in the way in which national sovereignty was viewed by the international community.

At the time of the United Nations Bretton Woods Conference of 1944, there existed a widespread consensus that the earlier episode of internationalism of the 1920s had been flawed. After the First World War international monetary cooperation had largely relied on independent central banks, who had imposed what the makers of Bretton Woods regarded as a false religion of monetary stability at the expense of domestic objectives, and in the early 1930s the system had collapsed. Central banks were to be largely excluded from the new institutional setting, and the IMF was made and owned by Finance Ministries rather than by central banks. But there was also a great regard for the principle of national sovereignty, which was increased by the need in 1944 to produce a settlement that the USSR would not feel as an imposition of U.S. institutions and capitalistic practices on the rest of the world (especially that part of the world that it hoped to dominate itself).

This vision quickly lost relevance in the Cold War, when the United States began to view multilateralism as a way of organizing a great political coalition and was not hesitant about overriding sovereignty when it got in the way of that objective: by the late 1940s, the United States was even talking about promoting a United States of Europe. Nevertheless, in Europe particularly, the United States needed to be careful of national sensibilities, and in practice, as Alan Milward (1984) has demonstrated, Europe arose out of the calculations of nation-states. Consequently, international institutions were sensitive too about European preoccupations with their national policy autonomy; and the cases discussed here in the 1950s (especially France and Spain) reflect that sensitivity.

Such sensitivity was not universal, however; and, especially in poorer (developing) countries with less sophisticated state structures, international institutions were much more inclined to play the whipping-boy function, especially in the early aftermath of decolonization, and local elites saw the institutions as a useful way to discharge themselves of responsibility without establishing new dependency on their former colonizers.

The end of the Cold War was brought about in large part as a result of a heightened awareness of the principles of self-determination. In line with that awareness, and also no doubt as part of the bitter legacy of the repeated failure of economic reform programs in contexts where they appeared to lack political legitimacy, the IMF talked once again much more about policy involvement. The new credo of post-communist reform involved the idea that a reform package could not work unless it reflected a domestic consensus, and that it could not simply be imposed from the outside. In many ways, this was a return to an earlier era of policy advice, and it is not surprising that the successful Polish reforms of the early 1990s look similar to those implemented (equally successfully) in France and Spain in the 1950s.

Some readers of the following argument might feel that there is another type of explanation that could be given for the successes of one type of (essentially self-managed) reform and the failures of (imposed) reform. Is it not, it might be said, that the successes are European – in the 1950s and the 1990s – and the failures are those of much poorer societies with less developed state systems? There are actually some dramatic successes outside Europe, the most notable being in South Korea, which had almost continual Fund standby programs from 1965, and where they represented an important element in Korea's highly successful growth strategy. Long-term involvements with the IMF thus did not necessarily breed a destructive type of "welfare dependence." The determining factor in the choice of approach lies in great measure with the kind of country, and its institutions, as well as reflecting more general choices on the part of international organizations about civic involvement.

This chapter looks first at some of the cases of early stabilizations in industrial countries, in which what would now be termed "ownership" was a central feature of the diplomacy needed to convince quite autocratic leaders of the need for reform; then at probably the most famous country case of contested relations with the IMF (relating to Jamaica), in which a long experience with the Fund produced little except mutual bad feelings; and, finally, at two contrasting post-communist experiences, in Poland and Russia, in both of which the ownership issue was central to discussions about the IMF program.

National sovereignty and stabilizations in the 1950s

For the first decade of its existence, the IMF played a largely subdued and quite peripheral role in international economic relations. By the mid-1950s, many thought that it had no longer had any significant function and that it should be allowed to fade away quietly. After 1956, in large part as a response to the international political crisis that divided France and Britain from the United States over the Suez crisis, it revived, and it played an important part in the transition of the industrial countries to current account convertibility (see Boughton 2000: 273–91). A central role was played here by Per Jacobsson, a Swedish economist who had been the major intellectual figure in the Bank for International Settlements (BIS) in the 1930s and in 1956 became the third Managing Director of the IMF.

An early stabilization program not involving the IMF proved an inspiration for much of the IMF's activity under the Managing Directorship of Per Jacobsson, a period which marked a definite type of approach to the politics of the conditionality problem. In 1950, a first crisis shook the new European

Payments Union (EPU) as the German balance of payments deteriorated. German imports surged as a result of a rapid recovery, made more intense in the wake of a German relaxation of German credit controls, which set in with the investment boom accompanying the Korean War (which had broken out in June 1950) (Milward 1992: 102). The Allied High Commissioner in Germany, John McCloy, advised the suspension of the liberalization program and the imposition of trade controls. But an EPU delegation composed of the Swedish economist Per Jacobsson (from the BIS) and the Briton Alec Cairncross recommended strongly against this course and in favor of using monetary policy (a discount rate rise) to deal with the German balance of payments. Jacobsson was a committed liberalizer; Cairncross took a more pragmatic stance, but saw in the German situation a "straightforward liquidity crisis in an otherwise healthy economy," simply the result of too much monetary growth in Germany, which produced an unsustainable demand for dollar liquidity (E. Jacobsson 1979: 243). Their advice was backed by a special EPU credit of $120 million. This combination of immediate balance of payments assistance with a commitment to progressive liberalization later came to be seen as an extremely attractive precedent for IMF stabilization programs, especially at the end of the 1950s, when Per Jacobsson was in Washington as Managing Director of the IMF. Against the opposition of both the American authorities and Federal Chancellor Konrad Adenauer, the German central bank (then called the Bank deutscher Länder) eventually accepted the EPU recommendation and took the road to economic liberalism. Jacobsson wrote to Roger Auboin, the General Manager of the BIS:

> I had one and a half hours with the Americans and I pointed out that there are some very favorable tendencies as regards German trade and added that if liberalization were discarded by Germany, people would say that another measure pressed on Europe by the Americans had shown itself unsuitable and impossible (as in 1947 the convertibility of sterling).
>
> (E. Jacobsson 1979: 239)

The Jacobsson/Cairncross course proved to be completely correct, and its success greatly strengthened the impetus to liberalization within the EPU. In retrospect, the experience appeared as an almost ideal model of an adjustment program, in which successful adjustment was followed by impressive growth. Once the process began, liberalization and the lifting of trade controls acquired a momentum of their own (see Buchheim 1990).

Jacobsson applied a very similar philosophy in dealing with the European country – and the European statesman – who believed most emphatically in the principle of national sovereignty. By the later half of the 1950s France also faced a quite stark choice domestically: either she could proceed with liberalization and modernization, or the "Malthusian" "stalemate society" of interwar France would reassert itself. Modernization required both an agreement on exports and markets for French goods and, in political terms, a security framework that would guarantee the stability of Franco-German relations. Internal reform and external policy as a result became closely identified with each other. The veteran planner of the postwar period, Jean Monnet, commented that

> France is on the way to becoming a *pays neuf*. The internal changes are part of France's modern revolution. They have led her to endorse the wider changes of a united Europe…Europe must contribute more nearly equally with America to the development of the West. United, Europe can do it. Separately, its nations cannot. The six countries have opened the way and we hope others will join their common effort.
>
> (Jean Monnet 1958)

The European Economic Community (EEC) had barely begun operating, and the French stabilization program had barely had time to operate, when France was engulfed once more by political instability. Faced with a mutiny of the army in Algeria and the threat of a military coup in France, in May 1958 General de Gaulle took power – for the moment as Prime Minister. He appointed as Finance Minister Antoine Pinay, a fiscal conservative who in 1952 had been the author of one of the Fourth Republic's more successful stabilization efforts, in which budgetary measures had been accompanied by a domestic loan. In June 1958 Pinay launched a new version of this plan: a tax-free loan, with the promise of an amnesty for returned flight capital that might be subscribed. At the time the loan was issued, the economist Jacques Rueff brought Pinay a memorandum couched in apocalyptic terms ("the existence of France is threatened") and advocating a total liberalization of the Banque de France's policy. The Banque should not try to impose quantitative credit ceilings, but should operate only through changes in discount rates and leave the allocation of credit to the market mechanism. If there were no French stabilization, Rueff believed, there would inevitably be a "new effort at international begging, which would bring, even if it did not fail, humiliation and loss of independence."[1] Rueff convinced Pinay, but the Banque de France opposed a stabilization package.

In the course of 1958, Jacobsson acted as a go-between between Pinay, the Governor of the Banque Wilfrid Baumgartner, and General de Gaulle. He took Pinay's program to the General, spoke about the success of the loan, and then began with the only language de Gaulle really understood: that of power politics. He warned de Gaulle against being concerned only with the pressing issue of Algeria: "No country can gain international esteem if it has not a good currency. That the French franc has not been a strong currency has been very damaging to French prestige in recent years." He then appealed to the memory of the Emperor Napoleon, whose gold franc had survived two revolutions (in 1848 and 1871) and a war (in 1870):

> The French are a hard-working and saving people. If they have monetary stability they can stand a great deal of political instability. But after 1919

they had to endure both monetary and political instability and that is too much even for the French.

France in 1958 was threatened by political unrest. "Therefore it will be important to do as Napoleon did – to give France again a strong currency." Then Jacobsson spoke about the role of international institutions in the world order. The IMF had been created to deal with monetary problems. It was true that it and the World Bank were "dominated by the Americans":

> Of course, the Americans have put up most – almost all – of the money so far – and ought to have influence – and are very decent and helpful. But Europe has already more influence – and will have even more if it can contribute. But to that [*sic*] European countries have to have sound monetary systems.

For an effective French participation in the EEC, Jacobsson said, "a strong French franc was essential." De Gaulle replied that the Common Market was "probably a good thing. But he added that he does not like supernational structures – he prefers '*arrangements entre Etats*'."[2]

The result was a devaluation of the franc (in reality a regularization of the August 1957 measures) and the introduction of a realistic exchange rate, in combination with the implementation of the Rueff reform proposals. On December 27, 1958, France established a par value with the IMF for the first time since 1946. In November 1958 Rueff had been summoned to see de Gaulle. In 1960 a commission under his leadership diagnosed that since 1945 the major obstacle to French economic expansion had been the blocked and manipulated interest rates (see Rueff 1972: 287–448). De Gaulle's France had established an identity between liberalization, economic expansion, and the assertion of national power.

French convertibility was supported by the establishment of swap credit lines from European central banks and also by a standby credit of $200 million from a private U.S. bank consortium. It was also immediately followed by the entry into effect of the European Monetary Agreement (December 28, 1958), which provided a framework of margins for currency movements. The European currencies could move within a bank of 1.5 per cent relative to the U.S. dollar, and within 3 per cent margins relative to each other.

With the French stabilization completed, it rapidly became apparent to many policy-makers that currency liberalization and stabilization offered a way to a better future. Probably the most extraordinary and surprising of all the European liberalizations at the end of the decade occurred in Spain. The Nationalist regime of General Francisco Franco, which had been victorious in the Civil War of the 1930s, committed itself to traditional, anti-urban values, and to a regimented nationalist corporatism. It had tried to cut Spain off from the world economy and "international capitalism" and dependence. Spain survived into the 1950s as a relic of the attempts at autarkic planning

characteristic of the 1930s, to which the spirit of Bretton Woods had stood in
fundamental antagonism. In fact, import licenses on machine tools, fuels and
fertilizers produced a slow strangulation of the Spanish economy. Industrial
wages declined – in accordance with the ideological preferences of the
regime. But even agricultural production stagnated.

By the late 1950s it had become clear to many Spaniards that economic
nationalism was unsustainable. The combination of high rates of inflation,
produced by unlimited central bank discounting of government debt, with
government regulation of pay in accordance with the principles of corporatism provoked major unrest in the industrial centers of Catalonia and the
Basque country. At the same time, some policy-makers, notably in the Banco
de España and the Ministry of Commerce, began to argue against the idea of
Spanish difference and a peculiar Spanish economic policy (Varela 1989–90:
45). They wanted to use the possibility of Spanish membership of international institutions as a way of securing and supporting a fundamental reform.
Spain became an associate member of the Organization for European
Economic Cooperation (OEEC), and in 1958 joined the IMF and the World
Bank.

The missions sent in the process of the membership negotiations emphasized
the need to suppress unnecessary restrictions, regulation, and interventions, and
to improve productivity by engaging in competition on the world market. On
June 25, 1959, Franco received Per Jacobsson and Hans Karl von Mangoldt, the
General Manager of the European Monetary Agreement; both men persuaded
him of the benefits of convertibility and the devaluation of the peseta to a realistic rate (Varela 1989–90: 48). In a television interview, Jacobsson explained that
membership of the Fund provided additional reserves, which would protect
against the need to combat balance of payments problems by means of "severe
and damaging import restrictions." But he also explained that sometimes deep-
seated problems required "a fundamental stabilization program…to restore the
balance of the economy." His formulation of how Spain might be helped has a
surprisingly modern tone:

> I must emphasize that such programs can only succeed if there is the will to
> succeed in the countries themselves. The Fund has always found people in
> these countries who know very well what needs to be done. The Fund does
> not impose conditions on countries; they themselves freely have come to the
> conclusion that the measures they arrange to take – even when they are
> sometimes harsh – are in the best interests of their own countries.
>
> (Jacobsson 1959)

At the end of June, the Spanish government presented the IMF and the OEEC
with a memorandum in which it set out the basis of a stabilization plan:

> the time has come to redirect economic policy in order to place the Spanish
> economy in line with the countries of the Western world, and to free it from

the interventions inherited from the past which do not correspond to the needs of the present situation.

Public-sector expenditure would be limited; government securities would no longer automatically be treated as collateral by the central bank; commercial credit would be limited; and a more liberal trade and payments regime instituted.[3]

With the help of an IMF drawing and an additional standby agreement, the National Stabilization Plan was launched one month later (Ullastres 1959). Spain joined the European Monetary Agreement and provided a first list of liberalized imports, mostly foodstuffs and other raw materials, covering over half of Spain's foreign trade. By 1961 almost all barriers had been lifted. In addition, foreign investment was now permitted up to 50 per cent of the capital of a Spanish company (and in some cases even higher).

The reform initially produced a distinct economic and social cost. Some industries suffered heavily from the initial effects of foreign competition (Varela 1989–90: 52). In 1960 real gross national product (GNP) fell by 0.5 per cent. But then a great boom began. In 1961 real GNP rose by 3.7 per cent, and in 1962 by 7.0 per cent. As the economy grew, it drew in large volumes of imports (especially engineering goods and machine tools); but the resulting trade deficit was paid through large investment inflows. Most observers consider the 1960s the date of "the true industrialization of Spain."[4] Economic success of a spectacular variety also in the longer run generated an increased pressure for political liberalization in the wake of the economic reforms. One economist in 1969 expressed very eloquently the new mood created by successful structural adjustment: "The last third of the twentieth century will be extremely difficult for any country which does not accept the rhythms of rapid technological and social change and the rational criticism and democracy that make them possible…. The future of economic development in Spain will depend on our ability to force the retreat of conservative forces."

The experience of 1959 made a profound impact, and helped to shape the course of the reforms and adjustment pursued after General Franco's death.[5]

Both these cases raise an interesting question about the relationship between the "ownership" discussion and the structure of domestic politics. Franco was a dictator, and de Gaulle an autocrat with a plebiscitary approach to politics; both believed that their leadership style uniquely incarnated the better values of their nations. Their experience of economic reform invites an observation often made in the 1970s and 1980s, but rarely made in the 1990s, that reform is easier for un- or semi-democratic polities – Chile, Korea, and Singapore are examples of such reforms, with quite different relations with the international financial institutions (quite autonomous for Singapore, and very close for Korea). One of the reasons that these countries stood out is that they offered a dramatic contrast to the bulk of newly democratic and newly independent countries, in which weak institutions invited the whipping-boy approach.

Developing countries and long-term IMF dependence

The European programs of the 1950s provide a very marked contrast with a great deal of developing country experience in the 1960s and 1970s. The experience of Jamaica has frequently been used, literally as a textbook case of bad relations with the Fund – of the dire consequences of either (or both) political insensitivity on the part of the Fund or misguided radical populism on the side of the government of a poor country (see, for instance, Meier 1982: 159–74). The Jamaican economy had grown very quickly in the 1960s, at an average real rate of growth in gross domestic product (GDP) of 6 per cent, developing tourism and bauxite production. But the growth was not matched by employment creation, and in 1972 unemployment stood at 23.5 per cent. The new Prime Minister elected in that year, Michael Manley, promised to solve the labor surplus by implementing "democratic socialism." Bauxite production would be expanded with the help of foreign capital as well as development assistance. In practice, Manley built up a large public sector and implemented new social programs. When the economy was hit by the oil price shock, the government attempted to minimize the effect on living standards by an expansive monetary policy designed to allow higher consumption. Investment fell abruptly, the unemployment rate returned to 24 per cent (1976), and by 1977 real per capita GDP was 20 per cent below the level of 1972.

In the December 1976 elections, the opposition attacked Manley with the allegation that he had accepted devaluation as part of an IMF program, and he responded with a campaign against "IMF impositions." After a new victory, in 1977 his party's National Executive Council prepared a paper recommending that Jamaica should stay as a member of the Fund, but work towards the creation of a New International Economic Order. The essence of the Jamaican position was explained by Foreign Minister Percival J. Patterson to the UN General Assembly:

> Unfortunately, developing countries which take a really serious view of their obligation to divert resources to meet the needs of their underprivileged find little sympathy or understanding among developed countries and certain international institutions. If we devote domestic resources primarily to meeting these needs and have to seek temporary foreign-exchange assistance from the international monetary agencies, those agencies ignore or discount the social objectives and apply rigid and anachronistic yardsticks to the credit application; stigmatize our Governments as having frittered away our resources and provide limited amounts of credit only on condition that the vital social programmes are cut back. All this is done in the name of sound financial practice.
>
> (United Nations General Assembly 1977: 260)

At the beginning of January 1977, Manley told parliament:

> This government, on behalf of our people, will not accept anybody anywhere in the world telling us what to do in our country. We are the masters in our house and in our house there shall be no other master but ourselves. Above all we are not for sale.

The parliament began to develop a non-IMF alternative Emergency Production Plan for self-reliant development with an increased emphasis on agriculture and closer relations with socialist economies, but eventually turned to the IMF instead, while still engaging in a harsh criticism of the international economic order.[6] The goal of the government was to use the international authority as the scapegoat for the imposition of an unavoidable, but unavoidably unpopular program. This was the background to a 64 million SDR ($75 million) two-year stabilization program negotiated with the IMF in August 1977. Although the program specified a flexible external rate and a real depreciation, in practice currency controls remained and the exchange rate was overvalued, especially as wages rose further. Other performance criteria were not met, and in December 1977 the Fund suspended Jamaica's drawing rights under the program.

The suspension alarmed Jamaica's private creditors, and the banks formed a syndicate organized by the Bank of Nova Scotia. At a meeting with the Jamaican Finance Minister (who appealed for further funds) and IMF representatives, the bankers discussed the possibilities for solving Jamaica's debt crisis. Essentially they hoped for a bailout from the official sector. They expected that official development assistance might help Jamaica, that the World Bank might participate with some program financing, and that the U.S. Exim Bank would grant some debt relief. But the fundamental strategy involved linking further private credit to the Fund's conditionality. The banks proposed to refinance 87.5 per cent of the credits maturing in 1979 and 1980, "subject to the negotiation of a suitable program under the Fund's Extended Facility."[7] The Extended Fund Facility (EFF) program was indeed negotiated during 1977–8, in a wide-ranging set of discussions designed by the IMF to involve as many Jamaicans, both officials and politicians, as possible in the formulation of an improved economic strategy in order to avoid the Fund being used as a scapegoat. The IMF would provide 200 million SDR ($250 million) over three years. Regular devaluations ("a crawling peg") would guarantee a realistic exchange rate. Subsidies would be cut, and prices and taxes increased.

In fact, in the first year of the program balance of payments problems persisted, and there was little substantial economic growth. In mid-1978 the crawling peg devaluations were suspended, with a Jamaican assurance that wage policy would tighten. In 1979 some indicators showed a modest recovery, but the economy was then hit by the second oil shock, and the IMF now extended additional facilities for commodity and buffer stock financing. Attempts to agree on a new refinancing with the private banks failed. The Fund staff urged a renegotiation of the EFF, with a concentration on microeconomic adjustment, with a slimmed down public sector providing only "basic services," the identification of a number of specific production and investment bottlenecks, and the creation of taskforces with business, labor, and government participation to tackle them.

Macro-adjustment had repeatedly failed in the case of Jamaica. As a consequence, the concept of conditionality came to include ever more details about the appropriate course of economic management. But this might appear like a new intrusion, especially when linked with the identification by the IMF team of a large J\$170 million gap in the budget plan for 1980–1. The IMF was used again as the bearer of bad news. At first, Jamaica tried to obtain a "waiver," under which the Fund would overlook the breach of performance criteria and which would avoid the necessity of negotiating a new program. But the government found it impossible to deal with the budget gap, and the waiver negotiations broke down.

Manley, on March 2, 1980, as a response proposed new elections before the adoption of a new EFF program. Once again, as riots broke out outside food stores, Manley mounted an anti-IMF campaign, in which the EFF became the object of a political ballgame. Some U.S. Congressmen joined in the criticism of the "harshness" of the IMF, and the Managing Director responded with a personal letter to Manley in which he explained that the fact that "Jamaica has received more Fund financing, relative to its quota, than any other country in the Fund's history is evidence of our readiness to assist Jamaica."[8] At the end of March, the Prime Minister announced that he would hold no further talks with the IMF, and on March 30 he delivered a speech asking whether the IMF had any "genuine value to the Third World."[9] The opposition Jamaica Labour Party campaigned on a promise of sounder economic management, smaller and more efficient government, an improved environment for private enterprise, and a resulting creation of jobs. It won a massive majority in the elections, eventually held in October 1980, and the new government of Edward Seaga began negotiations with multilateral institutions and also with U.S. aid authorities. Relations with international agencies as a result improved dramatically for a while, although the fundamental problem remained of how to accept a painful adjustment program which appeared to promise little recovery.

A staff memorandum prepared in the IMF explained the Jamaican experience in the following terms: "The Fund staff can perhaps be faulted for an over-optimistic assessment, in the earlier stages of the exercise, of the political commitment to the program; and for its over-estimation of the management capabilities of the administration."[10] Longer-term adjustment created too many problems for governments concerned with short-run popularity and obsessed with distributing elsewhere the blame for poor performance and unpopular measures.

Looking at the situation from the perspective of the 1980s, many observers concluded in consequence that developing democracies did not fit easily with economic reform and liberalization. This is a completely opposite view to the majority view of the 1990s – that democracy provided an important element that made reform sustainable. The most important reason for this remarkable shift lies in the experience of Central and Eastern Europe's transition from communism, though Latin America also provided examples of a coincidence of democratization and economic reform.

Post-communist transition and debate about civil society

The IMF played a quite central role in the communist and post-communist transition, and the challenge provoked another of the periodic remakes that have characterized the history of the institution. In part, its role was as a scary monster, and the international community applied this role quite deliberately. In 1989 the East German communist regime was spurred to begin both political and economic reform because its security apparat had come to the conclusion that otherwise the precarious debt and trade situation would mean that it would become dependent on the IMF. One of the last government documents of the German Democratic Republic (GDR) stated: "The consequence of the immediately imminent incapacity to pay would be a moratorium in which the International Monetary Fund would determine what would happen in the GDR.... It is necessary to do everything to avoid taking this course."[11] In 1990, at the Houston Summit of the Group of Seven, the U.S. wanted the IMF to play a leading role in dealing with the Soviet Union in order to demonstrate to the Soviet leadership that reform was difficult and costly. But the most important role of the IMF was as a provider of policy advice, backed by funding, and it was that role that brought an engagement with the discussion about the domestic backing of reform and its sustainability.

In making parallel steps to democracy and market economies in the aftermath of communism, it was clear that the "ownership" issue would be a central issue in the legitimacy of economic reform programs. The political importance of this issue had already become clear in the last years of the communist systems, when governments and opposition movements struggled (particularly visibly in the case of Poland) over the contents of reform packages.

In the 1970s, under First Secretary Edward Gierek, the Polish Communist Party had attempted to promote modernization. As in Hungary, the oil shocks in the Western economies constituted a caesura. Growth rates fell off after the mid-1970s. Social resistance to the reduction of consumption levels constrained the Polish regime even more than had been the case in Hungary. Government attempts to raise prices not only formed a leitmotif running through Poland's economic and social experience between 1970 and 1990, but were also a fundamental cause of political change.

The government had been shaken by working-class protest in 1970, when Gierek's predecessor Wladislaw Gomulka had been forced to resign. While in the first half of the 1970s the average annual rate of real consumption increase was 9 per cent, in the second half of the decade it fell to 4 per cent. The regime knew its weakness, and saw its unpopularity limiting the possibility for effective action. In 1976, confronted with popular demonstrations, it backed down on an attempt to increase prices. Instead it encouraged a build-up of Western debt, a substantial proportion of which was used to finance increased consumption. From 1977–80, 34 per cent of credits are estimated to have been used in this way, the largest part of them to pay for purchases of agricultural goods.[12] Poland became the world's third-largest wheat importer. Some Poles suspected that after 1978 an increasingly political motive underlay the enthusiasm of Western governments for loans. The German Chancellor, Helmut Schmidt, who publicly urged German banks to extend credits to Eastern Europe, hoped that credit would contribute to political stabilization and the implementation of gradual reform. There also existed a purely commercial motive. A combination of prompt service payments, skillful debt management by a limited number of state-owned banks, and the widespread assumption by creditors that there existed a Soviet "guarantee" or "umbrella," made Poland appear a model debtor.

Gierek's attempt to buy popularity with foreign money succeeded only in raising consumption levels. It brought none of the hoped-for macroeconomic gains and almost no increases in productivity levels. Prices remained distorted, and an attempt to correct them provided the trigger to the crisis of legitimacy of the Polish regime that developed in the course of 1979 and 1980.

Poland became one of the first states to be shaken by the international debt crisis. As in other debtor countries, maturities shortened in the early 1980s, and the surge of interest rates increased the cost of service (Antowska-Bartosiewicz and Malecki 1992: 10). In order to deal with the unanticipated decline in foreign lending, the Prime Minister, Edward Babiuch, attempted a drastic adjustment program aimed at eliminating the Polish trade deficit in the course of a year and repaying foreign debt. In 1980 the government repaid about one-fifth of its long- and medium-term debts (*c.* $5.2 billion) in addition to paying $2 billion in interest. France agreed to a rescheduling of official credits. The domestic side of adjustment was to be accomplished through price increases, which the government hoped to camouflage by undertaking quality reductions of goods, which would stay at the same price, and by introducing the "reforms" at the start of the summer holiday season.[13] Initial strikes against the price hike were successful in obtaining wage increases. The initial victories of the workers' opposition groups helped to create a national movement (Solidarity) which demanded the creation of free trade unions, the right to strike, and freedom of speech and publication (MacDonald 1981: 102–9).

For some time in 1981 it appeared that it might be possible, given skillful negotiating by both the government and the opposition, to produce a consensus around economic reform, coupled with some measure of political liberalization. Both sides agreed on the desirability of some measure of liberalization. But the opposition found it hard to accept responsibility for a harsh stabilization that the government was attempting to impose on it, while the regime was stalling on demands for further political liberalization. Solidarity leaders insisted, rightly, on some measure of power: they did not simply want to take on the hard task of selling an initially unpleasant liberalization package. They worked out their own plans. There was even a detailed blueprint prepared by Professor Leszek Balcerowicz of the Warsaw School of Planning and Statistics, drawn up on the basis of discussions that had been taking place since 1978. Its main suggestion was an operation of independent firms, run on a self-made basis, within a market and cut off from central planning. This plan had been drawn up in the knowledge that it represented a second-best solution – but the basic premise of the would-be reformers was that they needed to stay within the boundaries of "our understanding of political realism." At this time, this included remaining within the Council for Mutual Economic Assistance (CMEA) and not introducing private property (Balcerowicz 1992: 10–13).

Some elements of reform were realized between September 1981 and February 1982. Large economic supra-enterprise organizations and the so-called "branch ministries" were abolished, and responsibility decentralized to the enterprise level. Firms were given greater autonomy in setting wages. A unified external exchange rate was introduced. But in its essentials, the program brought by the government to the Polish parliament on December 1, 1981 (termed the "*provizorium*"), ignored Solidarity's suggestions. To emphasize the fact that the decrees were not the result of negotiation with the domestic opposition, the government announced them during a meeting of Warsaw Pact Defense Ministers in Moscow. In fact, it was the world political scene that shaped the outcome of the upheavals of 1980–1. A different international context might have made possible an agreement on more far-ranging reform, including both political and economic elements. Some Solidarity activists, and others, advocated a Marshall Plan-style aid package that would make bearable the costs of reform. In November 1981, the Polish government applied for readmission to the IMF.

In fact, however, the reform endeavor came to an abrupt halt on December 13, 1981, with the imposition of martial law and the banning of Solidarity. This visibly and brutally destroyed both the domestic and the international basis for consensus on reform. The U.S. imposed economic sanctions, including a veto of Polish membership of the IMF. This threatened the process of debt negotiation.

Debt had played a crucial part in the shifting balance between an Eastern and Western orientation in Polish politics. Until April 1981 Poland was regularly servicing her debt, despite the disruptions to output caused by the political turmoil. Since the USSR reduced its deposits in Western banks between December 1980 and March 1981 by $3.1 billion, it was assumed by Poland's creditors that their loans were being repaid with Soviet help. In fact, the USSR advised against some Polish suggestions that they should declare a unilateral default, and provided the means to continue payments (Schröder 1981: 74). On August 31, 1981, Poland's medium- and long-term foreign liabilities had stood at $23.4 billion. They included $8.5 billion non-guaranteed debt to private creditors (501 banks), with the largest claims held by German banks (*c.* $2 billion). The German banks had adequate reserves against potential losses in Eastern Europe, and the exposure of bankers in other countries was insufficient to create a systemic threat of the kind posed one year later by Mexican developments (the largest exposure of a U.S. bank amounted to 8 per cent of its capital).[14] In the Paris Club rescheduling of debt in April 1981, in the face of the political uncertainty surrounding the rise of Solidarity, a clause had been added (Article IV,

Paragraph 3) providing for the suspension of the agreement without notice in the case of "exceptional circumstances." These were understood to include both "the entry of foreign troops into Poland, whether they were invited by the Polish government or not," and "the emergence of violence among Poles." Most creditors believed that General Jaruzelski's imposition of martial law unambiguously constituted the latter. After December 1981, the imposition of Western economic sanctions by the major creditor countries meant that new foreign funds were unavailable (apart from some officially guaranteed credits from Austria).

Jaruzelski's government tried to muddle through. After 1982 economic growth resumed, at an annual rate of some 4 per cent, but output never reached the peak levels of the later 1970s. Military expenditure increased. The government recognized that reform was needed, and at the same time it knew that it was too weak to make the necessary moves on its own.

The price for international assistance, however, was a domestic political as well as economic liberalization. The U.S. attitude involved a leveraging of economic change into political adaptation. In 1986 the U.S. government lifted its embargo on Polish membership of the IMF and, as a result of one of the conditions imposed by the U.S. for IMF membership, the Polish government freed all of its 225 political prisoners and declared a general amnesty.

The movement of Poland towards the international economy continued to be carefully analyzed by the underground Solidarity organization. In September 1985 the Solidarity office in Brussels sent a message to the IMF's Managing Director stating that the movement welcomed Polish membership and urging that "the IMF should familiarize itself with the numerous reform projects worked out in 1981" (such as the Balcerowicz plan). It also added that "only extensive, all-embracing economic reforms can achieve positive results and that partial modifications, on the other hand, can only achieve results opposite to the expected."[15]

The results of partial reform became apparent in 1988–9. Throughout 1987, the government puzzled over the problem of how to make economic reform acceptable. One of the more innovative solutions involved a range of opinion surveys intended to impress on the public the inevitability of some kind of price rise ("Do you prefer a 50 per cent rise in the price of bread and 100 per cent for gasoline, or 60 per cent for gasoline and 100 per cent for bread?"). There was also a referendum on economic reform. In late 1987, after a substantial delay, the second stage of the economic reform process envisaged in 1981–2 began to take effect. At the end of 1988 the government of Mieczyslaw Rakowski lifted restrictions on the establishment of private firms. Two obstacles stood in the way of further reforms at this stage: one international, the other domestic. The debt mountain had been increasing, as official debt piled up due to the suspension of debt servicing in 1982–4 and subsequent restrictions on debt servicing. The unpaid principal and interest were then capitalized into the sum of the outstanding debt, with the result that it rose from $25,950 million at the end of 1981 to $39,170 by 1988 (Antowska-Bartosiewicz and Malecki 1992: 8). But there could be no further inflows without an IMF program, and the IMF would not support an unsustainable program. Rakowski's realization that the government would be unable to meet its foreign debt obligations drove him to a consideration of more extensive domestic economic reform and liberalization. As elsewhere, the debt crisis proved to be a catalyst for a profound reorientation of economic policy as well as of political structures.

The second problem was domestic. The most contentious aspect of the reform was the "adjustment" (or elimination) of subsidies. The rate of price rises increased (the average of consumer prices rose by 25 per cent in 1987 and 60 per cent in 1988), sparking two waves of renewed labor unrest. Faced with these conditions, the government admitted Solidarity representatives to a Round Table to discuss the political future of Poland, then made the movement legal (April 1989) and allowed its candidates to contest a restricted number of seats in parliamentary elections (all of which the government lost). The General Secretary of the Soviet Communist Party, Mikhail Gorbachev, telephoned the Polish Prime Minister to urge him to abide by the election results. After a series of unsuccessful experiments in forming a communist-led government, a Solidarity-led government, with Tadeusz Mazowiecki as Prime Minister, was installed in September 1989. The effects of partial reform had augmented the political crisis and led to a complete collapse of the old order.

The Polish story, quite uniquely, has its own internal dynamic and is less dependent on international events (the fall of the Berlin Wall) than any other post-communist transition; that alone may go quite a long way to explaining its greater success. There is no case in fact in the post-communist world in which the character of a reform program as the product of an internal debate within civil society is so clear.

In its first months in power, the Mazowiecki government launched its own very radical version of a reform program. At the outset, Mazowiecki had remarked that "I am looking for my Ludwig Erhard!"[16] The man appointed as Finance Minister, Leszek Balcerowicz, had been the author of the influential 1981 program, and for over two years had been involved in intensive private discussions on economic reform involving privatization, currency convertibility, the liberalization of international trade, and the abandonment of notions of import substitution.[17] After the revolution, in the words of one observer, "economics revealed itself with a vengeance to be a key determinant of the political realm…. What is the essential point of reference, the short-hand designation, the symbol associated today with the Polish revolution?…It is the Balcerowicz plan."[18]

The fundamental threat to the plan was monetary. A partial financial reform at the beginning of 1989 had created a two-tier Western-style banking system, with a central bank and also a network of (fundamentally regional) commercial banks. The new banks were, however, in most areas in a practically monopolistic position, and they continued, without much control, to give credit to enterprises. Once price controls were lifted, the consequence of an uncontrolled explosion of enterprise credit would be inflation. In consequence, in late 1989, as a result of the combination of price liberalization and the fiscal aftermath of the previous regime's last-minute attempt to buy for itself political stability, Poland was threatened by hyperinflation. Between December 1988 and September 1989 open inflation rose to 230 per cent. In October it seemed that hyperinflation had arrived. Consumer prices increased by 54 per cent (an annualized rate of 17,000 per cent) (Sachs 1993: 40). Tackling this became the most urgent economic issue, as well as an opportunity for a much more broadly based reform. Pegging the zloty to an external standard could be the only guarantee of monetary control. Only ten days after the formation of the government, Balcerowicz traveled to Washington to lay out the details of the government's very radical reform and stabilization program in his speech at the IMF Annual Meeting.

Already in September, budget spending was reduced by cutting the coal subsidy. Credit to the non-government sector was cut. The gap between the official exchange rate and the market rate was reduced. Wages would be held in check by a tax of 100 to 200 per cent on wage increases in excess of a sum set at 80 per cent of the cost of living increase. The two principles underlying the reform package were that stabilization should be accomplished "quickly and decisively" and that there should be a move to market mechanisms: "We believe that speed is of the essence, so that the transitional stage – so hard on society – will be as short as possible. Radical change is also dictated by the bad experience with piecemeal reforms in the 1980s."[19]

The most radical phase of the reform, the Balcerowicz plan implemented in January 1990, was explicitly designed as a "shock treatment" and constructed in a deliberately tight timeframe. Balcerowicz believed that the government should use the political capital generated by the honeymoon period of transition to democracy in order to introduce reforms that would be beneficial in the long term but inevitably carry short-term costs. The outcome of liberalization, he thought, could not be predicted. No one could forecast how output, prices, and external trade would behave in a completely transformed situation. But the level of certainty about the outcome would not be increased if the reforms were applied more slowly. As a result, a rapid passage through government committees and through parliament, with an imposed deadline of January 1, offered an alternative far superior to unending negotiations about individual details of the plan.

In addition, as a result of the democratic revolutions Poland stood as the focus of world attention, but she could not expect to occupy that place for long. The country should use her "five minutes of history," Balcerowicz thought, in order to introduce a program so ambitious that it would encourage creditors to accept a generous solution to the international debt issue. It was consciously devised as a program that would appear to the rest of the world as a model of the application of economic liberalism, a new version of Ludwig Erhard's achievement.

It included the achievement of fiscal balance in 1990, a sharp restriction of monetary growth, the continuation of a tax-based wage indexation policy, a lifting of price controls (with especially dramatic effects in energy: there was to be a fourfold increase of the coal price for industrial consumers and sixfold for retail customers; and a 300 per cent rise in electricity prices). The foreign exchange market was to be unified, in order to create greater incentives to export. Credit policy would be tightened (with the result that "some enterprises are likely to become bankrupt and close"). But the policy would also be supported by a Labor Fund, financed by a 2 per cent levy on the payroll of enterprises, to create a "protective shield" for those workers made redundant in the course of the transition and to pay for retraining and vocational training programs. Pensions benefits and family allowances would be reviewed on a quarterly basis. IMF drawings would be used primarily to build up Poland's foreign currency reserves. This was in essence a program largely produced in Poland – and not either an "IMF program" or one laid down by any one of the numerous foreign advisers who now descended on Warsaw, attracted by the possibility of making a significant contribution to a model program dealing with the economic aftermath of socialist planning. At this stage of the reform exercise, which is undoubtedly the one which has attracted the most attention in the literature on Polish reform, there was a multiplicity of foreign advice and advisers – much of it helpful in terms of clarifying issues and in propagandizing the idea of reform to other post-communist societies, but not essential to the cause of reform itself.

The total effect of the program was estimated to involve, in the immediate aftermath of the "shock," a drop in real wages of between 30 and 40 per cent. But it appeared to be strikingly popular. In an opinion poll held on January 4, 1990, over half of those surveyed claimed to be in favor of the "shock cure." The new government's approval ratings stood at 90 per cent.[20] When the IMF's Managing Director traveled to Poland in December 1989, he found support for the program from Solidarity, church leaders, parliamentarians, but also from the leaders of the former official (that is, communist) unions and from the President, General Jaruzelski.[21]

The IMF program (a 545 million SDR standby) approved in February 1990[22] was designed as a demonstration of external support, and as a reassurance and a catalyst for foreign investors initially hesitant about Poland's prospects for stability (in the light of the debt situation, which was not resolved for years and remained a major liability in the first years of post-communist transition). The Fund's preparations and the discussion on the Executive Board also emphasized that it was essential to protect the neediest groups in the population and to provide funds for retraining and unemployment benefits to cushion the process of transition to the market economy.[23] Some of the advocates of the reform plan even felt that the IMF should have taken a tougher stance on fiscal issues, and especially about the question of pensions, which later proved to be one of the most intractable difficulties facing the reform government. Within Poland, the idea of conditionality was not used by the government to justify its program – which it explained as being necessary for "our internal considerations" – but, rather, in terms of making the program internationally credible and achieving a debt reduction. Balcerowicz later argued that "this was not only truthful but also probably politically more effective than trying to push through tough measures on the pretext that the IMF had imposed them."[24]

In the beginning, no one knew quite how the key economic data would develop over the course of the transition. Most, including the major foreign economic advisers of the Solidarity government, assumed that the greatest problems would be in the first *months* rather than *years* of the restricting program (Sachs 1989: 29). In the first half of 1990 fiscal policies turned out to be even tighter than had been anticipated, as a result of the bracket-creep effect of inflation on tax rates. At the same time, the output collapse appeared greater than anticipated, although much of the fall proved to be an optical illusion brought about as a consequence of the exaggeration of production figures for 1989, and part of it was because statistical collection involved primarily the large state-owned factories most hit by the collapse. Thus the earliest official Polish figures gave the decline in GDP in 1990 as 18–20 per cent, but more recent calculations place it at between 5 and 10 per cent.[25] The result of a strong fiscal performance combined with an apparently dramatic output decline played into the hands of officials from the old planning authorities, who now began to argue that a demand-oriented policy on allegedly "Keynesian" lines should be applied in order to promote recovery. They did not want to modify the basic impetus toward liberalization and structural change of the reform; but, at the same time, they claimed that the shock had been "over-cooked." As a result, in the third quarter of 1990 fiscal policy relaxed, wages also began to increase at a faster rate than had been targeted, and the basis of the IMF program was endangered. Negotiating a new program in 1991 became much harder. The central bank's response to enterprises paying higher wages and to the new fiscal policy was monetary expansion. In addition, social pressures mounted. During the summer of 1991, in the run-up to elections, every morning the Ministry of Social Affairs received desperate phone calls from all over Poland requesting emergency resources for the support of the unemployed, funds which the government provided. But at the same time, the privatization program of share offerings for large enterprises and some 70 per cent of retail stores were transferred to private management. Very quickly, a vigorous private sector developed. The increase in the number of small businesses alone generated employment equivalent to 7 per cent of the workforce (Sachs 1993). The ending of the old "official rate" and the adoption of a realistic exchange rate in addition set off an export boom. Export earnings increased faster than had been anticipated, and the first estimates showed that in 1990 Poland had run a surplus on current account in convertible currencies of $700 million.[26]

As a result, it was possible to negotiate a waiver on the standby in December 1990, and then a larger three-year 1,224 million SDR EFF in April 1991.[27] This paved a way for a negotiated solution to the international debt problem. At a meeting of the Paris Club on April 19–21, 1991, the official creditors agreed to an extraordinary debt reduction on the $33 billion outstanding debt that was equivalent to 50 per cent of the net present value. The relief was to come in two stages, the second of which (in 1994) depended on continued compliance with Poland's commitments to the IMF. The debt plan thus secured a longer-term framework for the continued application of successful policies. The Paris Club agreement in turn also facilitated a solution to the problem of the (smaller) volume of outstanding bank debt, some $12 billion in capital and capitalized interest arrears.[28] The negotiation of a solution to the longstanding debt problem, as in other severely indebted countries, could only be accomplished adequately in the more general context of a reorientation and adjustment of the entire approach to economic management. A crucial Polish mistake, which acted as an irritant and a deterrent to new foreign investment, was the failure to reach agreement on the bank-held (London Club) foreign debt (there was eventually an agreement, but only in 1994). The early adoption of liberalization not only made debt negotiation easier; it also created a Polish model of how to carry out an economic transformation.

Renewed growth in Poland was delayed by the drastic fall in exports to the East as a result of the collapse of the Soviet Union (1990–1); but real GDP had already begun to grow again in 1992 (1.0 per cent), and rose at a much faster rate in 1993.[29] In 1992 the government of Hanna Suchocka began to pay greater attention to issues of micro-adjustment that had been relatively neglected in the rush to conclude the original stabilization plan. The first experimenter in Central Europe was also the first country to show sustained recovery and growth.

In the case of Russia, "ownership" was just as central to the discussion – but the reform issue was also tied in with broad geopolitical and security considerations, which substantially complicated and impaired the ability of governments to formulate their "own" economic strategies. Post-communist Russia went through three waves of attempted reforms, in each of which the IMF played a shaping role. In each of these, negotiations between the IMF and Russia always emphasized "ownership," that the reform programs had a Russian genesis and shape. In the first (1992–5), the IMF was widely criticized for not providing enough resources to cover a large fiscal deficit. The disagreements concerned the character of program design. In particular, the Russian authorities refused IMF suggestions that reform should be accompanied by the creation of a social security net that might absorb the unemployment created as a consequence of industrial reconstruction. The result was uncontrolled spending in state-owned enterprises, and state and intra-industry deficits that were monetized by the central bank, leading to sharply inflationary developments.

From 1995, Russia introduced a quite effective stabilization program, which in practice depended on an external currency peg. Inflation fell to an average of 2.7 per cent between 1996 and 1998. IMF assistance occurred, however, without effective fiscal controls. The markets judged the fact of an IMF presence combined with the political uncertainties about the 1996 election as a statement that "the West" was prepared to support Russia at any cost. From August 1996 an insurge of funds flowed into direct investment, but also into the high-yielding Treasury bond market.

The third stage was prompted by the collapse of an IMF package negotiated in July 1998, which brought an immediate end to the "moral hazard" issue: the Fund was no longer prepared to support Russia at any cost. It immediately produced a default and a sharp devaluation of the overvalued exchange rate (the crisis of August 17, 1998). Prices accelerated (consumer prices rose by 75 per cent in the last five months of 1998), foreign direct investment collapsed, and the government deficit surged again. At the beginning of 1999 Russia started to tighten monetary policy, and in April 1999 the IMF announced a new standby program.

The obsession with not intervening in Russian sovereignty produced bad programs – in the first place a neglect of essential accompaniments of an economic reform program, and in the second an over-enthusiastic endorsement that misled markets (and politicians) about the extent of Western support, which led to a substantial backlash against IMF involvement. Many reformers agreed with the observation of Grigor Yavlinsky that the IMF had obstructed effective reform. But these observations need not be confined to Russia. There are similar cases in the 1990s in which there was too much "ownership" for the good of the program. Perhaps the most spectacularly drawn-out case of such a failure is Argentina, where a solution (the Currency Board) was adopted, initially with much skepticism from the IMF, and where the IMF became – as in Russia – increasingly frustrated by the way it had been tied in to a bad exchange rate arrangement but could not leave for fear of being blamed as the party which destroyed a promising reform effort.

Conclusion

Can international institutions such as the IMF find a way out of a permanent pendulum swing of policy between over-reliance on external scapegoats and insufficient control for the sake of policy "ownership"? This is a dilemma that is not new – it has existed from the early days of the IMF (and helped to marginalize it in the first postwar decade), and only arises in new forms as thinking about civil society and its role in political and economic stability evolves. Many of the reform suggestions discussed with great intensity after the Asian crisis and its contagious effects in 1997–8 have attempted to deal with precisely this issue. Some of the most thorny cases seem to contain both elements in a "worst of all possible worlds" scenario: thus Argentina is now cited by the Fund as an example of too much ownership, and by Argentine and other radicals as an outcome of too much Fund diktat and austerity.

Would a greater involvement of regional authorities be helpful? One reading of the European success gives a great role to institutions in Europe, the EPU and above all the EEC and its successors, and blames the Asian crisis of 1997 in part on the U.S. blocking of a Japanese initiative for an Asian Monetary Fund.

At a fundamental level, the issue involved the weakness or incapacity of state institutions in many countries: if such national institutions were more efficient and less corrupt, international advice would be less needed. It is the weaker political entities that are most likely to demand the whipping-boy function. But the complexities of a globalized world are likely to produce more and more examples of failed or broken-down states; and many stable and advanced societies use analogous arguments to push through political reform (very obviously in the case of the European Union and the way it has been used to modernize states such as Italy and Greece).

A solution to the policy dilemma as regards the IMF and ownership can only be sketched out here. It depends on the following:

- pre-qualification, or the establishment of a good policy basis before the outbreak of crises as a basis for the speedy provision of resources in the event of a sudden and unexpected reversal of capital flows;
- extending the capacity of international institutions to deal with the legal consequences of debt problems, perhaps in the shape of some activity analogous to those of bankruptcy courts in a national setting, so that the IMF could decree debt write-downs;
- the establishment of a more rules-based and less discretionary basis to circumstances in which Fund resources will be made available;
- there should and will nevertheless always remain some scope for political fudges, and any realistic reform proposals need to exclude these as far as possible and at the same time to leave some room for maneuver.

If the last observation seems contradictory and absurd, it is at the same time a reality for the guidelines according to which international institutions will continue to operate in a world in which there is no extensive abdication of national sovereignty. (And it will be noted that suggestions for an international bankruptcy procedure imply a strong limiting of domestic national authority and legislation.)

It is now a commonplace to see the increasing prominence of the market in international economics in the last years of the twentieth century as a return to some of the features of the first really global economy that emerged in the last third of the nineteenth century. At that time, however, the political principles of national sovereignty and democracy were both very underdeveloped. International institutions are a twentieth-century effort to reconcile global interdependence with national sovereignty. It is not surprising that as interdependence increased at the end of the century, international financial institutions became at the same time more central to policy management and more politicized and controversial.

Unless national sovereignty breaks down completely, leaving the way free for new imperialisms, there will not be much choice but to have institutions that reflect a world community and its ideals in an advisory role. But it is safe to say that their role will always be controversial, because it grows in large part out of the inability of some political systems to produce sustainable answers to their own problems.

Notes

1 Rueff (1972: 154).
2 Jacobsson diaries 1958, the Per Jacobsson Papers, University of Basel manuscript collection.

3 IMF Central Files (1959).
4 Fontana and Nadal (1976: 522).
5 Rojo (1978: 178). See also Bermeo and García-Duran (forthcoming).
6 Levi and Manley (1989: 184–6); Kaufman (1985: 132–7).
7 IMF Central Files (1978).
8 IMF Central Files (1980a).
9 Keesings Contemporary Archives (1981: 30,751).
10 IMF Central Files (1980b).
11 IMF Central Files (1989a: 102–3).
12 Kaminski (1991: 130); Schröder (1982: 73).
13 Schröder (1982: 71); Garton Ash (1983: 33–4).
14 IMF Central Files (1991).
15 IMF Central Files (1985).
16 Garton Ash (1990: 43).
17 This was elaborated in a paper of May 1989: see Balcerowicz (1992: 17).
18 Gross (1992: 66).
19 IMF Central Files (1989b).
20 Garton Ash (1990: 45); *New York Times* (1992).
21 EBM (1989).
22 EBM (1990).
23 IMF (1990: 21).
24 Balcerowicz (1994: 175).
25 See Rajski (1992); Balcerowicz (1993: 12).
26 EBM (1991a).
27 EBM (1991b).
28 *Financial Times* (1993).
29 IMF (1993: 85).

References

Antowska-Bartosiewicz, I. and W. Malecki (1992) *Poland's External Debt Problem by the End of 1991*, Warsaw: Friedrich Ebert Foundation for Poland.

Balcerowicz, L. (1992) *800 Dni: Szok Kontrolowany*, Warsaw: Polska Oficyna Wydawnicza BGW.

Balcerowicz, L. (1993) *Eastern Europe: Economic, Social and Political Dynamics: A Lecture*, London: School of Slavonic and East European Studies.

Balcerowicz, L. (1994) "Poland," in J. Williamson (ed.) *The Political Economy of Policy Reform*, Washington, DC: Institute for International Economics.

Bermeo, N. and J. García-Duran (forthcoming) "The Political Economy of Structural Adjustment in New Democracies: The Case of Spain," in S. Haggard and S. Webb (eds.) *The Political Economy of Structural Adjustment in New Democracies*.

Boughton, J. (2000) "From Suez to Tequila: The IMF as Crisis Manager," *Economic Journal* 110: 273–91.

Buchheim, C. (1990) *Die Wiedereingliederung Westdeutschlands in die Weltwirtschaft 1945–1958*, Munich: Oldenbourg.

EBM (1989) 89/163, December 15 (IMF Executive Board Minutes).

EBM (1990) 90/14, February 5.

EBM (1991a) 91/60, March 18.

EBM (1991b) 91/57, April 18.

Financial Times (1993) May 29–30.

Fontana, J. and J. Nadal (1976) "Spain 1914–1970," in C. Cipolla (ed.) *The Fontana Economic History of Europe: Contemporary Economies 2*, Glasgow: Collins.

Garton Ash, T. (ed.) (1983) *The Polish Revolution: Solidarity 1980–1982*, London: Jonathan Cape.

Garton Ash, T. (1990) *The Magic Lantern: The Revolution of '89 Witnessed in Warsaw, Budapest, Berlin and Prague*, New York: Random House.

Gross, J. (1992) "Poland: From Civil Society to Political Nation," in I. Banac (ed.) *Eastern Europe in Revolution*, Ithaca, NY: Cornell University Press.

IMF (1990) *Annual Report*, Washington, DC.

IMF (1993) *World Economic Outlook*, October, Washington, DC.

IMF Central File (1959) Marian Navarro Rubio and Alberto Ullastres, Memorandum from the Spanish Government to the IMF and OEEC, June 30, IMF CF/Spain/1760.

IMF Central Files (1978) C/Jamaica/150.1, November 22, E. Walter Robichek memorandum.

IMF Central Files (1980a) C/Jamaica/810, February 15, de Larosière to Manley.

IMF Central Files (1980b) C/Jamaica/810, April 18, Albertelli: *Jamaica: Role of the Fund in Recent Stabilization Efforts*.

IMF Central Files (1985) C/Poland/000, September 17, Solidarity cable to Managing Director of IMF.

IMF Central Files (1989a) Memorandum of 30 October 1989, reproduced in *Der Spiegel* (1992) 45/44.

IMF Central Files (1989b) C/Poland/1760, December 22, Memorandum of Economic Policies.

IMF Central Files (1991) S1195, November 18, David Finch memorandum.

Jacobsson, E. (1979) *A Life for Sound Money: Per Jacobsson, His Biography*, Oxford: Oxford University Press.

Jacobsson, P. (1959) television interview: C/Spain/810, June 23.

Kaminski, B. (1991) *The Collapse of State Socialism: The Case of Poland*, Princeton, NJ: Princeton University Press.

Kaufman, M. (1985) *Jamaica under Manley: Dilemmas of Socialism and Democracy*, London: Zed Books.

Levi, D. and M. Manley (1989) *The Making of a Leader*, London: Andre Deutsch.

MacDonald, O. (1981) *The Polish August: Documents from the Beginnings of the Polish Workers' Rebellion, Gdansk, August 1980*, San Francisco, CA: Ztangi Press.

Meier, G. (1982) *Problems of a World Monetary Order*, New York: Oxford University Press.

Milward, A. (1984) *The Reconstruction of Western Europe 1945–1951*, Berkeley, CA: University of California Press.

Milward, A. (1992) "The Reconstruction," in J. Kaplan and G. Schleiminger (eds.) *The European Payments Union: Financial Diplomacy in the 1950s*, Oxford: Oxford University Press.

Monnet, J. (1958) "Statements on Financial Aid Program for France," *New York Times*, January 31.

Pauly, L. (1996) *The League of Nations and the Foreshadowing of the International Monetary Fund*, Essays in International Finance, no. 201, Princeton, NJ: Princeton University Department of Economics, International Finance Section.

Rajski, Z. (1992) "Produkt krajowy brutto," in L. Zienkowski (ed.) *Gospodarka polska w latach 1990–92*, Warsaw: Glownego Urzedu Statystycznego i Polskiej Akademii Nauk.

Rojo, L.A. (1978) "Panorama Económico," *España Perspectiva*, in J. Hombravella (ed.) *Trece Economistas Españoles*, Barcelona: Oikos-tau.

Rubio, M. and A. Ullastres (1959) C/Spain/1760, Memorandum from the Spanish Government to the IMF and OEEC, June 30.

Rueff, J. (1972) *Combats pour l'ordre financier: Mémoires et documents pour servir à l'histoire du dernier demi-siècle*, Paris: Plon.

Sachs, J. (1989) "My Plan for Poland," *International Economy*, December 1989–January 1990: 24–9.

Sachs, J. (1993) *Poland's Jump to the Market Economy*, Cambridge, MA: MIT Press.

Schröder, K. (1981) "Die Verschuldung Polens," *Życie gospodarcze* 28, Jul 21, no. 1556.

Schröder, K. (1982) "Die Verschuldung Polens im Westen," in H. Volle and W. Wagner (eds.) *Krise in Polen*, Bonn: Verlag für Internationale Politik.

Schröder, K. (1983) "Die Verschuldung Polens," in T. Garton Aslı (ed.) *The Polish Revolution: Solidarity 1980–1982*, London: Jonathan Cape.

Ullastres, A. (1959) "Plan de Estabilización: Discurso del Ministro de Comercio a las Cortes," in *Información Comercial Española*, Boletín Semanal, 643, July 30.

United Nations General Assembly (1977) *Official Records of the General Assembly*, vol. I, 32nd Session, 15th Plenary Meeting, September 30.

Varela, M. (1989–90) "El Plan de Estabilización como yo lo recuerdo," *Información Comercial Española* December 1989–January 1990.

Part II

Case studies

Physicians and politicians

4 Who lost Russia in 1998?

Nadezhda Ivanova and Charles Wyplosz[1]

On August 17, 1998, Russia's exchange and financial markets collapsed. In a few days, the ruble dropped to one-third of its value, the federal government was in default on its debt, and the stock market fell into a deep freeze. It took a few more days for the crisis to migrate to far-flung emerging markets: Central and Eastern Europe, but also South America cringed, and if South Asia could have fallen any further after its own crisis a year before, it would have.

The world looked with disbelief at the waste. Barely six years before, optimism was unbounded: the astounding collapse of the Soviet Union held the promise of a peaceful and affluent Russia. Soon, it was believed, Russia would be too well integrated into the global marketplace ever again to be a threat to world peace. And, indeed, Russia's approach to the world quickly changed and Western military spending was being slashed. To be sure, not everything was rosy in Russia. Poverty was spreading and life expectancy declined, a definite sign of the state's inability to protect its distressed citizens. Yet there was no discussion of turning back; the Russian people were hanging on to a tough transition. How had this disaster been allowed to occur, in spite of some $50 billion of international support? Didn't the policymakers and their money doctors see it coming? What advice was provided and was it listened to? In short, who lost Russia?

The collapse of the Soviet Union had been a momentous event, the undoing of the October Revolution, and it was immediately recognized as such. No Western leader failed to promise every effort to assist the new Russia in its new historical phase. The task of assisting Russia was subcontracted by the G7 to the International Monetary Fund (IMF) and the World Bank, and both relished the challenge. All kinds of experts flocked to Moscow, peddling ready-made solutions. Was all this wisdom misguided? Or was the correct advice given in good time but not listened to by the Russian authorities?

These are the questions that this chapter explores. It concludes that, for almost a year, no one could have ignored the fact that the situation was hopeless. A first attack in November 1997 provided a dress rehearsal of worse things to come, but was dismissed as pure contagion from the Asian crisis. Already then, Russia was ripe for its own collapse. The policymakers knew it but were divided by those who still hoped for an IMF-led miracle and those who were coolly calculating how to take financial advantage of the impending meltdown. By 1998 the private money doctors had lost any influence. The IMF was the only game in town and, for various reasons, was not going to advise any drastic measure like abandoning the crawling peg arrangement or organizing a pre-emptive default.[2]

The chapter is structured as follows. The first section presents the money doctors at work in Russia over the period 1992–8. The second section builds up the case that the crisis of 1998 was perfectly foreseeable, and the subsequent section explains that it was in fact foreseen, paying particular attention to the views expressed by the main actors, the policymakers, and the foreign advisers. The fourth section concludes.[3]

Money doctors in Russia

The early reformers who took over Russia in the last days of 1991 were unprepared for the task. They were mostly young, medium-level Communist Party members. Along with the underdog President of the Russian Federation, Boris Yeltsin, they had realized that Gorbachev's glasnost was a desperate attempt to save the regime and the costly Soviet empire. They were getting organized to take over, but they knew very little of politics and economics.[4] They were the world's best hope that the Cold War would end, they needed help, and they got more than they wanted.

Virtually from day one, official and self-appointed advisers poured into Moscow. The IMF and the World Bank rushed in, most Western governments undertook to provide financing for consultants. The best and the worst of consulting seized on the occasion and it was easy: money was available and top officials' doors were surprisingly wide open.

International financial institutions

The G7 did not fail to grasp the importance of the collapse of the Soviet Union and to anticipate that economic policy advice would be sorely needed, along with substantial resources. It soon put the IMF and the World Bank in charge of coordinating this dual effort. They responded with remarkable speed. Michel Camdessus, the IMF's Managing Director, imprudently maybe, stated that Russia's successful transformation would be the Fund's defining challenge. He went on to build a whole new department to deal exclusively with the Commonwealth of Independent States (CIS). The IMF and the World Bank quickly opened up offices in Moscow and sent all kinds of missions.[5]

The hope was to achieve a smooth transition to the market economy. Some experience had already been accumulated in Central and Eastern Europe and it was becoming clear that the process is highly unstable, easily giving way to a collapse of the state and to hyperinflation. This was the IMF's responsibility. The Fund's first representative in Moscow was Kathryn Burke-Dillon, and the first mission chief was Ernesto Hernandez-Cata. Both had extensive experience of Latin America. This reflected the Fund's early approach, both in the CIS and Central and Eastern Europe: that transition was about high inflation, privatization and weak policy institutions. This intuition was plausible but soon turned out to miss a number of unique characteristics of transition, such as the disruption of existing economic arrangements and the total absence of institutions supporting markets (banks and payment systems, basic legislation and courts). They were eventually both replaced by senior staff members with different experience.[6]

The IMF offered some early financing, SDR 2.8 billion over 1992–4, but, as "first-tranche" loans, this did not carry mandatory programs. The Fund's role was merely that of a benevolent adviser. It mainly developed a close relationship with the reformers, especially with Anatoly Chubais, who was put in charge of economic policies in late 1994 as Deputy Prime Minister. The IMF provided private training to Tatyana Paramonova, who succeeded Gerashenko at the helm of the central bank in 1994. Even though she was never confirmed by the Duma and had therefore to step down in 1996, she was in charge of monetary policy at the most crucial time, the successful disinflation of 1995, when the IMF first played an important role, with a standby credit of $6.8 billion. The IMF's advice was strictly orthodox, relying on monetary and fiscal policy tightening. The IMF did not even suggest using the exchange rate as an anchor; it merely supported the Russian decision to adopt the "corridor," a crawling peg.

The IMF's second large-scale program came in the run-up to the 1996 election, when monthly inflation had been brought to 2.8 per cent, down from 17.8 per cent in January 1995. It was clearly a sign of support for Yeltsin, an attempt at stabilizing the volatile political and economic situation, given Yeltsin's dismal showing at the polls and the apparent ineluctability of a Communist victory. For this reason, the conditions were quite vague, aiming at the medium term, while disbursement was to be done on a monthly basis, so it could be promptly stopped in case events turned bad. A new program was agreed upon in July 1998 as the crisis was already under way. We examine this important move in the section on "The crisis and the money doctors" (pp. 127–31).

The World Bank's representative, Charles Blitzer, developed close personal relationships with the reformers in government. Through these personal contacts, the Bank's influence was large in relation to the relatively small amounts of fresh money that it contributed. Over the whole period 1992–June 1998, the World Bank committed $10.9 billion for 41 projects.[7] In comparison, the European Bank for Reconstruction and Development (EBRD) has provided $3.1 billion for about 100 projects, the largest share of EBRD's commitments.

Western governments

In addition to many programs designed to deal with weapons and the ecology, the Western governments quickly set up macroeconomic advisory operations, mostly relying on private experts for the "big picture." This is described below (pp. 108–10). Several government agencies sent missions, and invited Russian officials, to provide advice on practical "small-picture" issues. These missions explained how to structure economic ministries, how to establish a Treasury, how to run money market operations, how to collect taxes, etc. To the best of our knowledge, there is no account of this multifaceted activity. Naturally, the embassies were in touch with government members and some opposition leaders.

Individual experts

A number of experts came to Moscow with official financing. The U.S. launched a large operation mostly through USAID, the European countries built up a new program, TACIS (Technical Assistance to the CIS countries), while some countries occasionally run their own activities, mostly Britain through its rapid action "Know How Fund" program and Sweden on an ad-hoc basis.

The USAID program was largely channeled through HIID (Harvard Institute for International Development). Andrew Schleifer and Jonathan Hay dealt with mass privatization (see below, pp. 110–11). They worked closely with Chubais, the minister in charge of mass privatization at the time. They came up with the blueprint and then drafted detailed legislation.[8] Jeffrey Sachs, Director of HIID, was responsible for macroeconomics. He teamed up with Anders Aslund, who was receiving support from the Swedish government. Together they formed the Monetary and Financial Unit (MFU), which was initially physically housed inside the Finance Ministry. This proximity generated opposition in Russian official circles and the MFU was soon moved to a nearby dismal property of the Finance Ministry. The MFU team included David Lipton, who had worked with Jeffrey Sachs in Poland, where they had been instrumental in charting, with Finance Minister Balcerowicz, the first transition program ever built up, and arguably the most successful one. Lipton subsequently worked as Assistant Deputy Secretary of Treasury under Larry Summers, in charge of the transition countries. Also present at MFU were some European economists (Daniel Cohen, Christian de Boissieu, Gaël de Pontbriand, Jacques Delpla, Brigitte Granville, Charles Wyplosz) financed by TACIS, as well as some U.S. specialists in Russian agriculture on secondment from the Department of Agriculture. An interesting aspect of MFU was the presence of several junior Russian and foreign economists (mostly graduate students), the latter mostly from the U.S. and Sweden.[9] Except for Aslund, the senior advisers were not based in Moscow, but were visiting very frequently.

During the glasnost period, Aslund, a specialist on Russia, had developed excellent contacts with both the Moscow-based Gaïdar group and the St. Petersburg-based Chubais group, who were then in the political wilderness. These contacts subsequently allowed MFU remarkable access to the top levels of the Russian government. On the other side, the relationship with the Central Bank of Russia (CBR), under Matukhin and next under Gerashenko, was acrimonious, even though many reliable contacts were established at a lower level. When Gaïdar was ousted and replaced by Chernomyrdin in December 1992, MFU's influence declined, but it remained significant, largely through Chubais, who remained in charge of mass privatization, and through Boris Fedorov, who became Minister of Finance. Sachs was closely involved in negotiations with the IMF, which he began to criticize heavily, dismayed by the absence of any large-scale program and feeling that its advice was far too stereotyped. When Fedorov was ousted in late 1993, Aslund and Sachs left, publishing an angry communiqué attacking Prime Minister Chernomyrdin personally. Their departure was motivated by their conviction that the President had not chosen unambiguously to support the reform program. They viewed the new Prime Minister as representing the "old guard," intent on keeping political and economic power in the hands of former Party apparatchiks. Concluding that their efforts were doomed to failure, and that they would be blamed for the failure, they decided to close down MFU. This ended an era and opened the way for another one.

The European Commission's TACIS program initially supported two operations. One of them was short lived: Daniel Gros undertook to advocate the maintenance of the Russian ruble throughout the CIS. After some initial success at the Bishkek conference in 1992, the mission lost its purpose when all CIS countries established their own currencies.

The other operation, run by Richard Layard, was the most enduring. Layard pursued a triple track. First he worked as an adviser to the Ministry of Labor. This activity gradually fizzled out, in part because the Ministry of Labor had little power and was not able to follow up the measures advocated by Layard. Second, Layard launched the publication *Russian Economic Trends*. At a time when the official statistical agency, Goskomstat, was both disorganized and slow to present its exhaustive information in a way compatible with market economies' national accounts, essential data on the Russian economy was not available. *Russian Economic Trends* quickly filled this vacuum, and it remained for years the best source of macroeconomic data. In addition, each month Layard would hold a press conference to present the latest data and offer a commentary. For several years, this press conference was heavily attended and widely reported in the Russian press. Finally, Layard undertook to send a few carefully selected students to the London School of Economics, quickly building up the first group of well-trained Russian economists.

When the MFU stopped operating in late 1993, TACIS saw a window of opportunity and undertook to replace it with a European bureau, the Russian–European Center for Economic Policy (RECEP).[10] RECEP brought together various advisers who were funded by TACIS, Layard's *Russian Economic Trends* team, the teams of Cohen *et al.* and of Wyplosz from the MFU, and a new group led by Peter Oppenheimer. Later on a fifth team, led by Erik Berglof and Damien Neven, joined RECEP.

At RECEP, the group in charge of macroeconomics was that of Wyplosz. It took up where MFU had left off, benefiting from the good channels to the government opened by MFU, although at a lower level, partly because of the change of personnel in government, and partly because top-level officials were now seeking to establish a distance from foreign advisers. The group also established good links with the CBR, which had become considerably more open to Western-type analysis once Paramonova had replaced Gerashenko. The team was closely involved in the disinflation program of 1995 and played a role in convincing the Russian authorities to adopt the exchange rate corridor in the face of the IMF's lukewarm attitude. Wyplosz left in early 1998 when the crisis appeared unavoidable and yet neither the Russian authorities nor the IMF were willing to consider the emergency measures which could have helped avoid it.

RECEP was reorganized in late 1997 under the leadership of Berglof. By then, most of the reformers had left government or were corrupt. Six years after the collapse of the Soviet Union, the Russian administration had learnt most of the ropes of policymaking. Quite logically, the emphasis at RECEP shifted from policy advice to research and the build-up of a team of young Russian scholars, drawing on the pool of talent emerging from top Western Ph.D. programs. A team led by Enrico Perotti provided advice on bank restructuring following the 1998 meltdown.

Many other experts offered their services, often without explicit public financing. It is not known precisely who they were and what their influence was. The best-known is probably Steven Hanke, from Johns Hopkins University, who has devoted his career to promoting currency boards. He visited Moscow early on during the high inflation period. A colorful figure of the Moscow scene was Jochen Wermuth, a young German, a graduate economics student from Oxford who started out in MFU and then moved to form the Economic Expert Group at the Ministry of Finance (MinFin), using a model of the federal budget developed at MFU. The Economic Expert Group was financed by a loan from the World Bank, as were some of the activities of the Bureau of Economic Analysis (BEA), a group of Russian economists led by Yevgeny Yasin (an influential academic who was Minister of Economics in 1994–7) with close connections to the center run by Yegor Gaïdar. The BEA occasionally used foreign economists for short-term projects. Finally, Andréi Illarionov ran his own, partly self-financed, office. Illarionov, the wunderkind of the Chubais team, had occupied a high position early on. But his personal style quickly brought him into conflict with Chubais, who made sure that Illarionov was sidelined. From the side, therefore, he offered strident criticism and bold advice, enchanting the media and touching many official raw nerves.[11]

The picture would be incomplete without mentioning the New Economic School (NES). This graduate program was created and financed single-handed by George Soros in 1992. Teaching was done by visiting academics drawn from the best universities in the world. Under the fatherly leadership of Gur Ofer, it quickly attracted scores of bright Russians – mostly trained in mathematics and thus both ready to learn quickly and reasonably free of Marxist influence. Upon graduation, they either went on to pursue doctoral studies abroad or worked in both the administration and the private sector. NES graduates now form the largest group of competent Russian economists and are quite influential.

Privatization

This chapter deals mostly with macroeconomic policies, but privatization has been a massive project and a crucial aspect of Russia's transition, so some indications need to be given. In contrast to countries like Hungary and the Czech Republic, which aimed at getting a fair price from privatization even if it meant that the process would be slow, Russia adopted early on the principle of mass privatization. For reasons beyond the scope of the present chapter (see Schleifer and Triesman 2000), speed was seen as essential for the reform process, so that, in the initial phase, proceeds were not seen as important. The emphasis was, rather, on quickly passing management responsibilities to the private sector in the hope of generating a new class of entrepreneurs with a stake in the reform process as well as of triggering the restructuring of Soviet-era corporations into market-oriented firms.

Mass privatization undoubtedly represents the most controversial of all Russian reforms. Naturally, many consulting firms and financial institutions have been involved. Early on, however, the emphasis being on speed, advice was mostly directed at designing the auction process. HIID's Director, Jeff Sachs, had been involved in designing the Polish version of mass privatization and offered some of the initial advice to then Privatization Minister Anatoly Chubais. As noted above, financed by USAID, HIID went on to play a key role, as Andrew Schleifer and Jonathan Hay designed key aspects of the project. They worked closely with a close adviser of Chubais, Maxim Boyko, a young economist who had spent a year in the U.S. conducting academic research at NBER's Cambridge offices.[12]

From the very beginning of reforms, foreign investors had regular contacts with the Russian authorities. They often offered advice, and, early on, some of it was taken. Credit Suisse-First Boston (CSFB) was the first large foreign private financial institution to play an important role in Russia. The CSFB manager in charge was Hans-Jörg Rüdlof, a veteran of privatizations in Eastern Europe. At the invitation of the EBRD, CSFB played a crucial role in organizing the privatization process. When a Treasury bill market was set up in 1995, CSFB became a major player. Rüdlof had brought with him a Russian émigré, Boris Jordan. Jordan went on to settle permanently in Moscow and create his own brokerage firm, arguably the largest in Russia.

In 1994, with a large loan from the World Bank and other international institutions, Boyko created the Russian Privatization Center (RPC). Set up as a private institution, the RPC opened several field offices throughout Russia. Its staff, which included Russian and foreign economists and management experts, identified firms to be privatized and then encouraged and prepared them for that step. The RPC also endeavored to establish contacts between Russian and foreign firms, hoping to nurture partnerships. Money doctors were not disinterested, then, but it is in the area of privatization that most advice has been given, and taken.

Foreign banks and consulting firms

A small number of foreign banks and financial institutions set up shop early in Russia, nearly all of them only in Moscow. Some of them were there to provide services to their customers trying to do business in Russia. A few operated on their own account. No foreign bank was given a license, so they had to limit themselves to investment. Given the quasi absence of property rights, investment in industry or joint ventures with local banks and financial institutions rapidly proved to be the easiest way to lose money in Russia. As a result, most of the activity was limited to acquiring Treasury papers, GKO and OFZ, and providing intelligence on the Russian economy for would-be investors. CSFB is a prime example of this approach.

A number of large international financial institutions were active in Russian securities and regularly sent staff members to meet with the Russian officials from the government and CBR, as well as with Russian financiers and foreign banks with permanent Moscow offices. (Among the 18 foreign banks operating in Russia before the crisis, the most visible in terms of activity were, in order of arrival: Crédit Lyonnais, Société Générale, BNP–Dresden Bank, CSFB, ING–Eurasia, Citybank, ABN–AMRO, Chase Manhattan, Raiffaseisenbank, Deutsche Bank. In addition, 13 other banks had a foreign minority ownership.) During these meetings Russians officials usually provided the investors with their current and forecasted macroeconomic figures, but also discussed the situation more broadly, inviting opinions on particular policies.[13]

A number of "local" financial institutions had a strong foreign flavor. Several were run by Russian repatriates, who quickly linked up with the political establishment. Troika Dialog Bank and Renaissance Capital are two examples of successful brokerages which survived the 1998 crisis. Another case is Brunswik, a brokerage firm set up by young Swedes (several of them coming from MFU) but locally based.

These firms could have played an important advisory role, at least informally, since they had built up competent professional staff, often including many well-trained foreigners or foreign-trained Russians. With few exceptions, this was not the case. Their influence was clearly limited by that of their competitors, the purely Russian banks run by the oligarchs who deeply penetrated the government and the media and had an agenda of their own. The best example of this last group is Vladimir Potanin, head of Unexim Bank, who served as Minister of Finance after the 1996 presidential election without resigning from his private bank position.

Motivations

There were many money doctors in Russia, but what was motivating them? Motivations are notoriously hard to assess, and what follow are inevitably guesses. The IMF and the World Bank, later the EBRD, saw Russia as the biggest lump of the whole transition process, the acid test of their usefulness. The U.S. considered that the end of the Soviet Union marked the successful end of the Cold War and the beginning of a new era. The priority was to prevent the nuclear arsenal from falling into unfriendly hands, be it the Russian government or rogue states and terrorist groups. But world peace would be mightily enhanced if Russia could become an affluent, Western-oriented country. Economic success was to be a key component, which motivated the scale of the effort. Influence over the shape that the Russian economic institutions would take was another powerful incentive to have many advisers on the ground.

Consulting firms are in the business of making money, and a large-scale advisory effort opened up a new market. Individual advisers were many and diverse, and so were their motivations; no generalization can be made. Some were drawn by the intellectual excitement of the challenge, along with the more vain hope of influencing a piece of history; this was clearly the spirit perceptible at MFU. One did not need to have profound knowledge to be able to dispense advice to the young reformers, who were initially ready to absorb all knowledge.[14] Others saw advisory work as a good way of entering the economic and political scene and eventually settling and earning a good living, as several did. The financial returns were varied (negligible at MFU, substantial under the European TACIS program, for instance), and so were the incentives. One could find among the money doctors, as among all doctors, those who did the job because they believed in its mission and those who were mostly driven by financial rewards, with different weights attached to both motivations.

Was the crisis foreseeable?

From 1992 to 1996: main events and characters

The new Moscow leaders were eager to embrace the capitalist world. The first Prime Minister, Yegor Gaïdar, had secretly been learning Western-style economics along with a group of young bright Moscow colleagues. They quickly teamed up with a group from Leningrad – renamed St. Petersburg – led by Anatoly Chubais. They were enthusiastic. In a few days they had freed many prices, and would soon complete that primal step. Two years later, Chubais started mass privatization, the biggest sale of state-owned enterprises ever.

Within a few weeks of price liberalization, one of the most abhorred traditions of Soviet times, dawn lines in front of food stores, were gone. Traditionally bare shops started to fill up. Still publicly owned, though, most stores were not ready to seize on the occasion, so streets filled up with rudimentary but well-stocked stalls. Soon enterprising dealers set up more comfortable kiosks. As Russians started to find all sorts of goods previously unavailable (previously reserved for the happy few of the *nomenklatura*, bananas became the symbol of the new era) they also discovered the meaning of "unaffordable," and its corollary, poverty. For decades, they had been able to buy everything that could be found in stores, but there was little there. Now everything was tantalizingly available, but beyond the means of most. And, ominously, it took just a few more weeks for the kiosks to fall prey to ransom by warring mafias. Bad habits came early.

With amazing speed, curbside exchange dealing developed into a well-organized foreign exchange market. Top-notch rocket engineers set up performing computer trading systems. At every street corner in Moscow, one could follow in real time the evolution of the ruble, and it was relentlessly going down. The dollar quickly became the store of value for every citizen, an amazing symbol of the demise of the system.

Meanwhile, firms were left to fend for themselves. For decades they had relied on central planning for giving orders, picking up goods and providing parts, and providing money for the workers' salaries. To be sure, the money of Soviet times was not real money, it was even called *bez-nalitchnyi*, literally "without value." It was a sort of unit of account used by the central planning bureau to track down the (non-)fulfillment of commitments. But at least the economic life of the country used to be organized, and this uneventful machinery suddenly dissipated. Managers stopped receiving orders. They had to invent a new way of operating: finding customers and collecting orders, ordering materials and parts, and, most difficult of all, finding cash to operate.[15] The main invention of the time was asset stripping, the transfer into private hands (those of the managers and their friends and protectors) of whatever was of value in their firms: equipment, buildings and dwellings, goods. Much of the Soviet economy was thus promptly "privatized" by uncontrolled and unscrupulous bosses whose sole allegiance had been to the Communist Party.[16] "Connections," a word synonymous with power and influence in the previous regimes, became a tool for private wealth accumulation. Most of the latter-day oligarchs started that way in these early hours of transition. Marx's primitive accumulation of wealth proceeded in the wild at full speed on the still burning ashes of collectivism.

Meanwhile, government offices were taken over by a few dozens of young reformers, the troops of Gaïdar and Chubais. Promoted to the ranks of ministers and deputy ministers, they were supposed to give instructions to hundreds of thousands of bureaucrats trained to deal with the complex intricacies of central planning. Dumbfounded by the speed of events, these bureaucrats were not only unable to execute orders that they did not understand, but they quickly tried to restore the only order they knew. They linked up with the firm bosses both to pilfer whatever was within reach and to sabotage the early moves toward a market economy. The young reformers quickly discovered that their seats were standing on quicksand.

The reformers attempted to govern by issuing decrees, the famed *ukaz*, but nobody was really paying attention. The most committed of them embarked on a gigantic task, that of building market institutions, possibly along with democracy. Others soon realized that money could be made, quickly and in vast amounts. Corruption, an old Russian tradition under all regimes, blossomed. Within a few months, the reform movement was rotten at the heart.

Meanwhile inflation exploded. The central bank considered that its role was to fill the gap left by the central planning bureau, to provide firms with cash. Bosses asked for money, and they got it straight from the CBR. What happened to this money is not hard to guess; nor is it surprising that more and more was requested. While a happy few were becoming rich, the masses saw their standard of living plummet, as wages, when they were paid, massively lagged behind prices. Gregory Matukhin, the President of the central bank, famously rejected the Western view that inflation is a monetary phenomenon. He claimed to be a strict market economist and explained that inflation was rising because demand exceeded supply: firms were unable to produce, he observed, because they did not have sufficient working capital. He characterized his job as that of a "supply-sider," supporting firms by means of virtually unlimited cash injections. His more savvy successor, Victor Gerashenko, adopted the same "supply-side" view, and refined it by providing cash to the CIS countries, ostensibly to maintain the ruble zone throughout the collapsed Soviet Union.

Within a year of its rebirth, Russia was in complete disarray and the reformers largely on the defensive. Gaïdar was soon sacrificed to political coalition-building. Inflation was out of control, and the federal budget was quickly contracting, hurting basic public services such as hospitals and schools. Standards of living were sharply down, throwing into poverty millions of people too old or too weak to adjust. Mafias of all sorts had established themselves and were waging violent turf battles. The Communist Party, initially knocked out and then dismembered, was pulling itself together behind the most uncharismatic leader, Gennady Zyuganov. Along with a fringe of far-leftists intent on restoring the Soviet Union, the Communists controlled the Duma, the parliament elected before the collapse of the Soviet Union. The Duma became the center of increasingly strident opposition to Yeltsin and his reforms. In October 1993, leftist groups attempted to control Moscow's main TV center, the Ostankino tower. Violent fights erupted and demonstrators went on a stampede. When they linked up with the Duma, Yeltsin saw signs of a coup and sent the army to crush the Duma. The number of casualties remains unknown.

Yeltsin's show of strength gave him some breathing space. The reformers made a comeback. Chubais launched mass privatization and oversaw a successful disinflation program partly based on anchoring the ruble to the dollar through a crawling peg arrangement, the corridor. Yeltsin's popularity sagged and a few months before the next presidential elections his positive rating stood at 6 per cent. While some of his shady advisers were pushing him simply to cancel the elections, the reformers were busily arranging for a Western-type election: lots of money, elaborate market research, and use of television and the media. The money was lavishly provided by the budding oligarchs, who were united in their fear of a Communist victory.[17]

Yeltsin was re-elected in 1996, and immediately suffered serious heart attacks. The Kremlin went into a deep freeze. Policy reforms stopped. The state further fell apart. Among other things, payment discipline – the central institution of a market economy – evaporated. Firms would not pay taxes and the government would not pay for its purchases. Firms and the state would pay salaries only with considerable delay. Payment arrears piled up. Meanwhile, the oligarchs who had bankrolled Yeltsin's election skillfully exploited the power vacuum. They were expanding everywhere: accumulating wealth in business, especially oil and minerals, moving funds around, mostly toward safe heavens, through their control of banks, and dominating politics by running TV stations and the popular press, sitting in the Duma and holding key government positions. The pilfering went on unchecked, with corruption reaching all levels of government in each corner of Russia's vast expanses.

Unsurprisingly, the state coffers gradually emptied. Debt finance, once the crucial instrument to bring inflation down by separating the budget from the printing press, became the normal way of making ends meet. Obviously the party would have to come to an end, and an ugly one. The crisis of 1998 was written on the wall.

The outlook in 1997: reasons for optimism

To be sure, not everything was bleak. In many respects, the reformers could boast a number of successes. They had managed to establish most of the preconditions for a successful transition, but they had failed in some important details and never were politically able to move on to the next steps. Transition was more suspended than botched up. Yet there were many positive signals.

Mass privatization is usually presented as an unmitigated disaster. As argued by Schleifer and Triesman (2000), this view ignores the alternatives. By late 1992 anti-market forces had regrouped around the Association of Industrialists. Led by Arkady Volsky, this association mobilized the managers of the huge Soviet-era conglomerates who used to be the regime's backbone and beneficiaries. They were fighting back and trying to reverse the market-oriented measures introduced by Gaïdar. With the active support of the CBR, they were the most dangerous force. Mass privatization shrewdly co-opted them: they were given for free 51 per cent of the shares and the possibility of buying the rest.[18] Once their wealth, until then only the notional present value of expected privileges, was transformed into effective ownership their interest in a reversal of market reforms disappeared and Yeltsin's power was consolidated. During 1993 alone, leaving aside the oil and mineral extraction industries not yet up for sale, 40 per cent of Russian industry (measured in terms of employees) was privatized. In 1997, 69 per cent of enterprises (including foreign ones) were private; 9 per cent had mixed ownership. True, there would be a heavy price to pay: appalling corporate governance. Most firms were in the incompetent and corrupt hands of the former "red barons," more skilled at seeking subsidies than at retooling uncompetitive businesses. The oligarchs would soon buy them out and spread into government. But once the step of privatization had been taken, any reversal of the market economy was ruled out. The true question, therefore, is whether the price has been excessive, keeping in mind that Russia might have been lost right there, for good.

Inflation was no longer the debilitating factor it used to be. The inflation rate for 1997 stood at 11 per cent, down from 2,500 per cent in 1992. Monetary policy was entirely dedicated to the pursuit of disinflation, aiming at a rate of 5 per cent by the end of 1998. Tatyana Paramonova, the acting CBR President, was entirely sold on the idea that inflation is a monetary phenomenon, an idea that her predecessors decried as a Western, anti-Russian fallacy. Her successor, Sergei Dubinin, a reformer, fully upheld this approach.

Real interest rates finally settled at more reasonable levels (Table 4.1). Massively negative during the years of near-hyperinflation, massively positive in the post-inflation and electoral year 1996, in the lower teens by the end of 1997, they were at a level which could represent the availability of funds and riskiness of capital.

Table 4.1 Inflation and interest rates

	Inflation rate	*Nominal interest rate (GKO)*	*Real interest rate*
1992	2,508.8		
1993	839.9	121.0	-707.5
1994	215.1	172.3	-83.6
1995	131.3	166.2	8.5
1996	21.8	87.6	64.7
1997	11.0	24.4	13.0
1998	84.4	48.1	34.7

Source: *Russian Economic Trends.*

The exchange rate had been brought into the corridor in July 1995. The programmed rate of daily depreciation was being gradually reduced, alongside inflation (Figure 4.1). As a sign of stabilization, three zeros had been dropped, giving the new ruble a luster that befitted its status as a "normal" currency. At the same time, the corridor was made horizontal, thus eliminating the pre-announced trend depreciation.

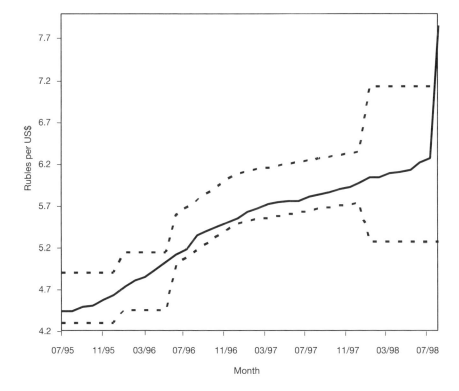

Figure 4.1 The ruble corridor, 1995–8

Source: *Russian Economic Trends.*

The current account balance never posed any threat. Oil, gas, and mineral exports were virtually guaranteed, at least in volume. This allowed the Russians to purchase Western goods deemed superior in quality, including bottled water and toothpaste.[19] Following liberalization, imports had risen sharply while non-oil, non-mineral, non-military exports were insignificant. Russian manufacturers were largely unable to compete on their own domestic markets, far less on foreign markets. The healthy current account acted as an anesthetic, concealing the failure of much of Russian industry.

Late 1997: mixed signals

Progress had been achieved over the period 1992–7, but much remained to be done on both the structural and macroeconomic levels, and, in some aspects, the Russian economy was rapidly deteriorating after the 1996 presidential election. The question is whether this deterioration was inexorably leading to a crisis and, if so, who saw it and why no remedial action was taken. This sub-section and the next ones describe the facts: we first look at ambiguous developments and then focus in on unmistakable signals that a crisis was on its way. The section which follows examines how the authorities and the money doctors interpreted them.

The federal budget had been in deficit from the beginning of the transition.[20] By early 1998 the situation was no better and no worse than before. At about 7 per cent of gross domestic product (GDP) (Table 4.2) the deficit was not unbearable, since the domestic public debt was nil to start with in 1992. The disinflation program of 1995 had relied on the end of monetary financing of the deficit, shifting instead to bond financing. The first debt instruments, short-term bills (GKO) had been issued in small quantities in May 1993. Pretty soon an efficient GKO market developed. The high real returns of 1996 made this instrument very appealing to Russian and foreign investors, even though the latter were not initially allowed and then had to hold their assets in special S-accounts which severely limited the repatriation of earnings. Clearly, debt could not be accumulated indefinitely. Some day, somehow, the deficit would have to be closed. Unsurprisingly, the IMF emphasized the need to bring the deficit down, but not as a matter of urgency. Similarly, GKO-holders did not seem extremely concerned, or considered that the returns were more than compensating for the risks.

A stock market had developed. Initially, relatively few companies were listed, but the list kept expanding. The market received a boost when oil and mineral-extracting companies were privatized at the end of 1995–6, starting with the infamous loan-for-shares deal.[21] By 1998, as privatization of oil and mineral-extracting companies continued, the Moscow stock market listed a number of highly attractive companies. Percentage limits on foreign ownership of the Russian gas, oil, and mineral resources companies were established, but some risk-seeking foreign investors worked their way around the restriction through friendly intermediaries. Unfortunately, there was no proper registry, which explains a number of dark events where minority shareholders (probably often representing foreign interests) were summarily dispossessed.

Table 4.2   The federal budget (% of GDP)

	Balance	Debt	Arrears due by federal government
1993	-7.0	0.1	n.a.
1994	-10.2	2.1	n.a.
1995	-5.4	4.7	n.a.
1996	-7.9	10.8	2.6
1997	-7.0	14.8	2.0
1998	-5.0	16.2 *	n.a.

Source: *Russian Economic Trends.*

Note:

*   for the first half of 1998.

Most transactions in the Russian stock market were conducted in dollars. Most trade volume was associated with foreign investors' activity, possibly including an unknown share of purely Russian funds operating from offshore tax-haven zones. From April 1996 to July 1997 equity prices increased by more than 550 per cent (Figure 4.2). The initial impetus was provided by the improving poll results of Yeltsin in the run-up to the presidential election. Over the first half of 1997 bullish sentiment further propelled the market, creating a feeling of Klondike-type euphoria. However, by late 1997 the stock market reflected a change in sentiment on the part of international investors scared by the Asian turmoil. A crisis was becoming an option.

The corridor started to raise eyebrows. Since July 1995, the exchange rate had been used as a key anchor to give credibility to disinflation. In many respects, it was a stunning success. It did affect expectations. Most crucially, it helped re-establish some credibility for the population, which had suffered several official and de facto confiscations of their cash holdings: in January 1991 when the Soviet authorities organized a forced exchange of 50-ruble and 100-ruble banknotes with a tight deadline that caught a number of citizens; then in July 1993 the CBR abruptly replaced Soviet rubles with new Russian banknotes, officially because vast quantities of forged Soviet notes were circulating in the CIS countries and were making their way back to Russia, a step that precipitated the end of the ruble zone;[22] obviously the great inflation of 1992–4 had robbed ordinary citizens of the rest of whatever savings they had been able to scrape together in better (Soviet) times. Trust in the ruble and the state, which had vanished, was being slowly restored.

The return to exchange rate stability was a potent symbol that the economic situation was under control. To further squeeze out inflation, the exchange rate was allowed to crawl every day, at a rate typically lower than inflation. A major real appreciation of the ruble took place during the hyperinflation period (877 per cent in 1992, 205 per cent in 1993, 41 per cent in January 1994–June 1995), largely as a catch-up from the collapse that took place immediately after the collapse of the Soviet Union. The real exchange rate continued to increase after

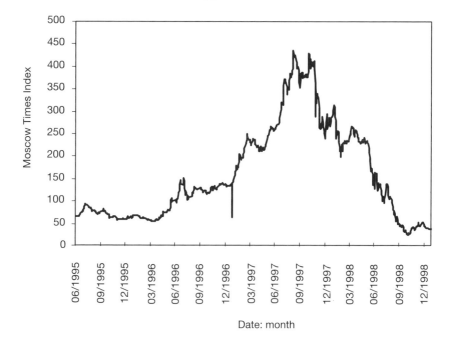

Figure 4.2 Stock prices
Source: Moscow Times.

the introduction of the corridor, as Figure 4.3 illustrates. This prompted a lively debate.

One view was that the ruble was overvalued,[23] the result of an excessively tight monetary policy which was strangling Russian firms. Table 4.1 shows that, in every single year from 1992 to 1997, inflation always exceeded nominal depreciation. Compared to both 1994 and 1998, in 1997 the ruble was massively overvalued.

Another view was that the ruble was at about its equilibrium value and that Russian firms would only be able to compete when they retooled. The current account was never in deficit. Quite possibly, Russia was a victim of a Dutch disease, but that does imply overvaluation. With such a short history with a market economy, whose first years had been marked by a calamitous near-hyperinflation, the evidence from Figure 4.3 was just too short to be interpreted and to pinpoint with any degree of precision where the ruble's equilibrium lay.[24]

Yet the economy remained heavily dollarized long after near-hyperinflation had been eradicated. Estimates of the amount of dollar banknotes in circulation by the end of 1997 vary from $40 billion to $120 billion, i.e. about 100 per cent to 300 per cent of ruble circulation. A portion of these dollar balances was circulating in the black economy, the rest being literally stored under mattresses.

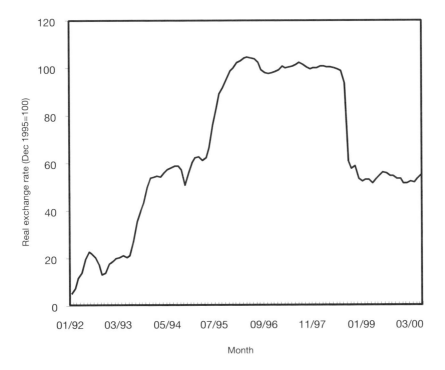

Figure 4.3 Real exchange rate

Source: Russian Economic Trends.

Unmistakable signals

Governance at both the government and corporate level emerged as a severe failure of transition. Russia was not alone in failing in this respect, but its record was much worse than in most non-CIS countries, and seriously deteriorating. By late 1997 the government was widely seen as being in the hands of "the family," the coterie of Yeltsin's advisers. Led by his daughter, Tatiana Dyachenko, this group included many reformers aligned with the oligarchs and shadowy figures like Boris Berezhovsky. They were visibly more interested in private wealth accumulation than in pursuing the complicated task of restructuring the country.

The oligarchs were at the helm of most large corporations and banks. Profits were not based on shrewd business plans but on proximity to power. The benefits came in many forms: the acquisition of state-owned interests, mostly in oil and mineral extraction, the possibility of not paying taxes, the ability of exporting ill-gotten money.

Policy proposals were assessed on the basis of their impact on the family's interests. In practice, this meant the status quo. Very few reforms were tried during the period that followed the 1996 presidential election, and even fewer were enacted. When the specter of a major crisis emerged in late 1997, the reaction of the family was to shelter its assets, possibly even to take advantage of the end-game. Prime Minister Chernomyrdin, never a part of that group,[25] was sacked and replaced by lesser figures unlikely to spoil the game.

Declining tax collection was the most visible and dangerous indicator of trouble. As previously noted, the budget deficit looked sustainable. The deficit numbers, however, were deceptive. As Table 4.3 shows, official tax revenues were apparently stable as a share of GDP. In fact, effective tax collection was plummeting. The tax authorities were following a time-honored tradition from Soviet times whereby those responsible for achieving planned targets invented all sorts of creative gimmicks to make it look as if they were fulfilling their commitments. In this case, two main loopholes grew larger. Tax offsets were arrangements between the tax authorities and firms whereby firms replaced tax payment in cash with deliveries of goods and services to the public sector. No one really knows how the prices of these goods and services were set, whether they were actually on order, simply bartered, or maybe even never delivered. The other loophole was tax arrears: firms were simply not paying, often arguing, with the vocal support of local and regional political leaders, that forcing them to pay taxes would lead to bankruptcy and result in massive layoffs. Measured on a cash accrual basis, the deficit was huge, and widening.

Table 4.3   Federal tax collection (% of GDP)

	Total tax collection	Tax collection in cash	Tax offsets	Arrears owed to federal government
1993				1.0
1994	7.9	7.6	0.3	1.5
1995	9.6	7.3	2.2	2.0
1996	8.9	4.9	4.0	3.2
1997	9.6	5.9	3.6	4.0
1998				6.0

Source: Russian Economic Trends.

Faced with a cash shortage, the federal government too was running up arrears (see Table 4.2). Any hope of closing the deficit rested on tax reform and spending cuts. The only visible effort at tax reform took the form of the preparation of a new tax code, long on legal details but short on practical measures. In preparation for more than three years, the tax code was bogged down in the quicksand of a hostile Duma which sensed that it was in a position of cornering the government and saw no reason to support even this modest step.[26] The need for spending cuts was not recognized until the end of 1997, once Asia was in crisis. The spending reduction program was completed too late – at the end of May 1998, when markets had already lost all confidence in the government.

Ominously, the value of the federal debt rested on the presumption that the government would be able, at some point, to swing its primary deficit into a surplus. With a primary surplus unlikely over any plausible horizon, sooner or later it would appear that the debt was valueless.

Interest rates on GKOs gradually factored in the risk that had to be attached to the debt. The process started in late 1997, at about the same time as the stock market was peaking, as Figures 4.2 and 4.4 show. In late January 1998, they rose to 44 per cent, while inflation was declining towards 10 per cent. The fear receded for a while, but by mid-May 1998 the climb had resumed, and it never stopped.

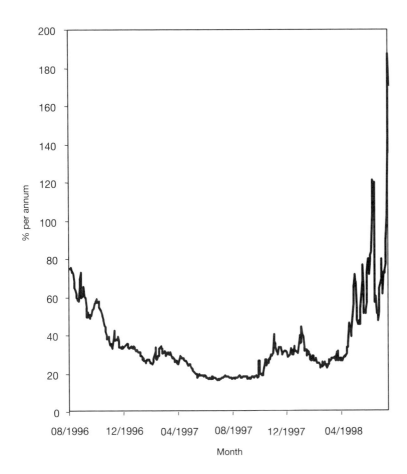

Figure 4.4 Interest rates on six-month GKOs
Source: Russian Economic Trends.

The interest rate rise was alarming for two reasons. First, it increased the debt service since most of the debt was short term. A vicious cycle was under way: every increase in interest rates was worsening the budget deficit, and every increase in the deficit was raising the risk premium on GKOs. Second, the risk premium also worked through the exchange rate. The specter of a debt default, increasingly plausible, put in doubt the ability to maintain the corridor policy. Using the interest rate to estimate the expected exchange rate, as explained below (see display), Table 4.4 presents the results. Table 4.4(a) shows in the first column the actual exchange rate (rubles per U.S.$) observed on selected days, the following ones display the expectation for that same day formed one, two, or three months before. Table 4.4(b) shows expectations for 1–12 months later, with the exchange rate observed on the due date indicated in brackets in each column. Both tables display worsening expectations, especially in late spring 1998, and then in August. In between, following the IMF loan discussed below, expectations temporarily improved.

Table 4.4　Exchange rate expectations

a)

Date	Actual (R / $)	Expectations formed …before				
		1 day	*1 week*	*1 month*	*2 months*	*3 months*
05/01/98	5.974	5.977	5.966	5.994	5.948	6.013
29/05/99	6.138	6.156	6.190	6.204	6.268	6.306
29/06/98	6.194	6.233	6.258	6.375	6.301	6.356
10/07/98	6.231	6.249	6.272	6.352	6.369	6.452
28/07/98	6.273	6.28	6.224	6.426	6.581	6.386
13/08/98	6.229	6.307	6.339	6.561	6.672	6.520
17/08/98	6.43	6.32	6.35	6.376	6.737	6.566
18/08/98	6.83		6.391	6.383	6.642	6.641

b)

Date when expectation made	Exchange rate expected …later (Actual exchange rate observed …later)				
	1 week	*1 month*	*2 months*	*3 months*	*1 year*
05/01/98	5.995	6.064	6.156	6.249	7.152
	(6.001)	(6.057)	(6.065)	(6.132)	(22.78)
30/01/98	6.081	6.193	6.341	6.492	8.032
	(6.059)	(6.045)	(6.0896)	(6.109)	(23.1)
29/05/98	6.185	6.343	6.556	6.775	9.11
	(6.178)	(6.225)	(6.278)	(12.89)	
29/06/98	6.253	6.453	6.724	7.005	10.113
	(6.231)	(6.276)	(12.89)	(16.052)	
28/07/99	6.331	6.528	6.794	7.07	10.124
	(6.283)	(12.89)	(15.97)	(16.8)	
13/08/98	6.372	6.622	6.962	7.319	11.482
	(6.995)	(8.901)	(15.049)	(18.2)	

Estimating exchange rate expectations

The uncovered interest parity assumption sets the expected rate of exchange at the n-month horizon equal to the current exchange rate adjusted by the ratio of the domestic and annualized interest rate factors (1 + the interest rate) over the same maturity n, adjusted for the length of the horizon period, adjusted for the presence of a country risk premium:

$$(1) \qquad E_t(S_{t+n}) = S_t \left(\frac{(1+i_{t,n})}{(1+i^*_{t,n})(1+RP_t)} \right)^{\frac{n}{12}}$$

where:

- $i_{t,n}$ is the annualized yield in month t on a GKO with maturity n, as observed on the secondary market;
- $i^*_{t,n}$ is the corresponding yield on a U.S. Treasury bill;
- S_t is the currently observed exchange rate (end of month) in rubles per U.S. dollar;
- $E_t(S_{t+n})$ is the market expectation in month t of the exchange rate in month $t + n$;
- RP_t is the country risk premium, i.e. risk on GKOs, in period t.

The risk premium is often hard to assess, as we need to disentangle the country from the currency risk. In the case of Russia we can measure it since there exist dollar-denominated Treasury bills, the MinFin bonds (which were issued as a replacement for Soviet Union debt taken over by Russia in late 1991):

$$(2) \qquad 1 + RP_t = \left(\frac{1 + i_{MinFin}}{1 + i^*} \right)$$

where i_{MinFin} is the yield on the third tranche of MinFin bonds, whose maturity date is May 14, 1999. In principle, we should use the same maturity for the MinFins as for the GKOs and Treasury bills. Unfortunately there are no short-term MinFins. As we substitute (2), we make an approximation unlikely to be of serious consequences. The risk premium is probably similar at all maturities and the U.S. rate is considerably less volatile than Russian rates. So in the end we work with:

$$(3) \qquad E_t(S_{t+n}) = S_t \left(\frac{1 + i_{t,n}}{1 + i_{MinFin}} \right)^{\frac{n}{12}}$$

i.e. we look at the ratio of interest rate factors on Russian public debt denominated in rubles and dollars to measure the expected exchange rate.

Foreign exchange reserves started to decline in the fall of 1997. Figure 4.5 displays the evolution of gross reserves, the amount of foreign currency available to the monetary authorities and of the net reserves that they own. The difference represents external borrowing by the monetary authorities. In the months leading up to August 1998, as net reserves were being exhausted, foreign borrowing was not sufficient to prevent a decline in the gross reserves. The central bank's ability to sustain the corridor was rapidly declining. The IMF loan of late July 1998 is visible, but clearly too small to make a difference.

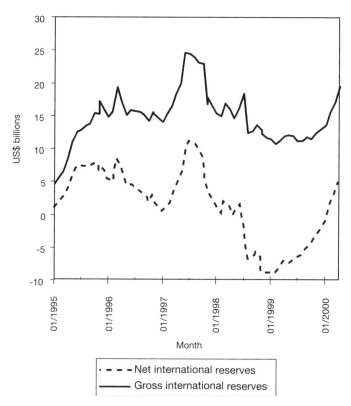

Figure 4.5 Foreign exchange reserves
Source: Central Bank of Russia.

Bad luck was also part of the story – it always is. To start with, oil prices, which had staged a comeback in 1995–6, started to decline quite abruptly in late 1997 (see Figure 4.6). The value of oil and gas exports fell from $38.8 billion in 1996 to $27.9 billion in 1998, a decline of nearly $11 billion (about 3 per cent of pre-crisis GDP). Most ominously, the decline in oil prices also affected tax revenues. In 1997 taxes paid by oil and gas companies (excluding foreign trade taxes) had contributed 35 per cent of all federal revenues. Not only did tax liabilities fall sharply, but actual payments in cash declined even faster. In the general climate of non tax-compliance, oil companies could easily pay even less than they owed, or not pay at all, and get away with it. As the deficit was quickly increasing, this blow may have been the last stroke that tipped the economy over the brink. Such bad luck is cruel when we realize that oil prices reached a trough shortly after the Russian crisis, and then increased threefold. Could Russia have been saved otherwise? Probably not.

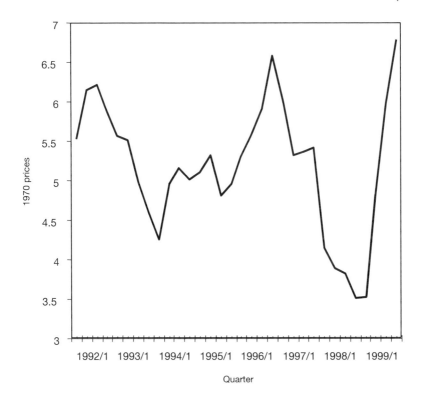

Figure 4.6 Real price of oil
Source: International Financial Statistics.

The other piece of bad luck was the Asian crisis of 1997–8. International investors grew significantly more cautious towards emerging economies in general, and countries with a suspicious governance record in particular. Independently of what was happening inside Russia, capital inflows had to decline anyway.

The crisis and the money doctors

On the way to the crisis

The wake-up call came in the last days of October 1997. As the Asian crisis was spreading, capital outflows from Russia, always large by international standards, intensified. The government found itself unable to raise money on the GKO market and had to secretly ask the CBR for help. Precisely at the same time, Chubais, then Finance Minister, was sacked because of a bizarre scandal on implausible advanced payments for a book yet to be written (and still not written in early 2003). To make matters worse, the current account balance turned negative (−$1.3 billion in the second half of 1997 and −$5.7 billion in the first half of 1998). Whether it was reflecting overvaluation or whether it was a consequence of declining world oil prices remains to be fully elucidated.

The Asian crisis frightened international investors, who became suspicious of all emerging economies. As they cut down on exposure to emerging markets, pressure on the ruble grew. Forced to intervene, the CBR lost $6.2 billion of foreign reserves in November 1997. It adopted temporary restrictions on capital movements and increased the interest rate. This vigorous defense temporarily restored some degree of ruble stability, providing the authorities with some breathing space to reconsider the exchange rate regime to be announced for 1998.

What the government knew and did

Following the first shot in November 1997, the immediate question was whether the exchange rate policy should be changed. Should the ruble be devalued? Or should its band of fluctuation be enlarged? Since March 1996, Russian authorities had operated under an IMF medium-term economic program, supported by a $10.1 billion loan. Nearly half of the loan had been disbursed by the end of 1997. Russian monetary policy remained driven by the exchange rate corridor. For the whole year 1997, the pre-announced rate of depreciation was set at 5–6 per cent. In addition to this "large" band, the CBR daily announced a "narrow" band (+/−0.75 per cent) which defined its points of intervention on MICEX (Moscow International Currency Exchange).

The CBR and the government quickly rejected the idea of a devaluation. There was almost no attempt to determine whether the exchange rate was overvalued or not. Rather, the logic was that a devaluation would shatter confidence and bring back inflation. There was also deep concern for the banking system, which had acquired (against all principles and without encumbrance from its regulator, the central bank) large dollar liabilities. On November 10, 1997, already after the first crisis had started, the Russian government and the CBR announced the exchange rate policy for 1998–2000. Reasonably enough, the "large" corridor was widened to +/−15 per cent around a now constant central rate of 6.2 rubles per dollar (Figure 4.1). Whatever flexibility was gained there was lost by the CBR's continued policy of pre-announcing a daily "narrow" band. De facto, Russia had adopted a fixed exchange rate at a time when it was already facing market pressure.

Some at the CBR thought that the band of fluctuation would have to be widened, but the time was never ripe. It was not ripe in November–December in the midst of the Asian crisis. In March the CBR thought the time had come, but then Chernomyrdin was dismissed from his position as Prime Minister. In May the CBR again wanted to move, but this is when the crisis gathered steam in Russia (see Figure 4.4) and it was then feared that any devaluation, or simply the removal of the narrow band, would dry up the GKO market and throw the financing of the budget into disarray. And so, again, it was felt preferable to stay on the sinking boat rather than to abandon it (Alexashenko 1999).

The government's reasoning was that the source of the problem was the budget and the evaporation of tax compliance. That was indeed the correct diagnosis. The solution, therefore, was to start with the budget, cutting expenditures and improving tax collection. There seems to have been a genuine belief that, with time, the budget could be turned around and the worst avoided.[27] So the government played for time. More precisely, it borrowed time by arranging with the CBR monetary financing of the deficits. This, of course, is what precipitated the crisis.

As matters grew worse, the government did not seem to realize the seriousness of the situation. It concentrated its effort on improving the budget, with no result. It then turned to the IMF to obtain more breathing space, which led to the July package discussed below (pp. 130–1). Drastic measures, such as devaluation, were seen as too dangerous both economically and politically. Apparently, debt default was never on the agenda. So the government could only slide into the crisis.

The crisis was well under way by early June. Equity prices were dropping sharply, to 60 per cent below the end-1997 level, yields on GKO reached 100 per cent, and, of course, the ruble was under persistent pressure: the exchange rate started systematically to hit the upper limit of the "narrow" corridor. Like a slow-motion movie, it unfolded step by step, accompanied by costly policy mistakes that were not always entirely innocent.

The government's publicly stated strategy, the July package, contained three main elements:

- a radical tightening of the federal budget, intended to solve once and for all persistent fiscal imbalances;
- an increase in international reserves;
- the lengthening of the debt maturity to reduce the vulnerability arising from the short-term structure of domestic debt.

The fiscal part of the package aimed at improving tax collection, reducing tax arrears, establishing treasury control on budget expenditure, and cutting federal expenditure commitments. In addition, the government pledged to submit to the Duma (more hostile than ever as it too smelled blood) tax legislation proposals aimed at quickly raising cash.

The GKO swap

With interest rates at three-digit levels, debt service was precipitously worsening and debt financing increasingly in doubt. The situation was not missed by the large taxpayers, whose payment discipline, very limited under normal conditions, vanished. In a panic effort at alleviating the burden of forthcoming repayments on domestic debt, in mid-July the Ministry of Finance converted a large portion of GKOs into foreign currency Eurobonds with longer maturities, at market prices.

The ruble defense

As soon as speculators saw that the CBR had started to sell reserves at the fixed exchange rate with fresh money from the IMF stabilization loan, they rushed in. In August gross international reserves decreased by $5.9 billion, almost exactly the amount provided to Russia over the same period.

On August 17, 1998, the Russian authorities threw in the towel. The ruble was set free, and depreciated by 60 per cent over the next few weeks. The government defaulted on its debt. Within days, Prime Minister Kyrienko was sacked and replaced by the fatherly figure of Yevgeny Primakov, the President of the CBR resigned, and the father of the great inflation of 1993–5, Victor Gerashenko, got his old job back. The banks collapsed. The oligarchs and the reformers – who had teamed up with the oligarchs – were gone.

What the money doctors said

By the end of 1997 most individual money doctors had left the scene or had lost any influence. The government was either committed to the oligarchs and their interests, or fully preoccupied with obtaining loans from the IMF, which had already provided a lot of advice. Anyway, the few individual money doctors were divided between those who claimed that it was too late to avoid a crisis and those who shared the government view that corrective fiscal measures could still spare Russia the unpalatable decision of devaluing the ruble. And Steven Hanke was back in town proposing a currency board.

So the only player was the IMF (with the World Bank playing second fiddle), and the IMF was in close contact with Larry Summers, the Deputy Secretary of the U.S. Treasury in 1995, and David Lipton, the Under Secretary of the Treasury for International Affairs.[28]

The ongoing Asian crisis was revealing the vulnerability of fixed exchange rate regimes in open economies with weak banking systems and poor governance. How could the IMF not recognize that Russia certainly fell into that category? Instead, the Fund repeatedly supported the fixed exchange rate policy, describing it as fundamentally on track. Never did it recommend letting the ruble float. When it approved, at the end of May 1998 (less than three months ahead of the crisis), yet another new set of fiscal "decisions"[29] and later the July package, the IMF felt the need to state publicly that the exchange rate policy was a key component of the policy package and that a devaluation of the ruble should be avoided.

The most surprising event is the July emergency package. By mid-June 1998 it was becoming increasingly clear that a storm would hit (Table 4.4). Then Chubais, back in government as Special Presidential Envoy, announced that

Russia would seek an emergency loan from the IMF to support the doomed ruble policy. Within three weeks the IMF decided to increase its financial support for 1998 by $11.2 billion, $4.8 billion of which was immediately disbursed with the explicitly stated aim of increasing foreign reserves. The World Bank was also called upon to lend $1.5 billion for structural reforms.

The conditions imposed were the same as before: correcting the budget and speeding up structural reforms. In the midst of the deteriorating situation, years of fiscal mismanagement could not conceivably be corrected in short order. Even in a stable environment, the proposed measures would have to signal a commitment to enforce the law and balance the budget, but by then the government had lost the political means to cut spending and enforce any measure of tax discipline. As for the structural reforms, they were those regularly requested by the Fund and turned down by the authorities. They were forced on a hapless government that had lost the power to implement them. Even if it did, the measures would have taken years to deliver tangible results.

Another part of the July package was the GKO swap. This is exactly what the Mexico authorities had done in 1994, a move fully recognized as deeply mistaken, possibly the main reason for the Mexican crisis a few weeks later. Everyone knew it, and the IMF better than anyone else.[30]

The IMF could not ignore that its actions were technically wrong and practically hopeless. Already under attack for its handling of the Asian crisis, the Fund would obviously want to steer a prudent course of action, not a multibillion-dollar gamble. So why did it act so apparently irresponsibly? The most plausible answer is that the IMF acted under intense pressure from the U.S. Treasury. For political reasons – and ignoring economic logic – the Treasury determined that everything had to be seen to be done not to lose Russia, even though David Lipton is reported to have expressed skepticism. Cynically perhaps, it was felt that a vigorous IMF defense, at Russian taxpayers' expense,[31] was just the kind of political signal that was needed. And the IMF obliged.

Domestic and foreign investors: victims or profiteers?

From the center of the storm, the financial markets made their views known. They had no doubt that Russia's macroeconomic fundamentals were good except for the fiscal problems and that a devaluation would be devastating. By mid-May 1998 they had concluded that the government would not be able to fix the situation on its own and that only a large IMF loan could restore confidence. Figure 4.4 shows that GKO yields hit new records after the government announced an expenditure-cutting package on May 26, and again after the anti-crisis program of June 23. Their view was that a devaluation of the ruble could only be avoided through a large-scale IMF loan. They saw the main threat as originating in the government's inability to service its debt and, unsurprisingly, argued that the solution would have to be a bailout.

When late in May interest rates rose to 150 per cent, President Yeltsin personally asked his Western counterparts (Clinton, Kohl, and Blair) for emergency financial aid. President Clinton publicly promised his support for fresh IMF and World Bank loans, but the following G7 Finance Ministers' Meeting in early June did not make any firm commitment. When the IMF followed up by expressing doubts that Russia needed help, the investors concluded that the ruble was doomed, they blamed the IMF for sending contradictory signals, and looked for another bailout.

The investors' next idea was that the government could solve the debt problem by converting short-term GKOs into longer-term dollar-denominated bonds, without a devaluation. The swap, a massive mistake in view of the previous experience in Mexico, was duly organized in mid-July, backed by an IMF promise to provide $22.6 billion over 1998–9, $5.6 billion of this in a few days. Immediately after the first tranche ($4.8 billion) was released the investors concluded that this was not enough, and the crisis soon occurred.

Who were the investors? First, there were the nonresident investors, who held about 30 per cent of state bonds (about $20 billion). They generally supported the GKO market longer than anybody else. Among the domestic bondholders, the CBR and Sberbank, which held about 50 per cent of GKOs, assisted the government by purchasing new GKO issues at the primary auctions. The remaining 20 per cent of GKOs were held by the domestic commercial banks, owned by the oligarchs, with considerable influence. Those whose interests were mostly in the oil and gas sector (Berezhovsky, Vyakhirev) publicly called for a devaluation.[32] The others, however, were mostly concerned by the dollar liabilities of the banks that they controlled, and they opposed a devaluation, calling instead for an IMF bailout. The latter group prevailed, partly because they were supported by the IMF, which still regarded exchange rate stability as a sacred cow.

The domestic investors

By late 1997 there were a few large "banks." They were not banks in the traditional sense of collecting deposits and lending to customers. They were holding companies in the hands of the oligarchs. They owned huge chunks of Russian industry and were financing the government by buying GKOs. They were also spiriting their profits abroad into shadowy subsidiaries based in Cyprus and other safe havens.

Their influence on the government was considerable, as many of their managers simultaneously held high-level official positions. They could be called the last money doctors if they were interested in helping the patient. But their preoccupation was elsewhere. They were the direct beneficiaries of the pre-crisis period. They were borrowing dollars at low interest and lending to the government at huge interest. They were selling futures contracts to concerned foreign investors at an enormous price. The profitability of these trades rested on the fixed exchange rate regime. They had convinced the government and the CBR that allowing the ruble to float would lead to a bank collapse. When they saw that the ruble and the government were going to collapse they moved to dispose of all their ruble holdings. When the money market dried out they convinced the authorities to ask for the July IMF package. When the $4 billion arrived in Moscow, the banks immediately sold an equivalent amount of rubles to the CBR, happy to avoid a bank crisis.

Of course, the banks went bust in the immediate aftermath of the crisis. By then they were loaded with massive dollar liabilities that they were delighted to default on, as explained. The assets had been safely stored abroad. The banks were bankrupt; the owners were rich. To this day, the situation has not been disentangled.

The foreign investors

Impressed by the Asian crisis, and then by the fear of possible devaluation, nonresidents started exiting the GKO market from the end of 1997. However, attracted by huge interest rates (Table 4.1), some foreigner investors preferred to stay. To hedge the risk they brought forward contracts from Russian banks despite serious doubts on the banks' creditworthiness. The amount of forward contracts that the Russian banks had to pay to foreign investors after August 17 has been estimated at $6 billion. All of that was forfeited when the Russian banks collapsed.

When the government devalued the ruble it froze the GKO market and announced a 90-day moratorium on principal repayments of foreign debts by the Russian commercial enterprises, including banks. The terms of the GKO restructuring were announced only one week later. Initially Russia offered to restructure nonresidents' frozen GKOs into 17-year dollar-denominated Eurobonds. The IMF tried to insist on an equal approach to resident and nonresident holders of GKOs, but the new Russian government of Yevgeny Primakov decided to offer different restructuring schemes. Later on Russia started negotiations on terms of its debt restructuring with 19 Western banks representing the interests of foreign investors.

Conclusion

So who lost Russia? Undoubtedly, the Russians did. They accumulated policy mistakes, which may not all have been innocent. Some policymakers were certainly doing the best that they could. In doing so, they received much advice from domestic and foreign money doctors. Most of the influential doctors came from the ranks of the oligarchs and saw the plundering of Russia as the easiest way to accumulate even more wealth. Bona fide Russian advisers were a few voices in the wilderness. Illarionov is remembered as the one who advocated devaluing the ruble well ahead of the crisis, but, because of his hostility towards Chubais, then the strong man, no one would listen.

The individual foreign money doctors have gradually faded away. Gone the first years of excitement, when the reformers were widely opening their ministerial doors to receive advice – probably with little discrimination between competent and incompetent economists – the Russian policymakers started to distance themselves from these money doctors. The advisers often failed fully to grasp Russian politics. Most were not resilient enough, willing to stay even when the reformers' clout was at a low ebb. Some were discouraged early on by the darker forces of corruption and compromise that were increasingly at work. The advice was often contradictory from one adviser to another, in effect raising suspicions that there was no good advice as such. The Russians also suspected that the advisers were primarily interested in making money, either as paid consultants or as actors in Russia's big privatization roulette. By 1995 old-fashioned Russian xenophobic sentiment was on the rise in many political circles, making contact with foreign advisers a potential liability. And, last but not least, many of the romantic reformers of the early 1990s had been captured by the oligarchs. Ministers' salaries were just too low to keep good intentions intact.

The IMF had one distinct advantage over private money doctors. The advice that it provided was not all that different, but it was also providing huge loans. And when private money doctors' advice was different from the IMF's it was used as an argument to negotiate with the IMF, not as an input to policy decisions, which were increasingly driven by the ever-shifting balance of power among the different factions who were vying for the ear of the President.

Did the IMF, and its masters at the U.S. Treasury, also lose Russia? Much of the advice given was correct, but the IMF was always very careful not to be held responsible for a failure. Instead, it developed an ever-lengthening list of dos and don'ts which were as standard as they were impractical in the Russian political environment. Negotiations eventually amounted to going down the list and checking what had been done (typically little) and scolding the authorities for what had not been taken on board. Focusing on smaller technical issues was a good way of staying out of firing range. Crucially, the IMF did not suggest pegging the ruble to the dollar in 1995, but approved of it when the Russians made that decision, and shared the credit for a wise move. It did not suggest unhinging the ruble as the crisis was gathering steam, for the move could have backfired. And the infamous July package was mostly a goodbye kiss to the IMF's good old friend Chubais, proof that everything had been done to avoid the worst. Sorry, it did not work out as intended, now you pay the bill.

In the end, there was a silver lining to the crisis. The oligarchs had played their hand too heavily. The heart of their system, the banks, was gone. Their allies in government were gone too. The new Prime Minister, Primakov, a thinly reformed holdout from the Soviet era, would not countenance doing business with them. And the "family" around the President was on the way out. Putin spent much of his first year in office at the Kremlin systematically extricating the government from the hold of the oligarchs. Today's Russia is considerably healthier than it was back then. Maybe the crisis was necessary after all.

Notes

1 The original version of this chapter was presented at the conference on "Money Doctors" in Paris on December 14–16, 2000. We gratefully acknowledge the conference participants, and especially Giannini Curzio, Marc Flandreau, and Nicolas

Jabko for useful comments and suggestions. In preparing the new version, we bene-fited from discussions with a number of Russian policymakers. Without implicating them, we thank for their insights Arkadiy Dvorkovich, Alexander Potemkin, Sergei Vasiliev, and Oleg Vyugin.

2 This chapter's title has already been used twice, as the title of a sub-section in Chapter 14 in Gros and Steinherr (1995) in a different context, and by Soros (2000), who had already used it in an article published in the *Moscow Times* on March 1, 2000. It is a reminder of Kissinger's question "Who Lost China?" Soros' point differs from ours. He argues that the West lost Russia not economically ("within a year the Russian GDP was higher than it had been before the financial crisis") but politically, as an open society. Like us, Soros traces Russia's failure to the influence of the oligarchs, the "robber capitalists" as he calls them, in particular to the loan-for-shares auctions of 1995 and the subsequent privatization auctions of 1996–7, but he also faults the Putin presidency, which he sees as fatally tainted by the support of the "family" and the war in Chechnya. On the money doctors, Soros sees the interna-tional financial institutions as "ill-suited for the job," calling for a more "direct and intrusive approach," like providing aids for paying social security benefits or direct support for democratic forces by his own charity activity.

3 As explained below, one of the authors was advising the monetary authorities between 1993 and 1997. The other author was part of his team as a junior economist from 1996 to 1997.

4 Freeland (2000) presents a lively description of the ascent to power of the "young reformers."

5 One concern was to avoid theft of nuclear material and technology as well as advanced weaponry. Chernobyl, where a nuclear leak had occurred just a few months before the collapse of the Soviet Union, was on everybody's mind as a symbol of the country's industrial decay and inability to cope with its own military and technolog-ical power. Russia was seen as a massive ecological world threat. The World Bank and many experts sent by Western governments provided both advice (a lot) and money (quite little).

6 Kathryn Burke-Dillon's successor was Thomas Wolf, who was later followed by Martin Gillman. Ernesto Hernandez-Cata was followed by Yusuke Horiguchi and next by Gerard Belanger.

7 Up to 1996, the amount per project rarely exceeded $200 million. The first Structural Adjustment Loan (SAL-1) project ($600 million) was only launched in June 1997. It was followed by a loan to the coal sector ($800 million) and the SAL-2 project ($800 million) in December 1997, as "compensation" for the suspended IMF tranche in the midst of the first wave of turmoil on Russian financial markets.

8 As is well known, Schleifer and Hay are currently under investigation by the U.S. authorities. They are suspected of having used privileged information for personal gain, an accusation that they strongly deny. In any event, Harvard University has disbanded HIID.

9 Most Swedish economists, Aslund's students, were fluent in Russian, which consider-ably helped them establish relationships of trust with Russian officials. Oddly enough, most of them had done their military service in an intelligence unit where they were specially trained to deal with Russia, hence their excellent knowledge of the country and its language.

10 A key actor in setting up RECEP was Michael Emerson, the European Union's ambassador in Moscow and a distinguished economist (who had earlier played an important role in the Commission during the preparation of monetary union).

11 When he became President, Putin appointed Illarionov as his official economic adviser.

12 Boyko was, perhaps, the only active Russian economist with publications in top academic reviews.

13 In particular, bankers regularly commented on MinFin's activity in the state bond market, offering detailed advice on how to conduct primary issues.

14 Many on the full-time staff of MFU and RECEP were either academics or graduate students who were planning to gather knowledge and material for their research and theses, respectively.

15 For a theoretical analysis, see Blanchard and Kremer (1997).

16 An account of this process can be found in Gros and Steinherr (1995).

17 See Freeland (2000).

18 More precisely, the personnel were given 51 per cent of the shares, but the managers received a significant portion of this and easily convinced lower-rank employees to sell their shares at a "nice" price.

19 Surprisingly, Russian bottled water only appeared in 1997, replacing the previous staple, an infamous-tasting Georgian product.

20 Local and regional governments were not allowed to run deficits and indeed managed to maintain a rough balance.

21 The idea of "loan-for-shares" auctions was legalized in the presidential decree on August 31, 1995. In the summer of 1995, ahead of the elections, the government was feeling the pinch of its deficit. Together with First Deputy Prime Minister Chubais, the oligarchs came up with a creative solution: they would lend $1.1 billion to the federal government, which would in turn mortgage some of the most profitable oil and mineral-extracting firms. If, within one year, the government would not repay the loans, ownership of these firms would be transferred to the lenders. No one ever doubted that the oligarchs had found a way of acquiring the cream of Russian mineral wealth on the cheap, and this is indeed what happened. The loan-for-shares auctions were held in November–December 1995.

22 On the list of monetary and financial cataclysms, including cash confiscation, organized by the Soviet and Russian state in the 20th century, see Illarionov (1998), who offers a sharp criticism of the policies followed by the government and the central bank in 1997–8.

23 Popov (1999) argues that the ruble overvaluation and balance of payments deficit were the main causes of the August 1998 collapse. He also rejects the claim that fiscal problems contributed to the crisis.

24 Halpern and Wyplosz (1997) provide estimates of equilibrium real exchange rates in the transition economies which indicate a minor overvaluation of the ruble.

25 Chernomyrdin came from the gas industry. He was leading Gazprom, the giant company regrouping virtually all of Russia's enormous gas production, which he created in the early transition period. Gazprom is a state in the state, and thus provided Chernomyrdin with his own power basis, almost on a par with Yeltsin and the "family."

26 Everyone remembered that Yeltsin, as President of Russia, had strangled Gorbachev, the head of the Soviet Union, by blocking federal tax revenues owed to the Soviet Union. Now Yeltsin, facing a Duma dominated by the Communists, was on the receiving end of that same strategy.

27 On the rationale behind government reasoning, see Bureau of Economic Analysis (1999).

28 David Lipton knew Russia well, as he had worked at MFU after being closely associated with Jeff Sachs's advisory work in Poland.

29 The government promised, once more, to cut appropriations and increase tax revenues.

30 Wyplosz and Yudaeva (1998) provide estimates of the cost of the swap.

31 The IMF's support is a loan, not a gift. It is to be fully reimbursed, capital and interest.

32 For instance, a newspaper controlled by Berezhovsky called for an immediate devaluation. It argued that a devaluation would boost exports and help reduce the debt. The

article also stressed that, while a devaluation would demand sacrifices, it could avoid radical anti-crisis measures.

References

Ahrend R. (1999) "Russia's Post-Stabilisation Decline, Crash and Revival," *Russian Economic Trends*, vol. 1.

Alexashenko, S. (1999) *Bitva za rubl (Struggle for Ruble)*, Moscow: Alma Mater.

Aslund, A. (1995) *How Russia Became a Market Economy*, Washington, DC: Brookings Institution.

Blanchard, O. and M. Kremer (1997) "Disorganization," *Quarterly Journal of Economics* 112(4): 1,091–126.

Bureau of Economic Analysis (1999) *Obzor economicheskoy politiki v Rossii za 1998 god (Survey on Economic Policy in Russia in 1998)*, Moscow: Rosspen.

Freeland, C. (2000) *Sale of the Century. The Inside Story of the Second Russian Revolution*, London: Little, Brown & Company.

Gros, D. and A. Steinherr (1995) *Winds of Change: Economic Transition in Central and Eastern Europe*, London: Longman.

Halpern, L. and C. Wyplosz (1997) "Equilibrium Exchange Rates in Transition Economies," *International Monetary Fund Staff Papers* 44(4): 430–61.

Illarionov, A. (1998) "Kak byl organizovan rossiyskiy finansoviy krizis" ("How the Russian Financial Crisis Was Organized"), *Voprosy Economiky* 11: 20–35; 12: 12–31.

Layard, R. and J. Parke (1996) *The Coming Russian Boom: A Guide to New Markets and Policies*, New York: Free Press.

Pinto, B., V. Drebentsov and A. Morozov (2000) "Give Growth and Macroeconomic Stability in Russia a Chance: Harden Budgets by Eliminating Nonpayments," *World Bank Working Paper*, no. 2324, April.

Popov, V. (1999) "Uroki valutnogo krizisa v Rossii i v drugih stranah" ("The Lessons of Financial Crisis in Russia and other countries"), *Voprosy Economiky* 6: 100–12.

Schleifer, A. and D. Triesman (2000) *Without a Map: Political Tactics and Economic Reform in Russia*, Cambridge: MIT Press.

Soros, G. (2000) "Who Lost Russia?," *New York Review of Books*, April 13.

Wyplosz, C. and K. Yudaeva (1998) "The Costs of Debt Conversion," *Russian Economic Trends*, 1998, vol. 4.

5 French money doctors, central banks, and politics in the 1920s

Kenneth Mouré[1]

The restoration of financial and monetary stability after the First World War posed unprecedented policy problems for many European governments. The suspension of gold convertibility in 1914 had opened the way to inflationary war finance; the authorities expected "normalcy" to be restored quickly after the war. Peace brought no respite. War-related monetary disorder increased as the authorities struggled to reconstruct devastated areas, repay wartime loans, arrange the payment of reparations, restore domestic financial stability, and rebuild the international monetary system. Arthur Salter, director of the Economic and Financial Section of the League of Nations from 1922 to 1931, recalled that in 1919

> the world of 1913 seemed to most of us a paradise from which we had for a time been excluded by a flaming sword. It seemed a sufficient goal for our efforts to win our way back to what we had lost.[2]

Restoring the pre-1914 world was believed to be desirable and possible. To restore "normalcy" – sound finance in the form of balanced budgets and sound currency in the form of stable currencies convertible into gold at a fixed value – established policy goals that admitted no serious dissent. The serious problems in the early 1920s were not in deciding the ultimate objectives for policy, but in finding practicable means to attain them.

The postwar financial and monetary disorder created opportunities for experts to play a role in the development and implementation of programs to restore stability. "Money doctors" brought their expertise to nations experiencing financial and monetary instability before the First World War. They were financial experts who worked within a hierarchical relationship in which economically advanced, capital-rich nations gave advice to less-industrialized, poorer nations, often parts of their formal or informal economic empire. Advice was tied to the provision of financial aid. "Money doctors" did not just prescribe the financial medicine necessary to restore domestic stability; they did so in order to establish conditions for international transfusions of capital.[3] The First World War shifted European countries into the category of those needing assistance, particularly in Central and Eastern Europe. As the scale of postwar

stabilization difficulties became evident in the early 1920s, stabilization planning abandoned the goal of restoring the pre-1914 world and tried instead to
construct a stable international system adapted to the new needs and problems
of the postwar world. The problems were not simply economic or financial.
The dominant issues of reparations, war debts, and reconstruction were
primarily political questions, and the roles for economic experts called on for
advice were distinctly subordinate.

French advisers did not figure prominently in the corps of experts called on to
help restore stability. Instability in France itself weakened the role for French
experts abroad and restricted the ability of the Paris market to provide financial
assistance. The de facto stabilization of the franc in December 1926 enabled the
Bank of France to reclaim a position as a leading central bank, and in January
1928 France lifted the postwar restrictions on the export of capital. At this point
French central bankers could contemplate playing a greater role in currency
stabilizations elsewhere in Europe, and Romania was their first case.

French leadership in stabilizing the Romanian leu in 1928–9 merits close
attention for three reasons. First, comparison of French aid to Romania and
advice on monetary policy in France and Romania provides a valuable perspective on the role of politics and political influence in the provision and influence
of economic advice, and on the degree to which politics and political rivalries
could affect the process of monetary reconstruction. This point is essential:
"experts" made their case for expertise on the grounds that financial and
economic order should be restored through the mobilization of objective, technical expertise, outside the subjective terrain of intense political rivalries and
animosities in postwar Europe. The degree to which this was not true in the
Romanian stabilization will be evident below. Second, Romania proved a problematic case for central bank cooperation. Recently available archival sources in
France highlight the degree to which political concerns pervaded the process for
international cooperation between central banks. Third, effective financial
supervision required more than simple advice. French technical advisers supervising the Romanian stabilization program found that without power over loan
disbursement they could have little influence on policy.

The first section of this chapter reviews the evolution of the process for
handling monetary stabilizations in the 1920s. It does so at length in order to
show that the unprecedented scale of the problems encouraged, and indeed
imposed, a process of improvisation. Countries suffering financial and monetary
instability in conjunction with serious shortages of food and raw materials
needed assistance from abroad. The League of Nations tried to provide help, but
it lacked the resources and expertise necessary to meet European needs on its
own. Authority for monetary stabilization shifted to central banks, chiefly to the
Bank of England, partly by default, but aided by a belief that central bankers
would provide disinterested, apolitical, technical assistance. This assistance
required closer contacts among central banks, and, as central bank efforts to
assist in currency stabilization developed, competition encroached upon cooperation. The course of earlier cooperative efforts is necessary to understand how

and why tensions between the central banks peaked during the Romanian stabilization.

The second section assesses the role of economic advice in the stabilization of the franc. France stabilized with little advice and no stabilization loan from abroad. As such, it does not fit the normal pattern of foreign "money doctors" arriving to "cure" monetary ills and provide capital transfusions. But foreign advice and capital were sought, particularly from the United States, and the French economists who advised on stabilization in France would be called on to act as "money doctors" in Romania. Their role in France was not large, indicating the importance of access to foreign capital if they were to be treated seriously as "money doctors." The third section explores the French purpose, politics, and program in French leadership of the stabilization effort for the Romanian leu in 1928. Here, the importance of political considerations and access to foreign lending played a powerful part in determining the choice of experts and the markets for stabilization aid, and in disrupting central bank cooperation. A final section reviews the problematic nature of the technical advice from the French counselors appointed to monitor Romanian finances, and provides conclusions on the significance of the French experience of money doctoring in Romania.

The Romanian stabilization illustrates the nature and the importance of three points. The first is the degree to which "money doctoring" can be understood as the provision of disinterested, technical advice independent of political considerations. In this case, clearly, it cannot. Political considerations predominated. The second is the identification of the purpose served by calling in a "money doctor." To make up for deficiencies in domestic expertise? To obtain foreign approval and thus open access to foreign credits and loans? To overcome domestic political resistance by appealing to the authority of foreign experts? More than one purpose could be served; the expertise offered was a means to an end, not an end in itself. In this case, the main objective was access to foreign loans with minimal outside supervision. The purpose to be served helped determine who would be asked for help, particularly when rival foreign centers offered expertise and financial support. The third point is noting the role offered to the "money doctors": a foreign appeal for advice to particular institutions and economists increased their professional prestige. It also provided an opportunity for influence and recognition they could not obtain on the same terms at home.

Postwar instability and the role for expertise

Salter described the First World War as "so shattering and stupendous an event that it seemed a sufficient explanation of all the distresses from which the world was suffering when it ended."[4] Decisions to suspend gold convertibility in August 1911 had been determined on a national basis, and national defense interests took precedence in setting financial policies during the war. This increased government borrowing significantly; rapid inflation and currency depreciation were staved off by wartime controls and pegged exchange rates. The scale of monetary and financial disorder only became evident after controls were lifted in 1919, revealing an unprecedented need for international coordination to restore international finance, trade, and payments. There was no structure or organization to coordinate action. The gold standard had come into existence since 1870 as an "additive" system, the product of separate national decisions regarding monetary regimes that produced an international system in which domestic concerns determined policy. Consistency in domestic policy produced implicit policy coordination so long as the system merely sought to maintain stability (Gallarotti 1995). Efforts to coordinate the return to prewar monetary and financial "normalcy" took place along two tracks, through the League of Nations and through cooperation among central banks. Benjamin Strong, governor of the Federal Reserve Bank of New York (FRBNY) 1914–28, had initiated efforts in 1916 for cooperative central bank policies to restore monetary stability after the war (Chandler 1958: 93–6). Wartime financial cooperation among the allied and associated powers included United States support of both the pound sterling and the franc, which was terminated abruptly in 1919. In the early 1920s Montagu Norman, governor of the Bank of England 1920–44, continued and extended Strong's efforts, encouraging the creation of independent central banks and dialogue between them in order to hasten stabilization efforts and coordinate monetary action.[5]

The League moved into the institutional vacuum, where stabilization planning was needed only after early efforts to provide international credits in 1919–20 had failed. The League had been assigned no specific goal to assist in financial and monetary reconstruction, merely a vague commission "to secure and maintain…equitable treatment for the commerce" among its members (Hill 1946: 11–23). Its first effort at a technical conference to deal with practical problems was the International Financial Conference in Brussels in 1920, which established commonsense principles for countries seeking to stabilize their finances and currency: reduce government expenditure, end money creation to cover budget deficits, check inflation, return currencies to gold (a distant goal), and abolish restrictions on trade and transport. It recommended the establishment of independent central banks of issue and the creation of a League committee to collect financial statistics and investigate currency policy.[6] These principles set a standard for stabilization plans, whether devised by the League itself or outside League auspices.[7] The most innovative provision, the ter Meulen plan for an International Credits Organization, resulted in the opening of a League office to organize international credits in London in 1920. It closed in June 1922 without having arranged any credits.

Another conference, convened in Genoa in April 1922, agreed on specific resolutions for the reconstruction of the international monetary system. These were intended to facilitate the restoration of a working gold standard and to improve its operation, encouraging central bank cooperation to economize scarce gold reserves, particularly through the use of a gold exchange standard by which central banks returning to gold could hold gold-convertible currencies as reserves. Credit policies would be coordinated "not only with a view to maintaining the currencies at par with one another, but also with a view to preventing undue fluctuations in the purchasing power of gold." Britain and France organized this conference rather than the League, in hopes (disappointed) that the United States would participate. The financial resolutions were of British origin.[8]

By 1922, Montagu Norman had taken up Benjamin Strong's mission to foster central bank cooperation. He formulated his own ideas on the organization of central banks and their role in monetary reconstruction in correspondence with Henry Strakosch, whose background was in finance and gold mining, with W.H. Clegg, chief accountant at the Bank of England and the first governor of the South African Reserve Bank in 1920, and with Strong.[9] Norman saw central banks as institutions that should not compete with commercial banks for business, should act as lender of last resort to their country's banking system, should serve as banker to their own governments, but also have independence in setting monetary policy. He began preaching this "gospel" of central banking abroad through personal contacts and by correspondence in mid-1921, seeking to create a network of central banks and to rally a professional caste of central bankers to coordinate international financial rehabilitation.

Norman believed that central banks should cooperate by consulting on matters of mutual interest, dealing exclusively with each other in their financial transactions in foreign centers, maintaining minimal balances in accounts with each other, and he believed it essential that they be independent from governments.[10] He attached great importance to central bank autonomy from political pressures, personally avoiding contact with foreign ministry of finance officials (Sayers 1976: 160). Treasury demands on central banks, national demands for reparation payments, and the international diplomacy of war debt repayment all encouraged him to look forward to a day when monetary and financial problems would escape the corrupting influence of political passions and would be solved outside politics by a coterie of technical banking experts. Like Strong, Norman sought to develop central bank cooperation "against the time when politics may come to give way to economics and finance."[11] "On the whole, I think the world is suffering more from politics and politicians than it is from economic disorders," Strong wrote in 1922;[12] both saw the problems of postwar stabilization and reconstruction as chiefly political.

Austria, devastated by the war and the dissolution of the Habsburg Empire, was the first country to appeal for international help, requesting League assistance via the ter Meulen plan in March 1921. But securing a credit required the agreement of all powers who held liens on Austrian assets, particularly the United States, and consent from the Reparations Commission. The League effort to offer international credits proved futile and was abandoned in June 1922.[13] Prospects for private and central bank credits diminished as Austrian financial conditions deteriorated. In August 1922 Austria appealed again for League assistance and declared its willingness to accept League controls. The Austrian crown had fallen to one-15,000th of its prewar gold value, and the budget deficit was "incapable of calculation" owing to currency depreciation (League of Nations 1926b: 75). Governor Norman had tried to avoid political conflict within the League by seeking central bank credits for Austria, but he had limited success and finally abandoned hope for this route. Accepting League intervention and stabilization planning in the fall of 1922 with skepticism, despite the influential role of British advisers on the League's Financial Committee, he gave support crucial to the plan's success.[14] The Austrian stabilization marked a new departure for the Bank of England, involving it in European reconstruction, in financial activity in conjunction with the League, and in the organization and personnel of the new Austrian National Bank (Sayers 1976: 169–71).

The League stabilization plan served to guarantee new foreign lending (£26 million) and required the creation of an independent central bank, a return to the gold standard, and strict measures to balance the state budget. The plan included the appointment of a League commissioner-general, Dr. Zimmerman, who would oversee the implementation of the League stabilization plan and influence policy through his control of the stabilization loan that would assist the Austrian government in balancing its budget. He was responsible to the League, and issued monthly reports on the Austrian government's actions (League of Nations 1926a: 23–7). The plan stabilized the Austrian crown and balanced the state budget. Its success encouraged popular confidence in League supervision when Hungary sought stabilization assistance in April 1923, having first sought aid from the Bank of England and been told to consult the League. When the League began implementing its plan there, the Hungarian crown had fallen to one-20,000th of its prewar value. As in Austria, the League arranged for a stabilization loan to finance the state budget deficit, stabilized the currency, and created a new, independent central bank, with the process supervised by a commissioner-general, Jeremiah Smith, responsible to the Council of the League.[15] Both plans were declared successful in restoring financial stability in June 1926, and the offices of commissioner-general ended on 30 June.

The success of these two plans established the League's reputation for technical competence and set a model for subsequent stabilization programs, but it was a model other countries sought to avoid. A key part of that model was the use of outside financial experts to assess, approve, and monitor stabilization. The experts included the French economists Charles Rist and Pierre Quesnay, who would later work for the Bank of France, and British advisers Harry Siepmann and Otto Niemeyer, who would join the Bank of England. The Bank of England played a vital role, acting on its own account and indirectly through the British representatives who played a determining role in the League's Financial Committee (Piétri 1983: 324–5). Some European countries looked to Britain for leadership based on its importance as the main prewar financial and trading market; the Bank of England recognized the need for leadership to reconstruct an international system and restore world trade and finance, and the City of London had powerful direct interests in speeding that reconstruction. But the combination of British interests and Norman's leadership would arouse suspicion and animosity, and be seen by those with differing interests as financial imperialism designed to favor the London market.

The stabilizations of the pound sterling and the German mark differed from the pattern set by the League. Both involved countries of Great Power status normally on the giving, not the receiving, end of international advice and assistance. Britain returned to gold in April 1925 at prewar parity, helped by advice and encouragement from Benjamin Strong, an FRBNY credit to the Bank of England and a private bank credit to the British government.[16] Sterling's return to gold marked a major step in restoring "normalcy," and the role of American advice and finance was small. The mark was an exceptional case for several reasons: the importance of the German economy to European stability, the complete collapse of the mark in 1923, and the public and political significance of German reparation payments to inter-Allied relations, reconstruction efforts, and enforcement of the Treaty of Versailles. Norman was committed to German reconstruction to restore European economic stability; he played a key role in coordinating the financial efforts to stabilize the mark and provide Germany with foreign loans to facilitate economic recovery. The part played by the Bank of England provides, as Sayers has emphasized, "an important example of the unreality of any rigid line between central banking and international politics."[17] The German case featured stricter planning and supervision than League plans in Austria and Hungary, and was dealt with outside the League because of its importance and the need for American participation. Austria and Hungary had been treated as subordinate powers; Germany was a once and future equal. In Austria and Hungary, foreign loans had been arranged under League auspices in conjunction with their stabilization plans and a foreign adviser had been placed on the board of directors of each central bank. German borrowing was a product of international negotiation to reschedule reparation payments under the Dawes Plan in 1924, and the Reichsbank was reformed (by a law of 30 August 1924, passed in return for the reduction in reparation payments) to limit government control and access to credit. The new legislation required that seven members of the Reichsbank's fourteen-member general council and a new commissioner for the note issue be foreigners (Holtfrerich 1988: 117–23).

The stabilization of the franc

The French franc, the last major currency to stabilize, de facto in December 1926, de jure in June 1928, was another exception to the League pattern. Charles Rist and Pierre Quesnay both assisted in the de facto stabilization of the franc before going to Romania as "money doctors" in 1928. Rist was a renowned economist, co-editor of the *Revue d'économie politique* and professor of political economy at the University of Paris; he had assessed the economic situation in Austria for the Carnegie Foundation in 1922 and reported on the financial situation in Austria for the League of Nations in 1925.[18] In France, he had been an early critic of the deflationary policies promoted by the Bank of France to return the franc to its prewar parity, campaigning against deflation from 1921 to 1923 in the *Moniteur des intérêts matériels*, and developing his arguments at length in *La*

Déflation en pratique (first published in 1924). After surveying deflationary experience abroad, Rist argued that the deflationary program in France, seeking to repay the Bank of France wartime advances at a rate of at least 2 billion francs per year in order reduce the money supply and prices, could not work. Rist urged direct action: balance the budget in order to end capital flight and exchange depreciation. Flight capital would return to France, improving the exchange rate, lowering domestic interest rates, fostering economic expansion, and facilitating the repayment of Bank advances (Rist 1927).

French finances improved from 1920 to 1926 as reconstruction and economic recovery advanced and monetary crises prompted tougher tax legislation.[19] But passing a budget balanced on paper in April 1926 and negotiating a war debt settlement with the United States brought renewed decline of the franc. In desperation, Minister of Finance Raoul Péret appointed a committee of experts to plan financial and monetary stabilization at the end of May.[20] Rist, serving on the committee as both a leading economist and an outspoken critic of deflation, drafted the section of the report on monetary stabilization, recommending a prompt return to gold with the assistance of international credits, and abandonment of the effort to "revalorize" the franc to its prewar parity. This policy was exactly contrary to that pursued since 1920 by the Bank of France.

Bank leadership would be critical to stabilization. Governor Robineau was committed even at this late date to restoring the prewar parity of the franc. He obstructed the last efforts of the moderate-left Cartel des Gauches (elected in May 1924) to stabilize the franc, including the efforts of the committee of experts.[21] The minister of finance, Joseph Caillaux, had wished to remove Robineau from the Bank's governorship in 1925 (Jeanneney 1976: 242). The Bank's apparent role in the fall of the Briand government (which had appointed the committee of experts) gave him a reason to do so. On June 26 he removed Robineau and named Émile Moreau, governor of the Banque de l'Algérie and a member of the committee of experts, to head the Bank of France. Rist, appreciated for his strong views against deflation on the committee of experts, was appointed deputy governor.[22] Pierre Quesnay, a student of Rist's who had worked for the League Reparations Commission from 1920 to 1922, assisted in the stabilization of the Austrian crown in 1923, accompanied Rist on his League mission to Austria in 1925, and served as secretary to the committee of experts on Rist's recommendation, was invited to direct Moreau's *cabinet* at the Bank of France. After the death of Jules Décamps in August 1926, Quesnay was named director of the Bank's economic studies section. Moreau, Rist, and Quesnay would between them decide the stabilization policy of the Bank of France.

Rist and Quesnay advocated prompt stabilization. They supported Moreau's reversal of Bank policy on stabilization, abandoning Robineau's wish to return to prewar parity. They urged a strong stance on Bank autonomy. In August 1926, Quesnay drew up a preliminary plan for stabilization, which he and Rist discussed in detail with Benjamin Strong. Strong's advice came at a critical juncture: the Bank of France sought to re-establish its independence and obtain control of the decision making process for a rapid stabilization. Rist and

Quesnay paid close heed to Strong's recommendations, knowing his approval would be critical in obtaining foreign credits to assure defense of the franc after stabilization (Mouré 1998: 61–3). After talks with both Strong and Montagu Norman in July, Moreau sought a formal agreement with the state to assure continuity in direction of the Bank, a strong Bank voice in deciding the timing and level of stabilization, greater Bank control of domestic credit, and the negotiation of an international credit to assist stabilization (Mouré 1998: 59–60). Poincaré, however, having just returned to power leading a Union Nationale coalition to save the franc from collapse, had no intention of yielding command of stabilization to the Bank. He was also in no hurry to secure foreign credits in order to stabilize the franc at a fraction of its prewar value.

From August to December 1926, Moreau, Rist, and Quesnay were caught up in a struggle to determine how much control over monetary policy and stabilization they could wrest from Poincaré. Poincaré sought Bank intervention in the exchange market to reduce exchange rate fluctuations while permitting a steady rise of the franc. Moreau refused to intervene without first establishing a clear guarantee of Bank autonomy and a definite plan for stabilization (Mouré 1998: 63–8). The test of wills between Moreau and Poincaré was an unequal contest. Moreau could bristle at Poincaré's demands, but Poincaré and the government had the greater power, and Moreau could only increase his influence if Poincaré made political errors that weakened his position. Bank non-intervention in the exchange market allowed renewed appreciation of the franc, which took on alarming proportions in December 1926, threatening the spectacular French economic recovery. Rather than push non-intervention to its limit, in hopes a sharp economic crisis would wring concessions from Poincaré, Moreau intervened from December 20 to keep the franc from rising above 120 frs./£. Initially a temporary measure, this became a de facto stabilization lasting eighteen months and determined the ultimate level of stabilization (Mouré 1998: 70–5).

As experts, Rist and Quesnay were relatively powerless in this process. Both advocated prompt stabilization. In November 1926 Rist supported Poincaré's demand for Bank intervention to slow the appreciation of the franc and threatened to resign when Moreau remained obstinately opposed. Rist and Quesnay favored stabilization at about 150 frs./£, and were perturbed by the franc's appreciation above that mark in November and unhappy with the de facto stabilization at 122 frs./£. In January 1927 Rist analyzed the technical differences between stabilization at 125 and 150 and reported to Moreau that the lower rate of 150 frs./£ would increase the value of the Bank's gold reserves, forestall the need for lower prices, and reduce the burden of taxation. "In my opinion," he concluded, "the figure of 125 should not be considered under any circumstances, and we should do everything we can to retain the possibility of returning to a rate of about 150."[23] But as technical advisers in a country no longer in crisis they could not play a determining role in policy decisions. Neither expert advice nor foreign credits were needed unless the situation took a turn for the worse. The Bank itself was in a relatively weak position, and even within the Bank, Rist and Quesnay could not impose their policies. They could submit their views to the governor and disagree with his policy choices, but the governor decided policy based on his institutional and political, as well as economic, objectives.[24] With confidence and stability restored, economists' advice could be ignored. Foreign assistance, too, was no longer necessary. The advice of American bankers had been sought with great interest when a stabilization loan was believed necessary, but after de facto stabilization Moreau took pleasure in telling J.P. Morgan partners that France was no longer interested. He termed American financial assistance a "trap," especially if negotiated from a position of need.[25]

The de facto stabilization proved an immediate success. It was accomplished with minimal outside expertise and without foreign credits. Domestic expertise played a limited role: the stabilization planning by the committee of experts and the advice of Rist and Quesnay provided some assistance, but their recommendations were followed only in part. The nature, the rate, and the timing of the stabilization were determined in the contest of wills between Moreau and Poincaré, and relied upon the political authority with which Poincaré restored confidence in government financial management (Mouré 1998: 75–85). Rist acknowledged that Poincaré's contribution in this regard was crucial (1952: 65–6). Advice from Rist and Quesnay had been most important when seeking a way out of the crisis in the spring of 1926. But the political solution to that crisis when Poincaré took office, and the priority Moreau attached thereafter to Bank autonomy, reduced the role for expert advice.

France and the Romanian stabilization problem

The French maneuvers to direct the stabilization of the Romanian leu in 1928 should be understood in the context of growing cooperation among central banks and the weak position of the Bank of France prior to stabilization of the franc. Moreau acted immediately after his appointment as governor to establish regular contact with other central banks. He met Norman briefly on July 29, and described him in an oft-quoted diary entry as profoundly English, a dedicated imperialist seeking British advantage in all his actions and ardently anti-French (Moreau 1954: 48–9, 52–3). Moreau's views were influenced by Quesnay, who had spent four years working for the Financial Committee of the League of Nations and had described Norman's imperialist "secret intentions" to Moreau (1954: 24). Moreau's efforts to improve the reputation of the Bank of France developed on the international front with a clear sense that he would have to compete with the Bank of England. His suspicions of Norman were not groundless. Norman was skeptical of the institutional independence of the Bank of France and disliked the French government's strict enforcement policies with regard to German reparations. His efforts to foster central bank contacts and cooperation advanced on an essentially bilateral basis from the Bank of England, selecting a circle of preferred central bank governors with whom he tried to meet regularly. These included Benjamin Strong, Victor Moll of the Riksbank, Gerard Vissering of the Nederlandsche Bank, and Hjalmar Schacht of the

Reichsbank. Schacht and Vissering had planned to come to London during Strong's visit there in May 1926, but the British general strike caused them to cancel.[26] There was no question of including Robineau. France was not on gold and the Bank of France lacked sufficient independence from the Treasury to meet Norman's criteria for admission to his unofficial club of central bankers.

When Moreau took over as governor he demanded better treatment and sought to establish his bank as equal to the Bank of England. With the franc stabilized de facto and Bank of France sterling reserves climbing rapidly in 1927, Moreau arranged repayment of a wartime loan in order to secure the return of French gold from London. In May he bought gold in London in an attempt to force Norman to raise the bank rate, which Moreau thought unjustifiably low, thereby encouraging continental speculation on the franc. This contretemps earned Moreau an invitation to a meeting that Strong, Norman and Schacht had planned for Long Island, New York, in July 1927. Rist attended in place of Moreau, who did not speak English. The serious discussions there took place on a bilateral basis. Rist and Schacht spent no time together (Sayers 1976: 340). Strong later noted "the need for each of the three visitors to express views to me privately which they were unwilling to express in the presence of all of the others."[27] Strong was the one governor who held the confidence, financial power, and prestige essential to lead central bank efforts at policy coordination and system management. His influence was limited by the FRBNY's institutional situation and by his failing health.

The transition from financial reconstruction to management of the international monetary system proved difficult because central bankers disagreed on the nature of the system and the degree of management it required. Central bank cooperation had so far concentrated on stabilizing currencies on gold. The final currency stabilizations in Europe tested the limits of central bank cooperation, with stabilization plans and the organization of central bank credits demonstrating the prestige and the political influence of the central bank playing the lead role. Norman had been the key organizer of central bank credits for the Belgian and Italian stabilizations in October 1926 and December 1927. In both cases, domestic efforts had restored stability; foreign advice and supervision were not essential to the stabilization plans. The Bank of France was invited to join the central bank credit to Belgium almost as an afterthought, in the final stages of discussions led by Norman (Meyer 1970: 30–1). In the Italian case, the FRBNY and the Bank of France took shares in the credit equal to the Bank of England's but had no part in evaluating the stabilization program (see Meyer 1970: 53–7). Moreau saw this as a precedent for French leadership without consultation in the Romanian stabilization.

The Polish case also provided a precedent, in that American bankers took the lead, against Norman's wishes. Poland did need foreign advice and financial assistance. The Polish government solicited the aid of Professor Edwin W. Kemmerer through their financial agents in the United States, Dillon, Read & Company (Meyer 1970: 63–8). Their interest in employing Kemmerer as a "money doctor" was not so much that he offered expertise unavailable elsewhere, but that he offered an alternative to League control and central bank supervision, which could prove stricter in its stabilization demands, and because he could adapt his program to facilitate Polish borrowing and encourage their reliance on Dillon, Read (Pease 1986: 65, 78–9). The Polish government did not wish to work through the League. Norman stated clearly that League supervision was the proper route for their case. Strong thought the League too political, and supported an American-directed program; Moreau saw the effort to enlist American support as a way to escape "the veritable tyranny exercised by the Bank of England over European banks of issue." When the Polish stabilization was on the brink of collapse in May 1927, Moreau believed Norman responsible, seeking to demonstrate the indispensability of his support for currency stabilization planning in Europe.[28] The zloty was stabilized in October 1927, with a program and credits put together under the direction of the FRBNY, and with reluctant British participation in order to maintain a facade of cooperation.[29]

The stabilization of Balkan currencies posed greater difficulties. Action by the Bank of England in the Balkans challenged French influence in a region where France had longstanding diplomatic interests. Initially a technical problem, the stabilization of the Romanian leu turned into a test case for French political influence in the region and for the Bank of France's ability to demonstrate its parity with the Bank of England. The case offers a remarkable example of a central banker insisting on the politicization of central bank action rather than complaining of political interference. French prestige and political influence were important to the Bank of France, in this case perhaps more important to the bank than to the government.

Romania had remained neutral until mid-1916, then declared war on the Central Powers, who occupied half the country. Romania signed a separate peace in April 1918 after Russia's withdrawal from the war, then rejoined the Entente war effort in the closing days of the war in November 1918. At the Paris Peace Conference a Greater Romania was created, more than doubling the 1914 territory and population of the "Old Kingdom." After the war, the enlarged state had to integrate into one currency the four that circulated in its territory during the war: Austrian crowns, Russian rubles, and Romanian currency issued by two central banks, the National Bank of Romania and a German-controlled central bank, the Banque Générale Roumaine (see Angelesco 1928: 34–7). The state relied on advances from the Banque Nationale to cover expenditure in the immediate postwar years; the notes in circulation increased sixfold from 1918 to 1922, and prices had increased more than tenfold since 1914. When state finances were reordered to end state borrowing from the central bank, appeals to the bank via rediscounting continued the increase in money supply, although at a slower rate, until a maximum of 21 billion lei was fixed for the note circulation in May 1925 (Angelesco 1928: 149–66).

Romania needed foreign capital for domestic economic development. Both agriculture and industry had been hurt by the shortage of capital and high interest rates; politicians were divided not on whether the country needed foreign capital, but on where and how it should be obtained (Pasvolsky 1928: 433–8). Romanian commercial banks had traditionally lent mainly for agricultural development, while foreign loans provided most of the funds for industrial development, particularly for the petroleum industry. The National Liberal party dominated government from 1922 to 1928, and pursued a strict policy of retrenchment, seeking to balance the budget and revalorize the leu. Their policies were hardly "liberal"; they engaged in electoral manipulation, strong state direction of industry at the expense of agriculture, and protectionist policies that included export as well as import duties. The National Peasant Party challenged Liberal control; its leader, Iuliu Maniu, and key economic adviser, Virgil Madgearu, opposed the Liberal retrenchment policies and the foreign loans being sought to stabilize the leu (Roberts 1969: 116–29, 156–69). But both parties recognized that foreign assistance was essential to develop Romanian industry and infrastructure, and monetary stabilization was a prerequisite for a resumption of foreign lending.

Romania initially sought international loans to improve its railroad system, since the lack of transportation infrastructure was a major obstacle to economic development and the Romanian railroads could not finance investment on their own.[30] League stabilization plans in Austria and Hungary had arranged loans to governments to cover budget deficits during stabilization, in order to lay secure foundations for future private foreign borrowing. When Romania sounded out the League of Nations unofficially in December 1926, it quickly decided League financial controls would be too stringent.[31] The Romanian government tried to arrange a loan through Schröders Bank in London, discussing with Frank Tiarks of Schröders, who was also a director of the Bank of England, a £10 million stabilization loan, of which £6 million would remain on deposit in London as reserves for the National Bank of Romania.[32] Ion Brătianu's return to power in 1927 halted this effort: he did not trust the British or Schröders, especially since Schröders operated out of Budapest, seeking to extend British hegemony in the Balkans from there.[33] Romanian bankers then sought a French loan and were told that currency stabilization should precede foreign borrowing. But the French recognized that Romania did not wish to work through the League of Nations.[34] Romanian inquiries were made in London and New York, where they were told that monetary stabilization would be a prior condition for any loan.[35]

Vintilă Brătianu, the Romanian minister of finance, told Rist in September 1927 that he wished to avoid the "draconian" terms that would be imposed by the League of Nations, the route that British advisers – Salter, Niemeyer, and Strakosch – now encouraged him to follow. Brătianu wished to borrow abroad to finance economic improvements and delay currency stabilization until the economy had strengthened. Rist agreed with the British: currency stabilization should precede borrowing, as any loans would be obtained on better terms after stabilization. But he sympathized with Brătianu's desire to avoid the "authoritarian" League. Rist explained the method used in the Polish stabilization, in which foreign stabilization loans had been arranged through consultation with the FRBNY, bypassing the League's Financial Committee.[36] The Romanian authorities accepted the need for currency stabilization and claimed to be willing to work through the League in mid-November 1927.[37]

The French government offered to arrange a loan of up to $60 million for development of the Romanian railroads if Romania did *not* go through the League of Nations.[38] The French would accept a delay in the stabilization of the leu, but they expected a Romanian commitment to spend at least $10 million in France. French banks would provide $20 million of the total loan, and the Bank of France would oversee the stabilization arrangements, following the example set by the FRBNY in the Polish stabilization. Rist made it clear in his communications at this time that FRBNY support was essential to the success of a French-led stabilization.[39] French advisers were invited to visit Romania: Gaston Jèze to review the Romanian financial situation, Raoul Dautry to report on the railroads, and Pierre Quesnay to discuss currency stabilization.[40]

The leu had achieved de facto stability in March 1927 at about one-thirty-third of its prewar gold value; fiscal retrenchment since 1922 kept the national budget in surplus from 1924 to 1928 and there had been a trade surplus since 1922. Romania had not been able to meet its foreign debt payments.[41] Quesnay was not called in to develop a program to cure Romanian inflation and deficit spending, as inflation and the budget were both under control; he was called to provide independent approval of Romanian stabilization measures and the control exercised by the central bank, and thus to open Romanian access to foreign financial markets. Quesnay's report to the Romanian government on monetary stabilization concentrated on establishing the autonomy of the National Bank of Romania along the lines of the legislation governing the Bank of France, and on specifying that the profit from revaluing the Romanian gold reserve would be used principally to pay off central bank advances to the government.[42]

In Bucharest Quesnay stressed that, having requested Moreau's assistance, the National Bank would have to trust to Moreau's judgment about stabilization. Moreau would work in conjunction with Benjamin Strong to arrange a stabilization credit, but this effort could be jeopardized by interference from Norman and the Bank of England. When Norman, aware of Quesnay's visit, wrote to the Bank of Romania's governor, Dmitri Burillianu, asking to be kept posted on Romanian plans, the Bank of France vetted the Romanian reply, which stated merely that France had sent experts at their request.[43] The stabilization program and the plans for a central bank credit were modeled on earlier stabilization plans, with the Bank of France seeking to direct the operation as Norman had done for stabilization in Italy, and, in order to do so, seeking to exclude the Bank of England. In order for the program to succeed, Benjamin Strong's support was essential.[44] The prestige of the FRBNY would make the program more readily acceptable to other central banks and would aid Romanian access to the New York market.

The political impulse behind the French stabilization initiative clearly came from the bank. Moreau explained to Poincaré that British domination of the League's Financial Committee, British financial controllers in European central banks, and the stabilization programs developed in regions of French political interest were dividing the world into a two-tiered currency system. First-class currencies based on gold would dominate second-class currencies based on the dollar and sterling, and the countries with second-class currencies would suffer in their degree of financial and political independence. The Bank of England sought European domination, and the Financial Committee had been "the instrument of this policy." It had gained significant influence in Austria, Hungary, Belgium, Norway, and Italy; Yugoslavia and Romania were its next targets. It was essential for France to work with the United States and turn countries experiencing mone- tary difficulties away from the League Financial Committee. French sterling holdings gave the Bank of France a means of pressuring the Bank of England:

> We now have powerful means of pressure on the Bank of England. Shouldn't we have a serious conversation with Monsieur Norman to try to divide Europe into two zones of financial influence, to be attributed respec- tively to France and to England?[45]

Moreau planned to confront Norman over the Romanian stabilization, using French sterling balances to threaten massive gold withdrawals from London.

Poincaré explained the situation to his minister of foreign affairs, Louis Barthou, stating that the Bank of England was not happy at the Bank of France leading a Romanian stabilization and had sought to turn Governor Strong against the French plan by having Sir Otto Niemeyer convey observations on French intentions that were "completely erroneous." Although Moreau did not intend to withdraw gold from London, making Norman aware of his power to do so was one means of restoring balance to relations between the central banks: "Awareness of our strength will likely lead him to accept the close and friendly collaboration proposed by the Bank of France."[46]

Rist shared Moreau's ambitions, laying out the stakes with regard to central bank cooperation: postwar monetary instability in France had once obliged the Bank of France to show great reserve in its relations with other central banks, but now the stabilization of the franc and the strength of French reserves allowed the Bank of France and the Paris market to resume a role in world financial affairs equal to that of London and New York. The Bank could insist on being treated as an equal, including leadership in currency stabilization, holding central bank reserves for smaller countries and having French financial controllers appointed to foreign central banks.[47] Joseph Avenol and Moreau spoke of the mission to London in terms of battle: the Bank of England would not accord equal position to the Bank of France "without a fight," Avenol observed.[48] Moreau posed the conflict as one in which he would offer Norman a choice between peace and war: "All our influence in Central Europe is at stake."[49]

Norman was ill when Moreau tried to see him in London (Clay 1957: 260). Although Moreau suspected a ruse, he met with Deputy Governor Cecil Lubbock, and obtained a sympathetic hearing for his grievances. Lubbock stated that the Bank of England would endorse a stabilization scheme for Romania if it was recommended by the Bank of France and the FRBNY, and would treat the

Bank of France as an equal. Poincaré reported to Barthou that the Bank of England agreed that the Bank of France had played an insufficient role in currency stabilizations and would share in technical advising with the Bank of England, which would rally to French plans in Romania and participate in any credit "without any separate examination" if the plan had FRBNY support.[50] But Norman objected to the accord immediately, writing the next day to the governor of the National Bank of Romania and directing Siepmann to write to Quesnay that the Bank of England was *not* prepared to follow the Italian precedent and acquiesce in French leadership. It would endorse a Romanian stabilization plan only if recommended *jointly* by the Bank of France and the FRBNY.[51] In response, Quesnay asked, by letter and in a meeting with Siepmann, whether Norman was disavowing the commitment made by Lubbock.[52]

In New York, Strong and Harrison did not know that the French needed their support for the French stabilization plan to provide Romania with loans and to obtain central bank endorsement of their plan. They were caught between British demands that the Romanian case be handled by the League of Nations and French insistence on their right to follow the precedent set by the Bank of England in the Italian stabilization.[53] Harrison, having worked on the Polish stabilization, was sensitive to European suspicions of Norman. The FRBNY wished neither to pronounce on French plans for the benefit of other central banks nor to be enlisted by the British to push Romania to a League solution.[54] Rist and Quesnay traveled to New York in March to clear up misunderstandings there; they reported back to Moreau that Strong approved the French plan and would support it regardless of Norman's view, but that he nonetheless wished to persuade Norman to join. They commended Strong's efforts: bringing Norman on side would oblige him to recognize the Bank of France's right of initiative in stabilization planning.[55] The resulting exchanges between the FRBNY and the Bank of England failed to allay Norman's hostility. Some of the telegrams sent between London and New York were passed on to the Bank of France, but these notes were written to be seen by the French, and supplemented by explanatory notes between the Bank of England and the FRBNY very different in tone, which made the statements passed on to the Bank of France appear deliberately misleading (see Meyer 1970: 114–17). Strong and Harrison sought to make it clear that their participation did not constitute an endorsement of the French-directed plan,[56] although the French clearly wished it to be seen as such by the other central banks from which they sought support.

Norman and Moreau confronted each other in late April. Their meetings generated considerable heat, but brought closer understanding.[57] Moreau objected to Bank of England machinations to obstruct French direction of the Romanian stabilization; Norman invoked procedural questions to explain his opposition. Neither governor took the other's concerns seriously.[58] Norman promised, however, to abide by Lubbock's February commitment to Moreau, and explained that the fundamental British difficulty was the Romanian loan in 1913 that had been removed from the official list of the British Stock Exchange Committee in 1924 because Romania had not been making its payments.

Moreau promised to assist in negotiating payment to British – but not German – debt holders.[59] A week later, Norman agreed in principle to participate in the central bank credit, subject to the government of Romania arranging for the re-listing of the 1913 loan on the London stock exchange (Moreau 1954: 553). Negotiating a solution for prewar Romanian loans delayed the conclusion of a stabilization agreement with other central banks, particularly in Berlin, but satisfactory arrangements had been concluded by July 1928.

The National Bank of Romania looked forward, in its annual report of February 19, 1928, to "a period of expansion hitherto undreamed of in our national economy, the just reward of continuous labor and untiring efforts since the close of the war."[60] But the favorable circumstances of early 1928 deteriorated rapidly. The National Bank had to borrow foreign exchange from the Bank of England and the Bank of France in June, its foreign exchange reserves falling as a result of a poor harvest in 1927, a rising trade deficit, and excessive domestic lending.[61] Brătianu's Liberal Party lost popular support, and opposition to the stabilization loan in combination with another poor harvest in 1928 brought the National Peasant Party to power in November. This delayed passage of the monetary reform law, which meant that the central bank credit offer had to be extended from December 1928 to March 1929.[62] Peasant Party leader V.N. Madgearu preferred to stabilize with assistance from the Financial Committee of the League of Nations, believing this would allow Romanian borrowing under more advantageous conditions.[63] In power, the National Peasant Party chose to honor existing stabilization arrangements, but it had to deal with an increasing budget deficit. Rist pressed for and obtained a public confirmation of their fiscal and monetary orthodoxy and their desire to complete the delayed monetary stabilization and the international borrowing it was meant to facilitate.[64] The National Bank repaid its credit from the Bank of England by borrowing in Italy,[65] but borrowed more foreign exchange from the Bank of England in December. Norman took the opportunity to renew pressure on Romania to go to the League for stabilization assistance and to arrange a loan in London. Moreau warned that doing so would delay stabilization and borrowing, with "serious consequences" for the stability of the leu.[66]

Stabilization was accomplished according to the French plan on February 7, 1929. Thirteen central banks contributed a credit of $25 million, and private bankers arranged a thirty-year loan of $101 million to the Romanian government, to be used in part for railroad development and public works.[67] A French technical adviser would be appointed to the National Bank of Romania for three years, where his role would be purely advisory. The stabilization came with Romania already feeling the effects of the global slump, agricultural prices having been in decline since 1926. Thus the purpose of the stabilization, access to foreign capital for domestic economic development, would be frustrated in part by economic circumstances. High interest rates in New York not only made new borrowing there impossible; the part of the international loan used to repay domestic government debt flowed out rather than being reinvested in Romania.[68]

Meyer concluded that in the Romanian stabilization central bankers joined "in an effort in which they really had no confidence and, in the process, went a long way toward destroying any realistic basis for meaningful cooperation."[69] The Bank of France records indicate that the French stabilization initiative was chiefly political. To establish the Bank of France's equality with the Bank of England was the primary concern, and French planning understated the domestic difficulties in Romania in order to facilitate a central bank credit and to increase French influence in the Balkans. French actions did not destroy the basis for meaningful cooperation, but central bank relations suffered from the political rivalry between the central banks.

Strong found the handling of the Romanian stabilization disconcerting. When he met with Governor Norman at Cherbourg in May 1928, he was exasperated by Norman's tortuous evasions over his differences with the Bank of France. At the end of their conversations, Strong recorded that he was going to Paris "with absolutely nothing from Norman but generalities and disclaimers of knowledge and the reassertion of a lot of vague principles, some of which we had never heard before."[70] In Paris, he found he could discuss the Romanian stabilization and difficulties between the two banks "in every detail and aspect and with the utmost candour and frankness and with an astonishing display of good intentions and good will on the part of Governor Moreau."[71] The difference owed a great deal to the personalities of the governors. Strong's annoyance with Norman was based in part on a misunderstanding,[72] but the combination of personalities and misunderstandings complicated efforts at improved cooperation. Strong relayed news of his Cherbourg meeting to New York with the comment that "the outstanding problem is one of personalities," with Moreau and Norman "so fundamentally different in character and methods" that true cooperation between them was virtually impossible, and that the relations between their central banks "must not be allowed to depend for their success upon questions of personality."[73]

Strong discussed relations between the Bank of England and the Bank of France with Dr. Walter W. Stewart, an American economist from the FRBNY, seconded as an adviser to the Bank of England from 1928 to 1930. Stewart confessed to dismay regarding Norman's practice, which included extensive unofficial correspondence and meetings with European banks of issue by Niemeyer and Siepmann that Norman could disavow at any time – a situation "dangerous in the extreme" – and the exercise of substantial influence in Central Europe through London private banks and through Peter Bark, chairman of the Anglo-Austrian Bank in Vienna.[74] Strong thought Norman's treatment of the Bank of France "stupid beyond understanding," allowing a minor issue of stabilization credits to strain relations between them "at a time when London was absolutely dependent on the good will of the Bank of France for protection against a raid on its gold."[75] Even Hjalmar Schacht expressed concern regarding Norman's "serious blunders" in dealing with the Bank of France; Norman's actions were drawing the Reichsbank and the Bank of France closer together, and Schacht praised Moreau's efforts in Romania.[76]

Siepmann, head of the Central Banking Section in the Bank of England, told Strong of his own reservations about Norman's methods and of a "fundamental hostility and mistrust" between the Bank of England and the Bank of France. He admitted the Bank of France "on the whole had had a more correct policy in their relations than had the Bank of England" in the Romanian stabilization. Siepmann and Quesnay agreed that deep mistrust between their two institutions hampered cooperation: they were ready to do all they could to improve relations but, "because of the overshadowing influence of political considerations in Europe as a whole, they were almost helpless."[77] Clearly political considerations did not overshadow, but rather were an essential part of, central bank relations. Siepmann and Quesnay may have felt helpless, but the central bank governors could have done better.

Stabilization and supervision

One key French objective in leading the Romanian stabilization had been to place a French technical adviser in Romania, for reasons of prestige and influence. Romania acquiesced to the requirement of a technical adviser with great reluctance, insisting that his role be strictly limited: appointed to the National Bank of Romania, where he would have only an advisory vote on the board of directors and play a consultative role, with no authority or control over government policy or over Romanian use of the foreign loan that remained the main purpose of the stabilization. This was in marked contrast to the League's use of commissioners-general who controlled loan disbursement.[78] Finding an appropriate adviser proved difficult. Charles Rist agreed to make periodic visits to Bucharest; he would take the role for the first year of a three-year term without taking up residence in Bucharest, and Roger Auboin would complete the term.[79] Two inspectors from the Bank of France were appointed to the National Bank of Romania to assist Rist and Auboin, and the French Ministry of Finance sent a finance inspector to the Romanian Treasury. Their roles were strictly advisory, and they would write quarterly reports (League reports had been monthly) on the monetary measures taken and the results obtained. The clear intention was to obtain authoritative reports on the monetary situation in Romania in order to reassure prospective international lenders without having the advisers influence policy.

In his final report in 1932, surveying their three-year experience in Romania, Auboin stated that he and Rist had never held sufficient power to exercise effective supervision. They extended their influence in two ways, used "constantly" to fulfill their role: they threatened to criticize Romanian policy in their next quarterly report,[80] and they insisted that Romanian authorities take on competent French advisers in the central bank and Treasury. Renewal of the initial central bank credit for a second year in 1929 had offered an opportunity to strengthen the power of the technical adviser; but efforts to exploit the opportunity brought few results.[81] Despite their limited role, Auboin believed that French technical assistance (on the management of the Romanian railroads as well as at the

National Bank and the Treasury) had been essential to improve management and accomplish the necessary reforms.[82]

The French stabilization program did succeed in maintaining currency stability with adequate reserves, but the economic slump in 1929 sharply curtailed economic development. Obtaining international investment funds had been the fundamental purpose of the stabilization; the Depression tightened international lending and brought a collapse of agricultural prices that was devastating for an economy heavily biased towards agricultural production and export.[83] The Romanian economic situation deteriorated further when the financial crises in Central Europe and Britain in 1931 caused international capital withdrawals, domestic hoarding, bank failures, and default on agricultural loans. French technical advice, true to gold standard ideals, warned against breaking the link with gold and allowing the leu to depreciate: this would bring uncontrolled depreciation, domestic inflation, and a worsening external balance because debt repayment was often in terms of gold currencies. As the French adviser's term neared its end, Auboin and his assistants assessed whether their role should be extended beyond February 1932. The Romanian government desired a continued advisory function with reduced control, its real interest being to continue annual reports for two years in order to reassure financial markets.

Reviewing his service in a frank letter to the minister of finance, Auboin stated that if he had technically fulfilled the "essential goal" of his mission, maintaining the stability of the leu, his action "was often rendered very difficult by the great disproportion between the practical results to be obtained and the real powers [he] had been given." The success he had achieved was thanks to Rist's "great authority" during the first year of the mission. A prolongation of the role of technical adviser after February 7, 1932, would require choosing between two distinct alternatives. The first would be to retreat from all responsibility and simply serve as an observer providing objective annual reports. The second would be to make a serious effort to accomplish the reforms that had not been effected in the previous three years. This would require granting the technical adviser much greater authority in the government and the central bank, with his approval necessary on monetary and fiscal policy measures: in short, giving him the same role League commissioners-general had held in Austria and Hungary.[84]

The inspectors who assisted Auboin at the National Bank of Romania repeatedly lamented the weakness of the technical adviser's position. In February 1931, bank inspector Jean Bolgert wrote to Governor Moret that the authorities at the National Bank were eager to be rid of French supervision, weak as it was, and he recommended ending the French advisory role completely in 1932.[85] The 1929 monetary reform program had never been fully implemented, particularly the purging of the central bank's discount portfolio and the reform of its discounting practice. "The current organization burdens us with all the moral responsibility and all the unpopularity, without conferring on us sufficient authority to make our views prevail on the essential questions."[86] The banking crises in Romania in 1931 heightened Bolgert's skepticism;[87] in December he and inspector Guitard wrote to Moret, stressing that any serious advisory role after February 1932 would require the continued presence of French inspectors and increased powers for the technical adviser.[88] Little wonder that Moret opposed continued service by Bank of France inspectors at the National Bank of Romania.[89] Adequate control, Auboin specified, required supervision by an international organization. He recommended the League of Nations.[90] In May 1932, Romania adopted exchange controls and suspended gold convertibility.

Conclusion

French "money doctors" succeeded in their immediate task of stabilizing the Romanian leu on gold. Their experience in Romania permits observations on three aspects of money doctoring and the gold standard in the interwar period.

First, central bank conflict is the most obvious characteristic of the story told here, particularly the rivalry between the Bank of England and the Bank of France. That the issue of currency stabilization in a small, economically backward country should have caused such discord among the world's leading central banks demonstrates the degree to which concerns for political influence and institutional prestige could pervade central bank relations and management of the international monetary system. Efforts to encourage the establishment of new central banks and to ensure the autonomy of existing central banks had focused on insulating the banks from domestic political control in order to prevent inflation for political purposes. Little attention was paid to the potential for political tensions to disrupt central bank relations through the nationalist tempers within and the rivalries between the central banks. Norman and Strong had hoped that central bankers would be guided in their actions by technical expertise and escape the nationalist machinations of diplomats and elected politicians. But the major financial problems of the postwar era – reconstruction, war debt repayment, reparations, and cooperative efforts to stabilize finances and currencies – all included important political considerations that could not be ignored by central bankers. When politics gave way to economics and finance, it did so relatively, not absolutely. For all central bank governors, their first responsibilities were to their own country and market, not to the international monetary system.

Émile Moreau's frank account of his objectives in the Romanian stabilization provides strong evidence of the role played by political considerations in the French effort to lead stabilization there; archival evidence shows that Poincaré adopted Moreau's views. The political considerations behind other governors' actions were seldom articulated and generally much more subtle. Political considerations were not confined to the governors; they operated at lower levels of administration as well, as is evident in the actions and reports of Charles Rist and Pierre Quesnay. As officials of the Bank of France, they shared Moreau's ambition to enhance their bank's international profile and prestige. It is unlikely that the French bankers were exceptional in this regard. They may have been more blunt in their statements, and their feelings of institutional disadvantage owing to the financial imperialism of the Bank of England may have pushed them to stronger nationalist efforts, but national competition was inherent in the rebuilding of the international monetary system, and differences elsewhere are more likely to have been in degree than in kind.

Second, Romania sought foreign advice and undertook stabilization in order to obtain foreign loans to finance domestic economic development. The choice of French "money doctors" was determined not by their expertise, but by access to financial markets and, critically in this case, the opportunity to escape rigorous control on state budget policy and central bank monetary policy. France's eagerness to lead a currency stabilization for essentially political reasons resulted in a program that was hastily conceived, with no adequate enforcement mechanism for supervision of the stabilization program and loan.

Third, the influence of money doctors was clearly linked to the need for outside help, mainly a need for financial resources. Finance, rather than expertise, was the most powerful factor in determining where and how aid was sought; the "money doctors" were less important than the money to be obtained. France could not rival London or New York. Its efforts in Romania were possible only when limited French resources were linked, misleadingly, to support from the United States. The fact that stabilization in France had been accomplished in 1926 without foreign credits reduced not only the role for foreign advice there, but the influence of French economists' advice as well. Rist and Quesnay found that they had little power to influence stabilization decisions in France after the monetary crisis of July 1926 had been resolved. Romania offered a venue in which their advice would take on new, and perhaps greater, importance. But French influence in Romania was limited by the absence of a financial crisis in 1928; Rist and Quesnay served more as ambassadors negotiating between Romania and the central banks than as "money doctors." In the stabilization, France was unable to insist on a strong role for technical advice, and the advisory role filled by Rist and Auboin proved to be a bit part, easily cut when it was reviewed in 1932. It was ironic that Auboin should recommend consigning financial oversight to the League of Nations: he was completing a three-year term as the technical adviser on a plan intended to increase French influence by helping Romania to avoid League supervision.

Notes

1 I would like to thank Susan Howson for her comments on an earlier draft of this essay.
2 Salter (1961: 193).
3 The principal examples are U.S. assistance to Latin American countries and the Philippines, and British assistance to countries within its empire and its former colonies. See Rosenberg (1999), Drake (1994), and Curti and Birr (1954).
4 Salter (1961: 192).
5 See Clarke (1967), Sayers (1976, vol. 1: 153–201), and Mouré (1992: 259–79). I give a fuller account of central bank cooperation in the 1920s in Mouré (2002: ch. 6).
6 The "Resolutions of the Commission on Currency and Exchange" are reprinted in Sayers (1976, vol. 3: 69–73).
7 Hill (1946: 24–6), Salter (1961: 191–2).
8 See Clarke (1973: 4–18). On American skepticism about the conference and its outcome, see Schuker (1991: 95–122); on the British origins of the resolutions and R.G. Hawtrey's role, see Howson (1985: 153–6).

9 See the discussions of Norman's views in Sayers (1976, vol. 1: 153–63), Clay (1957: 282–5), Péteri (1992: 234–40), and Cottrell (1997: 29–43).

10 See Cottrell (1997: 33–40), and Sayers (1976, vol. 1: 157–60); see also H.A. Siepmann's retrospective survey, "Central Bank Co-operation," 19 July 1943, in Archives of the Bank of England [BoE], G14/33. Siepmann referred to central bank cooperation as a "gospel" with "apostles" and to central bankers as a separate "caste" from other government officials, marked by their professional, international solidarity. On the importance of personal contacts, see Siepmann, "Personal contact with central banks," 15 March 1928; BoE, OV50/3.

11 Norman to Clegg, 2 November 1921; BoE, G3/177, cited in Cottrell (1997: 40). Earlier Norman had written to Clegg that

> finance and economics are at the present moment too much in the hands of politicians for us Central Bankers to take any overt action, but I think the time may come when the boot will be on the other leg and the Central Banks will openly have to assist one another and so the community at large, and it is with that future aim that we are now trying to make a beginning.
>
> (Norman to Clegg, 13 October 1921; BoE, G3/177)

12 Strong to Norman, 2 October 1922; Central Records Office of the Federal Reserve Bank of New York [FRBNY], 1116.3/1.

13 *League of Nations Reconstruction Schemes*, 13–15, and Orde (1990: 124–30).

14 Norman termed the League plan for Austria "practically unworkable" and lamented that issues of currency and finance "are continually at the mercy of political and psychological and international and incalculable influences" (Norman to Strong, 31 Oct. 1922; Strong Papers, FRBNY, 1116.3/2). The FRBNY's inability to provide credits was a major discouragement for Norman. See Salter's comments on Norman's importance and ambivalence in Salter (1967: 72–3). British influence on the Financial Committee is stressed in Piétri (1983: 319–42). See also Orde (1990: 130–8) and Sayers (1976, vol. 1: 163–71).

15 League of Nations (1926b); and see Sayers (1976, vol. 1: 171) and Orde (1990: 266–74).

16 The credit arrangements were criticized for their potential to delay or dilute the policy measures required by gold standard discipline. If used in lieu of gold exports, the credits could "merely aggravate the mischief" they were intended to cure. Clarke (1967: 77–8) and Sayers (1976, vol. 1: 141–3).

17 Sayers (1976, vol. 1: 180).

18 See Rist (1955: 1,017–21), and Layton and Rist (1925).

19 For French budgets and taxation in this period, see Hautcoeur and Sicsic (1999: 25–56).

20 To be credible, such a committee had to draw on financial and monetary experts from the financial community. See Mouré (1998: 46–7) and Jeanneney (1976: 296–8).

21 See details in Mouré (1998: 43–54).

22 On the role of the committee and the change of leadership in the bank's direction, see Blancheton (2001: 360–71). Moreau explains his choice of Rist in Moreau (1954: 3).

23 Rist, "Différences au point de vue des facilités techniques d'une stabilisation, du choix du cours de 125 ou de 150 à la livre," 15 January 1927; Archives Nationales [AN] 374 AP 7.

24 See Moreau (1954: 140–1) for Rist's threat of resignation; see also Moreau (1954: 133–4, 166) for Rist's opposition to Moreau's refusal to intervene in the market.

25 Moreau (1954: 200–1, 213, 218); Mouré (1998: 74).

26 Extract from minutes of the Committee of Treasury, 5 May 1926; BoE G15/29; Norman diary, 3 and 5 May 1926; BoE, ADM20/15.

27 Strong to Jay, 10 November 1927; FRBNY, Strong Papers, 1012.3/1.

28 Moreau (1954: 191 (quote), 255, 269, 298–9) and Meyer (1970: 77–86).
29 Meyer (1970: 86–99), Clay (1957: 258–60), and Sayers (1976, vol. 1: 190–1).
30 See the report of the French commercial attaché to the Minister of Commerce and Industry, 3 Dec. 1927; Archives of the Ministère des Affaires Étrangères [MAE], Z Europe Roumanie 72; he reported new rail construction since 1918 as having been a mere 18 kilometers.
31 Chalendar to MAE, 27 Dec. 1926, for Sir Arthur Salter's first mention of an unofficial Romanian query; Briand to Georges Clinchant, 10 Jan. 1927 and Clinchant to Briand, 13 Jan. 1927 for a report on Romanian government intentions; MAE, SDN 1293.
32 "Memorandum Schroeder du 6 Avril 1927," record of a conversation between Burillianu and Tiarks; Archives de la Banque de France [BdF], 1370200006/11.
33 "Négociations anglo-roumaines pour l'émission d'un emprunt de stabilisation," Feb. 1928, and Poincaré to Briand, 24 Feb. 1928; MAE, SDN 1293; for Burillianu's explanation, see Dmitri Burillianu to Tiarks, 15 July 1927; BdF, 1370200006/11.
34 When the Romanian authorities first approached French banks asking if they would handle a Romanian loan of about $80 million, the French bankers sought the Bank of England's opinion. J.A.C. Osborne, "Roumania," 13 July 1927; BoE, OV114/2.
35 Niemeyer to Norman, 15 October 1927, and R.G. Howe to Sargent, 22 November 1927; BoE, OV114/2.
36 Rist to Quesnay, 13 September 1927; BdF, formerly 1370199702/ no carton number. [The Romanian files have been reorganized and given new series and carton numbers (series 1370200006) since my initial research; documents that I have been unable to find in the new system of classification are listed with their old series number and no carton number.] Rist noted that Brătianu very much wished to avoid alienating Montagu Norman. For Niemeyer's recommendations to Brătianu, see Niemeyer to Norman, 15 October 1927; BoE, OV114/2.
37 See "Conversation de Monsieur Rist avec M. Louis D[reyfus] du 21 Novembre 1927," 21 November 1927; and Moret (on behalf of Poincaré) to Briand, 22 November 1927; BdF, formerly 1370199702.
38 Moreau (1954: 432) [23 Nov. 1927]; Rist to Monnet, telegram, 24 November 1927 in BdF, 1370200006/11.
39 Rist to Monnet, 24 November 1927: "It seems to us difficult, if not impossible, to join this transaction to lei stabilisation taking pattern by Polish stabilisation. Bank of England is surely determined to make serious opposition to any attempt recommencing Polish experience. At any rate, success would only be possible if Federal Bank would give Bank of France earnest support or even take initiative as in precedent circumstance." See also Rist to V. Brătianu, 29 December 1927; BdF, 1370200006/11.
40 Poincaré to Briand, 28 December 1927; BdF, 1370200006/11.
41 See Spigler (1986: 126) and Pasvolsky (1928: 407–12). On dubious Liberal budget practices, see Lampe and Jackson (1982: 667, n.16).
42 "Notes remises au gouvernement romain pour l'établissement de son programme de stabilisation monétaire et de développement économique," 8 February 1928; BdF, 1370200006/5. One advance on French experience, reflecting Moreau's demands from 1926, was provision for the governor of the bank to be appointed for a fixed term of five years.
43 Norman to Burillianu, 25 January 1928; BoF., OV114/2; Quesnay to Rist, letter of 28 January continued 5 February 1928; Poincaré to Briand, 24 February 1928; and National Bank of Romania letter to Norman, 8 February 1928; BdF, 1370200006/5.
44 Quesnay to Rist, 28 January and 5 February 1928; and Rist telegram to Quesnay, 14 February 1928; BdF, 1370200006/5.
45 Moreau (1954: 488–9) [6 Feb. 1928], and the repetition of these ideas in Poincaré to Briand, 24 February 1928; MAE, SDN 1293.
46 Poincaré to Briand, 24 February 1928; MAE, SDN 1293.

47 Rist, "Aide-mémoire pour la visite à Londres du 21 février 1928," 17 February 1928; BdF, formerly 1370199702.

48 Avenol to Quesnay, 17 February 1928; BdF, formerly 1370199702.

49 Moreau (1954: 505) [21 Feb. 1928]; also Rist to Quesnay, 14 February 1928; and Rist, "Aide-mémoire pour la visite à Londres du 21 février 1928," 17 February 1928; BdF, formerly 1370199702.

50 Moreau (1954: 502, 504–7) [19, 20, and 22 February, 1928]; Poincaré to Briand, 24 February 1928; and Siepmann, "Note of a conversation held at the Bank of England on the 22nd February, 1928," 23 February 1928; BoE, OV45/79.

51 Siepmann to Quesnay, 24 February 1928, enclosing copy of Norman to Burillianu of same date; BoE, ADM25/1.

52 Quesnay to Siepmann, 27 February 1928, and 1 March 1928 enclosing a *compte rendu* of their meeting on that date; BdF, formerly 1370199702.

53 Niemeyer, in New York in February, argued that Romania was a League case, irritating Moreau, who saw this as British interference: Niemeyer knew considerably less about the situation in Romania than Quesnay, who had just returned from Bucharest. Strong to Moreau, no. 44, 16 February 1928, and Moreau to Strong, telegram, 18 February 1924; BdF, formerly 1370199702.

54 See "Memorandum re Bank of England – Bank of France Relations," 24 May 1928; FRBNY, Strong Papers, 1000.9.

55 See the cables, Rist and Quesnay to Moreau, received 19 and 21 March 1928; BdF, formerly 1370199702.

56 Strong explained to Dr. W.W. Stewart that they did not wish to play the role of expert adviser to the Bank of England on stabilization plans in Europe, nor to be seen as endorsing the plans made by the Bank of France. "Memorandum re Bank of England – Bank of France Relations," 24 May 1928; FRBNY, Strong Papers, 1000.9. The Bank of England avoided endorsing the plan in discussions with other central banks; Siepmann, "Roumania," 28 March 1928, and Norman to Bachman, 11 June 1928; BoE, OV114/2.

57 Separate accounts can be found in Moreau (1954: 544–7) [27 and 28 Apr. 1928], and Siepmann, "Note of conversations held in Paris on the 27th and 28th April, 1928," 2 May 1928, reproduced in Sayers (1976, vol. 3: 101–7).

58 Moreau charged that the Bank of England was circulating rumors that he, Rist, and Quesnay were going to resign; Norman dismissed such rumors as "tittle-tattle." Yet Strong stated that Otto Niemeyer had told him "exactly that" in New York. Sayers (1976, vol. 3: 105) and "Memorandum re Bank of England – Bank of France," 24 May 1928; FRBNY, Strong Papers, 1000.9.

59 Moreau, Rist, and Quesnay had been convinced that this was a sticking point in part because Norman wished to assure payment to German debt holders; they knew that when Norman supported the Schröder Bank loan negotiations with Romania in 1927, discussions had included arrangements to resume payment on the 1913 London loan and payment to German holders of prewar securities which the Treaty of Versailles had absolved Romania of any obligation to pay (for securities in the hands of former enemies). "Memorandum Schroeder du 6 Avril 1927," and translated "Télégramme Schroeder," 1 June 1927. Schröders had bought up Romanian prewar bonds at a very low price on the Berlin market, working in cooperation with the Deutsche Bank, deliberately confusing the issue of whether the bonds were held by British or German citizens. "Note redigée à la suite d'entretiens avec MM. Benard et Pleven (17 février 1928)," BdF, 1370200006/11.

60 Annual report reprinted in *Federal Reserve Bulletin* (August 1928): 584.

61 Reported by Rist in Rist to Harrison, 25 July 1928; BdF, 1370200006/11.

62 Moreau to Norman, 10 December 1928; BoE OV114/26.

63 V.N. Madgearu to Norman, 14 and 17 January 1928; BoE, OV114/2, for his attempt to see Norman; "Conversation avec Monsieur Madgearu du vendredi 20 janvier 1928," BdF, 1370200006/9.

64 The offer of a central bank credit negotiated by the Bank of France had to be renewed in December, with Romania still not prepared to stabilize; see Rist to Popovici and Rist to Moreau, 27 November 1928, Rist to Moreau, 29 November 1928, and Rist to Popovici, 10 and 11 December 1928; BdF, 1370200006/11.

65 Rist to Harrison, 28 September 1928; BdF, 1370200006/9.

66 Norman to Moreau, 28 December 1928; Moreau to the French representative in Bucharest, 9 January 1929; BdF, 1370200006/11.

67 American participation had been desired to bolster confidence in the stabilization plan *and* to tap American financial resources; Rist hoped at one point that the United States would take up $50 million of the projected loan; Strong to Harrison, 27 July 1928; FRBNY, 1000.9. The U.S. share of the loan in 1929 was only $10 million. The loan was offered at 81, thus yielding $82 million.

68 Annual report of the National Bank of Romania for 1929, reprinted in *Federal Reserve Bulletin* (September 1930): 551.

69 Meyer (1970: 137).

70 "Memorandum re Bank of England – Bank of France," 24 May 1928; FRBNY, Strong Papers, 1000.9.

71 "Memorandum re: Discussions with the Bank of France," 27 May 1928; FRBNY, Strong Papers, 1000.9.

72 Strong did not realize that the French had talked of the FRBNY as if it were sharing leadership in the stabilization plan. See Chandler (1958: 418–19) and Meyer (1970: 128–30).

73 Strong to Case, 26 May 1928; Box 15, George L. Harrison Collection, Butler Library, Columbia University.

74 The Bank had been taken over by the Bank of England, and Bark was understood to represent Bank of England views in European currency discussions. Tiarks' role with the Schröder Bank was another example directly relevant to the Romanian stabilization.

75 "Memorandum re Bank of England – Bank of France," 24 May 1928; FRBNY, Strong Papers, 1000.9.

76 Strong to Harrison, 13 July 1928; Harrison Collection, Box 15.

77 Strong to Harrison, 27 July 1928; FRBNY, Strong Papers, 1000.9.

78 Meyer gives a good summary of the problem in Meyer (1970: 134–5); unlike the commissioners-general in League stabilization schemes and in Poland, the adviser in Romania would have no real power.

79 On difficulties finding an adviser, see Siepmann, "Note of conversations in Paris on the 25th and 26th July 1928," 31 July 1928; BoE, OV114/2.

80 In Auboin's words, they would tell the government and the central bank:

> You are entirely free to take such a decision and I have no legal right of veto, but I am entirely free as well to say what I think in my report. In order to allow me to make a favorable report, let's come to some agreement.
>
> (Auboin to Governor Moret, Minister of Finance Flandin and Prime Minister Tardieu, 7 March 1932; BdF, 1370200006/5)

81 See Rist's letters on this point to Moreau, 26 and 27 November 1929; BdF, 1397199402/34.

82 Auboin to Moret, 20 December 1931 and 7 March 1932; BdF, 1370200006/5.

83 Auboin reported that agricultural prices fell by as much as 75 per cent from January 1929 to January 1932, and that state spending had been cut by roughly one third

from 1929/30 to 1932. Auboin to Moret, Flandin, and Tardieu, 7 March 1932; BdF, 1370200006/5.
84 Auboin to Flandin, 20 December 1931, and annex 3 to this letter, "Note sur le régime à prévoir pour la période de 1932–1933," BdF, 1370200006/5.
85 Bolgert to Moret, 9 February 1931; BdF, 1370200006/5.
86 Bolgert to Moret, 23 February 1931; BdF, 1370200006/5.
87 Bolgert to Moret, 5 August 1931, 18 October 1931; BdF, 1370200006/5.
88 Bolgert to Moret, 24 December 1931, Guitard to Moret, 29 December 1931, and Puaux to Rist, 20 December 1931; BdF, 1370200006/5.
89 Banque de France to Escallier, "Note relative à la mission du conseiller technique près la Banque Nationale de Roumanie," 5 January 1932; BdF, 1370200006/5, and Auboin, "Note sur le régime postérieur au 7 février," 31 January 1932; BdF, 1370200006/8.
90 Auboin to Flandin, 20 December 1931; BdF, 13702000006/5.

References

Angelesco, N. (1928) *L'Expérience monétaire roumaine (1914–1927)*, Paris: Marcel Giard.

Blancheton, B. (2001) *Le Pape et l'Empereur: La Banque de France, la direction du Trésor et la politique monétaire de la France (1914–1928)*, Paris: Albin Michel.

Chandler, L. (1958) *Benjamin Strong, Central Banker*, Washington, DC: Brookings Institution.

Clarke, S. (1967) *Central Bank Cooperation 1924–31*, New York: Federal Reserve Bank of New York.

Clarke, S. (1973) "The Reconstruction of the International Monetary System: The Attempts of 1922 and 1933," *Princeton Studies in International Finance*, no. 33, Princeton: International Finance Section.

Clay, H. (1957) *Lord Norman*, London: Macmillan.

Cottrell, P. (1997) "Norman, Strakosch and the Development of Central Banking: From Conception to Practice, 1919–1924," in P. Cottrell (ed.) *Rebuilding the Financial System in Central and Eastern Europe, 1918–1994*, Aldershot: Scolar Press.

Curti, M. and K. Birr (1954) *Prelude to Point Four: American Technical Missions Overseas 1838–1938*, Madison, WI: University of Wisconsin Press.

Drake, P. (ed.) (1994) *Money Doctors, Foreign Debts, and Economic Reforms in Latin America from the 1890s to the Present*, Wilmington, DE: Scholarly Resources.

Gallarotti, G. (1995) *The Anatomy of an International Monetary Regime: The Classical Gold Standard, 1880–1914*, Oxford: Oxford University Press.

Hautcoeur, P.-C. and P. Sicsic (1999) "Threat of a Capital Levy, Expected Devaluation and Interest Rates in France during the Interwar Period," *European Review of Economic History* 3: 25–56

Hill, M. (1946) *The Economic and Financial Organization of the League of Nations: A Survey of Twenty-Five Years' Experience*, Washington, DC: Carnegie Endowment for International Peace.

Holtfrerich, C.-L. (1988) "Relations between Monetary Authorities and Governmental Institutions: The Case of Germany from the 19th Century to the Present," in G. Toniolo (ed.) *Central Bank Independence in Historical Perspective*, Berlin: Walter de Gruyter.

Howson, S. (1985) "Hawtrey and the Real World," in G. Harcourt (ed.) *Keynes and His Contemporaries*, New York: St. Martin's Press.

Jeanneney, J.-N. (1976) *François de Wendel en République: l'Argent et le pouvoir 1914–1940*, Paris: Éditions du Seuil.

Lampe, J. and M. Jackson (1982) *Balkan Economic History, 1550–1950: From Imperial Border-lands to Developing Nations*, Bloomington, IN: Indiana University Press.

Layton, W. and C. Rist (1925) *The Economic Situation of Austria*, Geneva: League of Nations.

League of Nations (1926a) *The Financial Reconstruction of Austria. General Survey and Principal Documents*, Geneva: League of Nations.

League of Nations (1926b) *The Financial Reconstruction of Hungary. General Survey and Principal Documents*, Geneva: League of Nations.

Meyer, R. (1970) *Bankers' Diplomacy: Monetary Stabilization in the Twenties*, New York, Columbia University Press.

Moreau, E. (1954) *Souvenirs d'un Gouverneur de la Banque de France. Histoire de la stabilisation du franc (1926–1928)*, Paris: Editions M.-Th. Génin.

Mouré, K. (1992) "The Limits to Central Bank Co-operation, 1916–36," *Contemporary European History* I(3): 259–79.

Mouré, K. (1998) *La Politique du franc Poincaré: Perception de l'économie et contraintes politiques dans la stratégie monétaire de la France 1926–1936*, Paris: Albin Michel.

Mouré, K. (2002) *The Gold Standard Illusion: France, the Bank of France, and the International Gold Standard, 1914–1939*, Oxford: Oxford University Press.

Orde, A. (1990) *British Policy and European Reconstruction after the First World War*, Cambridge: Cambridge University Press.

Pasvolsky, L. (1928) *Economic Nationalism of the Danubian States*, New York: Macmillan; reprinted by the Johnson Reprint Corporation in 1972.

Pease, N. (1986) *Poland, the United States, and the Stabilization of Europe, 1919–1933*, Oxford: Oxford University Press.

Péteri, G. (1992) "Central Bank Diplomacy: Montagu Norman and Central Europe's Monetary Reconstruction after World War I," *Contemporary European History* I(3): 233–58.

Piétri, N. (1983) "L'Oeuvre d'un organisme technique de la Société des Nations: Le Comité financier et la reconstruction de l'Autriche (1921–1926)," in *La Société des Nations: Retrospective. Actes du Colloque*, Berlin: Walter de Gruyter.

Rist, C. (1927) *La Déflation en pratique*, 2nd edn., Paris: Marcel Giard.

Rist, C. (1952) "L'Expérience de 1926 et le franc d'aujourd'hui," in J. Lacour-Gayet (ed.) *Monnaie d'hier et de demain*, Paris: Éditions SPID.

Rist, C. (1955) "Notice biographique," *Revue d'économie politique* 65: 959–1,045.

Roberts, H. (1969) *Rumania: Political Problems of an Agrarian State*, New York: Archon Books; reprint of the edition published by Yale University Press in 1951.

Rosenberg, E. (1999) *Financial Missionaries to the World: The Politics and Culture of Dollar Diplomacy, 1900–1930*, Cambridge, MA: Harvard University Press.

Salter, A. (1961) *Memoirs of a Public Servant*, London: Faber & Faber.

Salter, A. (1967) *Slave of the Lamp, A Public Servant's Notebook*, London: Weidenfeld & Nicolson.

Sayers, R. (1976) *The Bank of England, 1890–1944*, 3 vols, Cambridge: Cambridge University Press.

Schuker, S. (1991) "American Policy toward Debts and Reconstruction at Genoa, 1922," in C. Fink, A. Frohm and J. Heideking (eds.) *Genoa, Rapallo, and European Reconstruction in 1922*, Cambridge: Cambridge University Press.

Spigler, I. (1986) "Public Finance," in M. Kaser and E. Radice (eds.) *The Economic History of Eastern Europe 1919–1975*, vol. II: *Interwar Policy, the War and Reconstruction*, Oxford: Clarendon Press.

6 Chile's monetarist money doctors, 1850–1988

Elisabeth Glaser

Currency stabilization and foreign financial advice in Chile have often gone hand in hand. But long-term stability has been rare or has been achieved only at considerable expense. Albert Hirschman, in his insightful survey of the causes and remedies of inflation in Chile, suggests that foreign financial advisors often aim too high and bring about the demise of their reforms themselves (Hirschman 1994: 133–46). The history of Chile's interactions with financial advisors or money doctors seems to prove this fact without question. The failure of the financial regimes worked out for the Andean country by the foreign experts that it chose to employ began in the nineteenth century. The early history has cast a long shadow. The demise of convertibility in 1878, a key symbol of financial orthodoxy and a liberal economy, symbolized for many Chileans the unreliability of foreign advisors. However, critics of Courcelle-Seneuil likely chose to blame the nation's first money doctor in order to avoid tackling such contentious issues as raising property taxes to avoid deficits. Things did not improve with time: the failed return to gold of 1898 ushered in an era of long-term inflation in the Andean country (Fetter 1931).

The fight against domestic inflation and for a stable national currency after World War I constituted the main motive for Chile to continue to consult foreign financial experts in the golden era of international money doctoring. The work of Jean-Gustave Courcelle-Seneuil in the 1850s and 1860s paved the way for the mission of Edwin Walter Kemmerer's team of 1925. Kemmerer's mission consisted of a group of experts, some of whom remained in the country for several years in order to implement the required measures. Following more than four decades of inflation, the Kemmerer mission constituted the first serious attempt to modernize Chile's finances through comprehensive reforms. After initial success, the reforms foundered when a growing deficit led to the country's default and the demise of financial orthodoxy. This in turn led the country into a long-term depression. The Klein–Saks mission, another team of American experts, attempted in 1955–8 to establish an anti-inflationary policy but likewise failed. From 1973 onward, the American-trained "Chicago boys" carried through comprehensive economic and financial reforms. The post-Allende financial regime constituted the first instance in Chilean history when American-trained Chilean experts took the reins. Their monetarist reform regime seemed more homegrown than outside advice. In addition, it initially received reinforcement from the dictatorial powers of the Pinochet regime, which both intimidated and effectively curbed the power of the labor unions. The Chicago boys' indisputable success eventually silenced their critics and brought to fruition the first long-term modernization policy since the days of Courcelle-Seneuil and Kemmerer. The Chicago boys' policy from 1973 onward, inspired by liberal free market ideas, aimed at radical reform of the Chilean economy at large.

In the first instances discussed here the leaders of the Andean country chose to consult foreign experts rather than their own. This suggests less that they sought real technical advice than that they sought to use foreign financial experts to promote domestic coalitions that would uphold the requisite politics of austerity and modernization. Starting with the invitation of Kemmerer's mission, the Chilean military acted as a power broker that paved the way for reforms that the legislature had blocked. Private experts did not have the power basis to be players in the domestic policy game, but were nevertheless prized for their independence. This changed only after 1973, after two failed attempts at stabilization, when the military again presided over the ultimately successful course of reforms. The reforms that Chile sought to enact therefore reflect more than the rise and demise of technical financial advice alone: they constitute signposts along Chile's difficult path toward financial and political modernization in accordance with Western models while maintaining the country's independence.

Jean-Gustave Courcelle-Seneuil

Beginning in 1855, the French liberal economist Courcelle-Seneuil, invited by the Chilean government, redrafted the country's banking laws. Trained as a lawyer and economist, he had published a pamphlet on money and banking, served during the 1848 Revolution in the French Finance Ministry, and became an avid proponent of classical economics following personal studies of the English fiscal system. In Chile Courcelle-Seneuil taught economics at the Instituto Nacional. His lectures on classical economics proved immensely popular. They constituted the first broad effort, apart from the launching of the journal *Mercurio*, to popularize the liberal teachings of Say and others. The teaching of economics in Chile, until Courcelle-Seneuil's arrival, had comprised little more than recitation of Say's *Traité d'économie politique*, as interpreted by law professors (Will 1964: 1–21). Courcelle-Seneuil's work in Chile took place during the heyday of the country's copper mining boom. At that time Chile hoped to emulate in part the economic developments of Western European countries. The Chilean tariff of 1864, drafted with the help of the French economist, embodied the principle of free trade and helped to link the Andean country to world commerce. Courcelle-Seneuil applied his free market ideas about banking when he redrafted Chile's banking law in 1860. Courcelle-Seneuil's initial plan did not include provisions for state supervision of the banks. Competition, rather than control, was to provide the ground rules for sound banking. The 1860 banking legislation provided for fractional silver coins and a gold coin, in order to keep the undervalued peso in circulation (Fetter 1931: 6). After the 1861 economic crisis, Chile's first "modern" crisis, Courcelle-Seneuil initiated a detailed examination of the nation's finances and called for fiscal accountability. A corresponding law was passed the same year. His four-volume work *Curso completo de contabilitad* served as the main blueprint for accounting of Chile's finance ministry. Those volumes and the accompanying legislation constituted a major advance and helped Chile to keep her credit good when the copper boom came to an end. Far from being limited to macroeconomic advice, Courcelle-Seneuil's work included proposals designed to establish an orthodox, liberal financial regime and to establish the basis for Chile's fiscal and economic independence.

In sum, Courcelle-Seneuil influenced Chile not only through his stewardship of legislation, but through influential publications that advocated the country's adherence to classical economics. That advocacy reflected the expert's steadfast belief in the effectiveness of competition as a regulatory mechanism and the avoidance of heavy-handed state intervention. Courcelle-Seneuil's *La Banque libre*, published in 1867, called for absolute liberty for the central banks and the commercial banks against state intervention.[1] Courcelle-Seneuil's liberal legislation and teachings proved both long lasting and contentious. While his drafts for the banking and tariff law set Chile's economic system within the framework of laissez-faire economic liberalism, Courcelle-Seneuil's subsequent reputation rose and declined along with the fortunes of the regime that he had advocated. With the demise of laissez-faire liberalism in Chile during the international economic crisis of the 1870s, the French economist became a scapegoat. A recession in mining and agriculture led to the failure of several banks in 1878. When it became apparent that the Banco de Chile could not withstand a run, convertibility was suspended. The banks had run out of specie; paper money became the new currency. With the crisis of 1878, Courcelle-Seneuil's measures fell into disrepute. Critics deemed them too liberal to prevent the bank failures that had occurred. Their author, meanwhile, undertook a temporary diversion from his liberal ideas: during the 1878 crisis the French economist called for a new tax on wealth in order to restore Chile's financial stability. Corresponding legislation failed to be enacted. Instead, the country, perhaps emulating European imperialism, took part in the War of the Pacific. Subsequently it embarked on nitrate production in the territories acquired as a result of the war. The outcome was expansion of the mining sector instead of diversification of the Chilean economy.[2] Five decades of inflation, coupled with a steadfast refusal of the Chilean elite to shoulder its proportionate share of the fiscal responsibility for stability, followed.

When Guillermo Subercasaux published his expert treatise on money and banking in Chile in 1922, he faulted Courcelle-Seneuil for having advocated European laissez-faire. This, he asserted, had undermined the practical conservatism of earlier Chilean governments. Subercasaux's scathing criticism went largely unchallenged.[3] By the end of World War I, Courcelle-Seneuil's work was out of vogue among many economists, even among the next generation of financial advisors in Chile. In his dissertation Frank Fetter, Kemmerer's student, devoted no more than half a page of his 213-page oeuvre on Chile's inflation to the work of the French economist. And that brief reference characteristically stigmatized his "extremely liberal and loose legislation."[4]

The Kemmerer mission[5]

Reform-oriented domestic forces that sought to follow the American and British model provided the initial impetus for Chile's return to sound money after World War I. The financial expertise came from Edwin Walter Kemmerer (1875–1945). Kemmerer had taught money and banking from 1906 to 1912 at Cornell. From 1912 onward he held a professorship for economic policy and international finance at Princeton. His first financial mission led him to the Philippines in 1903. Investigations into the monetary regimes of Mexico and Guatemala followed. The postwar inflation in Europe and Latin America induced him to develop a systematic theory of currency reform.[6]

The introduction of a gold-based monetary standard and of a modern central banking system figured as the cornerstones of the money doctor's scheme for restoring financial orthodoxy. Kemmerer began to implement monetary reforms in South America with his mission to Colombia in 1923. During the 1920s he won international fame as the "Money Doctor." Largely through Kemmerer's labors, the gold-exchange standard emerged as the chief medium of the reformed currencies during the interwar period.[7]

A military coup in 1924 that ousted president Arturo Alessandri and the subsequent creation of a new military government offered a fresh opportunity to revamp the Chilean currency in order to combat the postwar inflation. The junta called upon Kemmerer in late 1924 to carry out a reform similar to his reorganization of the Colombian monetary system in 1923. Simultaneously the Chilean Treasury devised several laws that aimed at a comprehensive reform of the financial sector, including a new income tax measure (Palma 1967, vol. II: 297–322). To untie the Gordian knot of parliamentary obstruction, the junta, led by Carlos del Campo Ibáñez and Marmaduke Grove, called Alessandri back in January 1925 and invested him with extraordinary powers to initiate reform. That move commanded widespread support among business circles since it promised to attract foreign money to Chile.[8] With the reinstatement of Alessandri by the second junta on 23 January 1925, Kemmerer's mission became part of a larger reform program under authoritarian presidential rule. The country's new constitution of 1925 expanded the power of the executive and provided for the separation of church and state.

Arriving as a foreign independent expert, the money doctor seemed ideally suited to act as disinterested mediator and financial advisor. Kemmerer directed the Chilean financial reform mission, designed the basic concept for its operation, and coordinated the work of its technical experts. The replacement of Chile's depreciated paper money by a gold-exchange standard currency, the institution of effective spending control, the establishment of an independent central bank, and oversight of the country's commercial banks constituted the principal elements of the reform plan. Kemmerer's aides investigated the state of Chilean finances and prepared the practical realization of the scheme.[9]

Kemmerer arrived in Valparaiso harbor on 2 July 1925. He was greeted on the docks by a large reception, consisting of the government, labor organizations, the army and navy, as well as business groups. The prefect had called off a demonstration of 15,000 workers. Thus the money doctor, hailed as the "*Salvador del pais*," found himself immediately confronted with the principal political forces of the Alessandri era. The work of the currency commission progressed quickly, thanks to a nod by Alessandri to Kemmerer "to do as he d*** pleases" and to act rapidly on the currency question.[10]

The establishment of a central bank and the new gold-exchange standard peso, with a fixed exchange rate of 6 pence to the pound sterling ($0.1217), figured as the centerpieces of the commission's project. The peso stood close to its current level. The commission determined the conversion rate from paper as 3:1. The bank reform received general support across the spectrum of Chile's political and business circles because Chilean experts themselves had adumbrated the underlying scheme as early as 1923. The founding of the central bank led to the creation of several other credit institutions under government control, such as the Caja de Crédito Agricola and the Caja Crédito Minero in 1926 and 1927. These banks advanced capital at reasonable rates and thus implemented an important desideratum of the Kemmerer mission.

Frank Fetter, Kemmerer's assistant at Princeton, developed the plan for a currency reserve and delineated the principal monetary policy guidelines.[11] The commission founded a bank control board and devised a legislative framework for budgetary controls. Kemmerer designed a new tax law that aimed to increase revenues by authorizing a levy on the production of iron and copper. In short, the commission elaborated a scheme to increase government revenues and to attract foreign and domestic capital for productive purposes. The Chilean government, however, refused to publish the commission's recommendations in their entirety, as the money doctor, well aware of how politics in Santiago were played, had urged. Once more Chile's government refused to follow the political advice of the financial experts it had consulted. Kemmerer was so annoyed about this refusal that he contemplated departing prematurely. Faced with the demise of Alessandri's presidency and Chile's overwhelming need for reform he chose instead to stay and to finish and preserve the essence of his monetary plan, even though it remained unclear whether the necessary accompanying fiscal measures would be implemented. After the Chilean government had introduced appropriate enabling legislation in parliament, Kemmerer and his staff departed on October 6.[12]

The founding of the central bank and the inception of the currency reform in 1926 proceeded relatively smoothly, despite a downturn in business activity. That slowdown came as an inevitable result of the change in the monetary unit and the temporary reduction of currency in circulation. It did not imply an overvaluation of the new peso that began to circulate in January 1926 (Fetter 1931:

173). Only a sharp and unanticipated decrease in nitrate shipments in 1926 and a parallel steep decline in the stock market after the inflation-fed boom of 1925 and early 1926 transformed the essentially innocuous transition slump into a serious recession.[13] The export crisis resulted primarily from coordinated political action by the nitrate producers, who in the hope of restoring profit margins sought in 1926 simultaneously to raise the price of their products and to force the Chilean government to reduce its nitrate export tax. They achieved nothing more than a slowdown in the decline of nitrate prices that resulted from the competition of German synthetic nitrate (see Table 6.1). The crisis lasted through the first half of 1927 (Montéon 1982: 148–59).

Table 6.1 Prices for Chilean nitrate, 1925–33 (current $ per 1,000 kg)

1925	1926	1927	1928	1929	1930	1931	1932	1933
48.01	47.42	41.27	40.95	38.08	32.08	24.85	15.61	20.80

Source: United Nations, Department of Economic Affairs (1951: 386).

As nitrate trade imposts remained the chief source of state income, the downturn caused a corresponding decline in the country's tax revenue, by 8.2 per cent from fiscal 1926 to fiscal 1927.[14] The reduction of revenue from the nitrate tax followed a substantial autonomous increase in government spending, thus occasioning a serious budget crisis. During 1925 the Alessandri administration had raised the salaries of state employees as well as of the military and the navy. At the same time it increased the overall number of state positions. Despite peso stability, the wages of civil service employees rose, according to individual classifications, by between 20 per cent and 100 per cent (Montéon 1982: 157–9). The new government apparently meant to compensate state employees and the military for the undue favoritism that the Liberal Alliance had shown earlier to the parliamentary class. This balancing act tended to alleviate the hardships that real income loss through the 1923–5 inflation and stabilization at the 3:1 rate had inflicted on government employees. The measure proved financially costly: in 1925 Chile showed a budget deficit of 143.7 million new pesos. The deficit seemed to challenge the political wisdom of the 1925 reform. One of its backers, ex-Secretary of the Treasury Muñoz Rodriguez, had already warned at the end of 1924 that the new currency could only succeed if the cabinet managed to balance the budget and find additional sources of revenue (Smythe 1986: 283–4).

Emiliano Figueroa Larraín, succeeding Alessandri as civil president and head of a coalition cabinet at the end of 1925, provided only superficial remedies for the intricate problems of the ongoing recession and a ballooning budget deficit. Owing to uncertain parliamentary support, the new president could only marshal enough forces to impose a balanced budget on paper. Official government statistics did not show an increasing deficit for 1926, thanks to a refunding loan by Hallgarten & Co. The proceeds partly paid for current government outlays and a new public works program. In February 1927 New York bankers demanded a moratorium of one year for new bond issues. The prolonged recession, combined with pressure from the military, led to Figueroa's resignation in April 1927.[15]

Ibáñez's (1927–31) subsequent victory in the presidential election of May 1927 ended the era of laissez-faire in Chilean politics. Ibáñez had figured as one of the moving spirits in the reformist junta of early 1925. At that time holding the rank of colonel, he became minister of war after Alessandri's return and continued in that position under Figueroa's presidency. Already then, observers felt that the military was running the country. Subsequently Ibáñez acceded to the office of the vice-president, and in early 1927 he served as minister of the interior. At first widely acclaimed for the sweeping changes that he prepared, the new president introduced governmental economic intervention, coupled with violent military measures to control social protest, into Chilean politics.

Once in power, Ibáñez could also reap the political benefits resulting from an upswing in the nitrate trade, the country's chief export and source of revenue. In July 1927 the domestic price-fixing agreement among nitrate producers came to an end, and the president did not urge its renewal. Simultaneously, the Chilean nitrate producers concluded an agreement with their German and English counterparts that for the time being assured Chile a guaranteed share of the world nitrate trade. In the following two years Chilean nitrate exports boomed (see Table 6.2).[16]

Table 6.2 Chile: production statistics, 1925–38 (in millions of pesos at 1940 prices)

Year	Gross GDP	Mineral production	Mineral production as percentage of GDP	Industrial production	Industrial production as percentage of GDP
1925	7,212	1,478	20.49	2,732	37.88
1926	7,028	1,370	19.49	2,577	36.66
1927	6,743	1,311	19.44	2,307	34.21
1928	8,180	1,869	22.84	2,546	31.12
1929	8,974	2,099	23.38	3,100	34.54
1930	8,431	1,493	17.70	3,100	36.76
1931	6,350	1,014	15.96	2,307	36.33
1932	6,280	552	8.78	2,626	41.81
1933	7,434	688	9.25	2,892	38.90
1938	9,469	1,608	16.98	4,056	42.83

Source: Pitts (1987: 83).

The Ibáñez administration profited financially from this temporary rebound of Chilean nitrate production, since the upsurge increased government incomes from nitrate export taxes (see also Table 6.3) (Montéon 1982: 165). The nitrate boom lasted from 1927 to 1929 and offered Ibáñez a window of opportunity to consolidate Chile's finances on a long-term basis.

Encouraging American loans to Chile formed one of the main, though implicit, motives of Kemmerer's reform mission to the Andean state (Hirschman 1994). Kemmerer, however, remained ambivalent toward those implications of

Table 6.3   Chile: percentage of nitrate and iodine taxes to ordinary state income, 1913–24

1913	*1914*	*1915*	*1916*	*1917*	*1918*	*1919*	*1920*	*1921*	*1922*	*1923*	*1924*
48.73	52.91	60.16	60.13	50.43	44.84	24.37	40.97	33.54	31.35	40.61	39.80

Source: Republica de Chile, Ministerio de Hacienda, "Porcentaje con que ha contribudo la industria salitrera en las rentas ordinarias de la nacion" (1925), Box 40, Public Finance, *Kemmerer Papers*.

his mission. During his labors in Chile, the money doctor had cautioned against large-scale foreign financing of public-works projects at high interest rates (Drake 1989: 106–7). Once the monetary reform had been completed, and nitrate exports grew, Chile nevertheless appeared as an attractive market for American and British capital. The country showed a solid record of steady repayments for the foreign loans it had contracted in the nineteenth century. In the analysis of international bankers involved in Latin American finance, Chile's wealth in raw materials guaranteed a revenue stream that made further lending seem advisable. With Kemmerer's reforms and the establishment of a sound currency, no major visible obstacles existed that could have induced foreign investors to turn away from Chile. This, after all, had been one of the major motives of the Chilean government in inviting the Kemmerer mission.

From 1926 on, the United States became Chile's chief lender, followed by Great Britain. Despite the inflow of foreign loans, Chile's finances in 1929 showed a current account deficit, owing to increased government spending. The deficit continued in 1930 (see Table 6.4). In its public statements the government avoided any hints about the looming deficit and stressed instead the increased customhouse receipts and the solidity of Chile's gold standard. As the secretary of the treasury put it at the end of 1929, in the face of a real current account deficit of 350 million pesos, "for the last three years the Government plan has signified experimental audacity."[17]

Table 6.4   Chilean loans, debts, and real current deficits 1927–30, in million new pesos ($0.1208) *

	Dollar loans contracted **	*Aggregate external debt* **	*Total public debt*	*Current deficits*
1927	228	2609.3	2766.7	
1928	513	3108.8	3419.6	
1929	83	3355.7	3820.9	362.5
1930	247	3597.2	4104.9	344.6

Note:

*   Calculated from Memorandum, Official Data Upon Revenues and Expenditures of Chile, ca. April 1930, DF 825.51/314; Memorandum by Stinson, "Chilean Financial Situation," 13 August 1931, DF 825.51/423. Both reports give carefully revised estimates of Chilean finances, based on the most detailed contemporary evidence. Current deficit figures do not correspond to the official Chilean budget figures and are derived from League of Nations, Economic Intelligence Service (1932: 251).

** Figures for dollar loans contracted and aggregate external debt do not correspond, owing to varying maturities and the nature of refunding operations.

Increased government outlays continued into 1930, although by that time it had become plain for all to see that Wall Street would limit future long-term loans. Clearly, after 1925 Chile had made a doubtful Faustian bargain by sacrificing budgetary discipline in order to build mass support for an authoritarian government that seemed to promise stability. While older studies suggest that the worldwide depression pushed Chile's economy and finances into the abyss beginning in 1930, in fact the country's financial problems had already become obvious to careful observers by 1929. One year later, at the inception of the Depression, Chile could only keep current on its foreign obligations by drawing down 69 million pesos from its gold reserve, thus circumventing the most basic rules established by Kemmerer's reform. From early 1930 on, the Andean country lived off its capital.[18] A look at Chile's key production figures (see Table 6.2) demonstrates that the steep decline in Chile's gross domestic product (GDP) occurred only in the second half of 1930 and in the wake of Chile's default. The chronology of the crisis does not point to external factors as the main causes of the Chilean depression. The first signs of the impending Chilean default came in the fall of 1930, when Julio Philippi, the new finance minister, openly criticized the government's free-spending ways. By the end of 1930 all public construction had to be stopped owing to lack of funds. At that time Chile's remittances to foreign debtors amounted to 25 per cent of the country's total expenditures. Ibáñez responded by shooting the messenger: in January 1931 he forced Philippi to resign. That step revealed dramatically to every Chilean citizen that a financial crisis was threatening the country. Ibáñez had once more chosen populist policies instead of the necessary reforms, but to no avail (Marichal 1989: 207). By February government deposits in Chile's central bank had sunk to 40 million pesos, enough to cover around two weeks of the government's ordinary expenses in 1928. Eventually the finance minister tried to bridge the gap by imposing a surtax on Chile's upper class. This step failed to raise additional revenue since the government lacked adequate collection mechanisms. Instead, the measure discouraged business circles and, on April 12, occasioned a stock market crash. In June the government claimed that it lacked the funds to pay debt installments of $3 million due to New York and $2 million due to London.

Right up to the last minute Chile's American and British bankers tried to keep the country afloat. In early July Ibáñez tried to reform his government in a face-saving manner without effecting political reforms. The situation in Santiago grew tense. Confronted with the impending default, Chile's foreign creditors sought to arrange quick relief. National City Bank's financial expert Garrard Winston, the former undersecretary of the U.S. Treasury, identified Chile's main problem as political and called for a revamping of Chile's government. Assistant Secretary Francis White, however, had to remind him "that obviously we could not take any part in the internal politics of Chile."

Meanwhile Rothschilds and National City Bank informally sought ways to achieve a short-term moratorium on Chile's upcoming July and August debt installments. This undertaking was inspired by the British Foreign Office. In June 1931, Undersecretary Robert Vansittart took the initiative to save Chile from defaulting by calling the Bank of England and Rothschilds to intervene. Only when the governor of the Bank of England learned that Chile had simultaneously asked the Federal Reserve Bank of New York to come to its rescue, did he opt for a "wait and see" attitude, since Chile's appeal to the United States seemed to preclude a rapid British intervention.

That mishap, owing to the lack of institutional cooperation and a common strategy for crisis intervention among the main creditors, constitutes the most serious factor in the Chilean default that could be attributed to its chief foreign lenders and their governments. However, even the failure to coordinate relief operations among the chief lending nations did not end efforts to help Chile: after that debacle Vansittart continued to urge financial assistance on Chile's behalf. Rothschilds responded by offering to extend a further short-term loan to Chile to enable it to pay the forthcoming debt installments. Rothschild's only safeguarding condition demanded that the Chilean government earmarked a part of its future revenue as security, not an uncommon request under the circumstances. The Chilean minister of finance, however, declined to do this. He argued, although other Latin American governments had entered into similar arrangements before, that this proposal seemed humiliating.

Still driven by financial populism at the cost of fiscal orthodoxy, Chile chose instead to default on its foreign obligations. On July 15 Chile defaulted on its foreign obligations to the tune of $265 million, £30 million sterling, and 84 million Swiss francs.[19] Chile's termination of foreign remittances caused a bigger loss to American investors than that of any other Latin American defaulter, as shown in Table 6.5.

Table 6.5 Argentina, Brazil, Chile: losses on Latin American dollar bonds issued between 1920 and 1931, in millions of current $

Country	*Nominal capital invested*	*Interest and reimbursement*	*Outstanding capital at market prices*	*Balance*
Argentina	694.8	615.6	258.0	178.7
Brazil	373.2	240.2	72.9	60.0
Chile	335.5	163.5	37.9	134.0

Source: United Nations, Department of Economic and Social Affairs, Economic Commission for Latin America (1965: 30).

The default also spelled the end of Ibáñez's mixed authoritarian and Keynesian economic policies, and the dictator fled the country on July 26.[20] A new round of inflation got underway which ultimately outlasted the Klein–Saks mission. Having defaulted on its foreign debt payments, the government had to look for new sources of liquid cash in Chile. It started to discount Treasury bills at the central bank, which in turn printed currency in corresponding amounts (Mamalakis 1976: 102–12). In September 1931 the government raised the maximum rate of Treasury bills relative to the bank's cash holdings from 20 per cent to 80 per cent. The authorities procured the foreign currency needed for the conduct of current business by reducing the required gold reserve from 50 per cent of currency holdings, as provided by the governing rules of 1925, to 35 per cent. By September 1932 the gold reserve had decreased by 24 per cent, while currency issues and deposits had increased by 43 per cent. The government thus degraded the central bank, the key institution in Kemmerer's monetary reform, to a political tool and thereby opened the floodgates to inflation. Chile's effort to maintain a greatly inappropriate official exchange rate led, as already indicated, to a rapid depreciation of the free exchange rate. As a result of the mismanagement, the real exchange rate had fallen even further by 1932 than the comparable Argentinean or Brazilian rates. (See Table 6.6.)

Table 6.6 Official and free-market valuation of monetary units as a percentage of the 1929 gold-parity valuation, yearly average figures, 1929–36

Year	Argentina, official	Argentina, free	Brazil, official	Brazil, free	Chile, official	Chile, free
1929	98.6		98.7		99.1	
1930	86.6		89.6		99.3	
1931	69.2		58.8		99.2	74.1
1932	60.6		59.5		65.0	22.8
1933	59.3		53.3		49.0	19.3
1934	47.2	35.8	42.0		49.7	19.7
1935	45.7	36.8	41.2	28.7	24.8	19.3
1936	46.2	38.8	42.4	28.5	24.9	17.4

Source: League of Nations (1941: Table 96).

The disproportionate decline in the purchasing power of Chile's currency prevented a quick financial recovery. While Chile had struggled to preserve the gold standard from July 1931 to April 19, 1932, it had operated it after the default so as to deplete the country's liquid and material resources, and had destroyed all confidence in its fragile capitalist system. After the return of Alessandri to power in 1932 and during the subsequent administrations from 1938–52, import substitution, help for domestic industry, and an often over-valued real exchange rate provided the means for domestic growth that was financed by growing inflation.[21]

Kemmerer commented only sparingly on the reasons for the breakdown of his reforms in Chile, which occurred shortly after he returned from another stabilization mission to Peru. In his characteristically restrained way, he hinted at the importance of political choices in causing Chile's financial catastrophe: high-employment public-works projects had pushed up workers' wages. Once foreign loans, which had constituted the financial basis for this policy choice, ceased, mass unemployment and political instability followed. As Kemmerer put it in September 1931, that outcome came as a complete surprise; he could not have anticipated it even in April 1931. The money doctor did not hide his disappointment and clearly attributed the crisis to political mismanagement.

> Our prophesies – or rather our warnings – in all of these countries, that the greatest danger to the gold standard was not an economic danger, but the danger of political exploitation, have certainly been justified. I am beginning to have my doubts as to whether any South American people is yet qualified to maintain a gold standard through difficult times, or, for that matter and for the same reasons, any stabilized standard. Had these countries been on a silver standard or on a managed paper standard, they would have broken in just the same way – probably in the case of a managed paper standard, much earlier than they have.
>
> (Kemmerer, quoted in Glaser n.d.)

Did Kemmerer and his team prescribe in 1925 a cure for Chile's financial ills that the country could not afford? The upsurge in exports and the inflow of foreign funds starting in 1926/7 do not suggest that the gold-exchange standard represented a burden for the Chilean economy. Kemmerer's student, Frank W. Fetter, also suggested discreetly that Chile's irresponsible use of loans figured as the main reason for its financial collapse. He concluded his 1931 dissertation on the Chilean inflation prophetically: "One of the lessons of Chilean history is that monetary theory cannot save those who do not want to be saved."[22]

The Klein–Saks mission and the end of an era

The Klein–Saks mission to Chile took place in a different phase of financial advising. After World War II and the inception of the Cold War, the International Monetary Fund (IMF), the Agency for International Development (AID), and the Import–Export Bank posed powerful allies to private financial emissaries like the Klein–Saks mission and would eventually replace them. Still, the private firm's mission in 1955–7 and its outcome show a marked resemblance to its predecessor's reforms and their subsequent fate, particularly when we examine the relationship between the mission and the Chilean government, which, since 1952, was again headed by Ibáñez. Chile's former dictator, after returning to power in the November 1952 election, beating the Popular Front's candidate Salvador Allende, had opted to govern democratically. He had campaigned on a promise to end inflation. The Chilean voters returned the old man to office because he seemed the only credible candidate to stop the decline in the currency. In the following years, however, Ibáñez proved unable to fulfill his promise because he lacked support in parliament.[23]

In 1955, in the third year of the second Ibáñez government, the hyperinflation had caused a domestic crisis. As a State Department paper described it: "Chile's economy is currently in a lamentable condition. The country is currently in the grip of galloping inflation: prices rose 71.85% between September 1953 and September 1954 and the government's budget is and for years has been hopelessly unbalanced." The State Department recommended in December 1954 that the IMF should put pressure on Chile to undertake economic and financial reforms.[24]

The winter of 1955 brought social unrest in Chile that seemed to threaten the country's stability. The government and leading business circles that had thought themselves to be relatively immune against the social results of hyperinflation began to rethink the situation, as did American diplomats.[25] A few weeks later, in January, the U.S. ambassador in Santiago, Willard L. Beaulac, suggested to Ibáñez that private investment should be encouraged "through improved treatment of the copper companies." Beaulac's advice did not go unheeded: In the spring of 1955 the Chilean Congress passed a bill that decreased taxation and Chilean government control of foreign copper companies.[26] Subsequently the well-known and respected financier Agustin Edwards, who had both supported and benefited from Kemmerer's mission, contacted the Klein–Saks financial consulting firm in the United States to conduct a study on Chile's finances with the aim of reforming the system. The sequence of the tax decrease on copper profits and the hiring of the financial consultants suggests that with the advent of hyperinflation the old system of give and take between the government and foreign corporations had outlived its usefulness. Indeed, the currency stabilization and stable exchange rates that resulted from the work of the Klein–Saks mission enabled the copper companies to make large profits in the first half of 1956. The mission hoped to find new ways through which the Chilean government could recoup part of that windfall.[27]

The Klein–Saks firm had previously worked for the Peruvian and Guatemalan governments and, thanks to the success of its financial missions there, had earned a solid reputation as financial advisors and advocates for inflation-threatened governments at the Southern cone. Its personnel consisted mainly of Julius Klein, formerly assistant secretary of commerce under Herbert Hoover, and Julian Saks, a financial economist. Herbert Hoover, Jr., emphasized in a meeting of the Operations Coordinating Board that the Klein–Saks firm was a "top-notch" firm.[28] The firm consented to the Chilean request, and Saks visited the country to prepare a preliminary study in the late spring of 1955. He contracted with the government in Santiago to undertake a mission to reform the country's exchange and financial system. This project seemed in harmony with a recent internal statement of the U.S. Department of State that Chile needed to adopt an anti-inflationary program, should it want further American aid. In September 1955 the Klein–Saks mission began its work in Chile. The reform undertaking enlisted the aid of the U.S. government. A delegation of the State Department visited Santiago in November and pressed the Chilean government to prepare "a coordinated program for combating inflation." In addition, the Klein–Saks firm should submit its program to the United States to obtain American aid for the implementation of the program.[29] Chile complied immediately with demonstrative measures: Minister of the Interior Benjamín Videla Vergara organized an army, the Comando Nacional contra la Especulacíon, to denounce violators of the recently enacted price-control law.

The Comando Nacional temporarily closed the Santiago clothing store Rosenblitts, as well as several others, for unlawful pricing (Bray 1961: 115–16).

Backed by the American promise of help, the presence of the Klein–Saks mission, and his demonstrative backing of anti-inflationary politics, Ibáñez managed to obtain the support of a majority in Congress, composed of Liberals, Conservatives, Independents, and Agrarian Laborites. For the first time since the beginning of Ibáñez's presidency his government commanded a working majority in the legislature. Owing to the new propitious political conditions, finance minister Oscar Herrera, with the help of the mission, drafted a bill that limited wage and salary readjustments to 50 per cent of 1955 adjustments. With the passage of Herrera's bill and the failure of a general strike in January 1956, the reform program could begin its work. The Klein–Saks group subsequently helped to build a congressional majority to pass minimum-wage legislation that aimed to mitigate the prospective income loss from the limited wage adjustments (Pisciotta 1987: 126–7). In sum, the mission's major accomplishment was a political, not a technical one, as Albert Hirschman (1994: 139–40) has reminded us. The Chilean left reacted to the mission's success and the failure of the general strike begun by the socialist–communist-dominated anti-Ibáñez Central Unica de Trabajadores de Chile (CUTCH) by creating the Frente de Acción Popular (FRAP). The popular front of Communist, Socialist, Popular Socialist and smaller leftist parties dominated Chile's left-wing politics (Pisciotta 1987: 127–8).

With basic legislation for an anti-inflationary program in place, the Klein–Saks delegation, headed by the retired president of the National City Bank, Prescott Carter, devised a combined financial reform (Hirschman 1994: 140). As the mission's report put it, "inflation was too deeply rooted to be dealt with by quick-acting drastic treatment." Still, for 1956 as a whole the Klein–Saks reforms cut the 1955 inflation rate of 90 per cent in half, although the government deficit remained large.[30] Further steps aimed at modernizing the Chilean economy by abolishing the old multiple exchange rate system and a large part of the country's import quotas and subsidies. Setting up an IMF stabilization fund for Chile constituted a collateral project. In addition, the Export–Import Bank authorized a $3.55 million loan to a Chilean steel company to build a modern steel mill in Huahipato. In February 1956 Congress passed exchange reform measures devised by the mission that consolidated export and import exchange rates into a single fluctuating rate that formed the basis for authorized trade transactions and invisible transactions in banking and brokers' markets. Once the Chilean Congress passed the exchange reform legislation, the Chilean government, backed by the U.S. State Department, obtained in March a standby loan of $37.5 million from the newly established IMF stabilization fund. Chile pledged that the proceeds of the standby would only finance operations in the banking market and would not operate "counter to economic trends." At the same time Santiago contracted with the United States to import agricultural goods at the value of $34.6 million.[31]

Additional legislative action foundered because Congress balked at passing the tax reform bill of August 1956 that the mission had devised and that aimed at tax enforcement, tax increases, and a reduction of public employees. The reform formed the necessary precondition to limit further inflation and thus to maintain the mission's work (Pisciotta 1987: 126–7). The tax battle led CUTCH to stage a strike at the Bank of London and South America. These seemed ominous signs: the failure of tax reform signified an impasse in the reform project.

Two further developments suggested that the reform movement had begun to run out of steam: Ibáñez fired Herrera, after the finance secretary had intimated that government price indexes were hiding the fact that the reforms had failed effectively to control price rises in all sectors of the economy. This came despite the fact that the Department of State had engineered a $15 million loan from the International Bank for Reconstruction and Development (IBRD) for the development of electrical power in Chile. Indeed, in a conversation with Henry F. Holland, U.S. undersecretary of state, Herrera had underlined the necessity to show concrete results for the budgetary restrictions that the government had imposed on the people. The IRBD loan came too late and was too little to save the minister. Apparently, to support the government's search for revenue the central bank refused to let the peso sink to its true value. The artificially high value of the peso seems to have helped to reverse the increase in copper prices and exports.[32] Copper prices, which had appreciated in the first half of 1956, started a downward slope in the second half of the year. The political era of goodwill between the government and the mission began visibly to wane. After Ibáñez fired Herrera, Prescott Carter gave a speech before the Budget Commission of the Chilean Congress asking for higher taxation of the rich in Chile. As Ibáñez put it to an American observer, this had the worst possible results, since it threatened his legislative reform coalition.[33] The drive to limit government expenses lost its momentum: at the end of the year it became clear that the Chilean government had failed to balance its budget, although the discrepancy between official and real figures for government expenses had been reduced relative to previous years.[34]

Ibáñez was facing a congressional election in March. This, in the face of the rising unpopularity of the Klein–Saks reforms, a severe draught, and the precariousness of his legislative reform coalition, could easily cost him congressional support. In November 1956 the president sought a meeting with the American ambassador and the director of the Export–Import Bank, Vance Brand. He complained about the political uncertainty in Chile, alluding to the fact that "Chile, like France, had far too many political parties," and asked Brand for loans for his agricultural development program. Brand declined to promise a loan before the anti-inflationary program had made further progress.[35] The political stalemate over tax reform, the agricultural slump, and the decline of copper prices plunged Chile into a severe recession that began at the end of 1956. The March election reflected the electorate's frustration with the austerity policy of the government in the face of the severe slump in business. Ibáñez parties lost out and did not return to the political scene. The Agrarian Laborite Party, one of the president's backers in Congress, suffered large losses. The president found himself without a political base. Worse, at the end of March, following Ibáñez's violent crackdown on Communist-backed student protests for lower bus fares, major riots occurred in Santiago that severely affected the country's international prestige.[36]

The domestic turmoil moved the Chilean ambassador in Washington, Mariano Puga, to address the precarious situation of his government openly. He reminded Secretary of State John Foster Dulles that 25 per cent of the money earned from copper and nitrate left the country. This seemed an obvious reminder that the Chilean government felt that in the face of falling copper prices it had lost out by decreasing taxation of foreign copper companies without having received the compensation that the mission had sought. Puga asked for a financial injection. Dulles reminded the ambassador that only long-term solutions to Chile's economic problems on recognized economic principles would be accepted by the U.S.[37] A further Chilean request for a "balance of payments loan" of $25 million underlined that the Klein–Saks mission had lost credibility with the government. The mission reacted by backing a Chilean government proposal to build subsidized public housing to counter Communist agitation against the financial reform, but initially balked against an American loan. However, in May it supported a Chilean request for a $40 million loan from the U.S. As the American ambassador in Santiago, Lyon, put it, for the first time since the inception of its work the mission seemed defeatist.

The contentious debate about a loan for Chile signified that the mission had lost its power as an advocate for Chile in Washington and as a political broker for fiscal discipline in Chile. The decision of the Export–Import Bank to grant Chile a loan of only $12.5 million, contingent upon Chile drawing the same amount from the IMF standby loan, left the Chilean government bitterly disappointed and the personnel of the Klein–Saks mission in Chile even more demoralized. In November Charles Knox of Klein–Saks stated in a conversation with State Department officials that exchange controls might be necessary, since "Chile's excessive dependence on copper would always subject the economy to swings of too great magnitude. Perhaps this made a free economy impracticable." Knox's proposal, as a State Department official observed, seemed to suggest throwing away all the progress that had been made.[38] In order to maintain the modernized exchange system in Chile, the State Department and the IMF arranged a further Chilean drawing on the IMF standby in 1958. But in January 1958 the Chilean government increased the minimum wage by 20 per cent, thus giving up one of the main principles of the Klein–Saks reforms. The fight against inflation had ended. Under the administration of Jorge Alessandri the budget deficit rose to 4.6 per cent of GDP from an average 2.6 per cent under the Ibáñez administration. Inflation increased to 200 per cent in six years. Still, some of the achievements of the mission outlasted it: it had helped to establish a unified exchange rate system that remained in place until the early 1960s. The principles of IMF and U.S. aid conditionality were there to stay.[39]

Conclusion? The Chicago boys' (counter) revolution

Although the Frei government made some progress in reducing the inflation rate, the regime under Allende launched an inflationary wave. Prices shot up by an unprecedented 605 per cent in 1973 alone. State intervention in the economy, a feature of Chilean life since the crisis of 1931, reached its peak.[40] The onset of hyperinflation led military and naval circles to demand thoroughgoing reform. One year before the successful coup against the Allende government, military circles began to encourage a fundamental economic revamping of the country. A cooperative program to train Chilean economists, which the Catholic University of Santiago had initiated with the University of Chicago as far back as 1956, provided a pool of well-trained experts ready to hand. Those who had arranged for the education of the Chilean economists responsible for the economic reforms after 1973 aimed chiefly at curbing the inflation that had stalked the land since 1931. The term Chicago, as Milton Friedman had pointed out, stood for the scientific belief in the efficacy of free markets, skepticism about government intervention, and emphasis on the quantity of money as the key factor in producing inflation. The military called in the monetarist policymakers for reasons similar to those that had led to the summoning of Kemmerer and other money doctors earlier: their impeccable scientific credentials and presumed impartiality promised success in resisting inflationary pressure and government inertia. Sergio de Castro became minister of the economy and subsequently, in 1976, finance minister. Pablo Baraona took the economics portfolio in 1976; Rolf Lüders succeeded him from 1982 to 1983. The Chicago boys operated in the shadow of a military government that split the powerful labor unions into small and comparatively powerless bodies. The absence of effective labor protest in the face of high unemployment proved to be a boon for the Chicago experiment in Chile. The economists took pride in their scientific approach. Their unprecedented experiment and its success gained them international recognition. A stream of foreign visitors, including Friedman, toured Chile to study the country's experiment and to aid with the implementation of a market economy (Valdès 1995: 65).

Despite the numerous challenges facing the reformers, the comprehensive monetarist reform program ultimately proved successful. However, the country had to weather two serious economic declines that severely tested the new regime: stabilization along orthodox lines ultimately remained a priority, but the continuation of anti-inflationary policy came at the expense of temporary real-wage declines. Initial reform measures, which mostly took effect between 1973 and 1975, included a price liberalization, an open regime in international trade and external financing, and a reduced government role in the economy. Fiscal tightening constituted the main instrument to reduce inflation (Valdès 1995: 18–21, 126–32). As a result, the annual inflation rate in 1980 stood at 31.2 per cent (Foxley 1983: 42–8). The drastic liberalization of the economic regime led initially to a worsening of the terms of trade as well as to high unemployment and a decline in real wages. The declining terms of trade, however, resulted mostly from external factors beyond the control of the Chilean government: a worldwide rise in oil prices and a decline in copper prices.

The liberalization of external trade through a lowering of the import tariff rates constituted an important precondition for the economic and financial reforms. Since the collapse of the earlier currency stabilization regime in 1929 the country had been largely isolated from the world economy. Chile possessed no foreign exchange reserves. The public-sector deficit stood at 25 per cent of GDP in 1973. The initial reforms of the new government quickly helped to undo the longstanding economic isolation of Chile. The maximum rate of protection declined from 220 per cent in December 1973 to 65 per cent in June 1976. As a result, the real value of exports grew at an average annual rate of 12 per cent, and nontraditional exports grew from 9.5 per cent of the total in 1971 to more than 35 per cent in 1981. Meanwhile the real exchange rate improved continuously (see Figure 6.1) (see Edwards and Cox-Edwards 1987: 109–29).

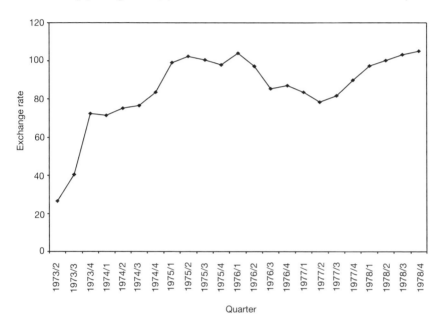

Figure 6.1 Chile: real exchange rate, 1973–8

Source: United Nations (1957: Table 160; 1960: Table 160); Edwards and Cox-Edwards (1987: 50–1).

The recession of 1975, which began after price controls had been abolished, led to renewed inflation and coincided with a decline in the price of copper. Concerns about the cost of anti-inflation measures for the wage-earner led to more drastic measures. The heretofore gradualist monetary policy gave way to a "shock" anti-inflationary policy that decreased government expenditures and real wages, combined with tax surcharges. In April 1975 Columbia-trained finance minister Jorge Cauas tightened monetary policy for the first time. As a result, the rate of growth of nominal money M1 declined in 1976 for the first time since the coup. A parallel tax reform aided the new monetary approach. Based on the belief that fiscally motivated domestic money creation provided the chief cause of inflation, the "shock" program did not try to manipulate the foreign exchange rate.

The "shock" anti-inflationary approach proved initially successful: the inflation rate dipped from 68 per cent in the second quarter of 1975 to 26 per cent in the fourth quarter of 1975. The initial decline, however, did not last: only in the second half of 1976, after a crawling peg devaluation, did the inflation rate begin permanently to decline. This proved to be the beginning of an active currency rate management policy in the service of stabilization. Pre-announced devaluations of the Chilean currency, in the form of the *tablita*, coupled with a proportional lowering of the Chilean tariff to counteract inflation, constituted the cornerstones of a new policy instituted by Sergio de Castro. That policy, which lasted until 1982, reduced the inflation rate to 7.7 per cent in the second quarter of 1979. Subsequently, in June 1979, the peso was tied to the dollar. The exchange-rate-based stabilization program stayed in force until June 1982 and led, combined with the effects of trade liberalization, to an overvaluation of the currency (Velasco 1994).

Following the establishment of the peso–dollar link in June 1979, the government relaxed the controls over capital flows. As a result, foreign indebtedness increased quickly. The reduced cost of foreign borrowing generated a boom similar to that of 1925–9. As had happened under the Kemmerer regime, the real overvaluation of the peso that resulted from pegging the exchange rate proved unsustainable, this time owing in large part to factors beyond Chile's control: record high interest rates, a worldwide recession, and widespread skepticism about the chances for a real recovery. In 1981–2 speculation against the peso began that foreshadowed perils for the new scheme of things. Capital imports fell off suddenly in early 1982. A serious recession followed that lasted until 1983. Mass unemployment ensued.

In response to the crisis, the previous policy of nonintervention was reversed in favor of active steps to save the currency through preferential exchange rates and endeavors to shore up the country's chief banks. De Castro resigned. The government intervened forcefully to take over thirteen banks, among them two of Chile's largest financial institutions. Some of the bank owners received jail sentences. Carlos Diaz-Alejandro has cynically described these measures as "Chile's road to a de facto socialism." But, equally significantly, Chile's central bank, instead of printing money, weathered the 1982–3 financial crisis by issuing foreign and domestic debt instruments, using non-monetary financing. Subsequently the Chilean government obtained funds by negotiating agreements with the IMF and leading commercial banks abroad. The government granted priority to foreign debt repayments. When a reshuffling of the economic portfolios threatened to produce a more populist policy, IMF pressure led to a reversal: in early 1985 Hernàn Buchi was newly appointed to the cabinet. Supported by a team of younger Chicago-trained economists, Buchi initiated a second round of strengthening the external sector, cutting tariffs, and broadening privatization. This, combined with a phase of domestic austerity, led to real devaluation, thus ending the overvaluation that had prevailed since 1979. External credit returned. As a result of the exchange rate depreciation, exports increased. After 1986 the economy began to recover, and in 1987 fiscal accounts showed a surplus.[41]

The Chicago boys succeeded in Chile in the post-Allende era because they elaborated for the first time a comprehensive reform program comprising elimination of the public sector deficit, liberalization of foreign trade, an opening of the economy, and an anti-inflationary policy. The reestablishment of financial orthodoxy was facilitated by the employment of Chilean experts – what the IMF would later call "ownership" of the adjustment program. Trade and social security reforms, linked with drastic curbing of the unions, promoted the transition toward an open economy. The positive interaction between experts trained in Chicago and domestically trained Chilean economists cemented the development of structures to sustain the changes made. These notably included an increased supervisory role of the central bank and new debt conversion schemes. The fact that Chile weathered the depression of 1982–3 underscores the success of the institutional and microeconomic reforms of the previous decade. Financial orthodoxy, paired with a brand of liberalism that had fallen into eclipse since Courcelle-Seneuil's day, returned to Chile at last.

Notes

1 Hernandez (1948: 14–15). For a description how the Banque de France used the rules of the game during the era of bimetallism to broaden its power of independent decision-making, see Flandreau (1995: 153–93).

2 Sater (1979: 67–99); for Courcelle-Seneuil's advocacy of a tax on wealth as an emergency measure in 1878, see O'Brien (1979: 101–21, particularly 104–5).

3 Review by Williams (1923: 140–2).

4 Fetter (1931: 8); for other one-man missions during the early phase of money doctoring, see Glaser (1988: 359–75).

5 Where not mentioned otherwise, see Glaser (n.d.).

6 Hirschman (1994: 133–46). The Kemmerer missions have been discussed by Drake (1989); see also Seidel (1972: 520–45). Additional useful information is derived from Montéon (1982), Mamalakis (1976), Stallings (1987), and Van Cleveland *et al.* (1985).

7 Translation of Report on the Chilean Finances by Secretary of the Treasury Fidel Muñoz Rodriguez, in American Embassy, Santiago to State Department, 4 November 1924, Decimal File (hereafter DF) 825.51/188, Records of the Department of State, RG 59, National Archives.

8 Hirschman (1994); Drake (1989: 80–5); Correa (1987, vol. 3: 597–602).

9 The currency reform is described in Drake (1989: 85–105).

10 7 Kemmerer diary, 8 July 1925, Edwin Walter Kemmerer Papers, Mudd Library, Princeton University.

11 Fetter (1931: 27–37); Palma (1985: 323).

12 Drake, (1989: 89–105); *El Mercurio*, 5 October 1925: 1 and 3.

13 Perhaps the Kemmerer mission can be faulted for not leaving a sufficient margin to take economic surprises into account. Then, as now, economic forecasting was not an exact science. British authorities, planning for the return to gold in the spring of 1925, likewise failed to predict the slowdown in coal exports that derived from sharp competition from newly refurbished mines in the Ruhr. See Moggridge (1972: 113–30).

14 Calculated from Great Britain, Department of Overseas Trade (hereafter GBDOT) (1931: 8). The fiscal year in Chile runs from July to June.

15 Republica de Chile (1929, vol. V: 4–5); Foreign Bondholders Protective Council, Inc. (1934: 150); Montéon (1982: 154).
16 Sales figures are in GBDOT (1931: 98). Montéon (1982: 165 and *passim*) errs when he argues that after 1926 the nitrate depression continued.
17 The quote can be found in *Bulletin of the Pan American Union*, February 1930: 295.
18 *New York Times*, 23 August 1929: 5. Drake (1989: 115–17) points to the economic crisis in Europe and the United States starting in 1929 as the main cause of Chile's depression; information about the Chilean budget and the balance of payments in 1930 derives from GBDOT (1931: 15–17).
19 For a review of the literature on the 1930–2 defaults, see Eichengreen (1991: 149–70).
20 Figures for the planned special budget of 1931 are in GBDOT (1931: 19); information about Chilean indebtedness derives from *Foreign Relations 1946*, vol. XI: 600–2; Palma (1967: 441–5), chronicles Ibáñez's fall and the decline of public confidence in his administration.
21 Drake (1978: 41–65); Velasco (1994: 379–411); see also Palma (2000: 43–70). Schuker (1988) examines the historical development of opportunistic defaults.
22 Fetter (1931: 184–85, 195 fn. 2); Thorp and Londoño (1984: 81–116, 102).
23 Pisciotta (1987: 107–20); Bray (1961: 18–23).
24 Paper presented to the Operations Coordinating Board: Courses of Action in Chile, 17 December 1954, Foreign Relations of the United States (FRUS), 1952–4, vol. IV (Washington: USGP, 1983): 758–63.
25 W. Empson, Santiago, to F.O., 10 September 1956, AC1102/2, FO371/119968, PRO, Kew, England.
26 Memorandum of a Conversation between President Ibáñez del Campo and the Ambassador in Chile (Beaulac), January 26, 1955, FRUS 1954, vol. VII: 777–80; Pisciotta (1987: 125).
27 AC1102/2, Empson, Santiago, to F.O.10 September1956; Beaulac to Belton, 14 March 1956, FRUS 1955–7, vol. VII: 811; see also Ffrench-Davis *et al.* (2000: 114–44).
28 Preliminary Notes on a Meeting of the Operations Coordinating Board, 13 April 1955, FRUS 1955–7: 787.
29 Special Report by the Operations Coordinating Board on Chile, 13 April 1955, FRUS 1955–7, vol. VII: 788–90; editorial note reproducing a part of Assistant of Secretary Holland's note of December 12, 1955, *ibid.*: 795–6.
30 Lyon to State Department, 5 January 1957, FRUS 1955–7, vol. VII: 821–2.
31 Minutes of the 242nd Meeting of the National Advisory Council on International Monetary and Financial Problems, Washington, March 6, 1956, FRUS 1955–7, vol. VII: 807–10. See also Nr. 393, editorial note, on the sale of American agricultural goods to Chile, *ibid.*: 810; and FN 2: 817, *ibid.*
32 Editorial Note, FRUS 1955–7, vol. VII: 816–17, on conversations between Assistant Secretary of State Holland with Oscar Herrera in early August 1956.
33 Memorandum of a conversation in Santiago, 14 November 1956, FRUS 1955–7, vol. VII: 817–20; Pisciotta (1987: 128).
34 Empson to F.O, 25 February 1957, Report on Chilean national budget for 1957. AC1114/2, FO371/126270.
35 Memorandum of a conversation in Santiago, 14 November 1956, FRUS 1955–7, vol. VII: 817–20.
36 Pisciotta (1987: 128–9); Bray (1961: 123–34); Empson to F.O., 27 January 1958, Annual Review for 1957, AC1011/1, FO371/132021.
37 Memorandum of a conversation, Department of State, 3 April 1957, FRUS 1955–7, vol. VII: 823–5.
38 Memorandum of a conversation, Department of State, 16 April 1957; Lyon to Rubottom, 14 May 1957; Memorandum from Rubottom, Acting Secretary of State for Inter-American Affairs, to Assistant Secretary of State for Economic Affairs, 4

June 1957; Rubottom to Lyon, 22 June 1957; Lyon to Rubottom, 11 July 1957; Memorandum of a conversation in Washington, July 31, 1957; Current Economic Development Issues No. 527, 3 September 1957; Memorandum of a Conversation, Department of State, Washington, 6 November 1957, all FRUS 1955–7, vol. VII: 831–54.

39 Velasco (1994); Edwards (1972). For subsequent developments, see Taffet (2001).
40 Edwards and Cox-Edwards (1987: 10); Valdès (1995: 18–21, 126–32).
41 Edwards and Cox-Edwards (1987: 49–90); Rudiger Dornbusch and Sebastian Edwards, "Exchange Rate Policy and Trade Strategy," in Bosworth *et al.* (1994: 81–115, 89); Valdès (1995: 261–5).

References

Bosworth, B., R. Dornbusch and R. Labán (eds.) (1994) *The Chilean Economy: Policy Lessons and Challenges*, Washington, DC: Brookings Institution.

Bray, D. (1961) *Chilean Politics during the Second Ibáñez Government*, Ph.D. Dissertation, Stanford University.

Cárdenas, E., J. Ocamp and R. Thorp (eds.) (2000) *An Economic History of Twentieth Century Latin America*, 3 vols., Basingstoke and New York: Palgrave.

Correa, G. (1987) *Historia de Chile (1891–1973)*, vol. III, Santiago de Chile: Editorial Santillana del Pacífico.

Department of State (n.d.) *Records of the Department of State. RG 59, Decimal File 825.51*, National Archives, College Park, MD.

Drake, P. (1978) *Socialism and Populism in Chile, 1932–52*, Urbana, IL: University of Illinois Press.Drake, P. (1989) *The Money Doctor in the Andes: The Kemmerer Missions, 1923–1933*, Durham, NC, and London: Duke University Press.

Drake, P. (1989) *The Money Doctor in the Andes: The Kemmere Missions, 1923–1933*, Durham, NC, and London: Duke University Press.

Edwards, S. and A. Cox-Edwards (1987) *Monetarism and Liberalization: The Chilean Experiment*, Cambridge, MA: Ballinger Publishing Company.

Edwards, T. (1972) *Economic Development and Reform in Chile: Progress under Frei*, East Lansing, MI: Latin American Studies Center, Michigan State University.

El Mercurio (1925–30) microfilm edition, Santiago de Chile.

Eichengreen, B. (1991) "Historical Research on International Lending and Debt," *Journal of Economic Perspectives* 5(2): 149–69.

Fetter, F. (1931) *Monetary Inflation in Chile*, Princeton, NJ: Princeton University Press.

Ffrench-Davis, R., O. Muñoz, J. Benavente and G. Crespi (2000) "The Industrialization of Chile during Protectionism, 1940–1982," in E. Cárdenas, J. Ocamp and R. Thorp (eds.) *An Economic History of Twentieth Century Latin America*, vol. 3, Basingstoke and New York: Palgrave.

Flandreau, M. (1995) *L'Or du monde; La France et la stabilité du système monétaire international 1848–1873*, Paris: Editions L'Harmattan.

Foreign Bondholders Protective Council, Inc. (1934) *Annual Report 1934*, New York: Foreign Bondholders Protective Council.

Foreign Office (Great Britain) (1906) *Political Department. General Correspondence from 1906. F.O.371*, Public Record Office, Kew, England.

Foxley, A. (1983) *Latin American Experiments in Neoconservative Economics*, Berkeley, Los Angeles, CA, and London: University of California Press.

Glaser, E. (n.d.) "Currency Reform and Debt Default in Chile, 1925–1932: Myth and Reality in the Great Depression," unpublished manuscript in possession of the author.

Glaser, E. (1988) "Amerikanische Währungsreformen in Ostasien und im karibischen Raum, 1900–1918," *Amerikastudien* 33: 359–75.

Great Britain, Department of Overseas Trade (1931) *Economic Conditions in Chile, 1930*, London: H.M. Stationery Office.

Hernandez, L. (1948) *Courcelle-Seneuil en Chile; Errores del Liberalismo Economico*, Santiago de Chile: Prensas de la Universidad de Chile.

Hirschman, A. (1994) "Inflation in Chile," reprinted in P. Drake (ed.) *Money Doctors, Foreign Debts, and Economic Reforms in Latin America from the 1890s to the Present*, Wilmington, DE: Scholarly Books.

Kemmerer, E. (n.d.) *Papers*, Mudd Library, Princeton University.

League of Nations, Economic Intelligence Service (1932) *Statistical Yearbook of the League of Nations*, Geneva: Economic Intelligence Service of the League of Nations.

League of Nations (1941) *Statistical Yearbook of the League of Nations, 1940/41*, Geneva: League of Nations.

Mamalakis, M. (1976) *The Growth and Structure of the Chilean Economy: From Independence to Allende*, New Haven, CT, and London: Yale University Press.

Marichal, C. (1989) *A Century of Debt Crises in Latin America: From Independence to the Great Depression*, Princeton, NJ: Princeton University Press.

Moggridge, D. (1972) *British Monetary Policy, 1924–1931: The Norman Conquest of $4.86*, Cambridge: Cambridge University Press.

Montéon, M. (1982) *Chile in the Nitrate Era: The Evolution of Economic Dependency, 1880–1930*, Madison, WI: University of Wisconsin Press.

New York Times (n.d.) Microfilm Edition.

O'Brien, T. (1979) "Chilean Elites and Foreign Investors: Chilean Nitrate Policy, 1880–1882," *Journal of Latin American Studies* 11(1): 101–21.

Palma, A. (1967) *Recuerdos de Gobierno*, Santiago de Chile: Editorial Nascimento.

Palma, G. (1985) "External Disequilibrium and Internal Industrialization: Chile, 1914–1935," in C. Abel and C.M. Lewis (eds.) *Latin America, Economic Imperialism and the State: The Political Economy of the External Connection from Independence to the Present*, London and Dover, NH: Athlone.

Palma, G. (2000) "From an Export-Led to an Import-Substitution Economy: Chile, 1914–1939," in E. Cárdenas, J. Ocamp and R. Thorp (eds.) *An Economic History of Latin America*, vol. II, Basingstoke and New York: Palgrave.

Pisciotta, J. (1987) *Development, Inflation, and Politics in Chile, 1938–1958*, New York and London: Garland.

Pitts, M.-A. (1987) *Economic Development in Chile under Two Growth Strategies, 1925–1968*, New York: Garland.

Republica de Chile (1929) *Estadistica Anual, Año 1928*, Santiago de Chile: La Dirección.

Sater, W. (1979) "Chile and the World Depression of the 1870's," *Journal of Latin American Studies* 11(1): 67–99.

Schuker, S. (1988) *American "Reparations" to Germany, 1919–1933: Implications for the Third World Debt Crisis*, Princeton Studies in International Finance, no. 61, Princeton, NJ: Princeton University.

Seidel, R. (1972) "American Reformers Abroad: The Kemmerer Missions in South America," *Journal of Economic History* 32(1): 520–45.

Smythe, D. (1986) *Pershing: General of the Armies*, Bloomington, IN: Indiana University Press.

Stallings, B. (1987) *Banker to the Third World: U.S. Portfolio Investments in Latin America, 1900–1986*, Berkeley, CA, and London: University of California Press.

Taffet, J. (2001) "Alliance for What? U.S. Development Assistance in Chile during the 1960s," unpublished Ph.D. Dissertation, Georgetown University.

Thorp, R. and C. Londoño (1984) "The Effect of the Great Depression on the Economies of Peru and Colombia," in R. Thorp (ed.) *Latin America in the 1930's: The Role of the Periphery in World Crisis*, Oxford: Macmillan in association with St. Antony's College.

United Nations, Department of Economic Affairs (1951) *Economic Survey of Latin America, 1949*, New York: United Nations.

United Nations, Department of Economic and Social Affairs, Economic Commission for Latin America (1965) *External Financing in Latin America*, New York: United Nations.

United Nations (1957) *Statistical Yearbooks 1957*, New York: United Nations.

United Nations (1960) *Statistical Yearbooks 1960*, New York: United Nations.

United States Department of State (1969) *Foreign Relations of the United States, 1946*, vol. XI, Washington, DC: Government Publishing Office.

United States Department of State (1983) *Foreign Relations of the United States, 1952–1954*, vol. IV, Washington, DC: Government Publishing Office.

United States Department of State (1987) *Foreign Relations of the United States, 1955–1957*, vol. VII, Washington, DC: Government Publishing Office.

Van Cleveland, H. and T. Huertas, with R. Strauber (1985) *Citibank, 1812–1970*, Cambridge, MA, and London: Harvard University Press.

Valdès, J. (1995) *Pinochet's Economists: The Chicago Boys in Chile*, Cambridge: Cambridge University Press.

Velasco, A. (1994) "The State and Economic Policy: Chile 1952–1959," in B. Bosworth *et al.* (1994) *The Chilean Economy: Policy Lessons and Challenges*, Washington, DC: Brookings Institution.

Will, R. (1964) "The Introduction of Classical Economics in Chile," *Hispanic American Historical Review* 44(1): 1–21.

Williams, J. (1923) "Review of Guillermo Subercasaux, El Sistema Monetario y la Organization Bancaria de Chile," *American Economic Review* 13(1): 140–2.

7 Advising, conditionality, culture

Money doctors in Bulgaria, 1900–2000

Roumen Avramov[1]

Bulgaria acquired independence from the Ottoman Empire in 1878. The country's financial experience went through several distinct phases: a strong expansion interrupted by sharp crises until World War I; a near hyperinflation after the war, followed by a short-lived macroeconomic stabilization in the second half of the 1920s; the Great Depression and the recovery of the late 1930s, followed by a second wave of war inflation; the communist era; the transition to a market economy in the 1990s, with a hesitant start and a clear acceleration after the introduction of a currency board arrangement in July 1997.

Small peripheral economies face international advice during episodes of financial distress. "Advice" in this context should be read as a euphemism and it seems more appropriate to talk of economic conditionality, for money doctors have always accompanied creditors. Money doctoring is thus defined here as the set of personal or institutional relations that design, support, and enforce those macroeconomic measures which are the counterpart of the needed capital inflow. This relation embeds the existing developmental gap between the behavioral standards of a mature market and those of a transition economy (whatever is meant by that). This chapter reviews the evolution of the conditionality relationship from the point of view of a small economy that has been subjected to a continuum of external control from 1900 to the present, drawing on the century-long experience of Bulgaria. The main focus is on the pre-World War II era. This period is interesting because it lays down many of the basic principles that re-emerged with the international financial institution (IFI)-based conditionality of the post-communist period. Archival evidence has been collected from Bulgarian sources, League of Nations documents, French government and private banks' archives, and the archives of the Inter-Allied Reparations Commission in Sofia (IARC) kept at the Archives Nationales in Paris.

Even allowing for cultural and historical specifics, Bulgaria may be treated as a representative case, typical of the small dependent transition economies of Southeastern Europe. The chapter is, correspondingly, an overview that deliberately favors more general conclusions and long trends, leaving aside many details. Relying on short case studies, we seek to delineate the multifaceted phenomenon of conditionality. As shall be seen, conditionality in Bulgaria involved a long string of actors. These were not only foreign money doctors, but also their Bulgarian counterparts as well as a Byzantine background of diplomats, politicians, civil servants, and bankers.

From a dynamic perspective, the evolution of conditionality in Bulgaria reflects a growing complexity. Instruments and tools for pressure have evolved, together with the sophistication of the markets and changing political context. Changes in conditionality culture also reflected the change in dominant theoretical paradigms and intellectual patterns. Yet, as shall be shown in the course of the chapter, one common theme runs through Bulgaria's varied experiences with money doctoring: it is the formula "money against reforms," which emerges as the main principle of economic conditionality as a political-economic bargain.

The remainder of the chapter is organized as follows: the first section establishes a typology of foreign conditionality; the next section discusses the enforcement mechanisms; and the third section focuses on some conceptual and personal aspects of conditionality.

Conditionalities: a typology

Bulgaria has experienced, in broad terms, five types of economic conditionality. The first foreign loan was extended to Bulgaria in 1888, followed by new loans in 1889, 1892, and 1896. Some minor short-term advances were also obtained until the end of the century.[2] All these arrangements did not involve any specific conditionality clauses related to macroeconomic policy monitoring or legal matters. Instead, they were secured through conventional covenants and the pledging of collateral.

A new era began with the underwriting of Bulgarian bonds by Banque de Paris et des Pays-Bas (Paribas)-led consortiums in 1902, 1904, and 1907. These specifically pledged key tax revenues as collateral and required the presence in the borrowing country of a representative of the bondholders. This personality rapidly became a pivotal figure in the local establishment and in the making of local economic policy. Instruments at his disposal were quite direct, namely the delivery of tobacco stamps[3] to the government against repayments of the loans.

The delegate of the bondholders was in very close contact with Paribas headquarters and the French government. This personal presence was essential in enforcing conditionality, suggesting that "standard" market monitoring was not enough and that a human presence was needed to manage control on a daily basis. The system survived almost without modifications, although in a more complicated context, until the mid-1930s. The bondholders delegate had a key position.[4] He was entrusted with protecting the interests of nearly 500,000 bondholders ("*porteurs*"), as well as supervising the fulfillment of the terms of the contract. His power was rooted in the strength of Paribas. The bulk of his correspondence was not with bondholders, but with Paribas headquarters. His personal promotion and numerous regalia were directly dependent on Paribas. At the same time, his appointment was a political matter. The application process was coordinated by the Ministry of Finance and the Quai d'Orsay, before being submitted to Paribas. The French government could revoke his mandate at any moment without compensation. The diplomatic formula, agreed upon after long discussions with the Bulgarian side, was that "the delegate is appointed by Paribas and notified to the Bulgarian Government by the French Legation in Sofia." The legal ground for such a treatment was the fact that the French government had authorized the loan's quotation on the Paris stock exchange under precise clauses and was correspondingly bound to assure their strict observation. As a whole, the "hybrid" institutional status of the delegate was that of a semi-civil servant, semi-bank employee recruited among the French administrative *nomenklatura*.

The delegate had large discretionary powers, including a de facto veto on monetary and fiscal policy decisions. He was entrusted with following the fiscal legislation (tax collection, tax laws, tobacco stamps, fraud) and reporting to Paribas. It was his duty to check for deviations or deficiencies in implementation. In effect, he also oversaw fiscal matters, since taxes had been pledged as collateral: the delegate could stop any amendment of the legislation. The agreement of the bondholders' representative was required for any change in the legal framework in which the Bulgarian National Bank (BNB) operated. The bank was not allowed to print paper money (except in the case of war) without the explicit permission of the delegate, since this would deteriorate the quality of the tax guarantees. The underlying idea was that currency devaluation (in metallic standard terms) and the eventual dilution of the collateral's value was a danger for creditors. The representative was requested to inform Paribas, the Bulgarian government, or (in the absence of adequate reaction) the French Legation about any measures that, in his view, undermined the exchange rate.

In order to execute all those instructions the delegate needed a broad information network. Personal contacts with the local establishment gave him insider knowledge. Beside, his position provided him unique access to data. The delegate's archives reveal a dense array of primary data sources that overcome the official bias and manipulations of the BNB and government balances. His office grew as a first-order macroeconomic observatory, which filtered the available economic information, aiming to assess the true creditworthiness of the country. By concentrating information, the delegate strengthened his position as one of the main poles of economic power in local society.

This kind of personal supervision was not, for all its closeness, of the same stuff as had characterized the Ottoman debt – a regime where national sovereignty on debt and tax matters had been completely surrendered.[5] The possibility of implementing this "extreme conditionality" in Bulgaria had been raised on various occasions as an intimidation (in 1899, 1904, and 1907). It was eventually implemented after the end of World War I, with the presence (from 1921 onwards) of the IARC in Sofia (this followed the 1919 Treaty of Neuilly). The role of the Commission was crucial in imposing fiscal and monetary orthodoxy. The Commission implemented strict monitoring of the overall macroeconomic policy as well as explicit requirements for certain institutional reforms. The IARC had vast prerogatives: they resulted in an explicit transfer of economic sovereignty to a foreign institution.

In 1919, the French occupation authorities had considered for a while a takeover of the Bulgarian Debt Directorate by the Allies. It was clearly understood (on the basis of the Ottoman Empire's experience) that control over the debt was the moot point for control over the entire economy. Later on the idea was abandoned and the IARC became the central agent of external control. The Commission's control covered every relevant economic matter – budget procedure, monetary policy, legislation. No major economic policy decision, including the budget, was allowed without the consent of the Commission.[6] It had, in particular, senior status among all Bulgarian creditors. This, de facto, ruled out the possibility of contracting other external loans without its consent.[7]

Moreover, the Commission's influence reached out much more broadly, as it became the stronghold of "market principles" in a strongly populist environment. For the local business elite the IARC was a champion of economic laissez-faire. In some instances IARC ended up overruling the arbitrary decisions the Bulgarian government was taking against prominent representatives of the Bulgarian bourgeoisie. The Commission had acted out of concern for the side-effects of those measures (capital flight and the destabilization of the national currency).

Eventually, many of the main features implemented by IARC became part of the "League of Nations' Financial Committee conditionality," as it resulted from the two stabilization loans of 1926 and 1928. With these arrangements, Bulgaria moved towards a more impersonal, bureaucratic style of conditionality that would again be characteristic of more recent experiences. The involvement of the League of Nations reinforced the political ingredient of conditionality, as monitoring was itself subject to a delicate balance of power between the spheres of influence of the leading countries. The League of Nations had sought to institute a multilateral forum for the discussion of global debt problems and of particular cases. Although it was not very successful in shaping broad international solutions,[8] it became the privileged instrument of a case-by-case approach that turned out to perform reasonably well in small countries.

An interesting modern ingredient in League of Nations conditionality was its quasi-role of rating agency. The inquiries by the League's Financial Committee were generally accepted by the bondholders as the relevant source of information regarding the solvency of a debtor country. As the Financial Committee took over from private creditors macroeconomic policy enforcement, it also began acquiring sensitive data and thus became a kind of informational intermediary. Meeting League of Nations' requests was tantamount to securing a strong official encouragement for foreign private investors, and this increased the leverage of its conditionality. This previewed the present-day model for countries with low creditworthiness needing the "warranty" of International Monetary Fund (IMF)-supported programs.

Despite the institutionalization of monitoring, the personal influence of the League Commissioner who was an adviser to the National Bank remained considerable. He was entrusted with managing the proceeds of stabilization loans. The Commissioner had a consultative vote at the Administrative and Executive Councils of the BNB. He assessed the conformity of the banks' management decisions with respect to the statutes, and could block any decision, forcing a formal arbitrage.[9] No amendment in the BNB statutes could be effected without the Commissioner's agreement. Finally, he had the exclusive right to approve short-term advances by the BNB to the Treasury.[10]

It was under League of Nations' monitoring that the formula "structural reforms against debt restructuring" was formalized. "Reforms," however, should be understood as a metaphor. In the 1920s, as now, what was meant by reform remained elusive, and requests for "reforming" the economy turned out to be a catch-all instrument. Bulgarian governments (as many others) tried to eschew reforms as much as they could. This is why prewar loans' bondholders were possibly wise in preferring pledges of tangible assets. They were probably right in complaining that macroeconomic conditionality and physical guarantees (or real losses) should not be treated on an equal footing.

The outbreak of World War II marked a turning point in foreign conditionality. The debacle of the League of Nations permitted emancipation from the Financial Committee's control. In May 1941 the League Commissioner and the adviser to the BNB left Bulgaria. In fact, since April 1940 foreign debt payments had been intermittent and subjected to occasional arrangements. Overall conditionality took a clear wartime look and was dominated by Germany. The German defeat opened an interregnum, which continued until 1949 and ended with the final default on outstanding Paribas debt.

The rapid postwar Sovietization of the country imposed a new, communist-type, foreign conditionality. Its features have not been systematically explored, as archival evidence became accessible only recently. In very broad terms, this foreign dependence was characterized by strict control by the USSR of every economic policy decision. "Shadow" institutions and an army of "advisers" exerted overview and coordination down to insignificant details. Nevertheless, this type of conditionality allowed some space for a bargaining process between the metropolis and its satellites. It was a primitive and direct bargain that fitted with the highly political nature of a de-monetized command economy.

The collapse of the communist system in the early 1990s gave way to standard IMF-based conditionality. More bureaucratized and impersonal than its League predecessor, the IMF conditionality introduced two innovations: first, unlike the League of Nations, the IMF manages its own resources; second, IMF-based conditionality rests on a clearer operational and conceptual framework, with a division of labor with other international financial institutions designed to monitor different facets of ongoing structural reforms.

For countries eligible to join the European Union, like Bulgaria, the main shift in the conditionality framework is expected to come from the overwhelmingly bureaucratized and institutionalized "harmonization process." This perspective broadens substantially the scope of conditionality. In fact, the accession monitoring incorporates a much wider societal philosophy. The ultimate goal of the process is enormously ambitious, focusing on the very cultural roots of the acceding society. Moreover, the "receiving" Union is changing its own set-up as it admits the new entrants.

This brief chronological review outlines some trends in conditionality culture. We observe a gradual bureaucratization, from the early, almost personal, supervision to the all-embracing European accession. A broadening of the scope of conditionality is also noticeable: over the long run, we found conditionality moving from narrow legal topics to national legislation; from constraints on fiscal to monetary policy; and from macroeconomic policy to reforming cultural, political, and institutional "fundamentals." And obviously there are reasons to believe that this Bulgarian experience is truly the reflection of a more general process.[11]

Enforcement: conditionality as a bargain

Monitoring procedures

The first conditionality regime relied on guarantees, which typically took the form of collateral along with fixed exchange rate clauses that insured against currency depreciation. The identification of the relevant "collateral" was at the heart of the conditionality relation. Historically, the practice began with the pledge of some material asset. Whatever the specific choice, the basic notion was always to identify some key asset whose monitoring would be an indirect way of monitoring the economy at large. Such was the case with the assets of the newly built infrastructure (railways or harbors) for the first loans in the late nineteenth century, or, for instance, the pledging of the revenues and assets of the vast network of agricultural banks in 1896. The use of tax revenues as collateral became widespread when the fiscal capacity of the state developed: then the most lucrative taxes (such as tobacco excises or customs duties) were used. The climax of this system was attained with the Treaty of Neuilly, whereby the entire national wealth was de facto pledged, since the IARC assumed complete economic control.

"Security" gradually acquired more intangible features. Visible already with the Paribas loans, this tendency became more clear cut with the macroeconomic policy conditionality imposed by the IARC. This approach was consecrated in the League of Nations and, much later, through IMF practice. At the same time, conditionality was always exercised through some form of direct control. For instance, part of the proceeds from the "French loans" was held in a special reserve account in the underwriting bank. Something similar was achieved in the stabilization loans of the 1920s, when the proceeds were placed under the authority of the creditors' representative. Modern market practice displays similar techniques to those of a century ago. Brady bonds, for instance, are partially secured with a pledge of U.S. securities held in a depositary bank. And the Bulgarian currency board arrangement in place since 1997 is cushioned by an important IMF-monitored fiscal surplus covering roughly one year of foreign debt installments.

Market-based instruments are another way of providing security to borrowers. At all times, premiums charged on Bulgarian loans were substantial in absolute terms, reflecting, among other things, a "geopolitical" risk related to the region's intrinsic instability. Their dynamics, however, also reflected the changing profile of the country risk. For instance, they captured (through declining interest rates for new loans) the growing creditworthiness of the country in 1902–12,[12] possibly the tighter guarantees as well. Indeed, fluctuations in the quotations of Bulgarian loans reflected not only "objective" risks but also the quality of the monitoring process and that of the assets pledged.[13] The 1926 and the 1928 stabilization loans commanded yields of respectively 144 and 166 base points higher than the relevant average interest levels on the American bond market.[14] This relatively low margin may suggest that the Financial Committee and IARC monitoring somewhat moderated the risk premium. This helps interpret foreign control as a counterpart of the lower prices paid by borrowers. In effect, the League of Nations umbrella put postwar loans' bondholders in a more favorable situation: after the 1932 partial Bulgarian default (until 1939), they managed to recover roughly 33 per cent of the nominal interest while prewar bondholders had to content themselves with 13–18 per cent. Similarly, the relatively more secured loans (the 1926 loan and the prewar loans with real pledges) performed better in the default context.[15] Sensitivity of the market conditions to the conditionality terms could be found even during the communist period.[16]

There is a question, however, whether pledges, barring actual external conditionality, can add sufficient guarantees. "Collaterals," when it comes to international lending, are of an intrinsically illusionary and evasive nature. Securities have been circumvented, ignored, or depreciated. When a major crisis between prewar bondholders and Bulgarian government struck in June 1932 the government simply threatened to take up the printing of tobacco stamps. Seizing the collateral could be difficult, be it a tangible pledge or an intangible security: this was illustrated in 1940, when the country suspended foreign debt payments without any possible retaliation on the part of creditors, and again in 1948, with the unilateral settlement with Paribas. The inflationary collapse of the gold standard after World War I undermined the fixed exchange rate clauses in earlier loan contracts. In the Bulgarian case, actual debt servicing never exceeded one-third of the pre-1914 interests' "gold value." Finally, in a different manner, the collapse of communism did away with stability and predictability, the Soviet system's main intangible asset from the creditors' point of view.

Institutional conditionality

The role of money doctors has often been to recommend institutional and legal reform in debtor countries. The focal points of the reform were the government budget and the central bank. On the fiscal side, control started in the early 1900s with close and direct monitoring of the tax pledged and the related legislation. Eventually, the IARC had complete discretionary power over the budget procedure and fiscal laws. The League of Nations continued this path by including as a basic conditionality principle the building of a consistent and transparent fiscal system and the realization of deep fiscal reforms. Despite the strict institutional control of the fiscal sector, it rapidly became evident that such monitoring was inefficient if it was not combined with control over monetary policy. Conversely, the control over monetization of deficit financing emerged as a central tool for the enforcement of fiscal discipline.

One recurrent problem which foreign investors faced was the fact that the issuing bank (the BNB) was widely utilized as a source of government finance. The point was perfectly caught by Georges Bousquet, the first bondholders' delegate in Sofia in 1908:

> The BNB is de facto a department of the Treasury…. This critical situation is due…to the easy access of the Government to the Bank's resources through the loans extended… This explains the deeply rooted reluctance of foreign financial institutions to extend not pledged loans to a Government that in a few months can borrow [from the BNB] 50 million without providing to its foreign creditors any preferential treatment with respect to the local ones.[17]

The government's obligation to consult the bondholders' delegate on decisions concerning the issuing policy of the BNB was an important – but not sufficient – enforcement instrument. Shutting down the national bank's window for government financing required a broad institutional reform. The idea was in the air, in line with the prevailing late-nineteenth-century doctrinal orthodoxy favoring an independent, privately owned bank of issue.[18] No strong political (and social) forces, however, were at work to separate the bank from the state. Instead, vested political interests and the dominant ideology inverted "politically correct" European values by exalting the "virtues" of the government-dependent BNB.

Plans to privatize the originally state-owned BNB were launched in the immediate aftermath of independence in 1878. In the years that followed, this highly controversial idea became the core of an intense national debate which also raised the problem of foreigners' participation in BNB capital. The issue has never been settled in favor of a private bank (Avramov 1999a, 1999b). The first project for a joint stock issuing bank was formulated by two Russian bankers in late 1879 and endorsed for a while by the Council of Ministers, before eventually being abandoned. Bulgarian politicians made a second attempt in 1883. The capital required was never raised, and the government finally opted for the alternative project in 1885. The law that was eventually enacted consecrated two fundamental principles in Bulgarian economic life – that the issuing bank should be state owned and that no foreign capital should be allowed to enter the institution.

Nevertheless, under strong foreign pressure the institution was deeply transformed after World War I. The first step was the adoption in June 1922 of a Law on the limitation of banknote issue and of the Treasury debt towards BNB imposed by the IARC. The Law set explicit and binding ceilings on the issue of banknotes and to the government debt to the BNB. It provides an excellent example of implicit "institutional conditionality."

These changes were occurring in a macroeconomic context that was characteristic of many countries in those years – especially defeated ones. The national currency had lost 97 per cent of its prewar "gold" value and hyperinflation was threatening. Diagnosis seemed straightforward: there was a wide national and international consensus that inflation had a fiscal source. The disputable point was whether this was the sole source. Interestingly, the conflict between Bulgarian authorities and the IARC took on "theoretical" issues. To accept that there were no other sources of inflation meant that the IARC should be legitimately empowered to take full control over fiscal policy. To accept additional sources implied that a degree of freedom could be left for the use of fiscal instruments. As in so many cases, "theory" meant power. The Bulgarian government thus challenged the IARC's monetarist interpretation and insisted that an important inflationary component was underestimated, namely the uncertainty surrounding the settlement of the reparation dispute. According to this view, the unknown volume of the forthcoming reparation debt burden fueled speculation against the lev. A purely fiscal approach could not solve the problem, and a fixed ceiling for direct deficit financing by the BNB would be inadequate.

While facts gave partial support to the Bulgarian point of view,[19] the focus on the fiscal sources of inflation was, however, by no means erroneous. Accordingly, the IARC faced the following choice: it could force an amendment of the BNB status or impose an explicit control on the money supply (e.g. through a ceiling on government deficit financing). In economic terms, both options boiled down to a kind of currency board arrangement.

The Commission eventually opted for the second option, which saved on legal transformations. It accommodated the strong public opposition to anything that might change the BNB as a kind of untouchable national symbol. At the same time, the IARC's approach illustrated the preference of Bulgaria's foreign monitors for direct instruments over institutional reforms. Reform plans were always seen as second-best solutions compared to explicit rules and criteria. The conditions for a large-scale reshuffling of BNB's status emerged only in 1926–8, when this reform became the bargaining chip for badly needed stabilization loans.

With the enactment of the 1922 Law, conflicts migrated into the difficult enforcement of deficit financing thresholds. At the start, both sides set unrealistic figures that seemed impossible to reconcile. The IARC then indicated that it was ready to accept a higher threshold, but with harder conditions for its revision. Money supply not covered by foreign reserves was limited through the ceiling of the government debt to BNB. Any decision on short-term extraordinary advances by the BNB to the government was to be approved by the IARC. One consequence of this debate was also a rationalization and objectification of statistical criteria. As in many other cases of conditionality, the conflict outlined the need for a more extensive and transparent set of economic and monetary data. Information means control, and it is not by chance that the IARC devoted much effort to progress in this direction. Statistics on foreign reserves became particularly relevant.

Nevertheless, the Law's disciplining impact on fiscal policy should be stressed. It was also the first step in a long-lasting effort to put order and some transparency into the budgetary procedure and the government fiscal account. There is no doubt that foreign monitoring played a crucial role in this process. The reform was completed by the BNB's institutional transformation, negotiated in exchange for the 1928 stabilization loan. The reform reshaped it into a pure bank of issue. It cut all those functions that had previously been utilized for government financing. The violent national debate accompanying the decision, and the final compromise, revealed – once more – the profound "statist" attitudes in Bulgarian society.[20]

To conclude, the 1922 Law was a piece of extremely effective conditionality enforcement. The key to its success was its comprehensiveness, which effectively constrained both monetary and fiscal policy. The 1928 reform completed the reforms by providing a new institutional framework to the 1922 measures. Later examples confirmed that partial approaches tend to perform considerably less effectively. The impossibility of controlling the debtor country without consistent, coordinated, and credible constraints imposed on both fiscal and monetary policy was illustrated once more by the aborted stabilization attempts in Bulgaria during the 1990s. By accommodating budget deficits in 1991–6 the central bank simply repeated an old practice. This parallel provides a perspective on the implementation of the currency board arrangement in 1997. With this step Bulgaria tried to overcome a chronic and century-long inconsistency in its macroeconomic policy. The conflict was settled by removing essential monetary functions from the BNB and transferring monetary sovereignty abroad. In this perspective, the Law of 1922 and the 1928 BNB Act emerge as precursors of the more recent currency board.

Conditionality: a view from the center

Creditors have never been a homogeneous community and this complexity increased, if anything, over the century. Until the end of World War I "creditors" were represented by the bondholders' delegate, the underwriting bank, and their home government (basically the Ministries of Foreign Affairs and of Finance). It is tempting to see the European banks as an acting arm of foreign politics, a view that was pioneered by Marxists and non-Marxists alike. The pre-World War I Bulgarian experience gives some credit to this view: politics were always in the background. The 1904 and 1907 loans, in particular, reflected the military rivalry between France and Germany, and its industrial translation in the field of the competition between Shneider and Krupp. At the same time, finance was not necessarily always the servant of politics: Paribas and Deutsche Bank, for example, cooperated in Bulgaria at some moments against prevailing foreign policy political trends.

Flandreau's characterization of "bankers as confessors" (Chapter 1) matches almost perfectly the Bulgarian experience, with only some minor retouches needed. One is the lesser degree of direct intercourse between the bank's upper management and Bulgarian authorities than he suggests was the norm. These close relations were probably more characteristic of middle-sized to large debtors. In more peripheral countries the local representative assumed the chief role in the contact with local authorities. This had consequences for the quality of information that reached the bank's headquarters – and, downstream, the markets – since representatives had a tendency to "go local." The Bulgarian experience also illustrates that borrowers often sought to escape from the monitoring of the "privileged bankers." No eternal alliances existed: the 1909 Bulgarian loan underwritten by Austrian banks against Paribas is a typical example. Of course such moves were gambles, with immediate gains often repaid by higher borrowing prices eventually. But the point is that governments, in a permanent search for fresh money, routinely undertook parallel talks with several banks at once: negotiations developed until the very last moment.

During the interwar period new institutions appeared. Ad-hoc associations of bondholders were constituted in order to deal with the problem of partial repudiation. The IARC, followed by the Committee of the League of Nations, emerged as the key agent of conditionality. These institutional arrangements were originally intended to manage, in a more or less orderly way, adjustments and cost sharing among creditors. Gradually, the conditionality world became so complex that it often produced more problems than solutions. Bulgarian interwar debt history clearly illustrates this intricate machinery. Archives show different creditor groups coming into conflict over goals, with rampant rivalries and interdependencies. For instance, in the 1920s conflicts of interest developed between pre-World War I debts, reparation debts, and stabilization loans issued under the auspices of the League of Nations. In the end, the reparation debt dominated the overall issue owing to the presence of the IARC.[21]

The experience of reparation debts outlined an important aspect of conditionality – namely that nothing could be got from a debtor if access to international finance was not restored first. This clearly illustrated that the most stubborn form of conditionality (that debtors should be isolated from capital markets as long as they had not paid) did not work. In effect, as outlined by Eichengreen (1988: 6), German reparation payments started only after capital flew in and the country was allowed to issue long-term bonds, thus rescheduling its debt. The key was thus to enable the transfer of resources from the debtors to the creditors through an initial reverse transfer that allowed reparations to be rolled over with capital inflows – a principle that had first been tested in the 1923 League-sponsored Austrian stabilization. Yet during this initial phase the need for close monitoring was paramount.

The experience of the early 1920s also demonstrated the impossibility of settling a debt crisis without a comprehensive arrangement that would be suitable for all categories of creditors, which meant they had to agree on a loss-sharing formula. The emergence of such a compromise during the 1920s was the backbone of Bulgaria's reparations settlement. It became possible when global arrangement among the major players was in sight and after consensus on the implied conditionality philosophy was reached. The stabilization loans of 1926 and 1928 also bore the imprint of the two major international economic problems of the time (reparations and the gold standard issue), and this was compounded by the magnified fight for financial power between France and Britain (see Chapter 5). The rising "Anglo-Saxon" strength meant a more flexible approach to the reparation problem, allowing greater capital inflow to debtor countries, in contrast with the strict requirement of the French to pay all debts, political or not, before fresh funds could be provided. The League of Nations stabilization loans (like the previous ones to Austria and Hungary or that to Romania, which would follow suit) were, from the outset, instruments of foreign policy. The rivalry between France and England (which took the shape of the conflict between their respective central banks) focused on the control of Bulgarian economic policy and of the future pledges. The situation was complicated by the intervention of prewar bondholders (mostly French), whom national authorities sought to protect: a possible bond issue by British and American banks was a threat to them. Finally, in the midst of this complex situation the League of Nations, the promoter and trustee of the future loans, had its own agenda, seeking to enhance its own prestige. As a result, the package was polished by the Financial Committee, the leading central banks, and the Federal Reserve Bank of New York, marking the eventual success of Anglo-Saxon plans (see Chapters 2 and 5).

Assessing the macroeconomic "success" of the stabilization loans is by no means an easy task. They achieved a diversification of the country's liability structure and restored Bulgaria's access to the by now British and American capital markets. Some authors have nonetheless criticized these loans, arguing that the well-known Romanian example involved many short-term costs but failed to achieve a sustainable stabilization (see Chapter 5). The Hungarian, Greek, and Bulgarian defaults of the early 1930s are also cited as an evidence of the failure of League's loans (see Chapter 2). A case could be made, however, that Bulgarian loans had a well-founded macroeconomic rationale, and were thus well intended: they correctly identified the badly needed institutional efforts that were precedents to restoring stability. The aftermath of the loans is a different story: their positive impact was bound to be short lived in the context of strong domestic pressures for "easy money" and of the eventual Great Depression.

Dealing with default

Bulgaria announced a partial default in April 1932. The decision followed similar moves in many Latin American and Central European countries. Attempts to find a global solution to the rampant debt problems of the early 1930s failed. As a result, each case was dealt with through negotiations between individual debtor countries and their respective bondholders (Eichengreen 1988). The search for solutions was further complicated by the ambiguous position of the League of Nations. The League's Financial Committee exerted macroeconomic conditionality (a "public good" for creditors) and was as a result a sort of supervisory agency. But as a trustee for the stabilization loans it also had its own vested interests. Since its influence could be detrimental to some categories of bondholders, creditors were prompt to emphasize that the League was not a neutral player, and the Bulgarian authorities often sought to take advantage of existing rivalries.[22]

Proposals to deal with the debt crisis came from various directions. The archives of the Service des archives économiques et financières (SAEF) bear evidence of a "funding plan" put forward in May 1932[23] by Colonel Enaux: an active figure in the lobby of Bulgaria's private creditors. Bulgarian archives and contemporary publications provide evidence of a similar plan formulated by the head of the Debt Directorate, Nikola Stoyanov. Both projects shared basic common features: a dramatic write-off of the debt in line with its sharply reduced market value (in 1934, quotations of Bulgarian bonds were at 5–12 per cent of their face value), achieved by a conversion of old bonds into new ones; and a right for the government to perform buybacks. But the market and the official financial community were not prepared to settle on such terms. A suggestion by Stoyanov along those lines at the September 1932 Conference in Stresa was just ignored.[24]

Bulgaria declared a second partial moratorium on its foreign debt payments in November 1934. The main difference from the 1932 episode was that in this case the Bulgarian decision was unilateral. Moreover, this time Bulgaria was isolated and this signaled it as an openly rogue country: it could no longer, as in 1932, find safety in numbers, and the creditors' stance became stronger. In this instance the bondholders of the pre-World War I and League loans acted in concert under the leadership of the Financial Committee. The conflicting interests between the two groups were ironed out. Bulgaria faced an unavoidable ultimatum and was forced to surrender – clear evidence that creditors' unity can reinforce their bargaining position.

The validity of the lessons from the interwar period was tested half a century later in a very different context. The cycle of the 1920s and 1930s almost repeated itself. In March 1990 the country ceased payments to private creditors. Bulgaria exited from communism in just the same way as Russia had entered it: by declaring default. After an initial "wait and see" period, a specifically tailored "Brady" deal was signed in June 1994. Its main features were remarkably similar to those outlined by the abovementioned Enaux and Stoyanov plans of the 1930s: after heavy provisioning by the creditor banks, the crisis was dealt with through large write-offs, buybacks, rescheduling, and maturity lengthening, with the support of the main classes of creditors (London club, Paris club, the international financial institutions). Thus, again, as in the 1930s, there was a gradual move to a flexible, market-based, and country-specific approach. The mediation and conditionality role of the IMF, on the other hand, closely resembled the role performed by the League of Nations in the 1920s and 1930s.[25]

Conditionality culture: ideas and people

Symbols and orthodoxies

Conditionality produces its own symbols and rites. Money doctoring is a highly hierarchical relationship. Creditors and doctors emphasize the "religious" aspects surrounding the lending ceremony, while creditors often seek to challenge the icons. This mechanism was illustrated early on in Bulgaria, in a context where the recently won independence was accompanied by effervescent nationalism. The public attention devoted to the debt issue might appear incomprehensible in retrospect, especially given the low amounts initially involved: every deal was considered a national trauma and accompanied by endless debates and political turmoil. They provoked at least four cabinet crises at the turn of the century. These tensions reflected the cultural break with the atavistic fears of a closed, archaic, and patriarchal Bulgarian society to move towards the "outside" world.[26] Those fears and its companion economic xenophobia were themselves based on suspicion of capital and capitalism. After World War I the problem was compounded by interference with reparation payments. Bulgarian opinion became extremely sensitive to the signs of national humiliation, and easily (if to an extent rightly) identified creditors' conditionality with war debts. As a result, the rejection of reparations legitimated a reluctance to repay all debts.

During the interwar period, the recurring requests by the League of Nations for a squeeze on the number of government employees were high on the list of symbolic conflicts stemming from material issues. Bulgarian officials and politicians alike counterattacked the measure as an inadmissible interference with national sovereignty. But the real challenge was the resulting constraint on clientelism and protected employment. Similarly, the pressures (during the Depression) for a decrease in public education expenditures provoked protests from the intelligentsia, fearing that the League of Nations would eliminate government-paid jobs for the educated elite. In a broader sense, it was considered that this requirement undermined some fundamental aspects of the Bulgarian modernization model. Since independence, Bulgaria had relied on mass education as an essential vehicle of modernization. Investment in human capital was important, indeed producing at some points an excess supply of qualified labor.

Two symbols became focal points of the public debate on conditionality before World War II: the constant irritation with the physical presence of foreign representatives and the status of the BNB. The status of the state-owned BNB, in particular, was broadly considered as the very essence of Bulgaria's "original" development model. Questioning its status was presented as a challenge to Bulgaria's identity. In fact, vested interests were a driving force behind support for the status quo.

It may be suggested that the gradual depersonalization and bureaucratization of today's conditionality to some extent undermines its symbolic dimension. Although nationalistic politicians exploit it, they have to point to more immaterial scapegoats: "globalization" then becomes the suspect, and the focus of symbolic wars gradually shifts towards anti-globalization activism, or, when it comes to European conditionality, to various forms of Euroscepticism.

As a rule, ideological money doctors are the acting arm of conventional economic orthodoxy. It has always been difficult for pre-communist Bulgarian opinion to accept the notion that adopting "outside" economic ideology is an unavoidable counterpart to getting creditors' money – it is the creditors' prerogative to assess the "appropriateness" of a debtor's policy since it influences the security of the investment. Obviously, assessment is performed according to creditors' values. The problem becomes acute when there are fundamental differences between "imported" and local economic values. The clash between the dominant liberal international money doctors' reference model and the traditionally strong statist and collectivist Bulgarian economic mentality was a major source of conflict throughout the entire century.

The conflict could be partly explained by the fact that, historically, liberalism was always coupled with the hardship of economic stabilization. Almost by definition, money doctors preach liberal economic reforms as medicine for financial distress, thus – wrongly but unavoidably – associating a certain philosophy with unpopular and painful measures in the public's eyes. But the traditionally marginal place of liberal ideology in Bulgaria has more profound roots. As Stoyan Bochev wrote in 1931:

> capitalism is unsympathetic to Bulgarians. If capitalism in the other countries, at least in its beginnings, was considered as a source of social welfare and had the energetic public and state support, it was considered [in Bulgaria] as an artificial addendum to the economic structure of the country.[27]

Alternative, "soft," ways exerted a constant appeal:

> We want to skip…the capitalistic stage of economic development, to obtain the fruits of the bourgeois and capitalist regime, but without capitalism itself, without the capitalistic organization of enterprises…. While everywhere cooperatives are considered as capitalism's correctives [in Bulgaria] they are seen as alternatives to the capitalist stage of development.[28]

These statements touched the very heart of the cultural roots of the Bulgarian economic mentality, and of the philosophy of national economic development.

It should be observed that the intensity of conflicts between money doctors and their local counterparts was not a simple mirror-image of their ideological differences. The key 1922 Law on the ceilings on money circulation, for instance, happened to be adopted by one of the most populist Bulgarian governments of the interwar period. On the other hand, it might have been expected that the semi-autocratic regime in place since May 1934 would be an easier and more reliable partner for the Financial Committee and the bondholders. Yet the succession of Bulgarian governments in the mid-1930s turned out to be less than cooperative and to favor confrontation.

Finally, in exploring the ideological dimensions of money doctoring, attention should be given to cases when a country becomes a test for new schemes. Then, the program itself becomes a symbol. Bulgaria twice found itself in this position. The first instance was in the 1920s when it integrated the small group of countries subjected to the League's stabilization experiments. The second instance is the present currency board arrangement – a rare monetary regime implemented in half a dozen countries. The Bulgarian experience supports the view that the status of a "test economy" changes the conditionality framework to some extent. First, the country is treated with a touch of cautious benevolence. Second, the specific status and the conceptual challenge tend to attract money doctors of a higher intellectual standard. Although this assertion could not be empirically proven, the association of first-order economists with the extreme cases of economic pathology is a fact of life.

Language

Conditionality also has a language. On the basis of Bulgarian experience, it is possible to follow the stylistic evolution of documents over time. Writing reflected the increasingly bureaucratic relationship. The reports of Paribas representatives in Sofia to their headquarters are rich in all kinds of information, and display a personal touch and grand style incomparable to the technocratic e-mail vernacular of today's bureaucrats. Similarly, League reports are much more ideologically stamped and confrontational than the formally neutral and diplomatic IMF "letters of intent."

In addition, in backward countries the money doctors' vocabulary typically arrives in a local vacuum. In the early twentieth century the limited domestic elite was not experienced in economic and financial matters; nor did it have any kind of cultural tradition that would have enabled it to develop its own concepts. The money doctors' language thus became the language of choice. A similar phenomenon was observed in the early 1990s with the inflow of the IMF slang in an almost completely Marxist-indoctrinated environment.

With the language of economics came the language of numbers. The assessment of a country's creditworthiness, for instance, is not possible without commonly agreed data. The most crucial material to construct relevant figures was typically, in the early twentieth century, hidden by the local authorities. In this way, the assessment of the amount of BNB gold reserves, the volume of government debt and deficits, or the money issue and cover ratio escaped scrutiny. In these "information wars" the contribution of foreign advisers was crucial for setting out a conceptual framework, which made the delivery of funds conditional upon the production of relevant numbers. As a result they contributed to providing a more comprehensive and explicit set of economic statistics. Fiscal and monetary data, in particular, have been developed to a great extent for the needs of foreign monitoring. In the early 1930s the focal point was the development of reliable and transparent fiscal returns that would consolidate the numerous "autonomous" accounts used as a means of relaxing the official fiscal restrictions. A similar exercise was repeated in the 1990s, when, beside reliable fiscal data, missing monetary statistics had to be created from scratch.

Money doctors in murky waters

An important area of foreign conditionality concerns the complex relationships with local politics. Money doctors are not outsiders in the local scene, but, rather, local representatives of the outside. Bulgarian politicians used them as favorite targets, orchestrating public campaigns against their physical presence and policy prescriptions. However, while using anti-conditionality slogans at home, they also exploited conditionality for domestic political pressure when necessary: conditionality requirements have always been a perfect alibi.[29]

Money doctors thus played an active role in the domestic political life of both borrowers and lenders. As power brokers, they have always had a temptation to influence public opinions, for instance through newspaper campaigns and the media. Léon Berger, the French head of Dette Publique Ottomane, for example, organized a successful hostile campaign in France to undermine the 1896 loan to the Bulgarian Agricultural Bank. The campaign was motivated by the interests of the Dette's French bondholders, who considered that Bulgaria should not obtain new credits while in arrears with payments due to their institution. In the same vein, with Paribas this time as the perpetrator, we find a curious series of six articles, prepared in 1901 and destined to be published in the Bulgarian press.[30] The articles were promoting a loan deal with the Bulgarian government, pledged by the concession of the tobacco monopoly ("*Régie du tabac*"). The wording, the tone, and the arguments exhibit a distinctive mass propaganda style. The unsigned texts were tailored with a good knowledge of the national psychology and of the most sensitive questions for public opinion. Similar endeavors may be found in more recent history as well. With the launch of the idea of a currency board for Bulgaria, in late 1996, the IMF inserted in the local media a set of simplistic articles meant to explain the merits of the arrangement to a virgin public opinion. They bear a surprisingly close resemblance to the 1901 specimens.

Creditors' bargaining position was arguably stronger when money doctors succeeded in building a close local network. Yet these connections bred corruption. The early twentieth century provides evidence of such problems. In the archives of Paribas, as well as in other French archives and reports of Bulgarian Parliamentary Inquiry Commissions, the identity of the suspects is revealed: local representatives of the foreign banks, international financial adventurers and lobbyists, top executives of big concerns. Their Bulgarian counterparts were ministers, members of parliament, and bankers. The semi-official status of the bondholders' delegate facilitated his implication in business deals. He sat on the boards of financial institutions affiliated to the creditors' banks. Thus remuneration for the traffic of influence took very different forms, from simple monetary payments to the arrangement of important business services.[31]

The corruption network was to an extent something that was commonly accepted as a fact of life on both sides. The interplay between politics and economic interests was often criticized by the opposition, but its roots were never really addressed, in part because everyone waited for his turn to come. In late 1918 the French occupation authorities produced a quite telling document in this respect.[32] They established a list of the joint stock companies created during World War I, and for each one reported the precise political clientelism that had led to its creation. The document outlined the indisputable influence of German interests during the war. What was missing, however, was a corresponding large-scale French endeavor of 1915 (known as the De Clozière Affair) to do the same.

The new conditionality style in the post-World War I period changed the position of the representatives. They acquired official diplomatic status and their presence was more institutionalized. However, this did not prevent conflicts of interest, or even rumors of corruption. The scandals merely shifted to the domain of international relations. One of the most publicized conflicts, for example, concerned the role of the League Commissioner (a Frenchman) in the attribution of public contracts by Bulgarian railways. It appeared that France had secretly bound the authorization for its portion of the 1928 stabilization loan to promises by the Bulgarian government to sign industrial contracts with French companies. The promise was made public and caused tensions with Czechoslovakia and Italy, which competed with France for these markets. Those events were not isolated cases confined to a small country. Corruption was a generalized phenomenon during the bond mania of the 1920s. U.S. Congressional hearings demonstrated that American banks offering underwriting of foreign securities were extremely active corrupting agents, just like European banks had been in the prewar years.[33]

Money doctors: backgrounds and profiles

The personality of money doctors is a matter that would seem better fitted to biographers and psychologists: it is difficult to generalize from personal details. Upon closer inspection, however, portraits of money doctors are less varied than might be expected.

There is a close correspondence, for instance, between the culture of the institutions enforcing conditionality and the people in charge. Bulgaria in the early 1900s illustrates the close links between the financial elite and the higher civil servants that was characteristic of the French Republic's *nomenklatura*. The transition between the two communities was easy, thanks to the traditional practice of "*pantouflage*."[34] French citizens continued almost exclusively to control the conditionality monitoring in Bulgaria during the entire pre-World War II period. Georges Bousquet and Marcel Charlot (representatives of the bondholders), as well as René Charron, Jean Watteau, and Pierre Cheysson (Commissioners of the League of Nations), played a crucial role in shaping Bulgaria's economic policy.

It is dangerous to generalize, but Bulgaria seems to have attracted two kinds of foreigners: end-career civil servants or ambitious beginners. Conditions in a peripheral country provide good career opportunities, especially for the eager young desirous of demonstrating their skills. This may explain the zeal which has typically characterized the presence of monitors: a tough stance towards debtors is not only a potentially comfortable position, but also a quality praised by hierarchical superiors. A guiding principle for foreign representatives has always been that it is better to have their ardor cooled by the home supervisor than to be blamed for a mild position towards the debtor country. In cases of tensions with local authorities or with the Paris headquarters, the representative could change himself into a more or less autonomous player in the creditors–debtors game, able to influence information and the decision-making process.[35]

Aside from the banker and the civil servant, another type of money doctor became more widespread in the interwar years: it was the academic doctor with a "theoretical" motivation. Such a type is well illustrated by Jacques Rueff and his 1927 mission in Bulgaria. Rueff was then a League official. He was serving what could be called in today's IFI jargon a "country mission" in Sofia, headed by Sir Otto Niemeyer. According to his memoirs, however, Rueff's goals were "scientific." They had later policy implications. By his own account, it was during these missions in Greece, Bulgaria, and Portugal that he shaped the basis of the conceptual approach he applied years later for the 1958 stabilization of the franc after De Gaulle came to power.[36]

While we find the French hands on in Bulgaria, the Britons were never far away and wielded considerable importance in the overall process. The macroeconomic ideology of the League was strongly influenced by personalities like Niemeyer, who at the same time closely followed Bulgarian debt affairs. The position of experts from smaller countries is more ambiguous. They were generally (if often wrongly) regarded as indirect representatives of their countries' sphere of influence. A typical case was the appointment, in 1932, of Nikolai Koestner as technical adviser of the BNB.[37] Koestner was an Estonian expert and his appointment came after the aforementioned clash between France and Britain over control of Bulgarian economic policy. A compromise was reached by finding a "politically neutral and technically adequate personality." Political neutrality, however, is always difficult to define. Because of his professional background the French considered Koestner as a vehicle for the Bank of England's influence. On the other side he was seen as suitable for his practical "experience at the issuing bank of an eminently agrarian country with a primitive civilization," as well as for his command of a Slavonic language. His appointment was finally part of a more comprehensive general deal. While France agreed to concede this technical position, it kept tight control of monetary policy in Romania – a country that was considered more important to French interests. It is worth noting that in retrospect the controversy proved superfluous. Koestner exercised his duties with loyalty and professionalism for almost a decade. This is a clear indication that money doctoring is perhaps better achieved, in an ideal world, when national passion and vested interests are kept at bay and tasks are performed in a professional, routine manner.

The post-World War II era pursued the interwar trend by seeking to minimize the numerous money doctors' potential conflicts of interests. In today's international financial institutions a clearer divide is set between the "theoretical" and "analytical" work and the "operational" responsibilities. This was achieved by introducing a division of labor between better-defined institutional units. Specific rules have tried to limit the overlap between business interests and economic advice to governments. The extent to which these newer arrangements have succeeded in improving the situation is controversial. A large-scale commercialization of macroeconomic reform packages has progressed together with post-communist transition, and the growing mobility between international financial institutions and the financial community has undermined the formal regulation of conflicts of interests.

In the present context, national specifics tend to fade away. A faceless cosmopolitan army of international bureaucrats, freelancers, and private consultants performs the job of foreign advising. The diversity of their institutional affiliations has grown impressively, ranging from non-governmental organizations (NGOs) to supranational structures. Yet behind this diversity is a spectacular doctrinal standardization fostered by the Washington consensus, the Brussels orthodoxy, and the burgeoning consultancy industry which lives on selling similar standardized "conceptual" products. The "politically correct" clichés on "good governance" are reproduced today by an infinite number of voices. The banalization of the economics profession produced a banalization of money doctoring itself. The personality of the foreign adviser has lost social weight, together with the tendency to standardize diagnostics and corresponding cures. The lack of strong personalities with a global vision (J.M. Keynes is the archetype) is a natural outcome in this context.[38]

The problems money doctors faced in the interwar period now seem less trivial: their pitfalls are nothing but a preview of modern problems. At the same time, old dilemmas are today approached in a new setting. Institution building is not the strength of today's mainstream economics. It is, rather, "market building," with the mastering of the corresponding sophisticated risk assessment and risk management instruments. Great reformist projects are over. The ongoing discussion on reshaping the international financial architecture, for example, is marked by a bureaucratic and "gray" approach where the room for theoretical creativity is extremely narrow. The essential point remains the balance of forces between leading countries, maintained through a careful distribution of top positions in the ever-growing pool of key international financial institutions.

Cross influences

The outline of the conditionality culture would not be complete if we only focused on foreign doctors. It has been rightly observed that external doctoring is always a bilateral learning process, involving the advisers' counterpart local authorities and experts.[39] Foreign advice is often provided as a means of importing reputedly "higher" foreign competence in a community lacking professional expertise. At the same time, a case could be made that the lack of technical expertise in Bulgaria has never been a major problem, at least beginning in the interwar years. The economic elite gradually gained know-how, partly through training abroad. By the early 1930s economic and financial analysis was at a decent level. The problems were of another nature. First, there was a lack of a critical mass of knowledge that would have served to develop a coherent homegrown paradigm. When a global vision was needed in order to face major policy challenges, the projects produced were either "plagiaries" of lending countries' dominant philosophy or social utopias with systematic biases towards state intervention and collectivist ideologies. On the other hand, the interface between expert knowledge and economic policy was never easy. Money doctors were powerful enough to design the framework of the reforms, but never to implement them in a consistent fashion.

Thus the role of the "IFI's man" in the host country, the privileged interlocutor of foreign money doctors, the main vehicle of their messages, and the translator of conflicting positions into a common conceptual language, was essential. This function was traditionally fulfilled by the Governor of the National Bank, or (to a lesser extent) by the Minister of Finance, who was, as a rule, more exposed to political pressures. The most successful Bulgarian negotiators were often professional bankers converted into civil servants or "neutral" experts. Their quality was of the utmost importance in determining the country's bargaining position. It was weakened when Bulgaria was represented by unconvincing and unprepared political figures.[40] Finding the right counterpart to foreign money doctors was by no means an easy task. A curious case occurred in 1934 when, for a while, the Bulgarian Minister of Finance suggested that the Financial Committee "provide any candidate deemed suitable [by the Financial Committee] for the vacant position of BNB Governor!"[41] Beyond personal qualities, however, most governments facing foreign conditionality reproduced a typical split – a handful of reformist technocrats outnumbered by cabinet members who followed their populist instinct, political agenda, and voters.

On the other hand, the local environment did influence the beliefs of foreign money doctors and thus made a decisive contribution to economic science. The Bulgarian experience offers two remarkable insights in this respect. From his mission in Bulgaria, J. Rueff emphasizes the idea that it was essential, for a successful stabilization to take place, to focus on the specific circumstances rather than proceed on dogmatic principles. The recipes for what he called the "incredibly Malthusian" Bulgarian economy could not be those for the general case, certainly not those he would apply to France thirty years later. Rueff preached conceptual humility – to stay on firm theoretical grounds, but to take on board the uniqueness of each particular case. "Do not hamper the profit-maximizing automatism by introducing a priori considerations that are pure financial aesthetic," he once wrote.[42]

From a different point of view, a well-informed American observer expressed a severe judgment on the dogmatic blindness of the League of Nations regarding central bank reform. His conclusion is worthy of being quoted at length:

> There is, to be sure, an important danger to be guarded against, the presence of which has been apparent, in some measure, in the League's relations with Bulgaria. It is the temptation on the part of foreign specialists to proceed too fast, to become impatient with the slowness with which basic reforms must necessarily be introduced in an economically more or less backward community. The controversy between the Bulgarian Government and the Financial Committee of the League over the transformation of the Bulgarian National Bank is an instance of this. It is difficult to see what useful purpose could be served in insisting upon the reorganization of the Bank into a privately owned corporation, when it already had, after the reforms of 1926 and 1928, ample safeguards from government interference in the management of its affairs. The mere fact that a quasi-private corporation is the form toward which the banks of issue have been tending in economically better developed countries is a very poor argument in the case of Bulgaria. The FC [Financial Committee] of the League would probably have done much better if it had taken from the start a more moderate position in this particular instance by proposing, for example, an equally effective but intermediate form of organization of the type in existence in many European countries, namely a joint stock company with government participation.[43]

Pasvolsky's lesson is still valid as a general principle, and still not fully digested in the present context.

Conclusion

The long historical perspective allows the continuity in money doctoring during the past century to be stressed. Many of the basic elements in today's conditionality could already be found in the scheme that accompanied the 1902 loan to Bulgaria. Similarly, it can be argued that by the late 1920s to the mid-1930s essential IMF-based conditionality principles were already in place. The interwar period was thus the laboratory of post-World War II practice.

Bulgaria never managed fully to escape foreign monitoring. For a short while, thanks to a coincidence of favorable economic and political factors, the country approached a "free" status with the loan of 1909 extended by Austrian banks. For the first and last time the contract did not mention any specific pledge or the presence of a special comptroller. However, this was a brief episode and, for a number of reasons, Bulgaria was forced to approach German banks in 1914, and very tight conditions were again imposed. Afterwards, the government's access to capital markets continued to be a permanent problem. For decades this access was granted through official intermediaries and at the price of direct conditionality. The last episode was the financial isolation of the country following the 1990 moratorium. Bulgaria had to rely for years on the resources of international financial institutions, and it is only after the debt problem was settled in 1994 and the economy stabilized in 1997 that the government regained the potential to float bonds.

In a medium-term perspective two major developments are likely to occur. Bulgaria is shifting gradually from the area of influence of the IMF to that of the European Union. The driving force of this process is the convergence process that paves the way to European monetary union. At the same time, the country will be more directly exposed to the discipline and appraisal imposed by the markets. Both processes are in conflict on many points. The outcome will undoubtedly be a new and original blend of conditionality culture.

Notes

1 I would like to thank Marc Flandreau for his careful reading of the draft and valuable suggestions.
2 Wynne (1951).
3 Tobacco stamps were printed in France and delivered to the Bulgarian Ministry of Finance in exchange for coupon payment. The Bulgarian authorities in turn sold the stamps to the public.
4 Banque de Paris et des Pays-Bas (Paribas), 4\Cabet-1\77, 83.
5 The model was applied in the Ottoman Empire, but also in Egypt and Greece.
6 The conflicts between the Commission and the Bulgarian authorities (as reflected in the French Archives Nationales /AAJ7/1–37/ and in Bulgarian archives) reveal the extreme form of external conditionality: conflicts developed over budget expenditures and the tax burden, the monetary policy stance, the scope of government intervention, the foreign debt maturities and arrears.
7 Although not in identical terms, this kind of conditionality on foreign debt has always been a familiar practice. The first loan contracts stipulated special provisions on the proceeds and feasibility of future credits to Bulgaria. Thresholds on new debt have routinely been included in IMF-supported programs.
8 See Chapter 2.
9 A formally symmetric, but truly cosmetic, Bulgarian government Commissioner with suspensive veto was also appointed.
10 Unsurprisingly, the influence of the Commissioner went well beyond his formal rights. For instance, René Charron, Commissioner from 1926 to 1932, remained a recognized authority on Bulgarian economic affairs long after he resigned from his position in 1931. His mediation has been sought on various occasions during crises in relations with the Financial Committee.
11 Different national conditionality "styles" can be outlined. The French system emphasized direct and personal control. In peaceful times the Germans have had a more disseminated, less visible, but highly effective presence in key positions in Bulgaria. During war episodes, as allies, their hard control was much like the Soviet type. The Anglo-Saxons have been more influential through the imposition of a conceptual, doctrinal, and institutional framework.
12 See Flandreau *et al.* (1998) and Chapter 1 in this volume.
13 Mintz (1951: 2).
14 *Handbook on American Underwriting of Foreign Securities* (1930: 41, 43, 104, 122).
15 Wynne (1951).
16 During the communist years the ultimate security accepted by Western creditors was of an essentially intangible nature: it was in fact the political stability of the regime and the implicit assurance that Bulgaria would be bailed out by the USSR in case of

distress. Such a bailout effectively happened at the start of the 1980s but failed in the next debt crisis at the end of the decade. Even taking into account some biasing political motives, creditors reacted by hardening the terms of rollover and by limiting access to credit, thus accelerating (with the USSR no longer a "payer of last resort") the Bulgarian moratorium of March 1990.

17 Banque de Paris et des Pays-Bas (Paribas), 4\Cabet-1\78.

18 See Flandreau *et al.* (1998) and Chapter 1 in this volume.

19 Even after the implementation of the 1922 Law depreciation of the currency continued. The final stabilization came only after the reparation debt problem was officially settled in March 1923 (with a tacit substantial reduction of the Treaty figures), and a complete monopoly of the BNB on foreign exchange transactions was introduced in December 1923.

20 Although the League's proposition adequately addressed the poor track record of BNB's relationships with the state, it felt bound to compromise in order to accommodate Bulgarian fears. One exotic proposal suggested that foreign shareholding should be ruled out, the bank's capital was to be divided into small shares, special preferences were foreseen for small shareholders at the public offer, the possible concentration of shares was strictly forbidden, and the general assembly was supposed to have the right to elect only four members of the board, the remaining four being appointed by professional associations. Even this strange design (close to a "mass privatization" scheme) was not adopted and the Bulgarian government preserved state ownership. See Protocole... (1928: annexes I and II).

21 The first agreement concerning Bulgarian reparations was signed on March 21, 1923. The Ruhr occupation and its failure underlined the limits of the Allies' extremist positions aiming at strict compliance with the Versailles system without consideration of the actual solvency of the "debtor" countries. The Bulgarian agreement was part of the precedent-setting game. It was made possible only after the evolution of views on German reparations.

22 Playing on conflicts among creditors is an evident temptation, but its opportunities are rarely manageable by debtors. There is no doubt that a debtor's bargaining position was cyclically sensitive, improving in a context of strong competition among lenders ("emerging markets" always present attractive investment opportunities).

23 SAEF, B33.651. Stoyanov (1932).

24 It seems, however, that the practice of undeclared market-based solutions through buybacks was surprisingly widespread. According to Eichengreen and Portes, a dozen debtor countries bought back 15–50 per cent of their bonds (1989: 45–6). In the case of Bulgaria, a buyback at a 90 per cent discount was formally allowed in the 1935 agreement with the bondholders. During the second half of the 1930s the government realized buybacks on a large scale.

25 The settlement of the Latin American debt crisis of the 1980s went through the same cycle, from extreme conditionality to market solutions. In the 1980s, as in the 1930s, the initial responses were of the tough sort. Creditors sought to isolate misbehaving debtors from capital markets. This policy was followed by the "Baker plan," which allowed some financial flows (mainly from the IMF) to be injected into debtors in distress in order to enhance their solvency. Finally, "Brady-type" solutions were designed: by relying on market perceptions, the Brady bonds enabled investors to break away from the initial approach. See Eichengreen and Portes (1989, 1995).

26 A number of irrational "symbolic wars" could be mentioned, ranging from insignificant details to essential principles. A tentative list includes such different topics as the location of the delegate's office, his diplomatic or tax status, the amount of his remuneration and of some benefits (paid out of the Bulgarian government budget), etc.

27 Bochev (1931: 102).

28 Bochev (1928: 72).

29 As has been observed, such a situation is not far away from James's analysis of the IMF as a "whipping boy" (see Chapter 3) or of the current relations between the European Commission and governments of the member countries.
30 Banque de Paris et des Pays-Bas (Paribas), 4\Cabet-1\80.
31 In a similar vein, it is highly symptomatic that such a respected and academically reputable figure as Kemmerer received a secret annual "commission" from the bank Dillon, Read & Co. (see Chapter 2). Let us note as well that the League's Financial Committee was made up of eminent bankers: an overlapping of business interests and economic policy prescriptions was almost inevitable.
32 SAEF, B31.578.
33 Mintz (1951: 68, 77).
34 A soft shift in the private (or state-owned) business, arranged for the caste of the top French civil servants that leave or are forced to leave their position.
35 The activities of Bousquet in Bulgaria (1902–12) are a classical case in this respect.
36 Rueff (1977: 63).
37 SAEF, B32.800.
38 It might also be emphasized that a widening gap between the promoted doctrine and the personal status of modern money doctors is noticeable. It is not so much (as in former times) their opulence in poor countries that irritates. It is often the fact that their personal status and institutional background seem closer to the old socialist values (job security, fringe benefits) than to the labor flexibility and market principles that they preach.
39 Rich archival evidence is available in this case. It is fortunate that the chief Bulgarian foreign debt negotiator from 1919 to 1939 was the unmovable Nikola Stoyanov – an extremely rare case of expert longevity in the national administration. He left an extraordinarily well-organized personal archive that is a first-order source for Bulgarian debt history. See Stoyanov (1932).
40 This was the case in the period of greatest tension in the negotiations with bondholders during the fall of 1934.
41 SAEF, B32.800.
42 Rueff (1977: 63).
43 Pasvolsky (1930: 296).

References

Archives Nationales, Commission des Réparations de Bulgarie (1922–31), Fonds AJ7/1–40.
Avramov, R. (1999a) "Central Banking in Bulgaria: A Historical Perspective," in *The Art of Central Banking in Eastern Europe in the 90s*, Conference on the occasion of the 120th anniversary of the Bulgarian National Bank, Sofia: Bulgarian National Bank.
Avramov, R. (ed.) (1999b) *120 Years of the Bulgarian National Bank, 1879–1999 (An Annotated Chronology)*, Sofia: Bulgarian National Bank.
Banque de Paris et des Pays-Bas (Paribas), Fonds d'archives.
Bochev, S. (1928) "Bulgaria and the Foreign Capitals," in *Capitalism in Bulgaria: Selected Economic Writings, 1911–1935* (in Bulgarian), edited, presented and compiled by Roumen Avramov, Sofia: Bulgarian Science and Culture Fund.
Bochev, S. (1931) "Capitalism in Bulgaria," in *Capitalism in Bulgaria: Selected Economic Writings, 1911–1935* (in Bulgarian), edited, presented and compiled by Roumen Avramov, Sofia: Bulgarian Science and Culture Fund.
Bulgarian National Bank (BNB) (1999, 2000, 2001) *Selected Documents, vol. I 1878–1900, vol. II 1901–1914, vol. III 1915–1929* (in Bulgarian), edited by R. Avramov, Sofia: National Archives of Bulgaria and Bulgarian National Bank.

Eichengreen, B. (1988) "Resolving Debt Crises: An Historical Perspective," *CEPR Discussion Papers Series*, no. 239, London: CEPR.

Eichengreen, B. and R. Portes (1989) *Dealing with Debt: The 1930s and the 1980s*, WPS 1989/August, Washington: World Bank.

Eichengreen, B. and R. Portes (1995) *Crisis? What Crisis? Orderly Workouts for Sovereign Debtors*, London: CEPR.

Flandreau, M., J. Le Cacheux and F. Zumer (1998) "Stability without a Pact? Lessons from the European Gold Standard," *Economic Policy* 13(26): 117–49.

Handbook on American Underwriting of Foreign Securities (1930) Washington: U.S. Department of Commerce.

Mintz, I. (1951) *Deterioration in the Quality of Foreign Bonds Issued in the United States, 1920–1930*, New York: National Bureau of Economic Research.

Pasvolsky, L. (1930) *Bulgaria's Economic Position*, Washington, DC: Brookings Institution.

Protocole (avec Annexes) approuvé par le Conseil de la Société des Nations et signé au nom du Gouvernement Bulgare le 10 mai 1928 (1928) Genève: C.338.M.961928.II [F.547].

Rueff, J. (1977) "De l'Aube au crépuscule. Autobiographie," in *Oeuvres completes*, vol. 1, Paris: Plon.

Service des Archives Économiques et Financières (SAEF). Paris: Direction du Trésor.

Sessions, G. (1992) *Prophesying upon the Bones: J. Reuben Clarck and the Foreign Debt Crisis 1933–1939*, Chicago, IL: University of Illinois Press.

Stoyanov, N. (1932) Personal Archives, State Historical Archives, Fund 1067, Folder 285.

Wynne, W. (1951) "Selected Case Histories of Governmental Foreign Bond Defaults and Debt Readjustment (Bulgaria)," in *State Insolvency and Foreign Bondholders*, vol. II, New Haven, CT: Yale University Press; reprinted by Garland Publishing Inc, New York & London, 1983.

Part III

Experts agree

International financial institutions
and macroeconomic orthodoxy

8 "Money talks"

Competition and cooperation with the League of Nations, 1929–40

Patricia Clavin[1]

There is a widely held assumption among social scientists that economics has had the strongest impact of any social science on the evolution of government policy thanks to "the elegant simplicity of its behavioural assumptions and from the possibilities of deductive reasoning and [the] formal analysis associated with them."[2] The time has come to interrogate this supposition more widely.[3] Historians and economists have devoted considerable attention to the making of economic policy, charting, in particular, the adoption and application of Keynesian and later non-Keynesian economic policies in the dominant western economies in the years after 1945.[4] But when it comes to the interwar period much remains to be done. While there has been some research into the contributions made by particular institutions and individuals to the development of economic policy, the attempt to draw the impact of economic advisors across national and institutional boundaries remains at an early stage.[5] Little attention also has been paid to the construction and application of policy advice in an international context. The majority of published work has focused on the rise and fall of central bank cooperation and its determining role in defining the character and success of Europe's economic and monetary reconstruction after the First World War.[6] This focus on the character and quality of central bank cooperation has caused us to neglect other aspects of informal cooperation like the exchange of ideas and personnel across national and institutional frontiers, which also shaped international financial cooperation.

The interwar period marked a watershed in the practice of international money doctoring in a number of important respects. Most significant was the creation of the League of Nations, a prime mover in the generation and dissemination of economic intelligence on an international scale. There remain notable gaps in our understanding of the contribution made by the Financial and Economic Committees of the League of Nations. These were the first international institutions dedicated to facilitating monetary and economic cooperation on a wide range of issues, contrasting with the few international institutions, like the Bank of International Settlements, that were founded later with a more focused agenda. These institutions not only helped to develop specific ideas and proposals, but produced intelligence and data that helped policy-makers interpret the world in which the policy was drafted and applied. Most published studies focus on specific outcomes of the committees' work: the contribution of the Financial Committees to the stabilization of the Austrian and Hungarian currencies in 1924; and the landmark Bruce Report of 1939, which proposed reforming the Economic and Financial wing of the League into an "autonomous" mechanism to challenge the rise of economic nationalism and to promote political disarmament.[7]

With their close focus on the "output" of the committees, however, these accounts offer no sustained appraisal of the limits of these institutions to shape international economic relations, nor sufficient materials to facilitate a comprehensive evaluation of their function and impact.[8] We must also move beyond the extensively used published accounts of key officials to the archival record of the League's interaction with nation-states, for such an approach would help to reconnect the history of international financial relations in the interwar period to those after 1945. What is needed is an integrated, structural, and process-oriented approach incorporating relevant primary materials focusing on the context of their establishment as committees; the selection of commissioners; the organizational structures; their strategies (content and implementation); and their subsequent impact on the "real world." While it is beyond the scope of this chapter to attempt a comprehensive response to this approach for the entire interwar period, the intention is to apply this analytical framework to explore the League's contribution to money doctoring during the Great Depression.[9]

Although the Covenant of the League of Nations was almost silent on the subject of its likely financial and economic activities, the financial upheaval occasioned by the First World War determined that this aspect of international cooperation could not be ignored for long.[10] The Financial and Economic Committee which ensued grew out of the Provisional Advisory Committee set up in 1919 and was incorporated into the permanent machinery of the League at the Brussels Conference of 1920. There subsequently emerged a subsidiary Economic, Financial and Transit Department (Section), comprised of distinct committees and directed by successive Britons, Walter Layton, Frank Nixon, and Arthur Salter. Another Briton, Alexander Loveday, went on to dominate its activities in the 1930s after the department underwent further reorganization in 1931.[11] (The consequence of this British domination of senior League positions also needs to be better understood.)[12]

At the outset, the composition and many of the ambitions of the Financial Committee were shaped by the past, comprising, as it did, men drawn from the ranks of private and central banks. Gradually, however, the legacy of nineteenth-century financial cooperation was challenged by the incorporation of civil servants from the finance ministries and treasuries of member states, supported by expert advisors drawn from academia. The Economic Committee was composed principally of the latter two groups: officials from member governments and private experts who had particular expertise in questions of tariffs, trade, the gold standard, public works, and so on. The employment of these new figures alone marked a significant extension of the diplomatic canvas of the nineteenth century and the diminution of traditional controls and hierarchies.[13]

As with all League appointments, the principal ambition was to secure the services of men who were well qualified in their individual capacities and who were loyal to the League. At the same time, it was essential for the prospects of international cooperation that the appointees both reflected the views of, and were held in some esteem by, their respective national governments.[14] The expertise and clout of these chosen individuals, it was hoped, would connect national political structures to the League and facilitate cooperation.[15] Indeed, the more efficacious their work for the League, the greater the risk to their reputation and influence within their "home" government.[16]

Measuring the performance of individual money doctors seconded to the League cuts to the heart of any attempt to assess either the historical role of particular advisors or the contribution made by the Financial Committee to the coordination of financial initiatives taken on a national or international level. The obvious way to measure the Financial Committee's contribution to policy development is to assess how far the Committee and its advisors were able to present feasible alternative proposals for action to deal with a specific issue and thereby alter the political decisions taken by nation-states. However, it is equally important to study the long-term educational impact of the Committee's work, be it in concrete educational developments like the creation of a Committee of Statistical Experts or in the admittedly more diffuse task of providing a clear, critical, imaginative, and sustained critique of government policy.[17]

So much for the wider context; now for specifics: this chapter seeks to explore two, interrelated questions. The first asks how far the Financial Committee of the League of Nations formed an integrated and effective part of international economic relations during the Great Depression. This bird's-eye view of international financial advising will tease out how far the League coordinated, complemented, duplicated, or competed with state and private institutions offering financial advice. It will focus on the years between 1929 and 1933 in an attempt to draw out the practical, political, and intellectual limitations of the League's efforts to coordinate international monetary policy to combat the depression.[18] Studying the contribution of the League of Nations to the dissemination and implementation of economic advice provides the opportunity of answering a secondary question: whether the League generated and promoted a transnational class of advisors. The chapter will explore some of the ways in which these individuals, working in the "borderlands," connected national political economies to the international economy as a whole. Specifically, we emphasize that money doctors also attempt to build connections to the general public, potentially widening the constituency in support of any change advocated by national or international authorities.[19] In addition, the chapter will illustrate that it is not easy to classify money doctors precisely as institutional or private agents given their sometimes simultaneous employment in a variety of institutions: universities, national and international committees, governments, charities, international foundations, think-tanks, and the media. The boundaries between these fields of employment are more porous than such categories suppose.

The Financial Committee and the Great Depression

In 1946 the Carnegie Endowment for International Peace published a short survey of the League of Nations' financial and economic activities in the interwar period. Written by Martin Hill, an official of the Economic and Financial Section of the League between 1927 and 1933, the book aimed to offer an "objective study of the facts" of international economic and financial cooperation to educate agents of international cooperation in the future.[20] The study has been used widely in a number of subsequent accounts of the Department's work.[21] But despite its grand claims to objectivity the text is clearly a prescriptive history, offering a critical reading of the past lessons of international cooperation with the intention of shaping future practice. Thanks to the pedigree of its author, and the extensive editorial input of Alexander Loveday, a former Director of the Economic, Financial and Transit Department of the League of Nations, the book also offers an insight into the League's perspective on both the nature of the economic and financial crisis which faced it after 1930 and the role of the League in facilitating recovery.

When it came to prioritizing the challenges confronting the economic and financial organization of the League, top of Hill's list came the collapse in primary prices, the burden of debt carried by particular central and eastern European states, and the restrictions to international trade. (Indeed, of the eleven problems identified by the League, eight of them related directly to the imposition of tariffs and quotas.) By contrast, the financial crisis of 1931 and the ensuing breakdown of the gold standard are summarized in one short paragraph (Hill 1946: 57–61). The priorities appear to stand in sharp contrast to what is now seen to be the pivotal role played by financial problems, notably the operation and ethos of the international gold standard, in the causes and course of the Great Depression. Recent studies of the Depression have underlined that countries that broke free of the gold standard enjoyed the most sustained economic recovery. It has also been proposed that a more enduring and widespread economic recovery may have been achieved if leading monetary powers had cooperated to launch a program to revalue currencies in relation to gold on a multilateral basis (Eichengreen 1995: 316–18). The opportunity for such an initiative existed at the time of the World Economic Conference in the summer of 1933. This gathering, sponsored and coordinated by the League of Nations, came at an opportune moment in the monetary history of the interwar period: by June 1933 it had become clear that Britain's departure from gold in September 1931 was not as "temporary" as the British government had claimed; a number of gold-linked currencies which had not yet opted for exchange controls were experiencing sustained speculatory pressure, notably the Dutch florin; and, most significantly, in April 1933 the United States dollar was floated in a deliberate break with past monetary orthodoxy.

The notion that a multilateral revaluation of currencies in relation to gold at the World Economic Conference would have triggered a more sustained global economic recovery than that achieved in the 1930s is more than just wishful thinking on the part of economists preoccupied with what *should* (rather than *could*) have been done to combat the Great Depression. The archival record in Britain and the United States reveals that in both countries money doctors, acting in a private and an institutional capacity, generated proposals that centered on the notion of a multilateral revaluation of currencies on the gold standard at the World Economic Conference. In Britain the Economic Advisory Council argued in favor of "an amicable international agreement, based on all-round devaluation."[22] The failure to initiate the right kind of cooperative international policies in the summer of 1933 cannot be explained by a lack of scientific progress. But a combination of domestic and international political and economic concerns meant that the Council's proposal never made it beyond the committee rooms in Whitehall. In the United States, two less well-studied proposals for a multilateral revaluation of currencies also failed to make much of an impact amid the whirlwind of Franklin D. Roosevelt's "Hundred Days." The more significant of the two, detailed in a memorandum by the International Economic Advisor to the State Department, Herbert Feis, again proposed a multilateral revaluation of currencies in relation to gold, and was sufficiently cogent to generate rumors in London in May of 1933 that the British government was about to launch a cooperative reflationary initiative with the United States at the forthcoming conference.[23] Lacking substantial political support in the context of their own national political economies, international monetary cooperation offered the potential for these solo voices (and there were others elsewhere) to form a chorus in favor of multilateral revaluation that could have shaped the discourse and the outcome of international monetary relations.

The League was uniquely well placed in the borderlands to draw out, amplify, and integrate such proposals for monetary innovation in a variety of League-sponsored initiatives and conferences intended to address economic and monetary problems which pre-dated, yet were exacerbated by, the Great Depression: the Gold Delegation Inquiry into the Purchasing Power of Gold, 1928–32; the Lausanne Conference of July 1932; the Stresa Conference held in September 1932; and the preparatory meetings for, and the convention of, the World Economic Conference, which lasted from July 1932 until October 1933. These League-sponsored ventures were a potential source of innovative economic advice, as well as serving as a more general reminder to nation-states of the benefits to be had from international cooperation. In practice, however, the role of the Financial and Economic Committees of the League of Nations in the planning and implementation of cooperative monetary initiatives to combat the depression was strongly circumscribed by its dependence on key nations (notably Britain); the process by which commissioners and advisors were appointed to the League; and its deference to, and lack of power over, the world's key monetary players, notably the central banks. These elements had profound consequences for the recovery strategies advocated by the League (content and implementation) and their subsequent impact on the "real world." In many ways, the failure of monetary cooperation at the World Economic Conference in 1933 was presaged by the history of an apparently less ambitious, and certainly less public, attempt at monetary cooperation: the Gold Delegation Inquiry into the Purchasing Power of Gold that ran from 1928 to 1932.

The Gold Delegation reports: practical, political and intellectual constraints

The origins of the League-sponsored Inquiry into the Purchasing Power of Gold, to give the initiative its full title (it soon became known as the Gold Delegation), lay in long-held, publicly expressed British disquiet regarding the shortage of gold reserves and the downward impact this was likely to have on world prices.[24] British interest in the topic was, in part, shaped by self-interest, notably the Bank of England's mounting anxieties regarding the adequacy of gold cover to meet legal requirements. But money doctors Gustav Cassel and Henry Strakosch also played a key role in informing a British critique which argued that shortages in the world's gold supply were likely to depress world prices to such a degree that the issue demanded immediate international attention (Sayers 1976: 346–8). At the end of 1927 the Bank of England, and to a lesser extent the British Treasury, supported the notion of an inquiry, albeit one undertaken by central banks. But when the Bank of England's direct overtures on the question drew a cool response from the Chairman of the Federal Reserve Board, Benjamin Strong, and a rather more hostile response from the Bank of France, rather than abandon the idea, the British chose to promote the call for an international inquiry through the Financial Committee of the League of Nations, where Strakosch, Sir Otto Niemeyer, and, of course, Arthur Salter, Director of the Economic and Financial Section of the League, were well ensconced.[25] On June 8, 1928, the Council of the League charged the Financial Committee to explore the "detrimental effect upon industry, agriculture and the conditions of employment due to fluctuations in the purchasing power of gold" thanks to the efforts of British officials, both within and without the Financial Committee, who demonstrated both their commitment to the cause and their mastery of the labyrinthine committee and commission structures of the League.[26]

The inquiry was to last more than four years, five if one takes into account the fact that its final report provided the basis for preparatory meetings of the 1933 World Economic Conference. It was never intended to last so long, but the practical, political, and intellectual problems that stood in its way were large and significant. Before exploring what these were, it is necessary to outline briefly the inquiry's history and its modest achievements. The work of the Gold Delegation, set up by the Financial Committee, comprised a number of meetings (lasting from three to six days) of between ten and twelve nominated economists and banking representatives from some of Europe's smaller states, as well as members of the Financial Committee. They met in the plush surroundings of the committee rooms of the Palais des Nations in Geneva, where, after a series of delays, the first session of the Gold Delegation opened on 26 August 1929. The second meeting was held in June 1930, with a further five sessions taking place at approximately six-monthly intervals until May 1932.[27] Early work focused on collating data on the main factors in the supply and demand for gold; determining the best criteria for measuring the purchasing power of gold; and defining what was, and should be, the relationship between the supply of gold, monetary policy, and the general level of prices. Setting these parameters was contentious in its own right. Much of the data was collated by the League's Secretariat, although delegates and unofficial organizations preoccupied with stable money also submitted their own intelligence.[28] Over the course of the inquiry, the documentation collected alone weighed in at some 3 kilograms. Sayers argued that the strategy of data collection reflected the delegation's hopes that once the intelligence was in, central bankers would want to become involved in shaping its recommendations.[29] But the step also reflected the broader ambitions of the delegation and its links with the League, which was coming to believe that the collation of – as far as possible, global – economic and monetary intelligence was one of the key contributions it could make to the prospects for international cooperation. By the late 1930s it had become a defining feature of the League's work.

Against the backdrop of a rapidly deteriorating world economy, and beset by a variety of practical, political, and intellectual problems, the Gold Delegation struggled to formulate a final report. Instead it opted, on September 8, 1930, to publish its *First Interim Report*. Aside from underlining that the demonstrated shortage of gold in the monetary system "could" cause prices to decline (note use of the conditional tense) and that it was important to economize on the use of gold, it sought to impress its readers by supplying a wealth of statistical information. The report contained a huge statistical index and was supplemented by the publication of additional reports by Strakosch; the American Oliver Sprague, Economic Advisor to the Bank of England; Jacques Rueff, Financial Attaché to the French Embassy in London; L.J.D Trip, former Governor of the Java Bank and Treasurer-General of the Netherlands; and the Polish economist Feliks Mlynarski. The report also included a comparative study of national legislation and statutes on gold reserves.[30] Tensions within the Gold Delegation, and between the Gold Delegation and the wider world became increasingly apparent when, on January 20, 1931, the Gold Delegation published yet another interim report. This was far less detailed than the first, bereft of a clear line of argument or lucid recommendations. It contained neither the detailed personal reflections of individual money doctors nor the statistical appendices that had characterized the first report. Most surprising of all, the document contained not one mention of the tumultuous economic context in which it was written – as far as the *Second Interim Report* was concerned, the Great Depression did not exist.

Finally, in June 1932, the Gold Delegation published its *Final Report*.[31] The title implied a unity of findings and recommendations that belied its contents, for the contention that had surrounded its creation and its work was mirrored in its final published outcome. The *Final Report* was divided into what became known as the "majority" and "minority" view, with the majority view dominating the main body of the text. Although it declares in its introduction that the Gold Delegation did not set out to study the "present economic and financial depression," the final majority section of the report offers a largely orthodox account of the crisis. Rooted in conventional theories on price equilibrium and on the benefits derived from a properly functioning gold standard, the report argued that the depression was caused by exogenous elements, namely the war and postwar inflation, while factors such as government overspending and price rigidities also challenged the smooth functioning of the gold standard. The majority view offered no clear recommendations for economic and monetary policy beyond the – hardly earth-shattering – recognition that unstable, and especially falling, prices were bad for economic health, and a vague call for greater international cooperation.

Quite how difficult it would be to achieve such international cooperation was exemplified in the *Final Report* itself. Not only was the majority section of the report in places vague and contradictory, but the latter part of the report contained two substantial notes of dissent: the first by the Belgian Albert Janssen, Chairman of the Gold Delegation, Reginald Mant of the Bank of England, and Henry Strakosch; the second by Gustav Cassel.[32] This became known as the "minority report." It made public for the first time a fundamental disagreement that had divided the work of the Gold Delegation from the outset: that monetary factors, notably the maldistribution of the world's gold reserves and the damaging rise in its price (especially since 1928), had triggered the economic crisis. It concluded that fundamental monetary reform alongside a program of credit expansion was the required remedy for the depression.[33] This view was implicitly critical of French and American monetary policy.

The minority view, unlike the majority report, contained a clear program of action centered on measures to both redistribute and economize on the world's gold reserves and a call for the leading "monetary authorities" to expand the supply of credit. (Interestingly, Strakosch, Mant, and Janssen cited the League's actions in central and eastern Europe as proof that it was possible to check inflation – there was no need to fear monetary expansion.)

Aspects of the minority critique, notably its emphasis on monetary causes of the crisis, continues to be reflected in accounts of the depression. (The majority view has not withstood the test of time.) It also stands as testimony to the energy and commitment of Henry Strakosch, the prime instigator, energizer, and supporter of the Gold Delegation, whose work illustrates that one well-placed money doctor can shape the discourse, if not the outcome, of international monetary diplomacy. Members of the majority group were at best irritated, at worst infuriated, at what they regarded as the special "care being taken over the presentation of the minority view."[34] At the time, they took comfort in the fact that the views of the minority group, including Cassel, were "completely one-sided and must condemn themselves."[35] Cassel later professed that he was profoundly bemused by the fact that the majority of the Gold Delegation had been "strangely incapable" of accepting the minority view – a bemusement that reflects an economist's sensitivity to the value of ideas rather than the practical, political, and intellectual context in which policy was generated and applied (Cassel 1936: 73). The minority report reflected just that in its contents: the *minority* view.

The scope of the inquiry indicated new ambitions on the part of the League's Financial Committee to address a financial topic of acute interest to all its members, for the Gold Delegation project was an unprecedented foray into international monetary policy on a multilateral basis. But the obstacles to success were manifold. First, there were a number of practical problems, such as the unwieldy structure of the League itself. During the interwar period the body was formed and re-formed a number of times to clarify its increasingly labyrinthine structure, but with limited success. Under the British-style bureaucratic structure that dominated until the mid-1930s there were no clear lines of authority or political power. This helped to increase the, already ripe, suspicions that the League (particularly the Financial Committee) was an entirely British-dominated institution, which challenged the League's claims to impartiality and clouded the motivation behind the League's move into monetary policy. Here, the position of the United States complicated matters further. Although not integrated into the workings of the League, the United States had achieved a semi-detached status thanks to its interest in, and power over, international financial relations. The League kept a wary eye on U.S. views and requirements.[36]

Coordination within the Gold Delegation also generated practical difficulties. The League had only limited powers to determine which delegates were seconded to the inquiry, and here national politics played a significant role.[37] Moreover, the length of the inquiry meant that few experts lasted the course; a good deal of energy was expended finding suitable replacements.[38] And, finally, the expert nature of the group frequently frustrated League officials. The economists serving the delegation brought with them a variety of national and intellectual perspectives to the gold inquiry. However, the character of their deliberations, notably the detailed arguments over the technical evidence, an unwillingness to compromise, and the determination of each economist to argue and promote his own views, meant that its work was increasingly perceived as overly technical, too academic, and bitterly divided by an increasingly unsympathetic audience of government officials and the general public.[39] Here, the inquiry's emphasis on the collation and dissemination of as much data as possible, whilst it was applauded in some political quarters (as a useful distraction from more sensitive issues), added to a public perception that the inquiry was too academic and removed from topics of immediate relevance or utility. League officials appeared to presuppose that data was neutral. But expert members of the Gold Delegation Inquiry certainly did not perceive them to be so, and the content of the supporting statistical materials triggered further wrangling among the experts.[40] The statistical work of the Gold Delegation served to detract from the policy discussions of the Delegation, and presented a confused picture of the League's ambition to contribute to international monetary cooperation. Did the League intend to critique and, where possible, promote a coordinated response to identified monetary problems? Or was its intention to collate statistical materials that would inform, and potentially shape, the decision of individual nation-states? On a more mundane level, the decision to publish statistical materials alongside the reports proper also helped to delay publication of the reports and to add to the general air of frustration and impatience with which the Gold Delegation's work was greeted after 1929.

Cassel was later to hold the League accountable for the lateness of an inquiry into the availability of gold and the deflationary effects of the reconstructed gold standard that, to his mind, should have been held sometime in the early 1920s (Cassel 1936: 57). But it was unfair to lay this charge at the League given the institution's dependence on "great" power support, the nature of the inquiry, and the variety of political opposition ranged against it. The inquiry marked a significant departure from previous attempts at money doctoring from the League, and it was met with powerful opposition. Although it was Montagu Norman who took up earlier calls for an investigation into the adequacy of gold reserves by supporting the notion of a League inquiry, the Governor of the Bank of England soon retreated when he found himself in the center of an unusually concerted and effective cooperative effort on the part of other central bankers to prevent the inquiry by an outside agency into a topic that was regarded as the sole purvey of central bankers.[41] Mouré, in particular, has drawn out how coordinated central bank opposition to the inquiry demonstrated the deep hostility with which central banks viewed any political or public opportunity to scrutinize their work and the rising suspicions of leading central bankers, notably those of France and the United States, as to both Norman's motives and the long-term viability of the gold *exchange* standard.[42] Despite Norman's protestations that the decision to study the purchasing power of gold was the result of "persistent, widespread and international" concerns, Moreau complained that the "whole occasion for the proposed inquiry is really domestic and English [*sic*] inquiry," which potentially threatened the independence of the Bank of France.[43] Here, the machinations of British League officials did little to help. When central bank support for the inquiry failed to materialize, Salter, in a clumsy effort to make Strong think again, argued that, given the current political climate in Britain in 1928 and 1929, the Bank of England would have to respond to any Gold Delegation Inquiry or face dire consequences for its independence, should a Labour government be elected. Strong was unimpressed. Like Moreau, the American believed that central bank independence was put at greater risk by the inquiry and both men made much of the fact that League officials enjoyed "power without responsibility."[44] (The charge prompted a spirited response from Niemeyer, who complained that not only did Moreau fail to understand "the League and its work," but he was mistaken in his belief that it was British dominated and that its involvement in monetary issues could be stopped.[45]) The history of the Gold Delegation, however, confirms the widespread League perception that it was burdened with the opposite: great expectations, but no power with which to meet them.

The Financial Committee of the League paid the price for its early dependence on British leadership and personnel. Britain undoubtedly presented its early support for the League as a generous and selfless act given French ambivalence and American hostility to the Geneva project. But by the late 1920s the close identification of the Financial Committee, in particular, with key objectives in the monetary policy of the British state did little to enhance the standing of the League's claim to act as an independent arbiter. Despite evidence that Strakosch, in particular, was motivated more by concern for the health and viability of the international monetary system as a whole than by consideration for British monetary well-being, his actions, whether inside or outside the League, were widely perceived to be driven by national self-interest.[46] The twists and turns in Norman's position – first supporting the inquiry, then backing away from it as both the depth of opposition among central bankers and the magnitude of the emerging monetary crisis became clear in late 1929 and 1930 – did little to help matters. If the inquiry was solely in Britain's interest, then Strakosch and Salter were entitled to much more consistent support from the British central bank and the government than they enjoyed during the lifetime of the Gold Delegation.

As we have seen, early Bank of England support for the Gold Delegation had turned to ambivalence in the face of widespread opposition from other central banks. The position of the British Treasury was more complex. In public, the Treasury attempted to maintain a steady demeanor of dispassionate interest in the inquiry's work. But privately its support for the Gold Delegation related directly to sterling's relationship with the gold exchange standard. Prior to September 1931, materials produced by the Gold Delegation were widely circulated and discussed within the British Treasury, where the views of Cassel and Strakosch had an influential following.[47] The *First Interim Report* and the early work of the Delegation were relatively well received in the Treasury, who harbored hopes of broadening the scope of the inquiry's work, including proposals for an international conference on the topic that included political representation.[48]

The publication of the vacuous *Second Interim Report* and mounting pressure on sterling changed all that. Just as the split between what were to become the majority and minority factions of the Gold Delegation grew increasingly pronounced, so the Treasury began to back away from endorsing the views of the minority camp, with which it previously had enjoyed an intimate, if private, association, because it wanted to avoid "an unsuitable controversy."[49] The reason was obvious: with sterling now floating free of the gold standard, the British government had lost interest in promoting an international settlement to its financial difficulties. As will be seen in the discussion which follows on preparations for the World Economic Conference, Britain did not want to draw further attention to its sterling policy (pp. 231–6). As Leith-Ross put it:

> Foreign holders of sterling are watching anxiously for indications of future currency policy…any suggestion that this policy will depart radically from orthodox conceptions or contain insufficient safeguards against the danger of inflation are likely to have a very adverse effect on the position of sterling.[50]

Now that British monetary policy had taken an innovative turn, it had to appear as orthodox as before. The Treasury now took the lead in arguing that

Britain should discourage Strakosch from pursuing what was now regarded as the dangerous and inflammatory route of publicizing his views in a separate and distinctive minority report to the *Final Report of the Gold Delegation*. There was grave concern (in sharp contrast to earlier Treasury assurances regarding the independence of the Financial Committee) that, while representatives to the Gold Delegation are

> appointed for technical qualifications and are in no sense representatives of the governments of which they are nationals…this fact is constantly over-looked and the minority report of the Gold Delegation will inevitably tend to be regarded as the expression of British Government policy.[51]

When the *Final Report* was published the British government and the Bank of England sided with the generality of the majority report.[52]

In the wake of sterling's depreciation, whatever international resonance Strakosch had hoped to achieve by promoting his views through the Gold Delegation were now dashed as the British government, as well as the Bank of England, sought to distance themselves from his views in the wake of sterling's depreciation. The saga of Strakosch's relations with these institutions alone illustrates some of the many political and economic obstacles that stood in the way of international monetary coordination and innovation during a global economic crisis. Strakosch certainly received little thanks from the British government or the League of Nations for the energy and commitment he gave to the Gold Delegation. Much of his time was given to recruiting members and cajoling them to attend the sessions in Geneva, and his work, after 1930, was consistently greeted with hostility by the very central banks he was hoping to influence. He was branded, alongside Cassel and Keynes, as an "irresponsible" influence for stirring up public opinion on monetary matters, in sharp contrast to "responsible" or "sound chaps," who did not challenge the wisdom of French or American monetary policy in private or in public.[53] Yet Strakosch remained committed to disseminating his view to elite and public opinion. Undeterred by Britain's cool response to his separate minority report, Strakosch ignored British Treasury and Foreign Office requests for discretion by working to ensure that the minority portion of the report received as much publicity as he could organize. Claiming that arrangements for the publication of the *Final Report* in Geneva had been "bungled," Strakosch took matters into his own hands by releasing the full report, alongside a detailed commentary on the minority portion, to the *Economist* periodical in London sometime before the *Final Report* was published in Geneva. Aside from earning him a swift rap across the knuckles from the Financial Committee, the episode showed he was a media-savvy money doctor and determined to secure the widest possible audience for his views.[54]

Strakosch's antics won him few friends in Geneva among League officials, who had become increasingly frustrated by the workings and outcome of the Gold Delegation. It had failed to offer a unified, if expert, perspective on the means by which the purchasing power of gold affected the performance of the gold standard or its broader contribution to world economic crisis. Not only had the delegation's well-publicized divisions done little to enhance the reputation of the Financial Committee of the League, its work had exposed League impotence in promoting central bank cooperation, disseminating policy knowledge, or accommodating political sensitivities.

But the Financial and Economic Committees of the League were not easily deterred. Instead, their strategies designed to promote cooperation began to change again. By early 1932 the League had become especially determined that the *Final Report* should appear in time for the meeting of the Lausanne Conference. This much was achieved, and aspects of the majority section of the final report were taken up in the fifth resolution of the Lausanne Conference, which called for the convocation of a World Economic Conference. However, many of the practical, political, and intellectual limitations which had dogged the work of the Gold Delegation returned to plague the League's efforts to promote international cooperation through the World Economic Conference. New, largely practical, steps were taken to improve the chances of cooperation. Greater efforts were made to ensure experts were, in some measure, representative of the governments who nominated them, and major meetings were held not just outside Geneva, but in the United States. As events were to demonstrate, the political and intellectual problems bedeviling cooperation were more intractable.

Policy coordination and the World Economic Conference

Conference diplomacy formed a major plank of the League of Nation's contribution to international monetary and economic relations in the first ten years after the First World War. This time the origins of the League's monetary initiatives lay not in the committee rooms of Geneva or the Bank of England, but in the office of William Castle, Under-Secretary of State to the State Department in Washington, DC. In December 1930 Castle, warmly supported by the U.S. Ambassador to Germany, Frederic Sackett, proposed that the American President Herbert Hoover should convene and lead a World Economic Conference to revive international "political and economic confidence." Stillborn in the winter of 1930 through a lack of political support on both sides of the Atlantic, the proposal for some kind of international conference was revived in the summer of 1931 in the wake of the financial crisis which had wide-ranging effects on international financial relations.[55]

During 1931 and 1932 the Financial and Economic Committees, while excited by the proposal for a world conference, waited for political representatives of powerful nation-states to take the lead. Although anxious to demonstrate its commitment to promoting economic and monetary cooperation, the desultory results of the Gold Delegation had underlined the Geneva-based institution's continued dependence on the "great" powers to initiate, as well as implement, any effort at international cooperation. This happened in the spring of 1932, when the British government, anxious to safeguard British commercial investments in Germany, called for an international conference to resolve the reparations issue. At the ensuing conference, held in Lausanne in June 1932, British and French delegates called on the League to convene a World Economic Conference.[56] Early signs of a new Franco-British unity on reparations were evident in the closing sessions of the Gold Delegation and in the British Treasury's warm endorsement of the majority section of the *Final Report of the Gold Delegation*'s emphasis on the need for "politicians to first clear the problems of reparations and war debts."[57]

Learning from the history of the Gold Delegation, the League waited until the agenda for the putative World Economic Conference was agreed between Britain and France before taking on a role in the coordination of international financial diplomacy in September 1932. This time political support came before League endorsement of the proposal. But anxious as ever to demonstrate their worth, League officials did not think through the potentially damaging consequences of acting as the principal coordinator, but not the author, of such an ambitious and wide-ranging agenda for the League's standing in international relations (Walters 1952: 7). Early preparatory work, too, was successful and gave little indication of the trouble that was to come, particularly after League officials successfully negotiated the terms on which the United States would participate in the conference.[58] Here, officials from the League Secretariat played an important role as intermediaries, better able than representatives of the British or French governments to ease American fears that the proposed world conference was merely a front to squeeze concessions from the U.S. The League also established the agenda and structure of the preparatory committees, mirroring its own structures by dividing the schedule into financial and economic issues. The more important monetary commission was presided over by the American Senator James Cox and was divided into two sub-committees. The first was to address so-called "immediate measures for financial reconstruction": credit policy, price levels, the limitation of monetary fluctuations, exchange control indebtedness, and the resumption of international lending. The second encompassed "permanent measures of the re-establishment of the international gold standard, addressing issues like central bank cooperation, the distribution of gold reserves and the price of silver." There was nothing new here then.[59]

The monetary portion of the agenda excited considerable interest in the fall of 1932, although the frisson of excitement in the world's finance ministries that greeted news of the preparatory commission program of work was not accompanied by an enthusiasm for policy development and innovation. Rather, preparations for and participation in the forthcoming World Economic Conference were welcomed by many who wished to interrogate British monetary policy. Indeed, the fact that so many senior representatives of the League were British heightened this expectation. Members of what were to become known as "gold bloc" and "pseudo gold bloc" countries were anxious for Britain to end what they claimed was a "temporary" floatation of sterling and wanted the British government to furnish specific details as to when it would return to the gold standard.

Yet an important conflict of interest was brewing for the League. The recently published *Report of the Gold Delegation*, coupled with the emphasis on monetary orthodoxy in the conference agenda, meant the League was promoting monetary policies in direct conflict with those now followed, although not openly advocated, by its principal member and sponsor of the conference – Great Britain. There were risks for Britain too. In promoting the World Economic Conference Britain invited international scrutiny at a crucial time in the evolution of its monetary policy, but it believed this could be controlled through the unique control the British government had secured over conference preparations as a whole. (In much the same way as Strakosch attempted to manage the early work of the Gold Delegation.) The Organizing Committee for the World Economic Conference was established, not by the League, but by the statesmen who attended the Lausanne Conference. It was chaired by the British Foreign Secretary John Simon, assisted by the energetic Cabinet Secretary Maurice Hankey, comprised foreign ministers and senior statesmen, and was charged with determining when, where, and how the conference met, securing the necessary financial support, and nominating delegates for monetary and economic commissions.[60] Crucially for the British government, Simon's leadership of the Organizing Committee gave Britain the power to determine when the preparatory committees and conference proper should convene. Interestingly, there is no evidence to suggest that other nations, or the League itself, recognized the significance of Britain's offer to take the lead in making arrangements. British influence explains why both the first meeting of the Preparatory Financial and Economic Committees and the conference proper were scheduled just days before war debt payments were due to the United States.[61] Competition between the League's objective of promoting international cooperation to fight the depression and Britain's determination to see off war debts was enshrined within the organizational structure of the conference. At the same time, it is unlikely that, without British energy and commitment to the world conference project, this belated, bloated, and, at the same time, feeble effort at money doctoring would have developed from the idle speculations of 1930 and 1931.

By October 1932 preparatory work for the conference was under way. In a departure from past practice, the conference was to bring together both expert and political actors. It was decided that while financial (and economic experts) should take the lead in defining the conference agenda at meetings of the Monetary Preparatory Committee – the engine house that was expected to deliver a detailed, agreed agenda and viable proposals for monetary action – politicians would be present at the final stages of the conference's work. Learning from the history of the Gold Delegation, it was hoped this arrangement would both discipline the experts to produce coherent proposals on time and ensure that their recommendations would, at the very least, secure the political support of the government they represented. Under this structure, there appeared to be less risk that an expert-generated agenda would be, as Per Jacobsson of the League described the Gold Delegation's final report, "a big garden which has been carefully laid out in detail, but without any general plan."[62] The next stage of preparations was for each nominated nation-state to select experts to send to the committee. As no country had what might be described as a designated "rapid reaction force" of international financial experts, determining who should be nominated sometimes triggered, as in Britain, serious interdepartmental rivalries between the Treasury, the Bank of England, and the Foreign Office. By the same token, because experts in international finance had to be appointed anew for each international conference, in theory the process gave nations, but crucially not the League, the opportunity to select experts who were at the cutting edge of their discipline.

There were hopes that providing the Monetary Preparatory Committee with "complete intellectual freedom" might create genuinely innovative and interesting proposals for international cooperation. But none of the great powers decided to avail themselves of this opportunity. The League supported this conservative approach thanks to the experience of the Gold Delegation, which had demonstrated the limitations of experts, who, while free from political accountability, were sometimes also without the political support to turn their intellectual efforts into action. The British government, for example, considered, but then rejected, the Cambridge economist John Maynard Keynes and Sir Ralph Hawtrey, Director of Financial Enquiries at the Treasury, as "too extreme" and "unreliable."[63] The British, like the Germans and French, opted for the "safe hands" of trusted civil servants or private money doctors who were known to be strongly sympathetic to the established contours of national monetary policy. These included Frederick Leith-Ross and Frederick Phillips of the British Treasury; Charles Rist, Deputy Governor of the Bank of France; Jean Parmentier, Director-General of the Ministry of Finance; and Wilhelm Vocke, a member of the Reichsbank Direktorium. Only the United States attempted to meet the Organizing Committee's call to appoint "independent" experts with sufficient "creative energy to escape traditional policy limitations" by appointing John Williams, Professor of Economics at Harvard University to the Monetary Committee.[64] True, Williams's credentials as an academic gave him a greater semblance of independence than the representatives appointed by Britain, France, and Germany, but this was contradicted by the fact that he was widely known to be an advisor and speechwriter for Ogden Mills, Assistant Secretary and then Secretary of State to the U.S. Treasury. Moreover, the majority of delegates at the meetings of the Preparatory Commission in Geneva, quite understandably, feared that whatever Williams proposed could be all too easily abdicated by a new American administration; they preferred to consult with members of the State Department who were ostensibly there to help Williams (and not the other way around). This problem became only more pronounced with the landslide election of Franklin D. Roosevelt on November 8, nine days after the Preparatory Monetary Committee began its deliberations. Developments at home left Williams isolated and, although he remained in post until January 1933, he was unable to answer the question that most interested the powers assembled at Geneva: what was the monetary policy of the new Democrat administration likely to be?

Discussions at the first meetings of the two monetary sub-committees, held in November 1932 and January 1933, were generally dominated by debates on how to reconstruct the international gold standard and, in particular, the issue of when Britain would return to gold. Here, at least, the League had no difficulty in coordinating the recovery strategies articulated by participants of the monetary commission. Despite the changed condition of the international economy, monetary relations between the major powers remained conditioned by years of commitment to the international gold standard. The League, too, was committed to the cause, an obligation underpinned by its role in the monetary stabilization of central and eastern Europe and the Gold Delegation of the League of Nations. The documentation submitted by the League on the question duplicated that of memoranda and proposals articulated by the participating nations – most of it centered on materials and arguments presented in the majority section of the *Final Report of the Gold Delegation*. But the League had much less success in broadening monetary discussions to embrace an issue of intimate concern to the League: the difficulties faced by central and eastern Europe since the cessation of international loans and the monetary pressures triggered by the depreciation of sterling and associated currencies. It did not attempt to take a leading role in the preparatory committees, but even its efforts at complementing the work of the nominated experts by introducing topics of interest to smaller powers unrepresented at the meetings met with little success (see Clavin 1996: 45–9).

A more glaring failure of the League's money doctoring was its inability to exploit the potential for monetary innovation by recognizing the benefits accrued by members of the sterling bloc since their floatation. But it would be unfair to lay this blame entirely at the door of the League. Neither "gold bloc" nor British policy helped. In the same way that Britain did not seek to coordinate the reflationary efforts of fellow members of the unofficial sterling bloc, it also refused to proselytize on the advantages of exchange depreciation for fear it would cut away Britain's new found competitive trading advantage and trigger "currency chaos" in central and eastern Europe. Hamstrung by its dependence on key nation-states to take the lead and its efforts to treat all pieces of expert advice as equal (witness its response to disputes within the Gold Delegation), the League made no sustained attempt to breach the differences between countries with floating currencies and those still committed to gold (Loveday 1938: 789). It also neglected to consider the implications for its own reputation or its broader policy objectives of allowing preparations for the conference to go forward. Sympathetic to claims that the world economy would recover if the issue of international indebtedness was addressed (even though it had been barred from the agenda), League officials did nothing to stop Britain from making repeated reference to the question of "political debts" during meetings of both monetary committees. Through inaction on this issue, the League's efforts at coordination implicitly favored the European perspective on the question of political debts – an inference not lost on the United States.

The League also had neither the power nor the political will to prevent Britain, in its capacity as chair of the Organizing Committee, from radically reshaping the role of the preparatory committees' work for the final conference. Deadlocked over monetary policy thanks to the refusal of Britain and other sterling bloc members to commit to restabilizing their currencies, the British government exploited its role as Chair of the Organizing Committee to redefine the remit of the future meetings of the Preparatory Monetary Committees to the production of a draft annotated agenda. It was a significant step away from the League's aspiration that the committees would produce firm proposals for the conference delegates to sign. The work of the two monetary sub-committees was also simplified by the decision to concentrate efforts on a theoretical examination of the gold standard. The step brought a number of immediate practical benefits for the second meetings of the League's Monetary Preparatory Sub-committees in January 1933: it reinforced the League's authority by drawing on its recently produced report from the Gold Delegation and it refocused the debate on abstract, technical issues on which it proved much easier to secure agreement. However, it also meant that in intellectual and political terms the hope for genuine cooperation and the exchange of innovative ideas to combat the crisis was abandoned. The meetings of the preparatory sub-committees generated a number of outcomes in January and February 1933. These included unanimity on a set of "rules" to guarantee the smooth operation of the gold standard that harked back to the first monetary conferences held after the end of the First World War, and a draft convention on central bank cooperation. In this sense the League had achieved, albeit superficially, its aims of coordinating the monetary policy of floating and stable currencies and of complementing the work of those committed to gold by making gold standard "values" the center of its portion of the annotated agenda.

But by side-stepping issues of serious contention in their monetary deliberations the preparatory sub-committees also rejected the opportunity to examine how and why the monetary policy of the sterling bloc differed from the rest or to interrogate the British proposal that the monetary portion of the conference agenda place the call for cheap money at its heart. Undoubtedly, the League's commitment to openness also limited the degree to which participants felt they could be candid with one another, as evidenced in the January and February 1933 discussions regarding the drafting of a central bank convention to be approved at the conference (Loveday 1938: 62–3). The same practical, political, and intellectual limitations that had dogged the work of the Gold Delegation were echoed in the monetary preparations for the conference.

Coordination becomes competition

By the spring of 1933, the rapidly changing political scene in Europe and the United States left the League struggling simply to ascertain the content of –

never mind coordinate – the monetary policies of new governments. Political developments in the United States were especially disruptive. As a consequence the League was pushed into an increasingly competitive role with key nation-states in its efforts to coordinate preparations for the conference. Hoover's talks with the newly elected Franklin D. Roosevelt in January 1933 first raised hopes that the outgoing and incoming administrations would coordinate U.S. policy in the Monetary Preparatory Sub-committees. It was always unlikely that the incoming administration would publicly accept policies and advice offered by the roundly defeated Hoover, but the talks also signaled that there was little chance that U.S. monetary policy would be shaped by any concern for the forthcoming World Economic Conference.

Two developments in American policy marked the beginning of the end for the Preparatory Monetary Committees' efforts to coordinate the policy proposals of the principal nation-states. First, Roosevelt invited all conference participants to come to Washington, DC, to engage in preparatory talks. Although the League applauded the move, this step also underlined the widespread view in British and American official circles, in particular, that it was only by moving conference deliberations away from Geneva that there was any chance of success. The second, more significant, development was Roosevelt's momentous decision to uncouple the U.S. dollar from gold. Given the emphasis on gold standard orthodoxy in the monetary proportion of the annotated agenda and the new fissures the step opened up between different "factions" of Roosevelt's administration, the League's efforts at international money doctoring, with their dated emphasis on exchange rate stability, were now out of step with all but the "gold bloc" countries.[65]

In theory, the floatation of the dollar did open up the opportunity for the sterling bloc, led by Britain, and the United States to launch a coordinated attempt at reflation – a possibility that was widely discussed, but dismissed, by the British Treasury. Fearing the monetary and political repercussions of what it termed "a further round of competitive depreciation and currency controls in the international economy," and determined to retain the reduction of war debts commensurate with the Lausanne reparations settlement, the British government avoided any substantial discussion of the new commonalties of Anglo-American monetary policy.[66] There was no League presence at the Washington talks (nor, at least officially, could there have been given the limitations of U.S.–League relations), which had very serious consequences for the League's role as coordinating money doctor – the commonalties and implications of Anglo-American reflation policies were not reflected upon.

By May 1933 the proposals contained within the draft annotated agenda were not just thin, but also hopelessly out of date. Their main champion was now France, although it, too, preferred to make its appeals for a return to the values and practices enshrined in the reconstructed international gold standard on its own terms, and not through the monetary sub-committees of the League. When the conference convened in the Geological Museum in London in June 1933, the League's role for the most part was confined to coordinating the practical, rather than the political or intellectual, dimension of the conference: much of its work, for example, was devoted to publicizing the work of the innumerable commissions and sub-committees, which met in private, through the publication of a daily journal. However, here, too, the League now found its authority undermined. Delegates, notably American ones, insisted on talking to the press, thereby confounding the League's aspirations that private meetings would afford the opportunity for statesmen to play to more than the home gallery. (All this must have been galling for League officials, who faced vociferous American criticism throughout the lifetime of the Gold Delegation that the League was far too open an institution to promote effective monetary cooperation.) Most damaging to both the prospects for the conference and the League's role as author of the agenda was the monetary drama played out beyond the conference hall during negotiations for a temporary stabilization agreement in the Bank of England.

The story of the breakdown of the stabilization negotiations in the Bank of England has often been told, but the League of Nations never appears as a protagonist. Notable during the course of these negotiations was the way that other nations began to cluster around the policy articulated by Britain or France. Norway, for example, was typical of those countries which had allied their currency fortunes to the floating pound; while members of the gold standard (including, for the most part, pseudo gold standard currencies) supported French determination to bring sterling and the dollar back to gold. The monetary portion of the annotated agenda was entirely hijacked by stabilization negotiations taking place some three miles away, and the League, given the priority afforded to the temporary stabilization agreement, was unable to draw the attention of the delegates or the world's press back to deliberations under way in the financial and economic commissions of the conference. This is a clear instance of the League's aspirations as money doctor competing with and losing out to the established lines of authority and power enjoyed by the world's leading central bankers. (Indeed, the word "competition" flatters the League here, for its efforts to compete with the bankers and promote negotiations centered on the established agenda were pretty feeble.)

When the stabilization talks reached their "last-ditch" phase it was Montagu Norman who stepped in in a final effort to forge an agreement. Although the negotiations for the temporary stabilization agreement collapsed in a dramatic failure with the announcement of Roosevelt's "bombshell message," Norman's intervention of July 4 formed the basis of the monetary commission's endorsement of the "rules of the gold standard game" that had also featured in the annotated agenda. But no one was fooled by the apparent unanimity achieved in the monetary portion of the conference's final report. Representatives from central and eastern Europe, notably those who had been the focus of the League's attentions, were bitter at the failure of both the League and the big powers to consider their interests.[67] The League did attempt to promote schemes to revive the supply of credit to eastern Europe, most prominent of which was the Franqui plan, which planned to establish a credit base of some $100 million with the power to issue debentures for $330–400 million. But the schemes had never enjoyed support from the major powers and received barely a cursory mention in the final report of the monetary commission. In a vain attempt to make up for the lack of financial help the League sponsored proposals for international public work schemes, which also failed because they were unable to attract the support of key players – the British, German, and American governments.

Conclusion

There is little in the history of the League's efforts to coordinate monetary policy for the Great Depression recounted here to contradict Schuker's findings, in this volume, that the League's ability to effect monetary cooperation independently of the "great" powers or leading central banks was severely limited, Flandreau's argument that the League's presentation of the key monetary challenges before them were shaped by the experience of the largest powers, or Pauly's assertion that when it comes to offering monetary "advice" international institutions act as "guardians of orthodoxy" not innovation.[68] But, while it is hard to distinguish a sustained and effective League contribution to money doctoring in the Depression, it is important not to appraise the historical record in such tightly defined terms. When the League's contribution to international diplomacy is taken more widely, there is potential for a more positive assessment.

First, the League did attempt to make good its failure to deliver anything of substance on the monetary agenda, by initiating some innovation in pursuit of its economic goals. In what was to become a radical break with past practice at international conferences, in the summer of 1933 League officials organized and coordinated issue-specific meetings regarding the supply, pricing, and trade of commodities: wheat, wine, cotton, lumber, sugar, tin, copper, and silver. Although only the silver negotiations produced an agreement at the world conference, agreements on other commodities were reached in future years. Moreover, the League's deep-seated frustration with the outcome of the world conference, and the opprobrium that came Geneva's way in its wake, encouraged a fundamental reappraisal of both the objectives of international monetary and economic cooperation and how to achieve those ends. In the wake of the Gold Delegation and the failure of the World Economic Conference, by 1935 the League had, partly by accident, partly by design, adopted a new strategy on financial and economic questions. Not only did the League now concentrate its efforts on coordinating national policies on specific commodities only, like wheat or quinine; it was also prepared to promote, when appropriate, multilateral as well as bilateral agreements.[69]

Published surveys of the League's contribution to international monetary relations in the 1930s also set great store by the educational impact of the Financial and Economic Committees' work, even when they appeared to have little concrete evidence to demonstrate its effect in the 1930s. League officials continued to be at their happiest, as they had been in the 1920s, when collecting and disseminating economic, social, and, to a lesser extent, financial intelligence, articulating their mission as one to enable "peoples and governments to learn something they did not know, to frame a judgement on evidence adequate for that purpose."[70] The point is worth reflecting on for it reasserts the League's value in helping to create a community, although Pauly's emphasis on the opportunities for social learning provided by former League employees like Jacques Polak needs further interrogation: at present the evidence is more circumstantial than conclusive.[71] But there can be no doubt that the Geneva institutions, echoing a theme raised in a number of chapters in this volume, helped to promote shared or common values that were central to effective international monetary cooperation in the interwar and postwar periods. The League's formal structures and, more importantly, the personnel seconded to work for them tied the Financial and Economic Organization of the League of Nations to banks, universities, foreign policy institutions, government departments, employers associations, industrialists, and the press. We need to know much more about these connections – apparent in the work of the Gold Delegation – to determine how far the League helped to facilitate the emergence of a transnational class of advisors and opinion-makers. For the time, the League also made a unique effort, notably through the League of Nations Union, to share the details of its activities and philosophies with the wider public.

This chapter has generated as many questions as answers. It has sought to establish the practical and intellectual limitations of League efforts to coordinate international monetary policy to combat the depression, and the degree to which, at least in terms of the Gold Delegation and the World Economic Conference, the success of any policy initiative depended upon the good grace of the great powers. However, it is clear that the League did play a central role in collating and disseminating monetary and economic data, and with it a League perspective on the value of international coordination and cooperation, ideally effected through an international institution with rather more clout and independence than the League enjoyed. We need to know much more about the content and character of this process and to work towards a recognition of the lines of continuity that run from the failed internationalism of the 1920s to its triumphant resurgence in the postwar period. The League also helped bring disparate money doctors together and, by operating in the borderlands between national state institutions, private banks, universities, and large businesses, sometimes reinforced connections which already existed, but also generated new networks and contacts.

Even in failure, the League continued to play an important role in the way each sector of the political economy thought about money doctoring in the international context. The experiences of the London Conference also underlined how a severe economic crisis generated a world of such heterogeneity, hostility, and polarization that it rendered the League's framework for the elaboration and implementation of cooperative programs almost entirely redundant. But this failure helped to generate a recognition that the creation of a stable, cooperative international system would require far greater changes in the behavior and attitude of national governments than either the Concert system or the League of the 1920s had ever demanded.

Schuker's contribution explores the relative successes and failures of the key participants in money doctoring during the interwar years – the League, central banks, and private advisors. But the cursory survey of some of the advisors participating in the work of the Gold Delegation or the preparatory meetings for the World Conference would suggest not only that the boundaries between these institutions are permeable, but that, even when the most influential period of a money doctor's career is over, she or he can continue to make an important contribution to the successful application of a remedy. It is not just the content of any policy advocated by the money doctors, be they individuals or institutions, that determines the final outcome, but the political context in which that policy is applied. Included in that political context are perceptions of recent monetary history, and the lessons to be drawn from it, articulated and promoted by money doctors.[72]

Although the League had fallen from grace as an agency of international financial cooperation after 1933, during the next thirty years the lessons from its failures in the interwar years that were articulated in publications and in lectures given by the very many men and women who had served the League helped to shape the questions that were asked of the new institutions, and the degree and character of public support for them, during the war and postwar years. During the Second World War, the "role of suasion," as Mouré emphasizes in Chapter 5, was recognized by the British and U.S. administrations to be crucial to the creation and support of any international economic institutions after the war. Former League employees played an important role in this process.[73] At the same time, it can be dangerous for those formulating any given monetary remedy to develop too great a preoccupation with history lessons. It can mean that entirely new elements in the international economy may be excluded or undervalued in any analysis – as were Britain's rapidly weakening financial circumstances after 1940 by America's postwar planners. As the mixture of historical and contemporary foci in this volume illustrates, understanding the present is not just about appreciating the past.

Notes

1 Special thanks go to Kenneth Mouré for his very helpful comments on an earlier draft of this chapter, Jens-Wilhelm Wessels for research on the Gold Delegation, and to the Arts and Humanities Board of Great Britain for financial support (B/RG/AN4009/APN12550).

2 O. Singer, "Knowledge and Politics in Economic Policy-Making. Official Economic Advisors in the USA, Great Britain and Germany," in Peters and Barker (1993: 73).

3 The role of expert advisors in the field of healthcare, nuclear research, and social policy dominates studies that explore the role of the economist in the policy-making process. Useful studies include Peters and Barker (1993) and Barker and Peters (1993). Wood (1993) is particularly lively and insightful as to character and the limits of academic expertise in the shaping of Presidential policy. Rose (1993) is a useful summary of how governments, in particular, seek to learn and how lessons are drawn in a national setting.

4 Hall (1989); Furner and Supple (1990). We know less about the role of international commissions more generally. A rare study of the contribution made by international

commissions is A. Langmann, "Policy Advice in Rearranging the North–South Relationship. The Fortunes of the Pearson, Tinbergen (RIO Project) and Brandt Commissions (1968–1980)," in Peters and Barker (1993: 98–114).

5 In the interwar period, relevant studies of Keynes's contribution as advisor include Thirlwall (1976, 1982). The work of William Barber, amongst others, has led to a new appreciation of the role of economic advisors in U.S. domestic policy. See Barber (1996). However, much more time and effort has been spent seeking to estab-lish specific policy lessons from recent economic history. For a typical example, see Fuhrer (1994).

6 For early studies, see Clarke, (1967); Meyer (1970); Costigliola (1972).

7 The hope was that, by uncoupling the Economic and Financial Committees from the League of Nations, non-League states, in particular the United States, would be encouraged to join. See Dubin (1983: 50–1).

8 Pauly and de Marchi were the first to argue that the League's contribution to interna-tional financial relations needs to be recognized and questions regarding its role to be cast more widely. See de Marchi (1991: 143–78) and Pauly (1996: 1).

9 A more sustained appreciation of these committees' work is now under way in a research project led by Patricia Clavin and funded by the British Arts and Humanities Research Board (AHRB), grant no. B/RG/AN4009/APN12550.

10 Article 23(e) of the Covenant simply stipulated that League members agree "to make provisions to secure…equitable treatment for the commerce of all Members of the League" (Hill 1946: 19–20).

11 Current accounts of the structure of the League offer conflicting accounts as to the evolution of its institutions. Compare, for example, P.-Y. Ghebali, "The Institutions of the League of Nations," in Groom and Taylor (1975), and de Marchi (1991: 146).

12 Pauly (1996: 6–10; 1998: 45–7).

13 N. Piétri, "L'Oeuvre d'un organisme technique de la Société des Nations: Le comité financier et la reconstruction de l'Autriche (1921–26)," in League of Nations Library (1983: 319–42).

14 Webster (1933: 226–8); J. Barros, "The Role of Sir Eric Drummond," in League of Nations Library (1983: 31–2).

15 It proved easier to appoint men of great talent and loyalty to the League than for these men to retain the confidence of the governments of the countries which they came from. J. Siotis, "The Institutions of the League of Nations," in League of Nations Library (1983: 26–7).

16 This point is echoed in Schuker's reflections on Hoover's perception that Strong was a "mental annex to Europe" in Chapter 2.

17 Pauly has undertaken some of the groundwork here in his appreciation of the degree to which the League's extensive publication and consultation program might be seen as a forerunner of the surveillance activities undertaken by the International Monetary Fund. See Pauly (1996: *passim*; 1998: 44–78).

18 van der Pijl (1998); Dubin (1983).

19 The need to engage with public opinion more broadly is underlined in the work of Langmann, in a rare study of the work of international commissions (to which the work of the League committees may be likened given their lack of political power). He argues that the Pearson, Tinbergen, and Brandt Commissions failed to shape either the educational context or the specific actions of decision-makers. The eminence of the commissioners counted for little in the face of the vested interests of powerful national actors. But, according to Langmann's analysis, these bodies squan-dered the chance to shape political decisions in the longer term. If they had focused their efforts on the education of policy-makers and the general public alike, they may well have made "a limited, but by no means insignificant, contribution to widening the constituency for structural change in world relationships." See A. Langmann, "Policy Advice on Rearranging the North–South Relationship. The Fortunes of the

Pearson, Tinbergen (RIO Project) and the Brandt Commissions (1968–1980)," in Peters and Barker (1993: 100).

20 Alexander Loveday in the preface to Hill (1946: ix).

21 Pauly's echo of Hill's claims in *Who Elected the Bankers?* (Pauly 1998: 75–6), while persuasive, requires further measurement against the archival record.

22 PRO CAB 29/140, 7th Report of the Economic Advisory Council, "The American Situation and the World Economic Conference," May 1933: 9.

23 Papers of the State Department, National Archives II, Washington, DC (hereafter NA SD), NA SD 550.S1/9, memorandum by Feis, 9 Sept. 1932. Keynes encouraged the rumors. See the Private Papers of John Maynard Keynes, King's College, Cambridge (hereafter JMK), JMK BR/2/129, Keynes to Lippmann, 26 May 1933. The second American proposal centers on the notion of "forcing" countries to initiate reflation through a vigorous denunciation of the international gold standard. See Clavin (2000: 158).

24 Boyce (1987: 158–86); Sayers (1976: 346–51); Peden (2000: 256); Mouré (2002: ch. 6).

25 Boyce argues that on June 4, 1928, Strakosch, thinking he had secured the support of the Bank of England for the enquiry, was rather taken aback by his "attitude of complete reserve" (1987: 169). Strakosch's surprise is understandable given that Niemeyer's public face was rather different from his private support for the enquiry. Political considerations determined Niemeyer's approach. He wrote to Frederick Phillips of the British Treasury: "I think the League enquiry is greatly disliked by many of the Central Banks, and is regarded by those Central Banks as a hindrance to cooperation rather than the contrary. You and I may think they are profoundly mistaken." See Archives of the Bank of England, London (hereafter BoE), BoE OV9/23, Niemeyer to Phillips, 17 March 1930. See also Niemeyer's response to Moreau's attack on the inquiry in BoE G/1/29, memorandum by Niemeyer, 2 Jan. 1929.

26 Archives of the League of Nations, United Nations Library, Geneva (hereafter LN), LN 10E/4704/4346/R2957, Report by the Financial Committee, "Monetary Stability and the Gold Standard," 4th June 1928. Boyce also cites June 4 as the starting point for the inquiry, but, strictly speaking, the official origins of the inquiry lie in the resolution proposing the inquiry passed through the Consultative Committee of the League's Economic Organization on 18 May 1928. See LN 10E/4346/R2957, Draft resolution by Consultative Committee, 18 May 1928.

27 Sessions two to seven lasted approximately a week each and were held as follows: November 1930, January 1931, August 1931, January 1932, and May 1932.

28 The topics were then itemized in further detail. See LN 10E/7227/4346/R2957, Memorandum on the Purchasing Power of Gold, Instructions to Secretariat from the Financial Committee, 2 Oct. 1928.

29 Sayers (1976: 349). For examples of additional documentation submitted to the committee, see, for example, memoranda and letters submitted by the International Labor Office to the delegation between 1928 and 1930 on "The Effects of Possible Inadequacy of the Means of Payment on Unemployment," in LN 10E/5888/4346/R2957.

30 Economic and Financial Organization (1930a); Economic and Financial Organization (1930b); Financial and Economic Organization (1930).

31 Economic and Financial Organization (1932).

32 Obfuscation in the majority report was not always enough to satisfy dissenting views. The majority section of the publication also contained three substantial addenda noting the disagreement of Mortiz Bonn, M.G.B. Roberts, and Guido Jung to portions of the report.

33 Economic and Financial Organization (1932: 61–6). Cassel largely endorsed the minority view but proposed a more radical break with the gold standard order. See Economic and Financial Organization (1932: 74–5) and Cassel (1936: 55–81).

34 LN 10E/34452/4346, Trip to van Walré de Bordes, 27 May 1932; LN 10E/34459/4346/R2962, Bonn to Trip, 24 May 1932.
35 LN 10E/34459/4346/R2962, Bonn to Trip, 24 May 1932.
36 See, for example, LN 10E/8626/4346/R2957, memorandum by Loveday, 21 Nov. 1928.
37 LN 10E/8626/4346/R2958, memorandum by the Financial Commission, 17 December 1928.
38 Including leading central bankers from smaller countries like Czechoslovakia and the Netherlands. See, for example, LN 10F/gold/92/R2962, Pospis to Gold Delegation, 29 April 1932.
39 The Gold Delegation was not oblivious to the problem. See LN 10E/34203/4346, Bonn, Mlynarski and de Chalendar to Chairman of Gold Delegation, 12 Jan. 1932.
40 The Italian Mario Alberti argued:

> Everyone is aware of the great difficulty in estimating in any way the amount of gold owned.... It was therefore necessary to be possessed of extraordinary audacity and to be persuaded that whatever issues from the mouth of an Englishman should be regarded by all the world as the quintessence of truth to publish a series of tables giving to the last farthing the production, consumption and requirements of gold.
>
> Article published in *La Tribuna*, 8 Oct. 1930, in the Private Papers of Frederick Leith-Ross, Public Record Office, London (hereafter PRO T188), PRO T188/15B, Leith-Ross to McKenna, 1 Nov. 1930.

41 The British Royal Commission on Indian Currency and Finance and the Royal Institute of International Affairs undertook similar investigations. For details of the central bank perspective, see Sayers (1976: 349–51); Boyce (1987: 166–72); Mouré (2002: 265–72).
42 Mouré (2002: ch. 6). Strong also secured the opposition of a range of European central bankers, including Vissering, Schacht, Bachmann, and Franck. See BoE EID/4/102, conversation between Salter and Strong, 25 May 1928. The gold exchange standard received an implicit endorsement in the work of the Gold Delegation given the incorporation of the Genoa resolutions into the League Council resolution which set it up. For details, see LN 10E 4346/4346/R2957.
43 BOE OV/9/263, Norman to Moreau, 8 Jan. 1929; BOE OV/48/2, Memorandum by Siepmann on conversation between Moreau and Salter, 20 Nov. 1928.
44 Boyce (1987: 169).
45 BoE G/1/29, memorandum by Niemeyer, 2 Jan 1929.
46 Although reflecting a perspective shared by British "internationalists" everywhere, Strakosch also believed that Britain was the least able of all monetary powers to retreat into a nationalist posture – hence, whatever he deemed was in the interests of the international economy was in British interests too.
47 The Treasury liaised both with Strakosch and with the Bank of England over the Gold Delegation's work. See, for example, BOE OV/9/263, Niemeyer to Phillips, 17 March 1930; PRO T188/15B, Strakosch to Leith-Ross, 22 Sept. 1930. The *First Interim Report* triggered a discussion between Bank and Treasury officials as to the merits of its conclusions. See PRO T188/15B, McKenna to Leith-Ross, 3 Nov. 1930.
48 PRO T188/15B, Waley to Leith-Ross, 10 Dec. 1930.
49 General Correspondence of the Foreign Office, Public Record Office, London (hereafter FO 371), FO 371/16452, W795/452/98, Vansittart to Strakosch, 8 Feb. 1932.
50 PRO FO 371/16452, W795/452/98, F.11986, Leith-Ross to Vansittart, 26 Jan. 1932.
51 *Ibid.*
52 See, for example, BOE, OV/48/4, Siepmann to Jacobsson, 25 June 1932.

53 Record of Conversation between Salter and Strong, 25 June 1929; Boyce (1987: 168–9).

54 LN 10E/34452/4346/R2962, Strakosch to Felkin, 22 June 1932.

55 These included the severely crippled banking systems of Germany and Austria, the postponement of war debt and reparation payments for twelve months under the Hoover Moratorium (in most cases these payments were not resumed), German commercial debts frozen under a complex arrangement of standstill agreements, and the landmark departure of sterling from the international gold standard.

56 The secret gentleman's agreement that accompanied the Lausanne settlement forestalled the ratification of the deal signed at Lausanne until a satisfactory deal was signed with the United States on war debts. See Clavin (1996: 30–5) and Kent (1986: 368–9).

57 LN 34452/4346/R2962, Mant to van Walré de Bordes, 28 May 1932; *Final Report of the Gold Delegation*: 7.

58 These were that war debts and tariff rates were left off the agenda, while silver production and bimetallism should be included.

59 Indeed, Loveday was later to bemoan the League's commitment to "general conventions to the system of applying to each problem the procedure which seems most likely to result in business being done." See Loveday (1938: 788).

60 FO 371/16418, W8609/8034/50, memorandum by Simon, 25 July 1932; T188/43, Simon to Leith-Ross, 27 May 1932; NA SD 550.S1/141, Atherton to Stimson, 20 Aug. 1932; Records of the Secretariat of the League of Nations (hereafter LN), LN C.764 M361 1932 II, Record of Organizing Committee, July 1932. The Organizing Committee comprised Constantin von Neurath (Germany), Massigli (France), Biancheri-Chiappari (Italy), Brandland (Norway), Swada (Japan), van Langenhove (Belgium), and Norman Davis (USA). Avenol, Alexander Loveday, and Stoppani represented the Secretariat of the League of Nations.

61 The Financial and Economic Preparatory Committees first convened on 31 October 1932 with war debt payments due to the United States on 15 December; the World Economic Conference proper opened on June 12, three days before the next war debt payment was due.

62 BoE OV/48/4, Jacobsson to Osborne, 8 July 1932.

63 LN 10A 3941/38756, correspondence between Leith-Ross and Stoppani, 18 and 20 October 1932.

64 See Committee's statement in PRO FO 371/16420, W12285/8034/50, memorandum by Trip, 8 Nov. 1932. For discussions of alternative U.S. nominations, see NA SD 550.S1/120 ½, Feis to Stimson, 2 Oct. 1932.

65 After taking office Roosevelt convened an informal advisory committee to oversee U.S. policy preparations for the world conference, which was soon riven with division over the direction of U.S. monetary policy and the value of an internationalist agenda. See Clavin (1996: 85).

66 PRO FO 371/17305, W4502/5/50, Leith-Ross to Simon, 26 April 1933.

67 For their views, see papers relating to the Ministerial Committee of the World Economic Conference, Public Record Office, Kew, Cab 29/142, notably the meeting between MacDonald, Beneš, and Hymans, 19 June 1933.

68 Chapters 1 and 10.

69 Loveday describes the League as becoming a "clearing house of ideas" (1938: 795). See also Walters (1952: 523–750); Hill (1946: 72–94); and Dubin (1983: 44–6).

70 Loveday (1938: 802).

71 Pauly (1996: 26–33); Jabko (2000); League of Nations Library (1983: 44–6).

72 O. Singer, "Knowledge and Politics in Economic Policy-Making. Official Economic Advisors in the USA, Great Britain and Germany," in Peters and Barker (1993: 72–86). The general conceptual framework is known as "discourse structuration." For an extended exposition, see Burns and Flam (1986: *passim*).

73 See, for example, publications by former League officials intended to shape planning for the new economic order to be established after war's end: Delegation on Economic Depression (1945); Economic, Financial and Transit Organization (1942); League of Nations, Information Section (1939); Economic, Financial and Transit Section (1944); League of Nations (1948); Tinbergen and Polak (1950).

References

Barber, W. (1996) *Designs within Disorder: Franklin D. Roosevelt, the Economists, and the Shaping of American Economic Policy, 1933–1945*, Cambridge and New York: Cambridge University Press.

Barker, A. and B. Peters (1993) *The Politics of Expert Advice. Creating, Using and Manipulating Scientific Knowledge for Public Policy*, Edinburgh: Edinburgh University Press.

Boyce, R. (1987) *British Capitalism at the Crossroads, 1919–1932: A Study in Politics, Economics and International Relations*, Cambridge: Cambridge University Press.

Burns, T. and H. Flam (1986) *The Shaping of Social Organisation: Social Rule Theory with Applications*, Beverly Hills, CA: Sage.

Cassel, G. (1936) *The Downfall of the Gold Standard*, Oxford: Clarendon Press.

Clarke, S. (1967) *Central Bank Co-operation, 1924–1931*, New York: Federal Reserve Bank of New York.

Clavin, P. (1996) *The Failure of Economic Diplomacy. Britain, Germany, France and the United States, 1931–36*, London: Macmillan.

Clavin, P. (2000) *The Great Depression in Europe*, London and New York: Palgrave.

Costigliola, F. (1972) "The Other Side of Isolationism: the Establishment of the World Bank, 1929–1930," *Journal of American History* 59: 602–20.

Delegation on Economic Depression (1945) *Report of the Delegation on Economic Depression*, pts. I and II, Geneva: League of Nations.

Dubin, M. (1983) "Toward the Bruce Report: The Economic and Social Programmes of the League of Nations in the Avenol Era," in League of Nations Library, *The League of Nations in Retrospect. Proceedings of the Symposium*, Berlin and New York: Walter de Gruyter.

Economic and Financial Organization (1930a) *Interim Report of the Gold Delegation of the Financial Committee*, Geneva: League of Nations.

Economic and Financial Organization (1930b) *Selected Documents Submitted to the Gold Delegation of the Financial Committee*, Geneva: League of Nations.

Economic and Financial Organization (1932) *Report of the Gold Delegation Financial Committee*, Geneva: League of Nations.

Economic, Financial and Transit Organization (1942) *Commercial Policy in the Interwar Period: International Proposals and National Policies*, Geneva: League of Nations.

Economic, Financial and Transit Section (1944) *Report to the Council on the Work of the 1943 Joint Session, Princeton, N.J., 1943*, Geneva: League of Nations.

Eichengreen, B. (1995) *Golden Fetters: The Gold Standard and the Great Depression, 1919–1939*, Oxford: Oxford University Press.

Financial and Economic Organization (1930) *Legislation on Gold*, Geneva: League of Nations.

Fuhrer, J. (ed.) (1994) *Goals, Guidelines and Constraints Facing Monetary Policymakers*, Boston, MA: Federal Reserve Bank.

Furner, M. and B. Supple (1990) *The State and Economic Knowledge*, Cambridge: Cambridge University Press.

Groom, A. and P. Taylor (eds.) (1975) *Functionalism. Theory and Practice in International Relations*, New York: Crane, Russak.

Hall, P. (1989) *The Political Power of Economic Ideas*, Princeton, NJ: Princeton University Press.

Hill, M. (1946) *The Economic and Financial Organization of the League of Nations. A Survey of Twenty-Five Years' Experience*, Washington, DC: Carnegie Endowment for International Peace.

Jabko, N. (2000) "European Community as Epistemic Community: The Case of Regional Development," mimeo.

Kent, B. (1986) *The Spoils of War. The Politics, Economics and Diplomacy of Reparations*, Oxford: Clarendon Press.

League of Nations (1948) *International Cartels: A League of Nations Memorandum*, prepared by Gertrud Lovasy, New York: United Nations, Lake Success.

League of Nations, Information Section (1939) *Towards a Better Economic World*, Geneva: League of Nations.

League of Nations Library (1983) *The League of Nations in Retrospect. Proceedings of the Symposium*, Berlin and New York: Walter de Gruyter.

Loveday, A. (1938) "The Economic and Financial Activities of the League," *International Affairs* 17: 788–808.

Marchi, N.de. (1991) "League of Nations Economists and the Ideal of Peaceful Change in the Decade of the 'Thirties'," in C. Goodwin (1991) *Economics and National Security. A History of their Interaction*, Annual Supplement to vol. 23, *History of the Political Economy*, Durham, NC, and London: Duke University Press.Meyer, R. (1970) *Bankers' Diplomacy: Monetary Stabilization in the Twenties*, New York: Columbia University Press.

Mouré, K. (2002) *The Gold Standard Illusion: France, the Bank of France and the International Gold Standard, 1914–1939*, Oxford: Oxford University Press.

Pauly, L. (1996) "The League of Nations and the Foreshadowing of the International Monetary Fund," *Essays in International Finance*, no. 201, December, Princeton, NJ: Princeton University Press, International Finance Section.

Pauly, L. (1998) *Who Elected the Bankers? Surveillance and Control in the World Economy*, Ithaca, NY, and London: Cornell University Press.

Peden, G. (2000) *The Treasury and British Public Policy, 1896–1959*, Oxford: Oxford University Press.

Peters, G. and A. Barker (eds.) (1993) *Advising Western European Governments. Inquiries, Expertise and Public Policy*, Edinburgh: Edinburgh University Press.

Rose, R. (1993) *Lesson-drawing in Public Policy. A Guide to Learning Across Time and Space*, Chatham, NJ: Chatham House Publishers.

Sayers, R. (1976) *The Bank of England, 1891–1944*, vol. 1, Cambridge: Cambridge University Press.

Thirlwall, A. (1976) *Keynes and International Monetary Relations*, Basingstoke: Macmillan.

Thirlwall, A. (1982) *Keynes as Policy Advisor*, Basingstoke: Macmillan.

Tinbergen, J. and J. Polak (1950) *The Dynamics of Business Cycles. A Study in Economic Fluctuations*, 2nd edn., London: Routledge, Kegan & Paul; first published in 1942.

van der Pijl, K. (1998) *Transnational Classes and International Relations*, London and New York: Routledge.

Walters, F. (1952) *A History of the League of Nations*, New York, Toronto, and London: Oxford University Press.

Webster, C. (1933) *The League of Nations in Theory and Practice*, London: George Allen & Unwin.

Wood, R. (1993) *Whatever Possessed the President. Academic Experts and Presidential Policy, 1960–1988*, Boston, MA: University of Massachusetts Press.

9 The Southern side of "embedded liberalism"

America's unorthodox money doctoring during the early post-1945 years

Eric Helleiner[1]

In an important 1983 article, John Ruggie (1983) highlighted the central role of the ideology of "embedded liberalism" in influencing the construction of the global monetary order after the Second World War. Embedded liberals sought to build quite a different kind of global monetary order from the gold standard that "classical liberals" had endorsed. Instead of celebrating the discipline of the gold standard, they sought to strengthen the capacity of national governments to pursue domestically oriented activist monetary policies (although still within the context of a multilateral world economy). National policy autonomy was bolstered through adjustable exchange rates, the provision of balance of payments financing, and the endorsement of capital controls. The international monetary system was now to be more of a "servant" of the domestic Keynesian and welfarist goals that had emerged so prominent across many industrial countries in the wake of the Great Depression of the 1930s (Helleiner 1993).

The role of Southern countries within the new "embedded liberal" international monetary order has received less attention than that of Northern countries. This neglect is unfortunate because dramatic monetary reforms took place in Southern countries in the early postwar years which were in keeping with the new "embedded liberal" commitment to domestic monetary autonomy. In the first few decades of the twentieth century, many independent Southern countries had created central banks whose mandate was one endorsed by classical liberals: maintaining an internationally convertible currency on the gold standard. In other parts of the South – particularly those regions that were colonized – currency boards had been introduced for the same purpose. During the early post-1945 years, however, policymakers in the many Southern countries followed their counterparts in the North in rejecting this "orthodox" approach to monetary policy.[2] In place of currency boards and the gold standard, they introduced capital controls, more flexible exchange rates, and powerful national central banks designed to serve the domestic goals of rapid industrial development and nation-building.

This chapter examines the politics that produced the post-1945 wave of Southern monetary reforms, calling special attention to the important role that

American "money doctors" played in promoting and supporting them. Despite their political importance, the activities of these money doctors have received little scholarly attention from historians of either U.S. foreign economic policy or international money doctoring. To the former, U.S. policy in this period is interesting because it marked a sharp break from the orthodox approach to money doctoring that the American Edwin Kemmerer had encouraged during the interwar period. To the latter, the episode should also be of interest because it highlights an episode in which the advice of money doctors was quite different from that traditionally associated with international "money doctoring" during the pre-1945 era or during the 1980s and 1990s.

In the first section of this chapter I outline the activities of American "money doctors" in this period and seek to explain their support for unorthodox monetary reforms in Southern countries. I argue that their support stemmed partly from their new commitment to "embedded liberal" ideas, but also from their recognition of the geo-strategic value of not challenging the growing power of Southern economic nationalism in the postwar period. In the second and third sections I suggest that the importance of U.S. support for unorthodox monetary reforms is highlighted well if we examine two contexts where it was not present: regions coming under British or French financial influence. The more orthodox approach to money doctoring adopted by these two financial powers, in combination with less strong support for nationalist ideas in some specific Southern countries, helps to explain why monetary reforms took a more limited and cautious form in some parts of the South in the postwar period. I conclude the chapter with a very brief discussion of the importance of this period for the study of international money doctoring.

America's new "money doctors" and Southern goals

To those familiar with U.S. foreign economic policy during the early twentieth century, U.S. policy towards monetary reform in Southern countries after the Second World War may seem surprising. In the pre-1931 era U.S. policymakers and private financiers had played a lead role in encouraging many Southern countries to adopt the gold standard and set up national monetary authorities that could guarantee its maintenance (e.g. Rosenberg 1985; Drake 1989). Indeed, the American Edwin Kemmerer became the most famous of the foreign "money doctors" promoting monetary reforms along these classical liberal lines across Latin America and other parts of the South in the interwar period. In the early post-1945 years, however, U.S. policymakers did an about-face. Explicitly rejecting Kemmerer's approach, they became leading critics of orthodox monetary policy in the Southern countries. Because of the dominant position of the U.S. in the postwar global monetary order, this policy reversal had an important impact on the direction of monetary reforms in many Southern countries in the postwar period.

The first sign of this reversal came from the Federal Reserve, which had been given the task of responding to a 1941 request for advice on monetary reform from the Paraguayan government. In response to this request, the chief of the Latin American section of the staff of the Federal Reserve's Board of Governors – Robert Triffin – launched an extensive process of consultation over several years with financial officials from the U.S., Paraguay, and other Latin American countries (Triffin 1966a: 16, 112–14). Out of this consultation process emerged the view among key Federal Reserve officials that a different approach to money doctoring would be necessary in the postwar period from that promoted by Kemmerer.

This new approach was first put into place in Paraguay in a set of monetary reforms in 1943–5 which the U.S. Federal Reserve described as "a fundamental departure from the central banking structures previously established in Latin America" (U.S. Federal Reserve 1945: 528). Triffin himself described the Paraguayan reforms as "revolutionary" (1946: 25). The Paraguayan model of reform was then promoted actively by Triffin and other U.S. officials in a series of "money doctoring" missions over the following decade in countries such as Ethiopia (1942–4), Guatemala (1945), the Dominican Republic (1947), Honduras (1950), the Philippines (1949), South Korea (1950), and Ceylon (1950).[3] In Kim's words, the new Bank of Paraguay's legislation "heralded much post-war central banking legislation that followed" (1965: 6).

Various publications by Federal Reserve officials in this period outline clearly their rationale for the new approach to money doctoring (U.S. Federal Reserve 1945; Triffin 1944, 1946, 1966a, 1966b). They argued that the interwar experience had highlighted the drawbacks of a passive monetary policy geared externally to respond automatically to changes in the balance of payments. In countries whose balance of payments were vulnerable to crop failures, dramatic changes in export markets, or volatile international capital movements, this "monetary automatism" was simply too costly in an economic and social sense. It magnified – rather than minimized – the impact of international instability on the domestic economy in this context.[4] In the 1920s, for example, orthodox central banks in Latin America reinforced the inflationary impact of sudden capital inflows by expanding the money supply in response to the large balance of payments surpluses these inflows produced. Then, when the balance of payments turned suddenly into deficit in the 1929–31 period (as capital flows suddenly collapsed and export markets dried up), orthodox central banks reinforced deflationary tendencies by contracting the money supply. In this way, orthodox monetary management subjected these economies to what Triffin called "unbearable and often unnecessary disruptions" (1946: 74).

Triffin (1946, 1966a) also noted that these adjustments might not even be equilibrating in the way that orthodox theory predicted:

> the very basis of the theory of automatic adjustments is open to serious objections in countries the export trade of which is highly concentrated in a few categories of products with inelastic demand. The pressures exerted upon the balance of payments often originate much more in the harvest within the country or in the movement of the business cycle in the

purchasing countries than in fundamental price and cost disparities with relation to competing markets.

(Triffin 1946: 79)

Similarly, he argued that traditional adjustment mechanisms might not be effective in poorer, trade-dependent countries where internal price levels were mostly determined by international prices of its exports and imports:

> It is possible that an increase in the means of payments would not be followed by a rise in domestic prices, the level of which remains fixed by international factors, but by a direct increase in imports, with a correlative deficit in the inflow and outflow of foreign exchange.

(Triffin 1946: 80)

He also noted that traditional adjustment mechanisms may be inappropriate in situations where a balance of payments deficit resulted not from price disparities or excessive credit, but from the preference of domestic consumers to import goods once a certain level of economic development had been reached.[5]

In the new American view, what was thus needed was a form of monetary management that *insulated* the national economy from international disruptions rather than *reinforced* the latter's impact on the former. Whereas Kemmerer's banks (and colonial currency boards) had prioritized the external stability of the currency and international equilibrium, the new priority was domestic economic development. In the Guatemalan reform of 1945, for example, the Federal Reserve highlighted that the goal was to create "guidance of monetary policy primarily by analysis of domestic developments, rather than in automatic response to changes in international reserves" (quoted in Laso 1957–8: 448). Similarly, one U.S. official involved in the 1950 Honduran reforms lamented how the monetary system had "not been used as an instrument to promote economic development" in the past, but that now it would be able "to assist the growth of the national economy" (Vinelli 1950–1: 420).

Indeed, this new domestic priority was clearly written into the constitutions of the central banks set up by the new U.S. money doctors. The Paraguayan central bank, which became the prototype of the new approach, described one of its key purposes as "the development of productive activities" (Triffin 1946: 115). A key goal of the new Philippine central bank established in 1948 was also "to promote a rising level of productive employment and real income in the Philippines." Similarly, Ceylon's new central bank set up in 1949 was designed to serve, among other things, "[t]he promotion and maintenance of a high level of production, employment, and real income in Ceylon, and [t]he encouragement and promotion of the full development of the productive resources of Ceylon" (quoted in Kim 1965: 15, fn. 2).

To achieve these new domestic objectives, central banks had to have quite different charters than those written by Kemmerer. To begin with, their note issue and deposit liabilities were no longer regulated by rigid provisions linking them to gold or foreign exchange reserves. With this external constraint loosened, the national currency could be managed without such a strict connection to the condition of the balance of payments. To ensure that international economy did not disrupt domestic goals, central banks were also allowed to adjust the exchange rate within limits in certain circumstances and to control capital inflows and outflows. Triffin (1966a: 141) acknowledged that many economic liberals would regard the endorsement of the latter in particular as "highly unorthodox," but he reminded them that the new IMF Articles of Agreement now permitted and even encouraged capital controls (by saying that IMF funds could not finance large capital outflows).[6] Indeed, the principle negotiators of the Bretton Woods agreements, Keynes and White, had seen capital controls as a central element of the new "embedded liberal" monetary order (Helleiner 1993).

Federal Reserve officials also insisted that central banks be equipped with strong powers to promote the development of their national economies.[7] Central banks set up with Kemmerer's advice had usually been expected to influence the money supply through mechanisms such as discount rate changes and open market operations. In most Southern countries (as well as the British Dominions), U.S. officials noted that these tools were quite ineffective because domestic financial markets were underdeveloped and the banking system was often dominated by foreign banks which responded primarily to monetary developments only in their home country. To become more effective, central banks needed to be able to impose reserve requirements on private banks and to control private lending, and perhaps even to lend directly to the public.[8]

Central bank involvement in lending to the public was advocated not just to strengthen central banks' ability to do national monetary management. It was also proposed as a means to promote developmental goals more directly. In contexts where foreign banks dominated the domestic banking system, there was often very little "developmental lending" for the domestic economy. A central bank could fill this void by taking on the role directly. Alternatively, it could play a key role in encouraging the establishment of domestically owned private financial institutions to do this kind of lending.

Interestingly, U.S. officials also did not oppose provisions which allowed central banks to lend to their own governments. The reasoning was that it was simply unrealistic to expect a central bank to behave otherwise in the context of many developing countries. As Triffin put it, "Few central banks are really in a position to deny assistance to the Treasury" (1946: 23).

One final recommendation of U.S. money doctors in this period is worth noting in the context of contemporary support for "dollarization." They encouraged Southern governments to eliminate the use of foreign currencies within their territory wherever that practice was widespread (e.g. such as the cases of Honduras, the Dominican Republic, Paraguay, and Ethiopia). It was impossible, U.S. officials argued, for a central bank to develop a strong and independent monetary policy devoted to national development unless the currency it issued held a monopoly position inside the country. In the Dominican Republic, for example, Wallich and Triffin (1953. 24) noted how difficult it was to control inflationary pressures deriving from a balance of payments surplus in a context where the U.S. dollar was the main currency in use (as it had been since 1905). In Paraguay, where an (outdated) Argentine currency standard was widely used, U.S. officials also argued that the use of a foreign standard "throws doubt upon the stability" of the national currency (Triffin 1946: 60).

The decision of U.S. Federal Reserve officials to turn their backs on Kemmerer and endorse quite unorthodox monetary policy and institutional reforms in Southern countries requires political explanation, especially since it was often quite controversial at the time among orthodox thinkers and some parts of the business community.[9] A key part of the explanation is the new ideological commitment of U.S. policymakers in this area to "embedded liberal" ideas. Triffin and other economists in the U.S. Federal Reserve were clearly influenced by the Keynesian revolution that was underway. Keynesian ideas were important not just in legitimating a more domestically oriented monetary policy geared to full employment and growth. In his earlier writings (particularly his 1913 recommendations for a central bank in India), Keynes had also advocated that central banks in developing countries become involved in the direct provision of credit for the support of domestic industry and agriculture (Chandavarkar 1996: 99). This approach to central banking – which had been rejected by British and U.S. officials in the 1920s – was the same as that now endorsed by the U.S. Federal Reserve.

Policymakers who were sympathetic to "embedded liberal" ideas had been strengthened politically inside the U.S. by the shift away from financial and monetary orthodoxy that took place within the country in the wake of the Great Depression in the early 1930s. I have described elsewhere how the opposition of New Dealers to the liberal financial world of the 1920s had considerable influence in turning U.S. Treasury officials away from orthodox international monetary policy during the years leading up to the Bretton Woods negotiations (Helleiner 1994: ch. 2). Indeed, Treasury officials may have played a role in encouraging U.S. support for unorthodox central banking in some Southern countries such as the Philippines (Hartendorp 1958: 255, 618). But the U.S. Federal Reserve had also been affected by the new thinking of the New Deal, particularly after it was headed by Marriner Eccles, a non-New York banker with quite unorthodox views.

Even if U.S. officials were not themselves convinced by the new monetary ideas unleashed by the 1930s experience and Keynesian revolution, they were forced to recognize the political power of these ideas abroad. Across the world, monetary policy had moved during the 1930s and wartime decisively away from the orthodox notion that monetary policy should be geared externally to respond automatically to changes in the balance of payments. In place of this "monetary automatism" was a new commitment to "autonomous monetary management" geared to *domestic* goals of monetary stability, full employment and rapid growth (Triffin 1946: 22). Triffin concluded from these changes that it was simply not politically feasible to try to return to orthodox policies: "Tomorrow's currencies will be managed currencies…. Any attempt to enforce rigid solutions patterned upon orthodox gold standard doctrines would be even more futile in the postwar than it already proved to be in the interwar period" (1966a: 144).

This shift away from orthodox monetary policies had been particularly striking in Latin America, the region which strongly influenced Triffin's and other Federal Reserve officials' early views. When declining export markets and the collapse of U.S. lending produced dramatic balance of payments crises in the early 1930s, most Latin American countries abandoned the gold standard and introduced exchange controls rather than undergo dramatic deflations. Many of them also began during the 1930s to experiment with more activist monetary policies aimed at financing government spending and producing domestic economic growth. Exchange controls, which had initially been introduced as temporary measures, were often made permanent in order to allow this kind of monetary policy to be pursued independently of external constraints. Governments also became more directly involved – often via the central bank – in directing credit to the private sector as a means of promoting economic growth.

These reforms were inspired by more of an "economic nationalist" ideology than the Keynesian ideology that guided Northern countries' reforms.[10] Their economic nationalism was similar to that of nineteenth-century thinkers such as List and Hamilton, who advocated rapid industrialization via strong state intervention in the economy. While List and Hamilton advocated tariffs and domestic subsidies to industry, economic nationalists in Southern countries in this era also promoted broader forms of state intervention in the economy, including that of active monetary management. In addition to supporting industrialization, these economic nationalists also saw the creation of a powerful central bank and a new national currency as tools of nation-building and important symbols of national sovereignty.

In the early 1940s, U.S. Federal Reserve officials displayed a detailed understanding of the various policy innovations in Latin America during the 1930s. Triffin (1944), in particular, was very knowledgeable about them and explicitly acknowledged that they had strongly influenced his thinking.[11] He made a special point of frequently citing his debt to Raul Prebisch's "pioneering work" in this area (Triffin 1966a: 141, fn. 2). Prebisch, who was head of the Argentine central bank between 1935 and 1943 and then became head of the UN Economic Commission for Latin America, was the leading theorist of the "structuralist" school that advocated economic nationalist policies of import-substitution industrialization. Triffin recognized his importance by consulting him in detail on the initial Paraguayan reforms.[12] Other Latin American governments, such as that in the Dominican Republic, also invited Prebisch for consultations with the Americans as part of the preparations for U.S.-led monetary reform programs (Wallich and Triffin 1953: 25).

U.S. officials were thus very familiar with the policy changes that had taken place across Latin America during the 1930s and understood the extent to which the new approach to monetary policymaking had become politically entrenched in the region. To challenge this approach might not just be futile but also detrimental to broader U.S. geo-strategic goals. In the important

Paraguayan case, for example, U.S. monetary consultations took place at a time when U.S. policymakers were actively seeking through aid packages and diplomatic efforts to prevent the Paraguayan government from allying itself too closely with the Axis powers. Accommodating the nationalist leanings of the country's government, rather than challenging them, was the U.S. priority. And to many nationalist Paraguay officials, monetary reform served not just the goal of industrialization but also the objective of consolidating an exclusive national currency for the first time. Indeed, U.S. advisors played to nationalist sentiments when they advocated the elimination of the use of the old Argentine monetary standard on the grounds that it would help the country "reaffirm its monetary independence and sovereignty" (U.S. Federal Reserve 1944: 46). They argued that the use of a foreign currency standard "ha[d] injured the prestige of the national currency both at home and abroad" (U.S. Federal Reserve 1944: 46) and they encouraged the naming of the new currency the "guarani," a name which "derives from the racial origins of the Paraguayan nation" (U.S. Federal Reserve 1944: 47).[13]

By the late 1940s, geo-strategic concerns in the new Cold War also encouraged an accommodating approach towards economic nationalism in the South.[14] In the Philippines, for example, local politicians after the war sought to replace the colonial currency board with a powerful central bank that would introduce capital controls and pursue expansionary monetary policies (Cullather 1994: 63–6). These local demands stemmed not just from the goal of rapid industrialization (and the pressing fiscal needs of the government), but also from broader nationalist sentiments that a currency board arrangement was "an unsuitable system for an independent Philippines."[15] Many U.S. officials were wary of the local demands for monetary reform and would have preferred to see more orthodox deflationary measures introduced by the late 1940s. But Cullather (1994: 64–71, 76, 81, 191) shows how Cold War fears of the growing power of left-wing rebels in the Philippines encouraged the U.S. to go along with local expansionary objectives and not to press for deflationary measures which might have given political strength to the rebels.

One further geo-strategic motivation deserves mention. In countries emerging from European colonial rule a more sympathetic approach to nationalist monetary reforms helped U.S. officials to gain influence in the newly independent countries. Some ex-British colonies, for example, explicitly sought out U.S. "money doctors" instead of British ones because the latter favored the maintenance of colonial boards (for reasons explained in the next section). In Ceylon, for example, the currency board "was looked upon as a financial appendage of colonial government and was recognized as part and parcel of the system of colonial administration" (Karunatilake 1973: 3). The construction of a central bank came to be seen by its supporters as necessary to achieve "economic freedom"; indeed, one supporter argued that was even more important than the Independence Bill (Karunatilake 1973: 8). Even the ability to adjust the national exchange rate – not possible under the currency board arrangements – was seen in political terms by the Minister of Finance in 1949 as creating a "free currency, the content of which, the value of which, we and we alone can determine according to the best interests of the people of Ceylon" (quoted in Karunatilake 1973: 13). Since U.S. officials were known to be more sympathetic to these nationalist goals,[16] they were invited – instead of Bank of England officials – to help construct the country's first central bank. Indeed, local policymakers wanted a central bank like that recently constructed under U.S. advice in Korea and the Philippines (Karunatilake 1973: 5).

In British-occupied Ethiopia during the early 1940s, a similar situation existed. At this time, the money in circulation within the country was a motley collection of currency issued by the Ethiopian state, Maria Theresa thalers, traditional commodity-based small-denomination money, and Italian and British currencies. Ethiopian policymakers sought to create an exclusive national currency for the first time in order to assert the state's authority over the whole country and to create a monetary system that could be mobilized to promote rapid economic growth. The British were supportive of the objective of consolidating the national currency, but they pushed for it to be managed on a currency board basis. To the Ethiopians, however, a currency board was unacceptable since it prevented them from pursuing their nationalist monetary goals. They also saw the British proposal in highly political terms as an attempt to turn the country into a protectorate or colony of the U.K.[17] To offset British influence, Ethiopian policymakers turned to U.S. officials for advice, recognizing correctly that the latter would support their goal of creating a powerful central bank guided by more nationalist thinking. Indeed, U.S. officials not only provided advice but also secretly printed Ethiopia's first notes and provided the central bank with its first governors until 1959 (Degefe 1995).[18]

U.S. support for the new approach to monetary policy thus had both ideological and geo-strategic political roots. Regardless of its sources, U.S. support was important in encouraging the trend of nationalist monetary reforms in the South. Its importance stemmed not so much from the specific content of the advice provided by U.S. money doctors. Most of the countries that received U.S. advice were, after all, already committed to the course that U.S. money doctors recommended.[19] The 1930s experience, the rise of economic nationalism, and broader anti-colonial sentiments had all played a role in encouraging Southern countries to reject the orthodox monetary economics. What was more important than the specifics of U.S. advice was the simple fact that the political weight of the world's dominant financial power would not stand in the way of nationalist reforms.

Discouraging "the wrong tendencies": British resistance to nationalist monetary reforms

The importance of U.S. support is highlighted well if we turn to examine some cases where it was not present. As mentioned already, British policymakers were quite opposed to nationalist monetary reforms and they went out of their way to advise newly independent, ex-British colonies not to implement them. Some countries – such as Ceylon and Ethiopia, as we have seen – simply ignored this advice, but others were forced to listen because of continuing close economic and political ties to Britain. In these latter cases the introduction of nationalist monetary reforms took place more cautiously and slowly.

Why were British policymakers so opposed to the new approach to monetary policy in Southern countries? The opposition was partly ideological. The institution that took charge of British foreign economy policy in this area in the early postwar period was the Bank of England. Alongside Kemmerer, Bank of England officials had been leaders of orthodox "money doctoring" during the interwar period (see, for example, Plumptre 1940). Despite the experience of the 1930s and the nationalization of the bank in 1944, its outlook remained largely orthodox throughout this period. The Bank of England's leading money doctors in the postwar period, such as J.B. Loynes, largely picked up where their predecessors had left off.

More important in explaining British policy was the goal of preserving the sterling area and Britain's privileged position within it.[20] The continued existence of the sterling area after the war provided Britain with not just international prestige but also important balance of payments support. This support came partly from the fact that sterling-area countries and colonial currency boards held very often considerable foreign exchange reserves in sterling and in London; indeed, in the case of currency boards Balogh noted that this arrangement ensured that any increase in the money supply within the Southern country resulted in a "*de facto* loan" to Britain (and often at below "market" rates since sterling balances earned very low rates of interest) (1966: 30). The absence of capital controls and exchange rate risk within the sterling area – when combined with limited local money markets – also encouraged private banks, companies, and individuals in many sterling-area countries to export savings and liquid funds to London markets. When this export of local savings was offset by long-term loans back to the colony from London there might be no net balance of payments benefit to Britain. But the arrangement still provided one further benefit of the sterling area to Britain: that of bolstering the City of London's role as an international financial center.

If countries turned to unorthodox policies these benefits of the sterling area to Britain would diminish. Activist domestic monetary management, for example, might produce balance of payments deficits that would force countries to drawn down their sterling reserves and sterling assets in London. Demand for sterling and sterling assets in London, and for sterling more generally, would also be reduced if national currencies were backed with less than 100 per cent reserves or if reserves were held in local government securities. Similarly, capital controls and the creation of domestic money and capital markets might reduce capital outflows to London and reduce the dependence of Southern borrowers on London financiers.

British hostility towards the new nationalist approaches to monetary policy initially took an interesting form: opposition to the creation of central banks in newly independent countries altogether. Throughout the 1940s and 1950s, at the same time that the U.S. was advocating the creation of powerful central banks, the Bank of England usually opposed their creation, and it was still promoting the creation of currency boards in countries such as Jordan and Libya in this period. In their various colonies, British officials went to great lengths to try to convince local policymakers not to create central banks and to maintain the colonial currency board arrangements after they attained independence.[21]

In some cases they even sought initially to keep together the large currency zones that had been administered by one currency board in colonial times, such as those in East Africa (Tanzania, Uganda, Kenya, Aden) or Malaya (Singapore, Malaysia, Brunei, Borneo, Sarawak).[22] In other regions such as West Africa, however, the British were willing to accept what Loynes called "prestige and appearance" reasons why countries would want to break up these zones and create national currencies immediately at independence (as Ghana did in 1957, Nigeria in 1958, Sierra Leone in 1963, and Gambia in 1964).[23] Most newly independent countries did, indeed, place considerable symbolic value on the creation of a national currency. As Ghana's Finance Minister put it, "no nation could be regarded as fully independent which shared a common currency with its former colonial neighbours."[24] But the British hoped that the creation of these national currencies would not lead to what Loynes called privately "the wrong tendencies." He hoped they would simply provide a "national façade for the currency."[25] As the Acting British Governor of Sierra Leone put it in 1960, "any reforms should be of a very conservative nature."[26]

In a further effort to prevent the creation of central banks, the British even began to reform currency boards to try to accommodate criticisms of their operations (see, for example, EACB 1967, 1972; Lee 1986: 20). Some currency boards, such as those in East Africa in 1955 and Malaya in 1960, were allowed to begin issuing some unbacked money in an effort to increase the flexibility of their operations. These currency boards were also permitted to invest their reserves in non-sterling assets such as local government securities and dollars around this time. The East African currency board also began in 1960 to cultivate a local money market by discounting activities in the local Treasury bill market, and by allowing banks to hold balances with it and offering clearance and settlement services. In addition, the headquarters of these operations were moved from London to the regions themselves and more local staff were recruited. Finally, colonial images on currency board notes and coins were replaced with iconography more appropriate to newly independent countries – in 1959 in the case of Malaya (the queen was replaced by a fishing craft) and 1964 in East Africa (Lake Victoria appeared on the notes).

The British opposition to central banks contrasted sharply not just with U.S. policy but also with the Bank of England's own policy during the interwar period. In that earlier era, the head of the Bank of England, Montagu Norman, had played a lead role in encouraging countries around the world to set up independent central banks where none yet existed (including in some colonized regions such as India). These banks, he had hoped, would help to insulate the management of money from political pressures and to preserve the international gold standard. Now that central banks had become associated with more activist monetary management, however, the Bank of England wanted nothing to do with them.

Central banks, it now argued, would only lead to inflationary pressures, as politicians controlled them to finance government deficits. Moreover, efforts to promote economic development with expansionist monetary policies could also lead to inflation and balance of payments crises. Capital controls, British officials argued, were often ineffective and would also discourage new inflows of capital (EACB 1966: 13). British officials also argued that modern central banking could not work in contexts where no local money and capital markets existed. If efforts were made to overcome this problem by involving the central bank directly in lending – as U.S. officials recommended – this would only risk undermining confidence in the bank if losses were sustained. As a final point, the British often stressed that, in comparison to currency boards, central banks were more expensive to run and required a kind of expertise that was often not available in newly independent countries (see, for example, EACB 1965: 7–11; Uche 1997).

It quickly became clear to British officials, however, that most Southern governments disregarded these arguments and planned to establish central banks anyway. In part, the desire of Southern policymakers for a modern central bank was symbolic. As Bangura notes in discussing nationalists in Africa, "they associated central banks with political maturity and independence" (1983: 49; see also Basu 1967: 52). Similarly, Schenck notes in the case of Malaya's decision to create a central bank in 1959: "For Malayan ministers, a central bank was overwhelmingly a political symbol rather than an instrument to wield real economic independence" (1993: 427).

Equally importantly, however, many policymakers in the South rejected currency boards because they precluded the kind of activist monetary policy that was seen as necessary to serve domestic goals of economic development. As Ghana's first Finance Minister put it, "a Currency Board is the financial hallmark of colonialism. And it is a dead thing as well, an automatic machine which has no volition of its own and could do nothing to assist in developing our own financial institutions" (Government of the Gold Coast 1956–7: 852).[27] President Nyerere in Tanzania explained the decision to create a national central bank on similar grounds: "We found that it is impossible to control our economy and achieve the maximum development while our currency and credit was outside our control" (quoted in Rothchild 1968: 234).

In defying British preferences these nationalists were sometimes supported by the U.S., as we have seen in the cases of Ceylon and Ethiopia. Also important was the role played by the U.S.-controlled international financial institutions, who made similar arguments to Triffin. In Nigeria, for example, the Bank of England was frustrated by a 1954 International Bank for Reconstruction and Development (IBRD) report that called for the creation of a central bank much more quickly than the bank was advising (Uche 1997). Similarly, the British were annoyed with an IBRD mission in Malaya during the next year that advocated the creation of a central bank with strong powers to pursue an autonomous domestic monetary policy and develop a local money market (Schenk 1993:

412–13). In addition to reserve requirements, the IBRD even recommended that the central bank be able to control the overseas assets of banks that are counterpart funds of Malay bank deposits. In Uganda in 1962, too, an IBRD report recommended the creation of central bank on similar grounds (World Bank 1962: 71–2). One final example comes from Sierra Leone, where Loynes was disappointed by the fact that, after he had recommended against the creation of a central bank, the government decided to get a second opinion from the International Monetary Fund (IMF) since it was known to favor the creation of central banks at this time (Uche 1996: 157, fn. 61).[28]

The IBRD and IMF were not the only external forces interfering with British efforts to preserve colonial monetary arrangements. Also important were some Northern academic experts who provided monetary advice to Southern governments at this time. One of the more prominent of these counter-establishment, unofficial "money doctors" was Thomas Balogh, a left-of-center economist from Oxford who was very critical of currency boards on the grounds that they served Britain's interests by reinforcing the export-oriented nature of Southern economies, encouraging capital outflows (both official and private), and leaving Southern countries dependent on the judgments of London financiers to determine their creditworthiness (Balogh 1959, 1966). His anti-imperialist analysis and his advocacy of powerful central banks in Southern countries appealed to many nationalist politicians in countries seeking to throw off British rule, and Balogh became involved in debates on monetary reform in various British colonies, such as Malta, Jamaica, and Malaya. In Jamaica, for example, he was invited in 1958 by the Jamaican government to support their arguments for a central bank, arguments that the British government was attempting to counter at the time. He was apparently very effective in this task, leaving one British colonial official to note privately that the "visit by Dr. T. Balogh has probably made it impossible ever to get things properly back."[29] When he intervened in debates in Malaya the next year, a Treasury official warned his colleague: "You may not be aware of the fact but Dr. Balogh has in fact been a considerable thorn in the flesh of the Colonial Office on a number of occasions when Colonial currency systems have been concerned."[30]

As it became clear that they could not resist the creation of central banks, British officials shifted their strategy. They accepted the case for a central bank, but insisted that it be managed in a conservative manner. The national currency should be backed by 100 per cent reserves, they argued, and its convertibility into sterling should be guaranteed. They also opposed giving the central bank large powers, such as the power to control capital movements or to force commercial banks to hold funds at the central bank (see, for example, Uche 1997). In the words of one British official in the Gold Coast (Ghana) in 1955, the objective was to ensure that the local government "does not set up a Frankenstein."[31]

British officials tried to appeal to nationalist sentiments in advancing these arguments in favor of an orthodox approach to monetary management. In the Gold Coast, Loynes, for example, argued that a stable and internationally convertible currency was crucial because "it is bound up with the international reputation of the Gold Coast as an independent country."[32] Other British officials were encouraged to stress how "[t]he world is strewn with unsatisfactory Central Banks and shaky currencies and the combination of the two in any country is simply to replace political dependence by economic dependence, exemplified in foreign aid."[33]

When one looks at the kinds of central banks established in many ex-British colonies, it appears that the British were quite successful in advancing these arguments. Most of the central banks set up – with the exception of Ceylon – had initially quite orthodox charters in contrast to those established under the U.S. Federal Reserve's guidance. They usually had only a limited fiduciary issue, no reserve requirements, strong sterling backing, and often no provisions for the use of capital controls or for direct lending by the central bank (Bangura 1983). This was even true of the central banks set up in countries such as Jamaica, where Balogh had initially had some influence, or Malaysia, where the IBRD had called for more radical measures. Indeed, domestic critics argued that these were not real central banks but just another name for the old currency boards (Government of the Gold Coast 1956–7: 705–6). As one Ghanaian critic put it, "if we are going to have a Central Bank we must have a Central Bank with 'teeth' and not a Central Bank which is only a channel for controlling the financial assets of their country by a foreign power" (Government of the Gold Coast 1956–7: 711).

The nature of these central banks partly reflected British pressure. But it also stemmed from the continued dependence of many of these countries on London financial markets and links to the British economy. Policymakers were particularly concerned to cultivate confidence in their new national currencies in order to prevent capital flight and encourage international lending to their country (Bangura 1983; Schenck 1993). A central bank with a conservative charter served this goal, as did public pronouncements of a commitment to orthodox policies at the time of its establishment. In Kenya, for example, the central bank was set up with what one observer called "the expression of sentiments of impeccable respectability in monetary matters of which Mr. Montagu Norman would have been proud" (Hazlewood 1979: 146). As President Kenyatta noted:

> One thing cannot be forgotten: currency issues and management is a real business and no magic. The bank cannot make something out of nothing and the Government cannot by order, or 'Fiat' grant to a piece of paper a value independent of the backing which it possesses. Such backing is provided by foreign exchange into which the Kenya currency will be convertible at its established par value.
>
> (President Kenyatta, quoted in EACB 1966: 118) [34]

If monetary reforms were usually quite limited at the time of independence in ex-British colonies, they often moved rapidly in a more nationalist direction in response to fiscal and economic pressures. In Ghana, for example, the government's desire in 1961 to accelerate economic growth and government spending led policymakers to allow the central bank to lend to the government more easily, to mobilize the foreign exchange reserves of Ghanaian residents, and to introduce capital controls (Bangura 1983: 99). Similar measures accompanied the introduction of Nigeria's 1962 development plan. Even conservative Kenya had begun deficit financing and tightened exchange controls by 1970. These episodes usually led to the results feared by British officials: the drawing down of sterling reserves, lessened dependence on London's financial market, and often a break from the sterling area itself.

Exception to the trend: the survival of the CFA franc zone

Not all newly independent Southern countries created national central banks guided by more domestic monetary objectives in the postwar period. One prominent exception among ex-British colonies was Singapore, which maintained a currency board backed by 100 per cent reserves (although a Monetary Authority was established in 1970 to fulfill some central banking functions unrelated to note issue). Its unique preference reflected partly its status as an international trading entrepôt, a status that gave it a strong reason to favor a stable currency. Singapore's Finance Minister from 1959 to 1971 also later made clear that the preference had ideological roots: "None of us [in Cabinet] believed that Keynesian economic policies could serve as Singapore's guide to economic well-being" (Goh 1995: 181).

The more dramatic exception, however, involved the ex-French colonies in West and Central Africa. At independence, most of these countries did not create national central banks and national currencies, but instead continued to be members of the two common currency zones that had existed under French colonial rule.[35] The post-independence CFA franc monetary zones functioned in a similar way as had their colonial predecessors (see, for example, Chipman 1989: 208–16). The CFA franc was convertible across the entire region, with no capital controls existing among member countries. The notes and coins in use across each zone were also almost identical, with no national emblems on them[36] (with the exception of those in Cameroon, which acquired its own note issue). All external payments of member countries were settled through an "operations account" held at the French Treasury, which continued to cover all deficits emerging in these accounts. Even the name CFA franc was the same as the colonial currency, although the meaning of CFA had been changed from "Colonies françaises d'Afrique" to "Communauté financière africaine."

How do we explain this anomalous experience among Southern countries? Part of the explanation is that the French government went to much greater lengths than the British government had to preserve the monetary structures in place in the colonial period. Chipman (1989) argues that the French government's desire to preserve the CFA zone was linked primarily to its broader concern with France's status as a world power after the war. But others note that the CFA zone also provided balance of payments support for France in much of the postwar period. As in the case of the sterling bloc, the absence of capital controls and exchange rate risk between France and CFA countries encouraged large private capital outflows from the latter to the former, outflows that usually exceeded public and private capital inflows (Joseph 1976; Balogh 1966: 46). Equally importantly, CFA countries earned continuous foreign exchange surpluses *vis-à-vis* the outside world in this period and these surpluses were controlled by the French Treasury, which used them to support the French balance of payments position (Joseph 1976).[37] More generally, an official French commission appointed to investigate the future of the CFA zone in 1960 reported that France–CFA trade was bolstered by the zone's existence because CFA francs were convertible only into French francs. Not only did this provide French companies with a protected export market (especially because the CFA franc was overvalued by this time), but France was also able to acquire raw material imports without having to use scarce foreign exchange.[38]

To increase the attractiveness of the CFA zone to African governments the French government undertook a series of reforms of its operations in the postwar period. The first reform was one that Britain had also introduced in a more limited way in its currency boards: after the Second World War, the prewar requirement that CFA currencies be backed with 100 per cent reserves in gold, French francs, or convertible currencies was changed to allow up to two-thirds of the reserve to be held in local assets (Onoh 1982: 29). The next key reform went much further than the British had contemplated in the sterling area. The French created regional central banks in Central Africa (1955) and West Africa (1959), which provided not only rediscount facilities for local banks but also short-term commercial credit (for example crop finance) and medium-term loans for development projects (Ezenwe 1983; Robson 1968: 201–7). After independence, the French went one step further in 1962 to transform the regional central banks into inter-governmental institutions with a majority of Africans on the board (although the headquarters remained in Paris until 1972 and France retained an effective veto). At this time, each member government was also given more input into the central banks' decisions on the overall level of credit being allocated to their country as well as decisions on how this credit would be distributed to banks and companies within their country.

In these ways, the French attempted to accommodate Southern goals of using the monetary system more actively to promote economic development. The 1960 report of the official commission looking into the future of the CFA zone explicitly acknowledged this objective; in the words of one British official, the report noted that the goal of reforms should be "to allow for the maximum expansion of economic activity in these countries, but nevertheless in such a way as to maintain their allegiance."[39] This last line highlighted the price of these economic reforms: the CFA zone remained a French-controlled monetary system. For this reason, many Africans continued to see CFA franc as "colonial money" and the CFA zone as a form of neocolonialism.[40] The extent of the 1962 economic reforms should also not be overstated. Credit from the central banks was refused to CFA countries which ran a consistent balance of payments deficit within the system, and CFA governments were still not allowed to run fiscal deficits (although French aid was available as a partial, albeit politically controlled, alternative to finance government spending).[41]

Given these constraints, it may seem surprising that more African governments did not break out on their own and create national currencies and national central banks as governments in ex-British colonies had done. To be sure, some countries such as Guinea and Mali did pursue this option, as is explained below. But the fact that more did not surprised many observers at the time, including a British Foreign Office official who was convinced that the situation would not last:

> In the longer term, the very conservatism of the Central Banks, and their inability under the present rules to play the part they ought to be playing in helping the countries they serve to establish their economic independence is, I should have thought, more likely to lead to moves of the kind Guinea and Mali have already taken.[42]

One reason so many African governments decided to remain in the CFA zone may have been that the French took a very tough stance towards countries that adopted a more independent course. Countries such as Guinea and Mali, which sought to break away from the CFA zone, found their broader security, trade, aid, and other economic links to France severed by the French government in ways that were very costly (Chipman 1989; Joseph 1976). African governments in the CFA zone thus appeared to face a starker choice than members of the sterling area had faced: either accept the CFA currency or face a sharp break in the relationship with France. For many elites, the prospects of losing security ties, aid support, and guaranteed access to the French market (as well as the stable and high prices paid by the French for these materials) were ones they were not willing to consider (Stasavage 2003).

This explanation is important, but it does not tell the whole story. It neglects the fact that the 1960 French commission examining potential reforms to the CFA actually opened the door to the possibility of France allowing distinct national currencies to be created. The commission even suggested that France would allow these currencies both to be devalued in situations of fundamental disequilibrium and to be defended by capital controls if such controls were necessary for economic development.[43] That African governments did not push more strongly for this kind of reform given French openness to it requires explanation. Indeed, when in 1961 the French government indicated its willingness to consider the creation of distinct national banknotes for each newly independent CFA country in West Africa, the proposal was actually opposed by every African government involved.[44]

To explain fully the choices made by CFA countries we must also examine the ideological roots of the decision. The governments of CFA countries were much less committed to the kind of "economic nationalist" thinking that was influential elsewhere in the South at this time. Most of the countries that stayed with the CFA zone were headed by conservative governments whose commitment to nationalist ideology was much weaker than in other Southern countries at this time. Many of their leaders had endorsed the goal of independence from France in only a luke-warm fashion, and they remained wedded to the assimilationist goals that the French had promoted in the colonial period (Chipman 1989; Alalade 1979). A national currency and national central bank thus appeared to hold much less symbolic value for these leaders than they had for policymakers elsewhere.

The importance of the ideological orientation of African governments is particularly clear when one examines the counter-cases of Guinea and Mali. Soon after their independence these two countries established a national central bank and national currency (in 1960 for Guinea and 1962 for Mali).[45] They also imposed capital controls, and the central banks were given considerable powers. In Guinea's case, for example, there was initially no provision for backing the currency whatsoever and no limitation on government borrowing from it. The five French banks in the country were also told to deposit 50 per cent of their foreign currency holdings with the central bank, and when four of them refused they were liquidated.[46]

This radically different approach to monetary reform from the other ex-French colonies was driven by the ideological goals of the two countries' leaders, Sekou Touré (Guinea) and Modibo Kéita (Mali). Unlike leaders in other ex-French African colonies, these two leaders were committed to a strong anti-colonial nationalism. In the economic sphere, their ideas were in fact much more radical than the nationalist ideas that were prominent in the ex-British colonies and the countries that the U.S. was advising at this time. Influenced by the French Marxist economist Charles Bettleheim, they sought to build not just a national industrial economy, but one that was organized on the basis of a revolutionary and ambitious form of national economic planning (Touré 1979; Zolberg 1967; Jones 1976).

Both leaders saw monetary reform as crucial to their political and economic projects. An independent national currency would not only enable effective capital controls to be introduced. It would also allow the country to mobilize the monetary system behind its planning objectives (Touré 1979: 371–9; Yansane 1979; Jones 1976). In broader nationalist terms, Touré also noted of the creation of Guinea's national currency and central bank:

> its importance is comparable, if not superior, to that of our choice of imme-diate independence in September 1958. This reform provides the basis upon which we can carry out our economic liberation, previously impeded by a financial system which remained that of the old régime, linked to the economic system of the colonizing country.
>
> (Touré 1979: 371)

Conclusion

The early postwar period witnessed a wave of monetary reform across many Southern countries that departed sharply from the orthodoxy of classical economic liberalism. In place of the external discipline of the gold standard, Southern policymakers sought to bolster the ability of national governments to use the monetary system in pursuit of the domestic objectives of rapid industrialization and nation-building. What explains this policy shift across the South?

As in Northern countries, the initial catalyst for the departure from orthodoxy was the painful experience of the 1930s. In regions that were independent at that time – especially Latin America – the collapse of international lending and world commodity prices forced a reevaluation of countries' commitment to orthodox approaches to monetary policy. Instead of accepting deflationary pressures, they chose to break with the gold standard and experiment with more interventionist, domestically oriented monetary policies. The rise of economic nationalist ideology, and its commitment to rapid industrialization, then reinforced this trend. In countries that were still colonized during the 1930s, reforms had to wait until independence came in the postwar period. But the experience of deflation under the colonial currency boards during the 1930s, when combined with broader political nationalist sentiments at the time of independence, also strengthened the case for monetary reforms in these countries.[47]

In addition, the rejection of monetary orthodoxy across the South in this period gained political strength from the fact that it was endorsed by the dominant financial power after the war. As I have shown, U.S. policymakers played a major role in promoting the new nationalist ideas through money doctoring missions from the early 1940s through the 1950s. The importance of U.S. support was highlighted well when we turned to examine some cases where it was not present. I showed, for example, how British and French policymakers were opposed to the ideas promoted by U.S. officials and went out of their way to advise their newly independent ex-colonies not to follow the new nationalist path. In British ex-colonies this advice was usually unwelcome, but it had some effect in ensuring that monetary reforms would be introduced more cautiously and slowly. In French ex-colonies in Central and West Africa, French advice in fact coincided with the conservative preferences of elite policymakers, resulting in the most dramatic exception to the trend of nationalist monetary reforms: the survival of colonial CFA franc zone.

The important role that American "money doctors" played in promoting and supporting unorthodox Southern monetary reforms deserves more attention than it has received in the existing scholarly literature. The activities of American "money doctors" in this period should be particularly interesting for historians of American foreign economic policy. As I have noted, they provide a marked contrast with the better-known activities of Kemmerer in the 1920s. They were also very different from the activities of American officials in the 1980s and 1990s. In this more recent period, the U.S. officials were much less sympathetic to the Southern monetary policies and institutions that Triffin and his colleagues had endorsed, such as capital controls, politically controlled central banks, and Keynesian domestic economic management. In the last few years, U.S. policymakers have even begun debating whether the U.S. should be encouraging Southern governments to "dollarize" their domestic monetary systems or introduce currency boards. In these respects, U.S. official attitudes today seem to be closer to those that existed in the pre-1931 period than those of the early post-1945 years.

The activities of U.S. money doctors in the early post-1945 years were unusual from the perspective not just of the history of American foreign economic policy but also of the history of international money doctoring more generally. Existing studies of international money doctoring demonstrate that the practice is usually associated with the dispensing of monetary advice that is consistent with liberal preferences for low inflation, fiscal discipline, and economic liberalization. In this period, however, the American money doctors offered advice which was regarded as quite unorthodox by economic liberals at the time and would be regarded the same way by many officials in the IMF and leading financial powers today. What explains this anomalous historical experience?

I have argued that the answer is partly that the American money doctors were influenced by the intellectual climate of their time. The experiences of the 1930s discredited classical economic liberalism and gave great political strength to those advocating more interventionist Keynesian or "embedded liberal" ideas. In the advice they gave Southern governments, American money doctors in this period were simply building upon ideas that U.S. officials had already endorsed as the key intellectual organizing principle for the international monetary order at Bretton Woods.

This ideational explanation, however, is not enough to account for U.S. behavior in this period. After all, British and French officials also endorsed the principle of embedded liberalism at Bretton Woods, but this did not prevent them from advising ex-colonies to adopt quite different policies designed to perpetuate colonial monetary practices. In their cases, this advice stemmed from national political and economic interests – such as the desire for international prestige and balance of payments support – that overrode any underlying ideological commitment to embedded liberalism. I have argued that the unorthodox nature of U.S. money doctoring in this period was also driven by some geopolitical interests. Specifically, the sympathy that U.S. officials exhibited towards the nationalist monetary goals of Southern governments often reflected their desire not to alienate key allies in the context of the Second World War and then the Cold War. It also helped them to gain influence in newly independent Southern countries, particularly in ex-British colonies. In these ways, the study of the early postwar period highlights the fact that the advice provided by international money doctors can reflect not just predominant economic ideologies but also the geopolitical projects of dominant financial powers.

Notes

1 I am very grateful to the Social Sciences and Humanities Research Council of Canada for helping to fund the research behind this work, as well as to Rachel Epstein, Marc Flandreau, Gerry Helleiner, Nicolas Jabko, Harold James, Jonathan Kirschner, Steven Schuker, and Jérôme Sgard for their helpful comments.

2 I use the term "orthodox" to refer to the monetary objectives of classical liberals in the pre-1945 period. These objectives included maintaining the international gold standard, preserving the free movement of capital across borders, and ensuring that domestic monetary policies were designed to maintain external convertibility of the national currency into gold.

3 Triffin (who was originally from Belgium), in his role as chief of the Latin American section of the Federal Reserve staff in the 1943–6 period, led many of these initial Federal Reserve "money doctoring" missions to Southern countries. Other U.S. officials involved in these missions included Bray Hammond, John Exter, Henry Wallich, David Grove, John DeBeers, Arthur Bloomfield, and John Jensen (Urquidi 1991; Kim 1965). For Honduras, see Vinelli (1950–1), Bulmer-Thomas (1987). For the Dominican Republic, see Wallich and Triffin (1953). For Korea, see Kim (1965). For the Philippines, see Castro (1960), Cullather (1994), Grove and Exter (1948), Hartendorp (1958). For Ceylon, see Karunatilake (1973), Gunasekera (1962). For Ethiopia, see Degefe (1995). The Ethiopian case is the one for which I have found the least information. Although the U.S. played an important role in supporting the country's 1942–4 monetary reforms, I have not yet been able to determine the detailed nature of their support, nor whether it was the Federal Reserve that was involved. I should also make clear that the new central banks set up under U.S. assistance did not always pursue the nationalist policies that U.S. money doctors advised.

4 The money supply might have been less dependent on changing balance of payments conditions if trends in private bank lending had counteracted the direction of monetary policy pursued by currency boards or central banks in Southern countries. In reality, however, private bank lending trends usually reinforced central bank or currency board policy because the banking sector was dominated by foreign banks that responded primarily to the needs of the foreign trade sector.

5 Triffin (1968) later developed a more detailed critique of the working of the classical gold standard from the standpoint of poorer countries. Other development economists also developed further critiques of the effectiveness of orthodox adjustment mechanisms in poorer countries, concentrating on other points than Triffin did at this time (for example the importance of supply rigidities).

6 Triffin acknowledged that capital controls had often been used for destructive nationalist purposes in the 1930s, but he noted:

> They have, however, enriched the apparatus through which monetary policy can be made effective. The situation calls for exorcism rather than for excommunication. The new weapons should not be scrapped indiscriminately – an objective on which general agreement would, anyway, be impossible – but harmonized and integrated, through international consultation, into the implementation of internationally defined monetary objectives.
>
> (Triffin 1966b: 178)

7 Indeed, in the case of Paraguay Triffin noted that the powers of the central bank were "almost without precedent" (1946: 72).

8 Acknowledging that there was a risk that direct credit lending by a central bank might compromise a central bank's monetary tasks, U.S. officials argued that it was crucial to make the Monetary Board the most important body in the new central banks (Triffin 1946: 19–20).

9 In the Philippines, for example, Cullather (1994: 81) notes the strong opposition of U.S. business to the introduction of capital controls in 1950 since it interfered with their ability to repatriate profits freely. The inflation that accompanied the monetary policy pursued by the new central bank of the Philippines was also strongly criticized by the U.S. business community (Hartendorp 1958: 255, 608).

10 For the post-1945 economic nationalism in Southern countries, see, for example, Seers (1983), Burnell (1986).

11 He also occasionally cited the experience of the British Dominions in highlighting the costs of not having a powerful central bank in contexts where only a small local capital market existed and foreign banks dominated the financial system (see, for example, Triffin 1946: 19). Plumptre's (1940) analysis of the Dominions' situation was similar to Triffin's in this respect and may have influenced the latter's thinking. Although Triffin does not mention them, some Middle Eastern countries, such as Iran (Minai 1961) and Turkey (Fry 1979), had also engaged in some policy innovations similar to those in Latin American countries during the 1930s. Also interesting was the experience of Korea under Japanese colonialism. Uniquely among colonial powers, Japan set up a central bank in Korea quite early in its colonial rule which pursued very unorthodox "developmentalist" policies, such as direct lending within the Korean economy (see, for example, Woo 1991).

12 The head of the Bank of Colombia (Enrique Davila) was also very involved in Paraguayan consultations with Triffin, and both he and Prebisch even spent three months in Paraguay in 1943 and 1945.

13 In the Dominican Republic, Triffin and Wallich also appealed to nationalist sentiment in making the case for the creation of an exclusive national currency: "In international affairs, it will strengthen the position of the Republic and put it on an equal footing with all other nations" (Wallich and Triffin 1953: 24).

14 I have shown elsewhere the influence of the Cold War in also encouraging U.S. officials to accept European and Japanese preferences for monetary and financial interventionism in the early postwar years (Helleiner 1994: ch. 3).

15 The quotation is from the U.S.–Philippine Finance Commission set up in 1946 to study the future of monetary arrangements (quoted in Golay 1961: 217). Interestingly, one U.S. business figure in the Philippines who opposed the goal of more activist monetary policy tried to turn this nationalist argument on its head, arguing that the introduction of such a policy was not in keeping with nationalism because it simply followed the example U.S. policymakers had set when they left the gold standard in 1933: "It would have been far less 'colonial' if the Philippine Government had truly struck out on its own and reestablished the gold standard" (Hartendorp 1958: 618).

16 Indeed, one analyst of the 1949 report of the Federal Reserve's money doctor John Exter (who went on to become the new central bank's first governor) notes: "Reading the Report, one is struck by the extensive criticism made of the Currency Board system" (Karunatilake 1973: 7).

17 These fears were intensified by the fact that the British made clear that the new currency would be called the Ethiopian pound and that the currency board's headquarters would be in London and be staffed with representatives not just of the Ethiopian government but also of the Bank of England and U.K. Treasury (Degefe 1995: 237).

18 The conflict between U.S. and U.K. money doctors emerged in a number of other places too, although with less influence on the outcome. In Saudi Arabia during the war, for example, U.S. officials strongly opposed the British effort to convince Saudi Arabia to introduce a currency board. In the end, neither piece of advice was followed (Young 1983: 14–15). As noted later (pp. 260–1), the U.S.-influenced IBRD and IMF often opposed British advice on monetary issues in ex-British colonies.

19 The same had been true of Kemmerer's missions (Drake 1989).

20 Bangura (1983) highlights convincingly that this goal was the central one in explaining British policy. Although Bank of England officials certainly remained committed to orthodox ideas, the influence of their ideological orientation should not be overstated. The British government often overruled Bank of England ideas when they did not suit British national economic needs in the early postwar years. This was

certainly true in British domestic economic policy, and it was also true in foreign monetary policy, where the very existence of a restrictive sterling bloc contravened orthodox thinking.

21 There were some exceptions. In the Gold Coast, Cecil Trevor (who had had experience with the Reserve Bank in India) had unexpectedly recommended the creation of a central bank in a 1951 report, a conclusion that greatly annoyed the Bank of England and led them to insist that he not be allowed to provide advice to Nigeria (Uche 1997). In the rest of West Africa the advice was consistent: the Bank of England's 1953 Fischer report for Nigeria recommended against a central bank, as did Loynes's 1961 report for Sierra Leone and Gambia (PRO 1025/127 E/57, March 1961).

22 These arrangements rarely lasted long, with the East African countries creating national currencies in 1965–7 and the Malayan common currency board breaking up completely by 1967.

23 The Loynes quotation is from his 1961 report to Sierra Leone (PRO CO 1025/127 E/57 March 1961: 8).

24 PRO CO1025/42 59/13/04, "Speech for the Minister of Finance on the Occasion of the Signing of the Currency Notes Contract Between the Gold Coast Govt and Messrs Thomas de la Rue and Co. Ltd, London, Sept. 15, 1955." He noted elsewhere: "The issuing by any country of its own distinctive currency is recognized as one of the outward and visible signs of sovereignty – as visible, indeed, as the national flag" (Government of the Gold Coast 1956–7: 860). Similarly, Sierra Leone's Finance Minister in his 1962 budget speech noted: "No independent country can regard itself as truly independent until it has its own national currency" (quoted in Uche 1996: 157, fn. 66).

25 The quotations are from Uche (1996: 151).

26 PRO CO 1025/127 S.F.P.9482, Acting Governor of SL to Galsworthy, Oct. 7, 1960.

27 See also Nkrumah (1965: 221), Bank of Sierra Leone (n.d.: 2–3).

28 The IMF did not favor the creation of central banks in every instance. An IMF mission to Libya in the early 1950s (co-headed by the American George Blowers, who had helped Ethiopia establish its central bank a decade earlier) came out in favor of a currency board, although it suggested that a central bank be set up at a later time (Blowers and McLeod 1952–3).

29 PRO CO1025/123, R.J. Vile to Mr. Marnham, April 30, 1958.

30 PRO T236/5149, C. Lucas to J. Rampton, Jan. 1, 1960.

31 PRO CO1025/42 59/13/04, "Gold Coast Currency and Banking: Notes for Meeting on Sept. 14, 1955": 4.

32 PRO CO1025/42 59/13/04, informal Report of J.B. Loynes to Minister of Finance, Feb. 21, 1956: 1.

33 PRO CO1025/42 59/13/04, "Gold Coast Currency and Banking: Notes for Meeting on Sept. 14, 1955": 4.

34 Similarly, Uganda's President opened its central bank with the following warning: "We must…work for every cent before the Bank can produce that one cent. The Bank is not, and will not be turned into a charity institution" (quoted in EACB 1966: 122).

35 The Central African CFA franc zone included Cameroon, Central African Republic, Chad, Congo, and Gabon, while the members of the West African CFA franc zone in the early years after independence were Ivory Coast, Dahomey, Mauritania, Niger, Senegal, and Upper Volta (as well as Togo after 1963).

36 In 1962 each CFA franc note acquired a small country identification code (a letter following the serial number) which enabled policymakers to analyze inter-country balance of payments situations. These payment situations were important in determining how much credit was allocated to each country by the regional central bank, as noted below (pp. 264–5) (Robson 1968).

37 Medhora (1992: 163) notes that an operations account offers an open-ended guarantee of foreign exchange, but that Central African countries had never used the overdraft facility and West African countries used it for the first time only in 1980.
38 BOE OV100/19, "Summary of the Report of the Conseil Economique et Social on the Revision of the Structure of the Franc Zone Published in March 1960," summary by M. Hailstone.
39 *Ibid.*: 3.
40 The quotation is from Joseph Tchunjang (quoted in Guyer 1995: 13). See also Nkrumah (1965: 20).
41 As the French government's Jeanneney Report of 1964 noted: "France in effect renounces the possibility of refusing to finance initiatives taken unilaterally by African governments, in return the States accept a certain monetary tutelage, particularly in the matter of deficit financing" (quoted in Robson 1968: 207). Credit from the IMF and World Bank to national governments also complicated the fiscal arrangements in the CFA zone.
42 BOE OV100/3, R.J. O'Neil (FO) to W. Pattinson (Treasury), Jan. 16, 1964.
43 BOE OV100/19, "Summary of the Report of the Conseil Economique et Social on the Revision of the Structure of the Franc Zone Published in March 1960," summary by M. Hailstone. Other newly independent countries which had been members of the broader franc zone had established central banks and national currencies at independence, such as Tunisia and Morocco. By the early 1960s they had also imposed exchange controls on transactions with France.
44 BOE OV100/20, C.M. Le Quesne to Foreign Office, Sept. 19, 1961: 3. My ability to explain the politics surrounding French policy in this period has been limited by the fact that I have not had time to consult French archives. For this reason, my arguments in this area should be seen as very tentative ones.
45 Mali's departure from the CFA zone was not permanent. It reestablished an operations account with France in 1968 and rejoined the CFA zone fully in 1984. Another country that pulled out of the CFA zone was Mauritania. It withdrew in 1973 and created a central bank in 1978 (Yansane 1984: 77).
46 BOE OV106/1, "Guinea," by J. Margetson, March 25, 1960; BOE OV106/1: 103–4.
47 Maddison (1990: 333–4) points out that many colonial regions, such as Indonesia, would probably have pursued the same policy course as did Latin America in the 1930s if they had been independent at the time. Instead, they were often forced into dramatic deflations, and some Europeans even seemed to approve of the way that colonial rule created "ideal conditions" to enforce a deflation that European workers would not accept (van Gelderen 1939: 11).

References

Alalade, F. (1979) "President Felix Houphouet-Boigny, the Ivory Coast and France," *Journal of African Studies* 6(3): 122–32.
Balogh, T. (1959) "A Note on the Monetary Controversy in Malaya," *Malaysian Economic Review*, October.
Balogh, T. (1966) "The Mechanism of Neo-Imperialism," in T. Balogh, *The Economics of Poverty*, London: Weidenfeld & Nicolson.
Bangura, Y. (1983) *Britain and Commonwealth Africa: The Politics of Economic Relations, 1951–1975*, Manchester: Manchester University Press.
Bank of Sierra Leone (n.d.) *Review of the General Manager's Department*, Freetown: Bank of Sierra Leone.
Basu, S.K. (1967) *Central Banking in the Emerging Countries*, Bombay: Asia Publishing House.
Blowers, G.A. and A.N. McLeod (1952–3) "Currency Unification in Libya," *IMF Staff Papers* 2: 439–67.

BOE – Bank of England Archives, Bank of England, London, U.K.

Bulmer-Thomas, V. (1987) *The Political Economy of Central America since 1920*, Cambridge: Cambridge University Press.

Burnell, P. (1986) *Economic Nationalism in the Third World*, Brighton: Wheatsheaf.

Castro, A. (1960) "Central Banking in the Philippines," in S.G. Davies (ed.) *Central Banking in South and East Asia*, Hong Kong: Hong Kong University Press.

Chandavarkar, A. (1996) *Central Banking in Developing Countries*, London: Macmillan.

Chipman, J. (1989) *French Power in Africa*, Oxford: Basil Blackwell.

Cullather, N. (1994) *Illusions of Influence: The Political Economy of United States–Philippines Relations, 1942–1960*, Stanford, CA: Stanford University Press.

Degefe, B. (1995) "The Development of Money, Monetary Institutions and Monetary Policy 1941–75," in S. Bekele (ed.) *An Economic History of Modern Ethiopia, vol.1: The Imperial Era 1941–74*, Senegal: Codesria.

Drake, P. (1989) *The Money Doctor in the Andes: The Kemmerer Missions 1923–1933*, Durham, NC: Duke University Press.

EACB (East African Currency Board) (1965) *Report*, Nairobi: EACB.

EACB (East African Currency Board) (1966) *Report*, Nairobi: EACB.

EACB (East African Currency Board) (1967) *Report*, Nairobi: EACB.

EACB (East African Currency Board) (1972) *Final Report of the East African Currency Board*, Nairobi: EACB.

Ezenwe, U. (1983) *ECOWAS and the Economic Integration of West Africa*, London: C. Hurst & Co.

Fry, M. (1979) *Money and Banking in Turkey*, Istanbul: Bogazici University Publications, no. 171.

Goh, K.S. (1995) "Why a Currency Board?," in L. Low (ed.) *Wealth of East Asian Nations: Speeches and Writings of Goh Keng Swee*, Singapore: Federal Publications.

Golay, F. (1961) *The Philippines: Public Policy and National Economic Development*, Ithaca, NY: Cornell University Press.

Government of the Gold Coast (1956–7) *Legislative Assembly Debates 1956–57*, 1st Series, vol. 3, Accra.

Grove, D. and J. Exter (1948) "The Philippines Central Bank Act," *Federal Reserve Bulletin* 34(8): 938–49.

Gunasekera, H.A. de S. (1962) *From Dependent Currency to Central Banking in Ceylon*, London: G. Bell & Sons.

Guyer, J. (1995) "Introduction," in J. Guyer (ed.) *Money Matters: Instability, Values and Social Payments in the Modern History of West African Communities*, London: James Currey.

Hartendorp, A.V.H. (1958) *History of Industry and Trade of the Philippines*, Manila: American Chamber of Commerce of the Philippines.

Hazlewood, A. (1979) *The Economy of Kenya: The Kenyatta Era*, Oxford: Oxford University Press.

Helleiner, E. (1993) "When Finance Was the Servant: International Capital Movements in the Bretton Woods Order," in P. Cerny (ed.) *Finance and World Politics: Markets, Regimes and States in the Post-Hegemonic Era*, Aldershot: Elgar.

Helleiner, E. (1994) *States and the Reemergence of Global Finance*, Ithaca, NY: Cornell University Press.

Helleiner, E. (1999) "Denationalizing Money? Economic Liberalism and the 'National Question' in Monetary Affairs," in E. Gilbert and E. Helleiner (eds.) *Nation-States and Money*, London: Routledge.

Jones, W. (1976) "Planning and Economic Policy in Mali," unpublished Ph.D. Université de Genève.

Joseph, R. (1976) "The Gaullist Legacy: Patterns of French Neo-colonialism," *Review of African Political Economy* (May–August) 6: 4–14.

Karunatilake, H.N.S. (1973) *Central Banking and Monetary Policy in Sri Lanka*, Colombo: Lake House Investment Ltd.

Kim, B.K. (1965) *Central Banking Experiment in a Developing Economy: Case Study of Korea*, Seoul: Korea Research Center.

Laso, E. (1957–8) "Financial Policies and Credit Control Techniques in Central America," *IMF Staff Papers* 6: 427–60.

Lee, S.-Y. (1986) *The Monetary and Banking Development of Singapore and Malaysia*, 2nd edn., Singapore: Singapore University Press.

Maddison, A. (1990) "Dutch Colonialism in Indonesia: A Comparative Perspective," in A. Booth, W.J. O'Malley and A. Weidermann (eds.) *Indonesian Economic History in the Dutch Colonial Era*, New Haven, CT: Yale University, South East Asia Studies.

Maxfield, S. (1997) *Gatekeepers of Growth: The International Political Economy of Central Banking in Developing Countries*, Princeton, NJ: Princeton University Press.

Medhora, R. (1992) "The West African Monetary Union," *Canadian Journal of Development Studies* 13(2): 151–79.

Minai, A. (1961) *Economic Development of Iran Under the Reign of Reza Shah 1926–1941*, Ph.D., the American University, Ann Arbor, MI: University Microfilms.

Nkrumah, K. (1965) *Neo-colonialism: The Last Stage of Imperialism*, London: Nelson.

Onoh, J.K. (1982) *Money and Banking in Africa*, London: Longman.

Plumptre, A. (1940) *Central Banking in the British Dominions*, Toronto: University of Toronto Press.

PRO – Public Record Office, London, U.K. CO (Colonial Files), T (Treasury Files).

Robson, P. (1968) *Economic Integration in Africa*, London: Allen & Unwin.

Rosenberg, E. (1985) "Foundations of US International Financial Power: Gold Standard Diplomacy, 1900–1905," *Business History Review* (summer) 59(2): 169–202.

Rothchild, D. (ed.) (1968) *Politics of Integration: An East African Documentary*, Nairobi: East African Publishing House.

Ruggie, J. (1983) "International Regimes, Transactions and Change," *International Organization* 36(2): 379–405.

Seers, D. (1983) *The Political Economy of Nationalism*, New York: Oxford University Press.

Schenk, C. (1993) "The Origins of a Central Bank in Malaysia and the Transition to Independence, 1954–59," *Journal of Imperial and Commonwealth History* 21(2): 409–31.

Stasavage, D. (2003) "When Do States Abandon Monetary Discretion?", in Jonathan Kirshner (ed.) *Monetary Orders*, Ithaca, NY: Cornell University Press.

Touré, A.S. (1979) *Africa on the Move*, London: Panaf.

Triffin, R. (1944) "Central Banking and Monetary Management in Latin America," in S. Harris (ed.) *Economic Problems of Latin America*, New York: McGraw-Hill.

Triffin, R. (1946) *Monetary and Banking Reform in Paraguay*, Washington, DC: Board of Governors of the Federal Reserve System.

Triffin, R. (1966a) "National Central Banking and the International Economy," in R. Triffin, *The World Money Maze: National Currencies in International Payments*, New Haven, CT: Yale University Press.

Triffin, R. (1966b) "International Versus Domestic Money," in R. Triffin, *The World Money Maze: National Currencies in International Payments*, New Haven, CT: Yale University Press.

Triffin, R. (1968) "The Myth and Realities of the So-Called Gold Standard," in R. Triffin, *Our International Monetary System*, New York: Random House.

Uche, C.U. (1996) "From Currency Board to Central Banking: The Politics of Change in Sierra Leone," *African Economic History* 24: 147–58.

Uche, C.U. (1997) "Bank of England vs. the IBRD: Did the Nigerian Colony Deserve a Central Bank?," *Explorations in Economic History* 34: 220–41.

Urquidi, V. (1991) "Monetary Management in Latin America," in A. Steinherr and D. Weiserbs (eds.) *Evolution of the International and Regional Monetary Systems*, London: Macmillan.

U.S. Federal Reserve (1944) "New Monetary and Banking Measures in Paraguay," *Federal Reserve Bulletin* (January): 42–51.

U.S. Federal Reserve (1945) "Monetary Developments in Latin America," *Federal Reserve Bulletin* (June) 31(6): 519–30.

van Gelderen, J. (1939) *The Recent Development of Economic Foreign Policy in the Netherlands East Indies*, London: Longmans, Green & Co.

Vinelli, P. (1950–1) "The Currency and Exchange System of Honduras," *IMF Staff Papers* 1: 420–31.

Wallich, H. and R. Triffin (1953) *Monetary and Banking Legislation of the Dominican Republic*, New York: Federal Reserve Bank of New York.

World Bank (1962) *The Economic Development of Uganda*, Baltimore, MD: John Hopkins Press.

Yansané, A. (1979) "Monetary Independence and Transition to Socialism in Guinea," *Journal of African Studies* 6(3): 132–43.

Yansané, A. (1984) *Decolonization in West African States with French Colonial Legacy*, Cambridge: Scheckman Publishing Co.

Young, A. (1983) *Saudi Arabia: The Making of a Financial Giant*, New York: New York University Press.

Woo, J.-E. (1991) *Race to the Swift: State and Finance in Korean Industrialization*, New York: Columbia University Press.

Zolberg, A. (1967) "The Political Use of Economic Planning in Mali," in H. Johnson (ed.) *Economic Nationalism in Old and New States*, Chicago, IL: University of Chicago Press.

10 New therapies from contemporary money doctors

The evolution of structural conditionality in the Bretton Woods institutions

Louis W. Pauly

When a state joins the International Monetary Fund (IMF) and the World Bank it accepts certain obligations to bring external considerations into its internal policy-making. At the very least, members of the Fund are bound to submit to a formal apparatus of surveillance over the economic consequences for other members of a full range of macroeconomic policies. When they accept financial assistance from the Fund or the Bank, moreover, the nature and scope of the obligations assumed can expand significantly. "Conditionality" is the term used to describe the practice of establishing those obligations and promoting compliance. The conferees at Bretton Woods in 1944 did not invent the practice, but the two institutions they helped establish later proved eminently adaptable. Since the 1970s, members have enlarged the scope of conditionality in both institutions and used it to encourage ever deeper adjustments in a wider range of policies. Members requiring high levels of financial assistance over long periods of time have found themselves drawn into an elaborate practice now commonly labeled "structural conditionality." The practice rendered such assistance conditional on negotiating and agreeing to implement plans for profound reform and adjustment in important national systems affecting economic stability and prospects for future prosperity. Since the boundary lines between the economic, political, and social realms blur at this level, structural conditionality has sparked intense controversy.

This chapter provides an overview of the evolution of that practice and the financial instruments within which it is embedded in the Fund and the Bank, the most prominent "money doctors" in the contemporary period.[1] Against this background, it proposes a political explanation for the emergence and elaboration of the practice during the watershed decade of the 1980s. That explanation emphasizes the importance of prior ideological and structural change inside the United States.

The puzzle of structural conditionality

International financial assistance conditional on structural adjustment can seem like an instrument of enforcement to its targets. Its development is puzzling in a world where sovereignty remains a key organizing principle and where global government is not obviously on the horizon.[2] Even if that principle has often been honored in the breach, for the strong directly to attempt deep domestic transformation in the weak has been rare since the end of the European colonial era. The inter-war experience of the League of Nations in certain Central European countries, the post-World War II experience of occupied Germany and Japan, and more recent interventions of an intrusive nature in certain failed states stand out as exceptions that prove the rule.[3] In the absence of military or humanitarian emergencies, international efforts aimed at recasting internal social and political arrangements within sovereign states have occurred very infrequently – that is, until recently. During the 1990s it became commonplace to see images of international financial diplomats apparently forcing the leaders of developing states, newly industrializing states, or states in transition from socialism to abandon traditional policies, open markets, and break domestic logjams to the kinds of reforms deemed necessary to integrate their national economies into a rapidly emerging global economy.

Why were the strong, who have led the Bretton Woods institutions since their inception, now so overtly trying to construct such an economy? And why were the weak, often despite public displays of resentment, now apparently more willing to go along with this? The way in which "structural conditionality" evolved within the Bank and the Fund suggests that the practice was driven by prior ideological and policy changes within their dominant member state, the United States. The crucial decade for those changes was the 1980s. In the end, the core challenge for the institutions and their key supporters was to draw lessons from the experience of that decade and apply them to debtor states. The principal underlying objective of that two-pronged effort, however, was to keep the United States engaged in the progressive internationalist project which the Fund and the Bank had represented ever since World War II. The Cold War obscured the nature of that project, but the denouement of that twilight struggle brought it back to the fore. It also brought back to prominence in American public policy debate longstanding conservative opposition to that project. Structural conditionality needs to be understood in this light. The key issue remained defining and maintaining the essential place of the United States in a globalizing economy. Changes within the United States as the Cold War stabilized and then receded needed to be accommodated if the overarching experiment giving rise to that economy was to endure. At the heart of that experiment was an attempt to reorient American foreign policy away from the pursuit of national interests narrowly defined and toward positive world order transformation guided by core American values. In the 1980s, the fundamental struggle inside the United States was over the redefinition of those values. For American conservatives, the issue of reconstructing the most effective means for defending those values arose in this context. For progressives, an agenda continuing to emphasize global transformation implied new mechanisms for promoting those values in a politically feasible way.

Contemporary money doctors as students, then teachers

In the early years after World War II, when the seeds of contemporary international markets were first sown, many hoped that the resumption of exports, imports, and accommodating portfolio investment would render recovering national economies interdependent. There was nothing automatic about this return to what some probably thought of as "normalcy." As careful analysts have convincingly shown, the dream of a liberal post-war order naturally moving a more fully capitalist world along a more peaceful path soon met the reality of communist intransigence, of new claims for the right to national self-determination, of irresistible demands for social protection at the national level, and of the necessity of coherent international leadership rooted in an adequate base of popular support. It would be convenient if the resulting experiment in reconstituting world order had proven neat and tidy. But history often seems messy and untidy. The record indicates that the elements of an intentional experiment emerged, especially after 1947. It was centered on active and continuing American engagement in the wider world, an engagement not simply conditioned on a narrow calculation of American national interests. It also succeeded in substantial part, at least if the avoidance of a reversion to global depression and great-power war may be taken as a reasonable indicator. Even with the advantage of historical hindsight, however, there seems no avoiding the conclusion that the experiment was an ideological and political muddle. Sympathetic scholars have tried to capture its essence with such evocative phrases as liberal internationalism, "the compromise of embedded liberalism," multilateral collaboration, democratic capitalism, the extension of Franklin Roosevelt's "New Deal" to the world, and "an empire by invitation."[4] And even opponents admit its existence, even if they favor terms like "hegemony" and "neo-imperialism."

The experiment rested on a deeply rooted, and still open, debate within the United States about its proper role in the world. Isolationism is commonly taken to inform one side of that debate, while the vision of the world converging inexorably toward the American way has long seemed to capture the other. As historians have convincingly demonstrated, however, if this sort of idealized ideological confrontation may once have had relevance, World War I rendered it irrelevant. The real debate inside the American polity after 1918 was between progressive internationalists, who saw the need for deep engagement far beyond U.S. borders aimed at nothing less than positive world-order transformation, and conservative internationalists, who wanted to keep foreign interventions limited and carefully calibrated to bounded and realistically conceived American interests.

My reading of the meandering path of this debate after World War I would focus on the progressive side losing decisively in the struggle over American participation in the League of Nations, the conservative side recalibrating its worldview in the midst of the storm unleashed by global depression and a new world war, a more "realistic" but still recognizably progressive vision coming to the fore at the start of the Cold War, and a conservative reaction to an open-ended external commitment as it came to an end.[5] The brief case histories presented below are consistent with just such a reading, and their interpretation here rests on a sense that the ebb and flow of that debate still shapes the changing character, scope, and authority of international institutions like the Fund and the Bank.[6]

During the 1970s, to be more specific regarding the contemporary period, not just expanding international trade but now also foreign direct investment and mushrooming short-term capital flows intensified pressures on idiosyncratic domestic structures and created markets that rewarded conformity to certain expectations of behavior broadly aligned with American norms. For countries seeking economic growth and prosperity, this now seemed to imply eventual agreement on more than the kinds of basic liberal economic rules associated with the 1944 Bretton Woods Agreement creating the Fund and the Bank. The alternative of revolutionizing the emerging structure of a globalizing economy itself was attempted during the troubled decade of the 1970s. Plans for a "New International Economic Order," one privileging local autonomy, national difference, and at least the possibility of assigning higher priority in national policies to social justice than to economic efficiency, came to naught. Whether the subsequent triumph of market liberalism in one developing country after another truly reflected a "silent revolution" within those countries remains the subject of debate. In any event, the trajectory of policy change seemed thereafter to imply convergence toward the way business is done, in the United States, or at least generally in conformity with liberal-market norms now shared across the richest countries in the system. Never mind the fact that certain specific and important business practices often differed among those countries.[7] Never mind the fact that idiosyncratic economic structures in the developing world reflected distinct histories, cultures, and politics. Never mind the fact that colonialism left persistent legacies across much of that world.

By the late 1980s, the main architects of the global economy – a handful of leading industrial states under the sometimes wavering but never seriously contested leadership of the United States – had constructed a system where international economic organizations appeared ever more assertively to promote deep structural change in countries needing financial assistance. By the end of the 1990s, the World Bank and especially the IMF were apparently now authorized to promote an expansive agenda of "sound economic policies" and "good governance." As the Managing Director of the Fund then stated in speech after speech, such a rubric now covered not simply prohibitions on outright corruption, but also prescriptions for financial market operations organized around objective commercial criteria, transparency in industrial conglomerates and in government–business relations more generally, the dismantling of monopolies, and the elimination of government-directed lending and procurement programs.[8]

The emerging global economy now seemed to require not simply voluntary adjustment in the context of gradually deepening interdependence across national economies, but also the external imposition of quite detailed normative standards in return for desperately needed financing. To radical critics from the left, what came to be known as "structural conditionality" as elaborated by the Fund and the Bank now cloaked a new form of imperialism. To their counterparts on the right, the tool of financing conditional on deep domestic reform proved a handy vehicle for the self-interested agendas of international bureaucrats, whose original purpose was rapidly being rendered obsolete by the liberated operation of private financial markets. To observers of a more moderately liberal persuasion, it seemed a defensible and rational response to new realities, a response embedded in a profound transformation in the ideological orientations of national policymakers in developing countries.[9] To political realists, it was simply a handy mechanism with which creditor states were trying to make the world safer for themselves.

Uncomplicated radical, liberal, or realist explanations may be attractive, but they are ultimately unsatisfying. The overarching questions are clear, but the easiest answers seem facile. Why did intergovernmental organizations of nearly universal membership and a founding ethos of political neutrality become the apparent enforcers of political preferences identified most clearly with a few rich countries, and especially with the United States? In a world where political authority remains dispersed but economic power is concentrated, why did a particular form of liberal internationalism develop whereby intermediaries originally organized precisely to allow members to retain a substantial degree of autonomy now became the guardians of a universal orthodoxy? Why did the strong not simply allow market pressures to overwhelm those intermediaries and force adjustment among the weak? If their political autonomy meant anything anymore, why did the weak not continue to resist?

The story of the emergence of structural conditionality in the Bank and the Fund revolves around such questions and sheds light on much larger themes in the history of "money doctoring." It also helps us deconstruct some of the images now associated with that nearly mystical word "globalization." Important ideological changes affecting the structures of governance *within* the political economy of the United States occurred in the decade when structural conditionality first emerged. Viewed in historical perspective, the connection seems more than coincidental. Of course, much more work would have to be done to prove a causal connection, but an exploration of the essential plausibility of just such a linkage is a necessary first step. Such a step would lead to the suggestion that in the wake of those ideological changes new ways had to be found to reinforce the American political commitment to progressive internationalism. Attentive to important shifts on both Wall Street and Main Street in the United States ever since the end of World War II, the Fund and the Bank adapted themselves to a new environment. Mixed motives abound in the real world of policy, but adjustment in the roles of those institutions had long been an important element in the fluid American-led experiment in world-order transformation first conceived while great-power war still raged in Europe and in the Pacific. A key objective, especially after the post-war experiment was reconceived in the mid-1970s, was the construction of a collaborative system of economic policymaking in which states would increasingly defer to signals emanating from more open markets, now including markets for money. Even though this new emphasis was quintessentially conservative (i.e. in the unique way American use that term; "liberal" in the sense that Europeans use it), progressives could continue to support the experiment as long as the actual operation of those markets did not entail a stark separation between social justice and economic efficiency, and as long as no more feasible mechanisms could promise peace, expanding prosperity, and increasing equity. The ultimate impact of more open markets remained unknowable, but the experiment itself continued to depend on American willingness to define national interests much more broadly than they had before 1940. In concrete terms, it required institutions capable of bridging the gap between conservative and progressive views of those interests.

From their earliest days, international financial institutions played an important role both in buffering and in bolstering American engagement in the wider world. Not coincidentally, they had to be Janus-faced. On one side, their existence limited the liability of American policymakers and citizens when other countries ran afoul of international markets. On the other side, they made those markets seem to the citizens of other states more cosmopolitan, less associated with particularistic national or class interests.

If the Americans did not desire an imperial order after 1945, even one mediated by the indirect instrumentality of markets, others did not desire market-based neo-colonialism. International financial markets ever more intensively linking still-national economies together confronted a particular kind of legitimacy problem, a problem that institutions like the Fund and the Bank promised to help assuage. The fact that their fundamental political role has never been entirely clear, the fact that jurisdictional disputes have always bedeviled them, and the fact that their operations have become more intrusive over time reflect deeper changes in the structure of power and authority within the United States. Adaptation within those institutions, in turn, reflect shifts in a long and continuing internal debate over the relationship between that structure and the international system as a whole. In a sense, the students of the strong become teachers of the weak. But, as any good scholar knows, learning is rarely a straightforward or transparent process.

Structural conditionality in the World Bank

In 1979 the World Bank first broke its standard practice of lending mainly for specific projects and began offering "structural adjustment loans." A major, and continuing, adaptation in the Bank's focus and mandate commenced. But the initial policy shift did not come out of the blue.

Financial conservatism had genetic roots in the Bank, roots that were embedded in the soil of American financial markets. The need to maintain its AAA credit rating, however, did not render the Bank an automaton. Just as ancient "sound money" orthodoxy dominated national economic policymaking in Britain and the United States in the 1940s, 1950s, and 1960s, the character of financial markets did not leave the Bank without room for maneuver. It needed that room, for it was a creature of its leading member states, few of whom would have appreciated the Bank foisting American values on them through policy-based lending. The Bank was forced to tread a fine line between satisfying the financial expectations of its funders and respecting the sovereign authority of its main clients.

In fact, the Bank was decidedly Keynesian in its formal and informal policy advice right through the 1960s.[10] Although stable macroeconomic frameworks inside client states were sought, that meant a reasonable equilibrium between internal and external balances. Excessive inflation, as in Brazil in the 1960s, could lead the Bank to halt its lending to that country, but the Bank did not question the legitimacy of the efforts of clients to steer markets, adopt and implement indicative economic plans, and control incoming and outgoing investment (Mason and Asher 1973: 662). It supported the IMF's mission of building up a global macroeconomy characterized by unified national exchange rate systems aimed at the kind of financial stability that promised to facilitate the expansion of international trade and long-term investment through well-functioning markets. Without compromising such objectives, however, the Bank was pragmatic in its judgment of the full range of policies we now label microeconomic. It was also generally cautious in its attempts to use financial leverage to encourage specific changes in macro policies.

A shift began to occur in the Bank when Robert McNamara assumed the presidency in 1968, but it was not a shift toward what one might call "Wall Street" values. In this respect, it is worth recalling the ideological baseline. In American political terms, the Bank and the Fund were emanations of Franklin Roosevelt's "New Deal."[11] The original plans for both institutions were anathema on Wall Street, for obvious reasons. After recovery from the ravages of war had occurred, the Fund and the Bank, as providers of financial assistance to countries in need, would be competitors to private financiers, and competitors with the very potent advantage of tacit safety nets from leading creditor states. Consequent distrust and resentment would pose larger challenges for the Bank than for the Fund, for the Bank was made dependent on private investors willing to hold its bonds, while the Fund was provided with substantial "own resources" through the quota subscriptions of its member states. That the Bank would attempt to accommodate Wall Street orthodoxies, therefore, is not as puzzling as the fact that it resisted such accommodation at all. In practice, its early presidents articulated a conservative vision and kept the Bank focused on projects of relatively limited scale not often directly competitive with the interests of private finance.

While some may in 1968 have expected the incoming President, Robert McNamara, to steer the Bank in an even more conservative direction, the opposite seems to have been his own intention. As McNamara made clear in later interviews with the Bank's historians, he always opposed fiscal indiscipline in the Bank's client states. But he also moved quite deliberately to expand the Bank's direct engagement with large-scale issues of poverty reduction, population control, and environmental-quality improvement. By way of implication, this engagement included the commitment of the Bank to harness and channel greater financial resource flows, including loans at concessionary rates effectively subsidized by creditor governments, and the necessity for the Bank to seek leverage points to guide allocation decisions inside client states. These two objectives existed in tension with one another, and success in raising new resources overshadowed aspirations for enduring policy influence.

During the heady and turbulent decade following McNamara's arrival, a vast expansion in the Bank's size and scope sought to keep pace with the rising expectations linked to vocal demands for a "New International Economic Order" and to simultaneously rising financing "gaps" associated with unprecedented oil price shocks. "The net result was that the 1970s (until their final year) were a period in which most of the Bank's policy-influencing efforts were upstaged and ineffective."[12] Inside the Bank, nevertheless, the ground was prepared for the Bank one day to refocus and reinvigorate an agenda for policy reform in its client states, not least because clients desperately seeking cash infusions during the 1970s had opened the door.

The "great bend in events," as the Bank's historians call it, occurred between 1979 and 1981. The cast of characters in the drama on the world stage is well known: Margaret Thatcher, Paul Volcker, Ronald Reagan, Milton Friedman, Walter Wriston. Against a changing ideological background, McNamara continued in his quest to expand the Bank's lendable resources, increasingly to be targeted at anti-poverty programs. (Curiously, McNamara's memoirs are silent on this period of his life, but speculation on his motivations at the time frequently and plausibly highlight the importance of his searing experience as U.S. Defense Secretary during the Vietnam War and its legacy of regret and atonement.[13]) Advising him and writing speeches for him were such well-known pro-development anti-poverty activists as Mahbub ul Haq, later Pakistan's Finance Minister. The Bank's Chief Economist, Hollis Chenery, helped construct the intellectual links between resource claims and deeper policy conditionality. Ernest Stern, the Bank's Chief Operating Officer after 1978, combined pragmatism with a clear vision of the need for policy reform inside the Bank's clients.

The Bank's new drama opened on May 10, 1979, with what must at the time have seemed like a fairly innocuous speech by McNamara to the UN Conference on Trade and Development then meeting in Manila:

> In order to benefit fully from an improved trade environment, the developing countries will need to carry out structural adjustments favoring their export sectors. This will require appropriate domestic policies and adequate external help. I would urge that the international community consider sympathetically the possibility of additional assistance to developing countries that undertake the needed structural adjustments for export promotion in line with their long-term comparative advantages. I am prepared to recommend to the Executive Directors that the World Bank consider such requests for assistance, and that it make available program lending in appropriate cases.
>
> (Kapur *et al.* 1997: 506–7)

During the next year, "structural adjustment loans" (SALs) would be formalized, just as demand for them would grow in tandem with rising balance of payments deficits occasioned by the second oil price shock.

The Bank's Board approved the new initiative early in 1980 and authorized structural adjustment lending in the range of $700 million during 1981. (The Board had authorized an increase in the Bank's capital stock from $41 billion to $85 billion.) Individual loans were to adopt the "program" model then used by the IMF. They were to be policy based, not project based. They would be phased in on a multi-year basis and would aim at basic reforms in longer-term economic structures. (The IMF, with whom the Bank pledged to coordinate its SALs, would continue to emphasize short-term adjustments needed to correct external payments imbalances.) Moreover, Bank documentation on the thinking behind SALs provided a broad set of examples of the types of policies that might be targeted for reform: policies shaping incentives, infrastructure, and marketing to encourage export diversification, policies affecting domestic resource mobilization, price incentives, and efficient resource use, and policies protecting inefficient industries and preventing the emergence of more competitive industries.[14]

As the SAL instrument developed, the irony is that what was originally advocated by anti-poverty activists trying to increase resource flows to developing countries soon proved quite attractive to parties long associated with economic orthodoxy. As if to symbolize the Bank's new enthusiasm for the reform agenda to be promoted through the instrument of SALs, a leading proponent of neoclassical economics, Anne Krueger, was appointed Chief Economist of the Bank in 1982. Between then and 1986 the Research Department led by her would undergo a major transformation, and its work would provide the rationale for the adoption of market-friendly policies by developing countries.[15]

Ernest Stern later recalled that this new form of lending was intended to accomplish three main things. It would

> support a program of specific policy changes and institutional reforms designed to reduce the current account deficit to sustainable levels, assist a country in meeting the transitional costs of structural changes in industry and agriculture by augmenting the supply of freely usable foreign exchange, and act as a catalyst for the inflow of other external capital to help ease the balance of payments situation.
>
> (Stern 1983: 89)[16]

The emphasis on the payments balance effectively subordinated Bank programs to IMF programs, but this apparently did not bother Stern. In practical terms, the actual procedures put in place to administer a Bank program mirrored those of the Fund. Stern described the underlying procedures that "may be called conditionality" as follows:

> The Bank must reach a firm understanding with each government on the monitorable action programs, specifying both the steps to be taken and the

studies required as a basis for further progress. The practice for this understanding is to be spelled out in detail in a Letter of Development Policies
that is explicitly referred to in the loan agreement. The tranching of
disbursement involves the identification of a few key actions that are specified as preconditions before the release of the second tranche. However,
satisfactory progress on the implementation of the overall program is also a
requirement.

(Stern 1983: 101)[17]

The practical shift allowing policy-based lending to occur through the Bank
reflected a clear tradeoff. New resources from creditor states implied new opportunities for constituents within those same states. Creditor states, mainly through
the private financiers of the Bank based within them, were expected to increase
the net resources at the disposal of the Bank. They needed an incentive of their
own. Even if policy reform could be depicted as inherently good for the Bank's
clients, whether they welcomed it or not in the short run, the reform agenda itself
bolstered a supportive coalition of beneficiaries within the creditor states. Exports
implied imports. The building and rebuilding of infrastructure in developing
countries promised opportunities for bankers, engineers, and equipment manufacturers in developed countries. Anti-protectionism in poor countries opened
markets for businesses based in rich countries. Moreover, as services became more
important in the economies of creditor states, the range of markets needing to be
opened in "emerging" countries broadened. The line between portfolio capital
flows needed to lubricate the machinery of trade in goods and flows constituting
in themselves trade in financial services began to blur.

There was nothing cynical about the new tradeoff. No conspiracy theory is
needed to explain it. Opening markets for goods and services in the Bank's client
states promised to open markets for financing in its creditor states. Market interdependence, not open national treasuries, promised to breed opportunities for
mutual gain. Capitalism tempered by a progressive internationalist vision, the
economic core of the post-war American-led experiment in world-order transformation, framed the Bank's operations from the beginning. As those markets
strengthened and neither the U.S. Treasury nor the U.S Congress showed any
interest in vastly expanding the role of direct governmental sources of development financing, the Bank adapted to the new situation. Progressives and
conservatives could both claim victory. That its legacy would come mainly to be
associated with conservatives, however, would be a function of the ideological
shading of the Bank's leaders finally catching up to that of mainstream
Washington in the 1980s.

The first use of the Bank's new structural lending tool happened to coincide
with a significant transition in its leadership, a transition that paralleled a much
broader ideological shift within its leading creditor state as well as in Great
Britain, a key player inside the Bretton Woods institutions since the beginning.
Reflecting on the images of Margaret Thatcher and Ronald Reagan, journalists
at the time commonly described the shift in terms of the death of Keynesianism

and the reemergence of laissez-faire liberalism and of classical "sound money" orthodoxy. In retrospect, that distinction is too stark. Excessive inflation, deepening fiscal imbalances, and threatened financial panics certainly shaped a new policy consensus across many states in the Organization for Economic Cooperation and Development (OECD). But Keynesianism, as conventionally conceived, survived. Indeed, in the United States it was given an enhanced military character and it thrived. Similarly, much to Milton Friedman's annoyance, an accompanying new monetarist fillip across much of the OECD was never truly orthodox or absolute. Still, classical economics came back into fashion – in the North American academy, in Washington policy circles, on Wall Street and in the City of London, and, hardly coincidentally, in a World Bank now led by the former Chief Executive Officer of the Bank of America. The SAL was a tool readily remolded in this light.

A reduced economic role for governments, an expanded role for more open markets, export expansion, import liberalization, the privatization of public enterprises, more flexible exchange rates, fiscal austerity, monetary targeting, expanding reliance on private financing flows and foreign direct investment – all of these policy reforms constituted the new agenda. And all of them implied deeper institutional change inside the Bank's client states. If the leaders of those states had once thought that structural adjustment loans represented a low-cost vehicle for increasing net inward resource transfers, they soon realized their mistake. Expanded Bank conditionality and a subtly threatened evolution of cross-conditionality with IMF lending programs promised heightened domestic political pressures. Likewise, however, free marketeers forecasting the dawn of a new, post-Keynesian era where efficient markets would ineluctably constrain such pressures would soon also be disappointed.

Bank SALs in practice turned out to be few, relatively small, and far between during the earliest phase of their implementation. An adapted version, targeted on specific sectors of a client's economy, also did not usher in a complete revolution in the way the Bank did its main business. Borrowers, unsurprisingly, turned out to be chary of accepting policy conditions deemed too intrusive, even when they needed the money badly. Before the debt crisis of the 1980s came into its fullest bloom, moreover, many middle-income countries most suitable as candidates for policy-based, reform-oriented Bank loans enjoyed access to other sources of financing – mainly foreign commercial bank loans, which generally came with no conditions except repayment with interest. What the Bank had done when it invented SALs, however, was to create a relatively quick-disbursing vehicle for partially replacing such sources of capital if and when they dried up.

SALs had a number of consequences inside the Bank during the 1980s. For one, their logic implied – and their character allowed – a proliferation in policy objectives. Getting incentives right inside client economies meant deeper and deeper structural adjustment. From a bureaucratic point of view, the short-term costs for the Bank to add conditions to its loans seemed very low. If those conditions were not met, however, or if they were regularly ignored, their long-term costs in terms of the Bank's own legitimacy could turn out to be very high. In fact, they deepened the necessity for expanded coordination between Bank and Fund programs. Money is fungible, and certain limited ideological, functional, and even cultural conflicts forced the two institutions to define and redefine their respective turfs over time.

The key example of where such conflicts could lead occurred in 1988 and 1989, and it involved Argentina. The story is well told elsewhere, from diverse points of view.[18] The essence, for our purposes, is that the IMF was trying to negotiate an adjustment program with Argentina that included tough fiscal austerity. New loans from the Bank, for a brief period and likely because of direct political pressure from the U.S. Treasury on its President (now Barber Conable, who had served in the U.S. Congress from 1965 until 1984), took the pressure off the Argentine government of the day. From the Fund's point of view, this new financing set back the cause of reform and financial stability. Others, including sitting members of the U.S. Congress, whose voices the U.S. Treasury does not even need to hear before it crafts pre-emptive policies, felt that it represented an emergency lifeline for a struggling democracy. When the pressure receded, however, the Bank reversed course, and a new rapprochement (glorified in a document labeled a "Concordat") between the two institutions was quickly negotiated on the basis of a now-traditional but always ambiguous distinction between the Fund's expertise in the area of relatively short-term balance of payments stabilization and adjustment and the Bank's expertise in long-term adjustment and development.[19] The incident focused attention on the receding difference between the two mandates and reminded creditor states of the irrationality of holding back public financing with one hand while providing it with another. More importantly, however, it underlined the new context. Public moneys merely primed the pump of private financing. Official creditors needed a strong and compelling rationale for pumping public money into a debtor country while private money was flowing out. Private markets themselves had become the central instrument available for creditor states committed to channeling increased financial flows to debtors. The Bank facilitated the process and, at the same time, buffered creditor states from more direct demands for financial resources. It should be emphasized in this regard that the leading creditor remained the United States, even if the actual source of most development financing had long since migrated from the Treasury and the Congress just up the street from the Bank to global networks with a principal node in downtown New York City.

It is worth quoting in substantial part the conclusion of the Bank's historians on the implications of the emergence of structural conditionality on the Bank itself:

> The turn toward heavier practice of macropolicy influence had major effects on the World Bank as an institution. It shaped the thrust of the Bank's work and program and surely gave many staff and managers a sense of power exercised. But the costs were heavy. With a higher profile, the institution was more exposed to attack…. The Bank helped cross-reference

policy discussion across countries, and the loans that carried [policy] messages sometimes tipped decision balances or facilitated implementation of reform....One reason the Bank was interesting as a policy promoter was that it was directed to be, and in considerable measure became, a financially powerful political eunuch....The zone of independence around the Bank diminished, when first...the Bank began to draw substantial public revenues, and second, began intruding more aggressively into [national] policy-making.

(Kapur et al. 1997: 588–9)

Structural conditionality in the IMF

The IMF was originally designed to monitor and defend a global exchange rate system. The underlying aim was to promote the expansion of world trade. Its financial role followed from the need to provide adequate resources in the short term to enable countries with external payments imbalances to adjust without resorting to system-destructive policies like competitive currency depreciation. Balance of payments *adjustment* was the key. In practice, the kinds of policy conditions that began to be attached to Fund credit in the mid-1950s focused on the stabilization of foreign exchange reserves. As practicable means for accomplishing such stabilization were sought, path-breaking research inside and outside the Fund pointed to the key role played by excessive domestic credit expansion. This soon translated into Fund programming aimed at the soundness of macroeconomic policies having the most obvious impact on that variable. In its early days, then, the words "growth" and "development" would have had no special place in the Fund's lexicon.[20]

The situation began to change very gradually after the first concessionary lending facility was created in 1963 in an attempt to help commodity-dependent countries stabilize their export proceeds in the face of increasingly turbulent international markets. There followed various adaptations in the Fund's standard lending arrangements: commodity financing facilities, buffer stock facilities, oil facilities, extended Fund facilities, "enlarged access" to routine funding. To make a long story short, a relatively straightforward line of policy development essentially moved Fund practice from an ethic that equated payments adjustment with monetary stabilization to one which attempted in principle to balance stabilization with long-term economic growth. That line starts with the inception in 1976 of a Trust Fund, essentially new financial resources for developing countries garnered from the sale of one-sixth of the IMF's gold reserves.

The U.S. Treasury proposed the Trust Fund in 1974, mainly as a relatively inexpensive means of building support among developing countries for its belated plan to legalize the post-1971 system of flexible exchange rates. (It also had the additional attraction of not requiring significant new commitments that needed to be authorized by the U.S. Congress.) Those countries were about to be disappointed by the refusal of the main creditor states to increase net aid flows by way of the free allocation of the IMF's fiat money, special drawing rights

(SDRs). That refusal, in turn, was rooted in concerns about excess-liquidity-induced global inflation, and the preference of the United States, Canada, Germany, and others not to obfuscate the issue of increasing foreign aid budgets directly. Loans granted under the terms of the Trust Fund did build in an aid element, however, for they were priced at below-market rates and came with relatively easy access conditions.

Ten years later, in 1986, when the original loans from the Trust Fund began to come due, the members of the IMF created a "Structural Adjustment Facility" to recycle the funds to the poorest developing countries, all of whom were asked to submit three-year adjustment programs to correct macroeconomic and structural problems impeding balance of payments adjustment and economic growth. As Harold James puts it,

> The new programs reflected the conviction that if adjustment were to succeed, it would require a medium-term orientation toward resumption of growth. This would be more feasible if a macroeconomic stabilization plan were associated with microeconomic reforms to stimulate enterprise and initiative at the local level.
>
> (James 1996: 526)[21]

One year later, an "Enhanced Structural Adjustment Facility" was established with grants from Japan, Canada, and others to provide financing at low cost and with long maturity periods to the poorest countries in the world, which soon numbered forty.

By this time the public rationalization for such facilities was to foster growth *and* to promote sustainable international payments balances. Such a rationalization signaled a potentially far-reaching shift in mandate. Economic growth – a profoundly political matter in both its causes and its consequences – had now achieved something like equivalence with the traditional balance of payments objectives of the Fund. Long criticized for forcing financial stringency on countries really requiring a stimulus to establish a virtuous cycle of economic growth, inward capital flows, and productive investment, the Fund would now be forced to move its adjustment time-horizons outward. Sustainable payments positions and sustainable development were acknowledged as interdependent goals. The Fund remained a global "monetary institution," but by increments it was also becoming an international development agency. For the true believers in politically neutral international organizations, such a transformation presaged much bigger dilemmas in the future. What constituted economic growth? A long series of ancillary questions arise from whatever answer is given, not least the following: if growth and development were now the appropriate targets for international financial institutions, could questions of economic justice be avoided?

The basic set of stabilization and adjustment policies the Fund had commonly come to advocate found their ultimate rationale during the 1980s in the idea of stable, long-term growth – "high quality" growth was the term later used by the Fund's Managing Director. The fact that the term was not innocuous can only be appreciated in retrospect. Traditionally, and in the simplest terms, the typical country coming to the Fund for assistance was driven there by an excess of its international payments over its international receipts, a cash shortfall that it could not easily finance on its own. The Fund was then charged with determining whether the shortfall was temporary, thus justifying the straightforward extension of short-term Fund credit, or fundamental, thus requiring an adjustment program likely facilitated in part by longer-term Fund credit. In either case, the alternative, assuming private financing, bilateral official development assistance, and other sources of funding were not available in sufficient amounts, was an immediate reduction in outgoing payments, typically payments for imports. In the case of fundamental problems, the ultimate implications for policies giving rise to them were generally the same. As the Fund's monetary approach to the balance of payments asserted, fundamental current account imbalances implied that underlying policies were generating excessive financial claims. Common sense seemed to lead to the conclusion that monetary stabilization required macroeconomic adjustments to address the imbalance, for example cuts in government spending, monetary tightening to rein in excess credit creation, and, if payments deficits were truly fundamental, changes in exchange rates to benefit exporters and discourage importers. (It takes little imagination to extrapolate the internal political consequences in the typical developing country exporting commodities and unfinished goods and importing finished goods, technology, equipment, and services. From the Fund's point of view, such consequences were inevitable, likely to be worsened in the absence of Fund financing, and, in any event, very much matters for "internal" distributive politics to manage.)

Common sense met hard experience in the 1980s, when middle-income developing countries, mainly in Latin America, confronted acute debt crises. As two respected critics of the Fund put it, the Fund's traditional approach risked "overkill" if reciprocal processes of adjustment were not undertaken in countries generating current account surpluses, or if the deeper causes of macroeconomic policy problems were "structural" in nature.[22] The latter term was already in use by the Fund to refer to difficulties not attributable to normal business cycles and generally resolvable only in the medium (3–5 years) or longer term. Throughout the 1980s and into the 1990s, notwithstanding its public image to the contrary, the Fund's staff, management, and Executive Board – often in conflict with one another – took such criticism seriously. The evolution of special financing facilities and more generalized adaptations in the actual practice of conditionality must be viewed in this light.

Small libraries were filled with analytical and policy research coming out of the Latin American debt crises of the 1980s. The standard view now holds that the basic problem in its early phase was misdiagnosed. As foreign bank lending, which dominated flows into many countries throughout the 1970s, suddenly dried up, the Fund and the world's main creditor countries thought they were dealing with a liquidity problem, albeit a serious one. The solution – embedded in the "Baker Plan," named for its chief architect, James Baker, then U.S. Treasury Secretary – was to bolster the confidence of private lenders, coordinate plans to lengthen debt maturities, and, in some cases, coerce lenders into continued lending. Baker himself put the plan's three main elements more diplomatically: the debtors "should adopt comprehensive macroeconomic and structural policies," the IMF should play a central role "in conjunction with increased and more effective structural adjustment lending by the multilateral development banks in support of the adoption of market-oriented policies for growth," and private banks "should increase their lending in support of comprehensive economic adjustment programs."[23] In the absence of an international lender of last resort, the Fund was available to act as the coordinator of efforts on the part of creditor governments to keep money flowing. Economic growth would eventually return, and a rising tide was clearly expected to lift all boats. The problem, after all, had occurred on Ronald Reagan's watch.

Alas, optimism can sometimes be excessive, even in the United States. Sufficient and enduring growth did not return to Latin America and the problem deepened. Moreover, the Fund had difficulty adapting to its emerging mandate of structural adjustment. Beyond its staff justifiably feeling out of their depth on microeconomic matters – from bank regulation to tax reform, to public procurement, to legal reform – skeptics in its management and executive ranks clearly saw the institutional risks inherent in the Fund setting itself up for a job that could prove impossible. The staff also considered themselves to be formally restricted by Conditionality Guidelines adopted by the Fund's Board in 1979, which specified a continuing focus on macroeconomic policies. Under the leadership of a dynamic Managing Director, who identified the urgent necessity for pragmatic adjustment within the Fund itself, those guidelines were to prove flexible, but disquiet remained among those who cherished the Fund's apolitical self-image.

The Baker Plan, in the end, met with very limited success, especially from the point of view of indebted countries unable to hold policy lines that continued to build up trade surpluses while growth sputtered and domestic political coalitions began to crumble. (Of course, it met with very great success if the core threat really arose from the probability of financial panics in the creditor countries, for the plan clearly gave the implicated banks enough time to get their developing country exposure down to manageable levels in relation to their capital resources.) Diagnosticians both inside and outside the Fund began to conclude that many heavily indebted countries faced solvency, not liquidity, crises.

As in any domestic context, insolvency seemed necessarily to imply debt "restructuring," a euphemism for outright debt reduction to sustainable levels. Such a solution lay at the heart of the next "plan" to resolve the regional crisis, this one identified with the name of Nicholas Brady, who had replaced Baker as U.S. Treasury Secretary. In the absence of an international bankruptcy court, the Fund was again called upon to coordinate national efforts, but this time to construct the functional equivalent of such a court. In short, creative debt workouts generally occurred under the umbrella of a Fund standby arrangement, which conditioned effective debt reductions on policy adjustment programs, emphasizing macroeconomic matters but increasingly encouraging changes in deeper internal economic structures. In practical terms, this entailed coordinating, even mutually negotiating, letters of agreement between the borrowing country and the Fund and between the borrowing country and the Bank. After 1989, moreover, many programs had longer time-horizons and were also implicitly linked to new money flows directly from creditor treasuries.

The adequacy of such flows is a matter of dispute to the present day, especially for the poorest debtor countries. But to cut to the chase in a long and continuing saga, few involved in the debt crises of the 1980s emerged happy, and everyone confronted but never clarified the fundamental political, economic, and legal ambiguities inherent in the core problem.[24] When economic growth returned in many of the indebted Latin American countries in the 1990s, optimists concluded that international cooperation had worked. This included many American banks, which did not face ruin from having their shareholders' equity completely wiped out by Latin American defaults, and members of the U.S. Congress, who were never called upon to help those banks directly and who never permitted themselves to be pushed in the direction of vastly increasing the official resources available to the Fund.[25] Pessimists, conversely, contended that the problem had merely gone into remission, and they agreed, on balance, that bankers and their regulators in creditor countries, as well as certain elites in debtor countries, had emerged as the true winners. In between those positions were the perplexed, who were left with a simple counterfactual issue to ponder. Would mass populations in Latin America have been better off under any other scenario? However they answered such a question, neither optimists nor pessimists could help observing that the trauma of the Latin American debt crises of the 1980s had profoundly transformed the Fund.

Structural conditionality, as opposed to technical advice touching on structural matters, would not become fully evident in the Fund until the 1990s. But evolving responses to the debt crises and other events during the 1980s presaged further adaptation of Fund practices along this very line. Throughout the decade, the focus of daily life for the Fund's management and staff, as well as for its Executive Board, shifted from overseeing adjustments in the system of current international payments to managing the more specific consequences of frictions in the flow of capital from international capital markets to middle-income developing countries. Incrementalism reigned. Pragmatic responses to individual cases cumulated. The Fund itself – that organization comprised of management, staff, and directors – was transformed by that cumulation. The reinterpretation of its legal mandate under political pressure, and the redirection of personnel, financial, and reputational resources were the end results. If a lack of clarity remained at the end of the decade – and it certainly did – it reflected the unwillingness of the Fund's member states to codify the transformation they themselves supported every step of the way. Here was the true "Washington consensus."

The capital-recycling mechanism at the heart of the global system of economic growth and adjustment could not be "reformed." Its underlying norms and rules could not be addressed explicitly. In short, no formal rules equivalent to those governing world trade could be agreed for world finance. Private intermediaries, regulated by national authorities, could not be regulated at the international level. No single international arbiter could be chosen. The die had been cast long ago, when financial regulatory authority was taken off the multilateral negotiating table and reserved for national governments, and when those governments began using that authority to give more liberty to non-domestic intermediaries than to domestic ones (Helleiner 1994). The subsequent policy priority assigned to financial markets in the allocation of international resources for development, a priority most clearly enshrined in American policy, was reinforced as most governments of rich countries intentionally reduced the relative and absolute volumes of public financing available for direct foreign aid. The consequences of increasingly free international capital flows through private channels could and would be addressed with available tools adapted for the purpose.

The historical record of international financial turmoil in the 1980s will, like all historical records, be subject to interpretation and debate for many years to come. As it stands now, however, most interpretations place the Latin American debt crisis at its center. In that context, they also strongly suggest that the expansion of the Fund's mandate into the realm of structural adjustment during that decade did not have a single, easily traceable source. It is true that strategic thinkers on the Fund's staff, most prominently in the Research Department, began arguing in the early 1980s that supply-side reforms were necessary to put leading debtor states on to a more sustainable financial track. Certainly not coincidentally, such views paralleled new thinking coming into vogue down Pennsylvania Avenue at a U.S. Treasury Department then led by firm supporters of the Reagan revolution.[26] Nevertheless, more than one executive director and many line staff members charged with designing and implementing actual country programs firmly rejected calls for a formal expansion in the Fund's responsibilities in this area. The record also indicates reticence on the part of the Executive Board to give Jacques de Larosière, Managing Director during the first half of the decade, its full and enthusiastic support for projecting the organization willy-nilly into the center of a crisis that was beginning to require major adjustments in some basic economic and political structures somewhere. Clearly, structures deep inside weak countries desperate for capital looked the most vulnerable. In 1981, 1986, 1987, and 1988, the Board directly addressed the question of explicitly including in its conditional lending instruments performance criteria related to those structures. Each time, however, it refused to authorize a formal binding role for the organization.

In 1981, Ariel Buira, then Mexico's Executive Director at the Fund, eloquently captured the skepticism the American-led ideological shift to the right was then engendering in the developing world. In reaction to a staff paper recommending a limited economic role for the state, Buira noted that, with regard to the "nineteenth century liberal concept in which the state has...no development responsibilities, [my authorities] did not expect Fund guidance on this matter."[27] By the end of the decade, however, enough directors from the developing world were in agreement to authorize the staff, in conjunction with their counterparts at the World Bank, to experiment with the concept of deeper adjustment in specific cases where structural reform appeared "essential for the achievement of external viability."[28]

Gradual movement in the direction of embedding a structural reform agenda into Fund lending programs did in fact occur for many Latin American debtors. Other significant cases bolstering the constituency for such an agenda include some ironies. In the case of South Africa, for example, the Fund designed a standby arrangement that wrapped a cloak of political neutrality and economic reasoning around an attack on labor market inefficiencies directly attributable to apartheid. Supporting structural adjustment in this sense was a broad constituency that included many developing countries. More controversially, signal Fund programs for Kenya, Tanzania, Uganda, and the Philippines during the 1980s edged very close to the inclusion of requirements for anti-corruption, privatization measures, and other structural measures, but formal performance criteria along these lines proved too controversial. Enforced policy liberalization, or "market-oriented" reform, would have to wait until the next decade. The necessity to adjust unsustainable current account deficits overrode rhetorical commitments to "adjustment *with* economic growth," at least in the short run. Formal commitments could still only be tied to that necessity. Throughout the decade, spokespeople for debtor nations continued to echo Buira's point, albeit with apparently declining enthusiasm: even if structural reforms were needed in many countries, it was beyond the authority and the competence of the Fund to enforce domestic institutional change. The Fund's historian puts the matter simply:

> Despite a universal agreement that growth was a 'primary objective of economic policy' and that adjustment would often fail if growth was too long in coming all efforts to link adjustment with growth foundered on this simple dilemma. Lacking a well-established and validated model of economic growth, the Fund could not require structural reforms as a condition of its credits. Not until domestic political support emerged for these reforms in their own right – not until the silent revolution was won – would the dichotomy between growth and stability finally fade away.
>
> (Boughton 2001: 614)

That may be, but it is again worth recalling that the adjective "structural" was used throughout the 1980s by Fund directors from poorer countries to refer not just to internal impediments to growth but also to external constraints on that growth. Low commodity prices, oil price shocks, turbulent exchange rates among leading currencies, closed markets for exports, and, again, the vagaries of privatized international finance – these surely constituted "structures" as well. Could reform of such structures really not be linked to adjustment strategies in developing countries? Apparently not. But, as we have seen, special funds and enhancements in standard financing arrangements could be established in the Fund partly to compensate for the one-sidedness of the process.

The Fund's historian sums up the experience of the organization during the 1980s in the following terms:

> The reliance of many low-income countries on short and medium-term financing from the Fund in the early 1980s and the attempt of many middle-income developing countries to rely on macroeconomic policy reforms in the mid-1980s exposed weaknesses in the coordination of multilateral assistance. Efforts by the Fund, the World Bank, and other agencies to collaborate more fully in the second half of the decade were only partially successful. That effort did, however, help prepare the institutions for the much greater level of coordination that would be required in the 1990s, when countries in transition from central planning would have to make comprehensive structural and macroeconomic reforms in a very short period of time....Throughout the 1980s, the Fund circumscribed its own scope for action by limiting explicit conditionality to macroeconomic policies and avoiding interference with policies that could be construed as politically rather than economically motivated. The initial success of countries that liberalized on their own – the silent revolution – drew the Fund out of that reluctance in ways that would enable it to play a more active role in promoting structural reform in the 1990s.
>
> (Boughton 2001: 50)

While the latter contention is plausible, it again begs the question of where the norms embedded in actual reform programs had come from, and why alternatives were infeasible. The continuation of the story into the 1990s draws attention back ever more insistently to the earlier and hardly silent "revolution" that had occurred in the United States.

The Bretton Woods institutions in the 1990s

The 1990s are still too fresh in historical memory to permit a balanced assessment. Key events included a remarkable boom in the American economy, a bursting financial bubble in Japan, a decisive move toward monetary union in Western Europe, the rise of what the Chinese called their socialist market economy, and an equally decisive shift away from socialism in Central and Eastern Europe. Linking those regional developments together was the vast expansion and increased volatility of international capital flows, but continuing national-level experiments with various measures to control or influence such flows.[29] In this context, the seeds of deliberate efforts to encourage, even to force, structural adjustment in developing countries that were sown in the 1980s flowered upon the terrain tended by the World Bank and the IMF. This occurred despite a relative decline in the financial size of the Fund and the Bank relative to those burgeoning international capital flows and despite rising political attacks on both organizations from the right and left of the political spectrum inside their leading member state.[30] Why? The story of the 1980s recounted above provides a clue.

There is no shortage of simple explanations on offer for the apparent emergence of the Fund and the Bank as the enforcers of structural adjustment in a new global regime. Even if not to the exclusion of all other factors, public choice analysts continue to emphasize the preservationist and expansionist instincts of their senior managers and employees. Fund and Bank historians assign significant weight to the conversion of national authorities in developing countries to sound economic orthodoxy as alternative strategies failed. Skeptics surmise a grand design orchestrated by the U.S. Treasury, or by faceless private financiers pulling the Treasury's strings.

Any such reading, on its own, does not fit comfortably with the full story of the 1980s. Taken together, they only help re-describe the mixed motivations of key actors and the ambiguous outcomes of the 1990s. Such an amalgamation does little to advance our deeper understanding; nor does it help us anticipate future developments.

In the early post-World War II period, the U.S. Congress needed to be convinced that U.S. taxpayers would not be left with the full bill for reconstructing economies destroyed by the war or for easing the transition of European colonies to political independence. In the absence of guarantees to that effect, the Bretton Woods institutions would never have seen the light of day. During each succeeding round of legislation required to allow those institutions to develop, new guarantees were required mainly to convince U.S. legislators that public money would not be wasted and that it would supplement, not substitute for, private financing. Conditionality itself was shaped in this context. Its strengthening and broadening into "structural" variants correlate almost perfectly with increasing reliance on private financial markets as the world's principal source of development finance, and with a declining American interest in international financial institutions except as they connected to those markets or were needed to compensate for deficiencies in those markets (Kahler 1990: 91–114).

In many member states, policy changes needed to participate in bolstering the resources of the Bank or adapting the formal mandate of the Fund are usually handled by the finance minister, the central bank governor, and a small set of elite bureaucrats.[31] Keeping national treasuries open and legislatures supportive is relatively easy. In the United States, this has never been the case. Over time, moreover, American financial officials had greater difficulty in maintaining control over such issues, much less in fostering strategic consistency. As the Cold War receded, the situation became even more difficult, as Congress came ever more obviously to the fore while the relative power of the presidency seemed to erode. Simultaneously, financial markets became much more prominent as the mechanisms through which key distributive decisions were taken within American society as a whole. Those markets also became much more important as mechanisms through which the American polity linked the interests of that society with the interests of both developed and "emerging" economies around the world.

American attention to the Fund and the Bank now clearly ebbs and flows with the absence or presence of crises in financial markets, or the absence or presence of security crises that can be addressed in part through easing the impact of financial market pressures. In other words, it correlates most obviously with the existence of external challenges that have become threatening enough to justify some kind of financial response but not yet so urgent as to demand the far less economical recourse to direct, unilateral aid from the U.S. Treasury. An upswing in this cycle occurred once again in the late 1990s, when the institutions were enlisted to oversee the orderly reduction of financial obligations in highly indebted poor countries (the so-called HIPC initiative). It also occurred in the wake of terrorist attacks in September 2001. In recent years American attention has sometimes also been heightened by the advocacy work of special-interest non-governmental organizations (NGOs). In line with the focus of this chapter, close observers have demonstrated how such advocacy has actually promoted the further elaboration of structural conditionality in the Fund and the Bank.[32]

Conclusion: reflections and speculations

If we take it as given that the United States continues to lead in the contemporary international system, the narrative histories outlined above suggest the following counterfactual question. Without the discourse on conditionality and structural adjustment, would the American political commitment to the Fund and the Bank increase? I doubt it. Indeed, the reverse seems much more plausible. Throughout the 1980s, the discourse itself arose directly out of American political debates on issues of world order. Both on the "left," with McNamara's commitment to poverty reduction, and on the right, with the rise of supply-side economics, the discourse of structural adjustment engaged or attempted to engage core American interests. Throughout the 1980s, certain interests became obvious as American financial intermediaries faced the prospect of catastrophe arising from their Latin American portfolios. In the 1990s, similar interests would be undeniable when countries in transition from communism as well as dynamic East Asian countries confronted a situation of sudden and catastrophic capital flight.

   Across the cases touched on in this chapter, demands for ever deeper structural change in borrowing countries became more insistent. As Miles Kahler points out, "Assuring the confidence of investors and nudging government toward prudent policies in the new environment had become the central task of multilateral institutions and industrialized-country governments in the 1990s."[33] This nudging really entailed promoting norm-governed behavior, with the norms drawn from an idealized version of American economic history and a close reading of contemporary American economic policy.[34] The Fund's Managing Director appealed directly to such norms whenever he advocated "financial market operations organized around objective commercial criteria, transparency in industrial conglomerates and in government-business relations more generally, the dismantling of monopolies, and the elimination of government-directed lending and procurement programs."[35] In truth, such norms described the actual history of no industrial country, including the United States.

They did, however, coincide clearly with the vision for a global market-system that came to be advocated by both government and business in the United States after World War II, and especially after the Cold War began to fade. The shift from "government managed to market-based mode of governance" within the international system has been widely noted (Kahler 1998). The view that this was logical, inevitable, and even unstoppable came to be widely embraced during the 1990s. Some analysts of the implications and prospects for developing countries have nevertheless adopted a less determinist position. Devesh Kapur, for example, sums up one such argument:

> [Norms can] serve as a fig-leaf for more prosaic material interests. There is an understandable skepticism that richer countries are long on norms when they are short on resources, and the increasing attention to norms of governance even as development budgets decline is perhaps not entirely coincidental. As long as the Cold War was on, "crony capitalism" in Indonesia was not considered a problem. Nor was it a problem while the East Asian "miracle" was being trumpeted. But when the Asia crisis of 1997–98 erupted, norms of corporate governance were strenuously advanced to deflect attention from broader issues of the nature and quality of international financial regulation.
>
> (Kapur n.d.)[36]

As it relates to the latest phase in the expansion of structural conditionality in the Bank and the Fund, Kapur's position appears eminently supportable. Pushing reflection on the larger post-World War II experience one step further, however, promises deeper insight into both the most significant cause of the shift toward market-based governance and the most likely challenges ahead. In short, the narrative of this chapter suggests that the shift mirrored precisely the central struggle within contemporary American capitalism since the early 1980s. That struggle may reasonably be interpreted as concerning the reconstruction of the middle ground inside the United States between an enduring commitment to a still-national economy and a decided preference for openness in the cause of system stabilization, at the very least, and in the cause of system transformation, at most. Consistent with a longstanding theme in American economic history, the customs, institutions, and processes involved in that reconstruction quite deliberately rendered opaque the borderlines between state and society. To a considerable extent, the struggle now revolved around questions concerning the appropriate limits of strict market principles within American society. In more concrete terms, it focused on the place of financial markets within that society, with all that this implies in terms of measuring important political and social outcomes in narrowly financial terms.

To be sure, the struggle did not begin when Ronald Reagan won the White House. Its terms had antecedents going back to the founding of the country. During the post-Great Depression period and right up to the 1970s, one set of answers to the principal dilemma created a relatively stable equilibrium: competitive markets centered on private corporations with diffuse (non-bank) owner-ship, fragmented financial markets (key parts of which now rested on implicit or explicit government guarantees), an overarching ideology combining free enter-prise with an expansion of public funding for social welfare, health, and educational programs. Often obscured but always highly significant was the role of government as system regulator, promoter of a massive defense-industrial base, and guarantor of a modicum of social equity.[37] In the 1980s, a new set of answers coursed through the American debate, the end result of which was to favor greater degrees of economic concentration, much less fragmented financial markets, a reduction in social welfare programs, and an ethic of underlying market supervision by government instead of overt market regulation. Occurring at the same time was a complicated expansion in the scale of implicit financial guarantees provided by government agencies and a deepening sense of disquiet about the moral hazards thereby entailed. When in 1998 the Federal Reserve and the Treasury facilitated the massive financial operation that stabilized and then in an orderly fashion unwound the Long Term Capital Management hedge fund, that sense of disquiet became quite palpable.

The rise of private intermediaries as the key providers of external financing for developing countries tracks a deeper transformation *within* the world's domi-nant economy. Here is the true taproot of the changing mandates of the main international financial institutions. The elaboration of their practice of struc-tural conditionality makes little sense if it is divorced from this context. Ideological and structural change within the system leader implies the need to accommodate change among those who seek to benefit from the system it leads, and who sense on the basis of experience little prospect for the near-term construction of an alternative system.

Certain outcomes are undeniable – the tiering of developing economies in terms of their creditworthiness, the increasing desperation of those countries deemed uncreditworthy, mounting pressures on national policies aimed at miti-gating income inequality, and the expansion in possibilities for exit for the owners of liquid capital. All such outcomes raise difficult international as well as domestic political difficulties, and those outcomes themselves summon a political response. The Fund and the Bank arose in the context of an experiment aiming to foster international economic interdependence without simultaneously creating a global government.[38] The contemporary elaboration of their mandates is a political response consistent with that experiment, even as it now relies on financial markets for its motor force.[39]

Since asymmetries of power are hard to overlook, difficult for the weak to accept, and important for the strong to obscure, international political buffers are necessary even in "market-led" systems.[40] In this light, the Fund and the Bank may be viewed as a gift of history, one that would be difficult to replicate if they had to be created *ab initio* today. They are led by the strong but give voice to the weak. They can learn lessons from leading members, and they can teach those lessons to followers. They can deflect blame and play the role of scape-goats when things do not go smoothly. They are useful surrogates for the imagined collectivity commonly now referred to by politicians and journalists as "the international community."

Because of their relatively modest size and their ambivalent record in actually serving as catalysts to private market solutions for basic economic problems, the Fund and the Bank can actually do little on their own to move the system toward what their founders called "symmetry."[41] It is not implausible to argue, however, that international economic inequities would be even worse in their absence. Such a view, of course, would be contentious, but the most sweeping positions currently being taken in related arguments over a "new international financial architecture" are surely misguided and misdirected. Skepticism is the appropriate response to calls for the abolition of the Bank and the Fund from the ideological left or the ideological right, to calls for a radical refocusing of institutional mandates across the two organizations, and to calls for their massive expansion. All such demands profoundly misunderstand the political underpinning of the international economy as it evolved after 1945.

A process of institutional adaptation at the international level has long been part of the experiment that began over half a century ago. In retrospect, it is but a step from the IMF's Trust Fund of 1976 to the HIPC initiative of today, and from the Bank's first SALs to today's Poverty Reduction Strategy Papers. The evolution of the practice of structural conditionality within both institutions has been almost perfectly attuned to developments within the state that continues in its role as leading proponent of that experiment. Those developments are not easily attributable to any one agency of American government or to any one sector of its national economy. They reflect instead the abiding interest of a complicated state and society in stability abroad but chary of paying its full cost.[42] At times, the historical record lets us catch a glimpse of an aspiration deep within that state and society for a progressive transformation of the world order. Whether it takes the Wilsonian form of trying to "make the world safe for democracy" or the more mundane form of promoting the American way of doing business, periodic expressions of that aspiration seem quickly to elicit a conservative reaction. That reaction is often mistaken for isolationism; in the contemporary period it is in practice the reassertion of a still-internationalist but more realistic impulse to correlate feasible ends with available means.

During the 1980s, the United States moved decisively to expand the scope for markets to resolve internal distributive problems. Other states and societies having recovered prominent positions in the hierarchy of world power since 1945 moved in a similar direction. But the system that bound them still required a leader, and the leader still required popular support for a durable policy of external engagement. Support could not be mustered inside the United States for an unambiguously progressive policy, say one that could work through significantly expanded multilateral institutions. But neither could support be maintained for a consistently conservative retrenchment.[43] In the continuing effort to strike a balance between these two positions lies the deeper structure now motivating adjustment elsewhere. The operations of more open capital markets and the ever more intimately related lending policies of leading international financial institutions remain rooted in that structure.

Notes

1   An early draft of this chapter was presented as a paper at a conference on "Critical Issues in Financial Reform," University of Toronto, June 1–2, 2000. A related presentation was made on February 2, 2000, in the Economic and Social Affairs Department of the United Nations in New York. I am grateful to Albert Berry, Eric Helleiner, Richard Webb, Gerry Helleiner, Barry Herman, and Gustavo Indart for constructive comments on the draft, and to the Social Sciences and Humanities Research Council of Canada for financial support. Very helpful advice on final revisions was offered by Marc Flandreau, Jérôme Sgard, and Nicholas Jabko.
2   For recent treatments of the theme, see Krasner (1999) and Caporaso (2000).
3   On the inter-war experience, see Santaella (1993).
4   Suggestive works in this tradition include Cooper (1968); Kindleberger (1973); de Cecco (1976: 381–99; 1979: 49–61); Keohane and Nye (1977: 195–231); Burley (1993: 125–56); Ikenberry (2001).
5   Knock (1992); Trachtenberg (1999); Friedberg (2000); Kennedy (1987); and Nau (2001).
6   For application of such an analysis to the Fund's core mandate, see Pauly (1997).
7   See, for example, Berger and Dore (1996).
8   See, for example, *IMF Survey* (1998).
9   "There is no separate economic truth that applies to developed, or to developing countries" (James 1996: 609).
10   For a subtle explication of this part of the original Keynesian vision itself, see Skidelsky (2000).
11   The fullest exploration of this theme can be found in Ruggie (1998).
12   Kapur *et al.* (1997: 472).
13   McNamara and Vandemark (1996).
14   Kapur *et al.* (1997: 510).
15   Rodgers and Cooley (1999: 1,405). Krueger was appointed Deputy Managing Director of the IMF in 2001, following the retirement of Stanley Fischer, who left shortly after Michel Camdessus stepped down as Managing Director.
16   See also James (1996: 327).
17   See also de Vries (1987: ch. 6).
18   Kapur *et al.* (1997: 528–31); Polak (1997); Boughton (2001: ch. 11).
19   For more on this issue, see Ahluwalia (1999: 1–26).
20   Polak (1991). A principal architect of the Fund's "monetary approach," Polak explores the background debate in Polak (2001).
21   See also Boughton (2001: 649-51).
22   Díaz-Alejandro (1981); and Dell (1983). See also Dell (1981).
23   Interim Committee Meeting, October 1985, cited in Boughton (2001: 417).
24   For an excellent exposition of these issues, see Cohen (1986).
25   In this regard, note Boughton's assertion that "the single greatest problem for the Fund in the 1980s was to garner the financial resources to meet the demand for its services" (Boughton 2001: 44).
26   Richard Erb, who held the key role of Deputy Managing Director of the Fund after 1984, began his policymaking career as staff assistant to Richard Nixon in 1971. After 1974, he worked intermittently at the U.S. Treasury and the conservative American Enterprise Institute. In 1981 he became U.S. Executive Director at the Fund. See Boughton (2001: 1,044).
27   IMF Executive Board Meeting Minutes, 81/62, April 20, 1981: 13–9; cited in Boughton (2001: 588–9).

302 *Louis W. Pauly*

28 From Managing Director's summing up of Board Review, December 18, 1987 (Boughton 2001: 590).
29 See Armijo (1999); and Andrews *et al.* (2002).
30 The critiques are thoroughly set out in: U.S. Congress (2000: chs. 2–3). See also the background paper by Bordo and James (1999).
31 The situation is similar in many developing countries, where the role of the central bank in particular has recently been gaining in political importance. See Maxfield (1997).
32 On the NGO–U.S. Congress–U.S. Treasury linkage and its impact on structural conditionality in the Bank, see Wade (2001).
33 Kahler (1998: 21).
34 On the notion of norm-governed behavioral change, see Ruggie (1983).
35 *IMF Survey* (1998).
36 See also Woods (1998: 81–106; 2001: 83–100).
37 See Roe (1994) and Doremus *et al.* (1998).
38 On the original political bargaining behind the Bretton Woods institutions, see Eichengreen (1996: ch. 4).
39 In this regard, planning for a Special Session of the UN General Assembly on "Financing for Development" in 2002 is relevant. For background, see United Nations (2000). For antecedent debates, see Krasner (1985).
40 The theme is cogently addressed in the international monetary arena in Cohen (1998).
41 See, for example, Hurrell and Woods (1999). Worth examining carefully in this regard are current debt-reduction efforts organized under the HIPC initiative creditor countries are coordinating through the Fund and the Bank.
42 This theme is explored in much recent research on international institution-building. See, for example, Luck (1999) and Hoopes and Brinkley (1997).
43 Witness the mixed signals in the first year of the Bush administration. Against the backdrop of electioneering that asserted the necessity of reining in the Bank and the Fund, and even after overseeing the installation of a more "conservative" team at the top of the Fund (including, again, Anne Krueger), a U.S. Treasury said to be hostile to structural conditionality as well as to any prominent role for the Fund and the Bank strongly supported a massive bailout of Turkey that involved detailed conditionality on a range of microeconomic issues. See *IMF Survey* (2001a, 2001b).

References

Ahluwalia, M.S. (1999) "The IMF and the World Bank in the New Financial Architecture," United Nations Conference on Trade and Development, *International Monetary and Financial Issues for the 1990s*, vol. 11, New York: United Nations.
Andrews, D., C. Randall Henning and L.W. Pauly (eds.) (2002) *Governing the World's Money*, Ithaca, NY: Cornell University Press.
Armijo, L.E. (ed.) (1999) *Financial Globalization and Democracy in Emerging Markets*, New York: St. Martin's Press.
Berger, S. and R. Dore (eds.) (1996) *National Diversity and Global Capitalism*, Ithaca, NY: Cornell University Press.
Bordo, M. and H. James (1999) "The International Monetary Fund: Its Present Role in Historical Perspective," November; available at http://phantom-x.gsia.cmu.edu/IFIAC/USWelcome.html.
Boughton, J. (2001) *Silent Revolution: The International Monetary Fund, 1979–1989*, Washington, DC: International Monetary Fund.

Burley, A.-M. (1993) "Regulating the World: Multilateralism, International Law, and the Projection of the New Deal Regulatory State," in J.G. Ruggie (ed.) *Multilateralism Matters*, New York: Columbia University Press.

Caporaso, J.A. (2000) "Changes in the Westphalian Order: Territory, Public Authority, and Sovereignty," *International Studies Review* (summer) 2(2): 1–28.

Cecco, M. de (1976) "International Financial Markets and U.S. Domestic Policy since 1945," *International Affairs* 52: 381–99.

Cecco, M. de (1979) "Origins of the Postwar Payments System," *Cambridge Journal of Economics* 2: 49–61.

Cohen, B.J. (1986) *In Whose Interest? International Banking and American Foreign Policy*, New Haven, CT: Yale University Press.

Cohen, B.J. (1998) *The Geography of Money*, Ithaca, NY: Cornell University Press.

Cooper, R.N. (1968) *The Economics of Interdependence*, New York: McGraw-Hill.

Dell, S. (1981) "On Being Grandmotherly: The Evolution of I.M.F. Conditionality," *Princeton Essays in International Finance*, no. 144, Princeton, NJ: Princeton University, International Finance Section, Department of Economics.

Dell, S. (1983) "Stabilization: The Political Economy of Overkill," in J. Williamson (ed.) *IMF Conditionality*, Washington, DC: Institute for International Economics.

Díaz-Alejandro, C. (1981) "Southern Cone Stabilization Plans," in W.R. Cline and S. Weintraub (eds.) *Economic Stabilization in Developing Countries*, Washington, DC: Brookings Institution.

Doremus, P.N., W. Keller, L.W. Pauly and S. Reich (1998) *The Myth of the Global Corporation*. Princeton, NJ: Princeton University Press.

Eichengreen, B. (1996) *Globalizing Capital*, Princeton, NJ: Princeton University Press.

Friedberg, A.L. (2000) *In the Shadow of the Garrison State*, Princeton, NJ: Princeton University Press.

Helleiner, E. (1994) *States and the Reemergence of Global Finance*, Ithaca, NY: Cornell University Press.

Hoopes, T. and D. Brinkley (1997) *FDR and the Creation of the U.N.*, New Haven, CT: Yale University Press.

Hurrell, A. and N. Woods (eds.) (1999) *Inequality, Globalization, and World Politics*, Oxford: Oxford University Press.

Ikenberry, G.J. (2001) *After Victory: Institutions, Strategic Restraint, and the Rebuilding of Order After Major Wars*, Princeton, NJ: Princeton University Press.

IMF Survey (1998) February 9.

IMF Survey (2001a) May 21.

IMF Survey (2001b) August 13.

James, H. (1996) *International Monetary Cooperation since Bretton Woods*, Washington, DC, and New York: International Monetary Fund and Oxford University Press.

Kahler, M. (1990) "The United States and the International Monetary Fund: Declining Influence or Declining Interest?," in M.P. Karns and K.A. Mingst (eds.) *The United States and Multilateral Institutions*, New York: Unwin Hyman.

Kahler, M. (1998) "Introduction: Capital Flows and Financial Crises in the 1990s," in M. Kahler (ed.) *Capital Flows and Financial Crises*, Ithaca, NY: Cornell University Press.

Kapur, D. (n.d.) "Processes of Change in International Organization," paper prepared for UNU/WIDER Project.

Kapur, D., J.P. Lewis and R. Webb (eds.) (1997) *The World Bank: Its First Half Century*, vol. 1, Washington, DC: Brookings Institution.

Kennedy, P.M. (1987) *The Rise and Fall of Great Powers*, New York: Random House.

Keohane, R.O. and J.S. Nye (1977) *Power and Interdependence*, Boston, MA: Little, Brown.

Kindleberger, C.P. (1973) *The World in Depression, 1929–1939*, Berkeley, CA: University of California Press.

Knock, T.J. (1992) *To End All Wars*, Princeton, NJ: Princeton University Press.

Krasner, S. (1985) *Structural Conflict: The Third World Against Global Liberalism*, Berkeley, CA: University of California Press.

Krasner, S. (1999) *Sovereignty: Organized Hypocrisy*, Princeton, NJ: Princeton University Press.

Luck, E. (1999) *Mixed Messages: American Politics and International Organizations, 1919–1939*, Washington, DC: Brookings Institution.

McNamara, R. and B. Vandemark (1996) *In Retrospect: The Tragedy and Lessons of Vietnam*, New York: Vintage Press.

Mason, E. and R.E. Asher (1973) *The World Bank since Bretton Woods*, Washington, DC: Brookings Institution.

Maxfield, S. (1997) *Gatekeepers of Growth: The International Political Economy of Central Banks in Developing Countries*, Princeton, NJ: Princeton University Press.

Nau, H.R. (2001) *At Home Abroad*, Ithaca, NY: Cornell University Press.

Pauly, L.W. (1997) *Who Elected the Bankers? Surveillance and Control in the World Economy*, Ithaca, NY: Cornell University Press.

Polak, J. (1991) "The Changing Nature of IMF Conditionality," *Princeton Essays in International Finance*, no. 184, Princeton, NJ: Princeton University, International Finance Section, Department of Economics.

Polak, J. (1997) "The World Bank and the IMF: A Changing Relationship," in D. Kapur, J.P. Lewis, and R. Webb (eds.) *The World Bank: Its First Half Century*, vol. 2, Washington, DC: Brookings Institution.

Polak, J. (2001) "The *Two* Monetary Approaches to the Balance of Payments: Keynesian and Johnsonian," *IMF Working Papers*, WP/01/100.

Rodgers, Y. and J. Cooley (1999) "Outstanding Female Economists in the Analysis and Practice of Development Economics," *World Development* 27(8): 1,397–411.

Roe, M.J. (1994) *Strong Managers, Weak Owners: The Political Roots of American Corporate Finance*, Princeton, NJ: Princeton University Press.

Ruggie, J.G. (1983) "International Regimes, Transactions, and Change: Embedded Liberalism in the Postwar Economic Order," in S. Krasner, *International Regimes*, Ithaca, NY: Cornell University Press.

Ruggie, J.G. (1998) *Constructing the World Polity*, London: Routledge.

Santaella, J.A. (1993) "Stabilization and External Enforcement," *IMF Staff Papers* 40(3), September: 584–621.

Skidelsky, R. (2000) *John Maynard Keynes: Fighting for Britain, 1937–1946*, London: Macmillan.

Stern, E. (1983) "World Bank Financing of Structural Adjustment," in J. Williamson (ed.) *IMF Conditionality*, Washington, DC: Institute for International Economics.

Trachtenberg, M. (1999) *A Constructed Peace*, Princeton, NJ: Princeton University Press.

United Nations (2000) "Towards a Stable International Financial System, Responsive to the Challenges of Development, Especially in the Developing Countries: Report of the Secretary General," General Assembly document A/55/187, July 27.

U.S. Congress (2000) *The Report of the International Financial Institutions Advisory Commission*, March.

Vries, B.A. de (1987) *Remaking the World Bank*, Washington, DC: Seven Locks Press.

Wade, R.H. (2001) "The U.S. Role in the Malaise at the World Bank," paper prepared for delivery at the annual meeting of the American Political Science Association, San Francisco, August 28–30.

Woods, N. (1998) "Governance in International Organization: The Case for Reforming the Bretton Woods Institutions," United Nations Conference on Trade and Development, *International Monetary and Financial Issues for the 1990s*, vol. 9, New York: United Nations.

Woods, N. (2001) "Making the IMF and World Bank More Accountable," *International Affairs* 77(1): 83–100.

Index

Page numbers in **bold** represent Figures and in *italics* Tables. {n} represents Endnotes.